# Between Desert and City:
# The Coptic Orthodox Church Today

# Between Desert and City: The Coptic Orthodox Church Today

Edited by
Nelly van Doorn-Harder
and Kari Vogt (eds.)

WIPF & STOCK · Eugene, Oregon

Wipf and Stock Publishers
199 W 8th Ave, Suite 3
Eugene, OR 97401

Between Desert and City: The Coptic Orthodox Church Today
By van Doorn-Harder, Nelly and Vogt, Kari
Copyright©1997 by van Doorn-Harder, Nelly
ISBN 13: 978-1-62032-080-8
Publication date 1/25/2012
Previously published by Novus Forlag, 1997

# Preface

It was in 1993, on a train between Luxor and Cairo, that the idea for this book first arose. As we toured the Coptic sites in the south of Egypt in search of new documentation concerning the contemporary Coptic Church, enthusiastic young Copts had lectured us tirelessly about their church's wisdom transmitted through the centuries. We were impressed by the way they had managed to reinhabit many a dilapidated monastery and to revive the interest in long forgotten saints and martyrs.

Going over all this information, we concluded that several themes about the Coptic tradition occur in recent research work (in Western languages), but without being available to a larger public. This is what made us decide to ask those working on the contemporary Coptic Orthodox Church to communicate some of their knowledge.

Among those who have been willing to share their inside knowledge with us, we particularly want to mention His Eminence, Bishop Athanasius of Beni Suef and Banha, whose ideas and suggestions recur throughout this book. We will never be able to thank him enough for his advice, lessons and many inspiring discussions.

We also thank His Holiness Patriarch Shenouda III for granting us a long and enlightening interview at his residence in Cairo, and for inviting us to the Monastery of St. Bishoy.

And, of course, this book would never have been written without the help of many other members of the Coptic community. We owe thanks to the bishops, priests, monks, nuns and lay people who helped us along the way.

Furthermore we owe thanks to Paddy Booz, Lance Castles, Paul Harder and Anne Hommes for reading the manuscript and correcting the English. Brian McNeil translated the French and several of the Norwegian articles into English. We also thank the writers for their patience and willingness to answer our endless questions about their contributions.

Last but not least, we thank *The Institute for Comparative Research in Human Culture*, Oslo, Norway, for making this publication possible.

Kari Vogt and Nelly van Doorn-Harder

# Contents

Preface .................................................................................................... 5
Introduction ........................................................................................... 9

1. The Renewal in Context: 1960-1990 ............................................. 15
   Maurice Martin

2. Changes in Relations between Copts and Muslims (1952-1994)
   in the Light of the Historical Experience ...................................... 22
   Christiaan van Nispen tot Sevenaer

3. Tradition and Renewal in Coptic Theology ................................. 36
   Samuel Rubenson

4. Coping with God: Coptic Monasticism in Egyptian Culture ............. 53
   Mark Francis Gruber

5. The Monastery as the Nexus of Coptic Cosmology ................................. 68
   Mark Francis Gruber

6. Discovering New Roles: Coptic Nuns and Church Revival .................. 84
   Nelly van Doorn-Harder

7. Talking through the Saints ........................................................ 101
   Anitra Bingham-Kolenkow

8. The Coptic Practice of the Jesus Prayer: A Tradition Revived ............ 113
   Kari Vogt ................................................................................................

9. The Era of Martyrs: Texts and Contexts of Religious Memory .......... 123
   Saphinaz-Amal Naguib

10. The Laity at the Heart of the Coptic Clerical Reform ............................ 143
   Dina el-Khawaga

11. Born in the Wrong Age: Coptic Women in a Changing Society ........ 168
   Berit Thorbjørnsrud

12. Becoming a Copt: The Integration of Coptic Children into
   the Church Community ............................................................................ 191
   Nora Stene

13. The Coptic Mouleds: Evolution of the Traditional Pilgrimages ........ 213
   Catherine Mayeur-Jaouen

14. Kyrillos VI (1902-1971): Planner, Patriarch and Saint .......................... 231
   Nelly van Doorn-Harder

15. Signposts to Biography - Pope Shenouda III ........................................ 244
   John Watson

16. Into the Lands of Immigration ................................................................ 255
   Nora Stene

17. The Copts in the United States of America .......................................... 266
   Anitra Bingham-Kolenkow

18. Coptic Art .................................................................................................... 275
   Mat Immerzeel

   List of Contributors ................................................................................... 291

Nelly van Doorn-Harder and Kari Vogt

# Introduction

"When we were fighting against Arius," or "When we went to Chalcedon," are remarks one regularly comes across during discussions with Copts about their faith, church or history. Copts see the long history and tradition of their church as "one whole indivisible unit,"[1] in which each of them has played and is playing an active part. Since the first century A.D., the Copts have developed a vivid tradition that continues strongly up to the present day. Nowadays, as the Coptic Church is witnessing a religious revival, this tradition is emphasized even more.

This book aims to represent several aspects of this revival. Since its most noticeable aspect seems to be renewed emphasis on and the use of the Coptic tradition, each article in this book tries to describe certain aspects of the revival as situated in the Coptic tradition.

The revival started in monastic circles and became visible in Coptic society when the efforts of priests, monks and other church leaders were combined with lay activities. Patriarch Kyrillos VI (1959-1971) can be pointed to as the one who merged together the disparate efforts to revive the Coptic Church into a consolidated enterprise that proved effective. This process is still going on as it was continued under his successor, the current Patriarch Shenouda III.

The Coptic Church traces the roots of its long history to the first century of Christianity when, according to Coptic tradition, the apostle Mark set foot in Alexandria sometime between the year 43 and 61.[2] Patriarch Shenouda III is considered the 117th patriarch in an uninterrupted line of succession that started with St. Mark. From the year 30 B.C. until the Arab invasion (642), Egypt was a province of the Roman Empire. Two elements in this historical situation stand out for their contribution to the distinctive character of the Coptic Church today: Roman persecution and the debate around the nature of Christ.

The first one, the recurring waves of persecution by some of the Roman emperors, left the Coptic Church with an abundance of martyrs who died for their Christian faith. All of these, named or unnamed, are still remembered and venerated. Nowadays the Copts feel (perhaps because of their position as a minority) strengthened by, and proud of, the host of martyrs and saints whom they can identify with and count on for protection.

The second point resulted in a theological split within the Roman Empire between two understandings about the nature of Christ: the imperial (Western) doctrine of the double Nature (Divine and human) and the so-called "Monophysite" view that was advocated by, among others, the Copts.[3] According to the Copts the nature of Christ consists of "two natures - divine and human - mystically united in one, without confusion, corruption or change."[4] The final split between the imperial and Coptic Church occurred during the Council of Chalcedon (451). Contact between the Coptic Church and other churches after 451 virtually came to a halt and until the beginning of the twentieth century the Coptic Church remained isolated from the rest of the Christian world.

After the Arab conquest (642), the number of Copts gradually declined until they definitely became a minority by the tenth century. Today the Copts constitute around 6% of the Egyptian population.[5] During the long centuries of co-existence, Muslims and Copts in Egypt naturally influenced each other's customs, habits and folklore. This contributed to the development of a distinctive Coptic culture.

The start of Egyptian modern history is counted from the beginning of the nineteenth century. The reign of Muhammad Ali (1805-1849) was favorable towards the Copts. He readily employed their skills and through the free market economy of his time several Coptic families became wealthy and influential. Egypt opened up to the outside world through which also the Coptic Church encountered new influences and challenges. At that time its religious life was lax and its priests uneducated. Only in the remote monasteries future members of the church hierarchy were trained and the Coptic faith was kept alive.

In the wake of the British occupiers (1882), Protestant missionaries came to Egypt. When their attempts to convert the Muslims failed, they devoted their energies to reforming the Coptic Church. Hence, nowadays there exist a Catholic and a Protestant Church in Egypt that in fact originated from Coptic Orthodox converts.[6]

Because of their education in schools established by the (Christian) Westerners, lay Copts gained an educational advantage over their still uneducated clergy. At the beginning of this century, many leading lay people started to press for reform of the Coptic Orthodox Church. Following the Protestant example, groups of lay Copts started Sunday schools to educate the believers, and these new schools became one of the main sources for future church leaders. During the 1940s and 1950s the lay movements gradually moved into the church structure. For example, many Sunday school teachers became monks or priests. Thus the leading role of the monasteries in the revival was underscored.

In the political domain, the Copts faced alternating climates. Before World War I, the climate in Egypt was one of nationalistic, pan-Arabic, and largely pro-Islamic feelings that frequently led to tensions between the Coptic and Muslim communities. After World War I, the atmosphere became more liberal as Copts and Muslims were united in their struggle for independence. By the 1940s the liberal and more secular climate had changed due to the rising influence of the Muslim Brotherhood that was founded in 1929. Egyptian society as a whole had become more Islamized as Islamic ideology started to prevail in the cultural, political and religious life. Copts lost their short-lived political influence, never to regain it again.

After the socialist revolution of President Nasser in 1952, due to land reform, many influential Coptic families lost their property which caused them to emigrate to the West. Another impact of Nasser's politics on Coptic demographics was that due to the system of free education, the number of Muslims with higher education increased. This meant that Copts were facing more competition in finding jobs, with the result that after the 1970s, many Copts left Egypt looking for better opportunities abroad. These waves of emigrants resulted in the building of Coptic churches outside Egypt, among others in Canada, U.S.A., Australia, and several European countries.

## Coptic tradition

Copts like to characterize their church as 'apostolic,' meaning that they strive to stay close to the teachings of the Bible and the early fathers. Hence it is not surprising that accentuating these original writings and teachings, including other works and words that are considered to form the Coptic tradition, has become one of the leading principles of the current revival.

The Copts consider the history of their church as an ongoing continuity because, so they reason, the work and guidance of the Holy Spirit is the same then and now. They stress that Jesus Christ did not write anything down, but his oral teachings were remembered and transmitted by his disciples. Furthermore, not everything Christ taught was eventually written down, so when the disciples forgot certain points, "the Holy Spirit reminded them."[7] This means that for the Copts the formation of their tradition is an ongoing process of teaching and learning that not only entails remembering, but also re-discovering, renewal and innovation. Copts can learn from their tradition through written, oral or living sources. A vision, dream, inspiration, or an apparition is considered a living source. An example of a living source is when St. Mary, the Mother of Christ, appeared to a nun in the Convent of Abu Saifein and instructed her to build a church in the convent's garden because on that spot the Holy Family had rested during their Flight to Egypt. The apparition served to initiate an appropriate revival project – the building of a church – and at the same time underscored the ancient Coptic traditions about the flight to Egypt.

Copts feel bound by their tradition because, on the one hand, it emphasizes their original Christian roots and identity, while on the other hand it confirms the teachings of their current leaders. Hence one can observe a flood of booklets being produced on different topics of Coptic theology and tradition. In monastic circles research is being done into the original writings of the great theologians. At the same time lay church members, for example, try to uncover the origins of their church building. When these turn out to have been the dwelling place of a hermit or a saint, consequently a booklet about this person's life is written and disseminated. Monks and nuns pore over texts concerning the life of their monastery's patron saints to reconstruct the proper biography and its related traditions in order to communicate these to the Coptic visitors. Among the manifold activities connected with the revival of tradition are: previously unknown saints and holy sites are rediscovered, new saints are being canonized and books with the saints' stories are rewritten for children. As a consequence of these new developments, Coptic iconography is developing and trying to transform the newly found materials into contemporary icons.

In the first part of this book, Maurice Martin introduces the current revival and places it in its historical, clerical and Muslim context, while Christiaan van Nispen tot Sevenaer outlines Coptic relations with its Muslim environment. The second part of the book focuses on the renewal from the clerical and monastic viewpoint. Samuel Rubenson introduces Coptic theology, with special attention to the writing of a leading contemporary theologian, Father Matta al-Miskin, the spiritual leader of the St. Macarius Monastery. Rubenson furthermore shows how deeply Coptic theology is rooted in the earliest Christian tradition. Gruber, van Doorn-Harder and Bingham-Kolenkow describe different aspects of the monastic life, and how religious recollection and rediscovering tradition is activated through the behavior and work of the contemporary monks and nuns. Mark Gruber shows in his first article, "Coping with God: Coptic Monasticism in Egyptian Culture," how the Coptic community turns to its monasteries to find the orientation to God. In his second article Gruber highlights the dynamics inside the monasteries. Kari Vogt gives an example of the process of rediscovering tradition by showing how the Jesus Prayer was reintroduced in Coptic religious life. Saphinaz Naguib closes this section with a theoretical contribution about how memories are kept alive within religious communities and accommodated to current times and needs.

In the third part the role of the Coptic believers, the laypeople, is discussed. Dina el-Khawaga shows how the Coptic Church has regained its control of lay activities through deliberate and conscious efforts to incorporate the lay workers into the clerical system. Nora Stene and Berit Thorbjørnsrud each highlight the position and condition of a specific group of church members: the children and young women. Catherine Mayeur observes in her article about the *moulid* (a festivity connected with the pilgrimage to the tombs of the saints), how the church hierarchy tries to incorporate this folkloric celebration into proper Coptic tradition and theology.

In the fourth part van Doorn-Harder and Watson portray two of the main proponents of this revival: Patriarch Kyrillos VI and his successor, Shenouda III. The two articles show how both patriarchs directed the Coptic Church into the modern age of technology, globalization and ecumenical approaches, while at the same time remaining faithful to their ancient traditions. With the fifth section the book closes with what could be considered new Coptic topics to be researched: Coptic churches in the lands of immigration (the situation in Europe by Nora Stene, and in NorthAmerica by Anitra Bingham-Kolenkow), and the development of modern icon painting by Mat Immerzeel.

## Notes

1. Iris Habib el Masri, *The Story of the Copts*, The Middle East Council of Churches (publ., no place), 1978, 9. On the same page El Masri also gives the often heard example of "...when we went to Chalcedon..."
2. Aziz S. Atiya, *A History of Eastern Christianity*, Millwood N.Y.: Kraus Reprint, 1980, 27 & Birger A. Pearson, "Earliest Christianity in Egypt: Some Observations," in: Birger A. Pearson & James E.Goehring (eds.) *The Roots of Egyptian Christianity*, Philadelphia: Fortress Press, 1986, 137 ff.
3. The Copts themselves never used the term "monophysite."
4. Atiya, *History*, 69.
5. The latest census of 1986 estimated the number of Egyptian Christians at slightly more than 6.3% (Central Agency for Public Mobilization and Statistics) *General Census of Population and Housing, all Egypt* (Cairo, 1986). This number is consistent with the census results of previous years: 1897, 7.3%, 1937, 8.2%, 1966, 6.7% and 1976, 6.3% In: E.J. Chitham, *The Coptic Community in Egypt. Spatial and Social*

*Change*, University of Durham: Centre for Middle Eastern and Islamic Studies, 1986, 25. Also see: Y. Courbage & P. Fargues, *Chrétiens et Juifs dans l'Islam arabe et turc*, Paris: Fayard, 1992, 283ff.
6. When the Coptic Church is mentioned in this book, this means the Coptic Orthodox Church. It will be indicated explicitly when the Catholic or Protestant Churches are referred to.
7. Interview with Patriarch Shenouda III, January 23, 1992.

Maurice Martin

# The Renewal in Context: 1960 – 1990

This essay will be rather like the progress of a tightrope walker: his safety depends on the balancing rod he holds in his hands, where the weight of the one pole must continually compensate and rectify the movement of the other. The comparison holds good in general for the situation of Egypt's Christians. Thus, when I attempt to identify the context of the current renewal of the Coptic community, it is not a question of minimizing the legitimate admiration – indeed, I should say the gratitude – which its rediscovered spiritual vigor must awaken in everyone who loves Egypt and in every Christian who knows how much of his or her own tradition is owed to the Egyptian sources. On the contrary, my intention is to locate this renewal in the conditions in which it is taking place, under the influence of its cultural and social environment, in order to make a contribution to the recording of its development.

To begin with, since we are dealing with a religious minority, I would like to draw attention to its demographic status. This is indeed the object of dispute, as is usual with all minorities, but the most recent studies seem to establish beyond doubt a diminution of the proportion of the Copts, from about 7% in the 1960s, when the renewer Kyrillos VI became Pope, to about 6% today.[1] But since the Egyptian population has more than doubled in size during this same period, it follows that its Christian minority has also roughly doubled in size, so that it is offered a much vaster and more varied field of internal action. When a homogenous social group crosses the threshold of two and then three millions, the result will be increasing demands on communal services. Thanks to the intensive communal bonds among the Copts these demands were met with appropriate services. This includes a growth in quality: demographic studies show in fact that the Coptic community tends to become urbanized earlier and more quickly than the Muslim peasantry, resulting in a denser Christian presence in the capital and the provincial towns of Middle and Upper Egypt (e.g. Minya 22%, Assiyut 33%). This leads also to the improvement of its cultural level, thanks to a greater sharing in education, including university studies, giving natural access to those professions most prized by the lower-middle and middle classes.

It is in this context, among the classes that recently found access to university educations, that the appeal for spiritual renewal was launched by Kyrillos VI (1959-1971). Supported by Kyrillos' image as a holy hermit, this movement was to find its greatest echo among the better educated Copts. It was from among this new class of educated Copts that he recruited his closest collaborators, the three "general bishops" whom he consecrated, significantly enough, to promote religious education, Coptic higher studies, and ecumenical and social activities. It is from the same background that the young bishops of the Coptic Church come too, after passing through a monastery – a point to which we shall return.

Since we are speaking now of the context from which the religious leaders of today's Coptic community come, it is relevant to reflect a moment on the cultural environment of their formation at school and university. This new milieu was assuredly very different from that of the lay leaders of the preceding generation, who were large landowners and members of the upper-middle class, often educated at "foreign" schools. These lay leaders had been exposed to the same political influences as their Muslim contemporaries during the relatively liberal religious and cultural climate at the time Egypt was struggling to attain its independence. With the advent of Nasserism, these people abandon the public stage, where new national actors arrive to play a wholly different role: and these come from precisely the middle class that we have just mentioned. It is perfectly natural that we see in the Coptic community what is happening in the nation as a whole.

At the government schools and the university departments, young Christians experience a fundamental change, beginning with the period of Nasser and quickly becoming more marked: it excludes them on the one hand, but it also includes them by giving motivation. Here we have the ascendancy of what is called today the Islamist ideology or movement, born with the Muslim Brotherhood, suppressed under Nasser, rather favored by Anwar al-Sadat, and all-pervasive today. It was at the university that this Islamist ideology developed, first by dominating the student elections and then surging onward to take over the direction of the trade unions of the professors, doctors, engineers, and lawyers. The Islamization of teaching, of culture and of the social structures marginalizes the Christian community, which had previously felt itself to be an active and indeed essential participant in Egyptian nationalism.

The Coptic students in the universities reacted to their rejection by a retreat to their communal religious identity. They met in fervent groups, "families" (*usar*) dedicated to prayer, to the study of their tradition and to serving the Sunday schools – i.e., the Christian education of the pupils of the government schools – where they became more and more numerous. It was in this environment of fervency that the general bishops, especially the future patriarch Shenouda III, who was responsible at that period for Coptic youth, found their collaborators to pursue their project of renewal; they formed the circle of volunteers (*khuddam*) of the church, a fertile nursery for monastic vocations. The arrival of numerous young graduates transformed the life of monasteries of men and women. Less than thirty years ago, these were poor, isolated and empty, surviving in the ruins of another world, but today they have become flourishing centers of Coptic culture.

In their structure and form, these agents of change returned to their communal religious identity by means available in the surrounding social culture. This process is not very different in the case of either Copts or Muslims who have had an identical formation at school and university, although the content of the renewal is different in each case. In both cases we find the rejection of a "westernized modernity," of its ideas and its praxis, while the intention is *ad fontes*, the return to the authenticity of one's own sources. These sources are sacred, eternally valid and clear, and therefore lie beyond all interpretation or modernization which might be brought to them by employing the human sciences of history, sociology or linguistic analysis – for such things are applicable only to human affairs, not to the affairs of God. In sum, this understanding is the source of the renewal; degradation and decadence have entered the body of society because people have departed from the original source of the religious tradition. Thus one must return to the eternal sources, by means of an exact repetition. A careful study of the sources indicates and enjoins an obvious and indisputable praxis.

Although this "fundamentalism" is common to the religious thinking of both groups, it is very clear that there is a profound difference in views: the intention to re-Islamize society includes a politics that goes so far as to call the state in question (e.g. "The Koran is our constitution," "Islam is the solution"). This fundamentalism also goes far beyond the national borders, since a similar movement is in process throughout the vast Muslim world. The re-Christianization in Egypt, on the other hand, is taking place within the narrow limits of a national church, and this Coptic project excludes the formation of a political party. Essentially, it is a question of promoting a spirituality which will shape the entire life of the faithful and will set its "mark" upon them. There is no great concern for keeping contact with the various other Christian communities of the country. Besides this, the other oriental rites in Egypt have de facto scarcely any significance today, and an old dispute encumbers the relationships with Protestant and Catholic Copts – these children torn away from their mother. These relations become even more complicated by the fact that the Orthodox Copts remain an overwhelming majority among Egyptian Christians.

As for the instruments of the current renewal, it is indeed true that the Christians (unlike the Muslims) do not have access to mass media, like radio and television, where there are very many religious programs. This is the most acutely felt sign of their exclusion. But the publication of numerous pious pamphlets about moral and religious practice, of the lives of Coptic saints, the narratives of their martyrdoms and their miracles, takes on great dimensions. These publications are accessible to all at church doors, in places of pilgrimage, in monastery shops; to these must be added cassettes of liturgical chant, of sermons or talks, and now also videos and posters. All this is impregnated by a piety strongly marked by the monastic spirit. It is superfluous here to speak of the primordial function of monasticism within the Coptic community, since it is the historical root of its identity, just as the monastery, where the ecclesiastical hierarchy is formed, is the proper place where the community gathers together at times of pilgrimage.

For an observer who comes from another religious world, it is a very delicate matter to give a proper appreciation of the Coptic "discourse" that is propagated in this way. We know that it is adapted in many aspects to a popular (or better: a traditional) consciousness, for which legends and miracles pose no problems, but on the contrary, express and symbolize profound convictions by giving these a material form. For example, it is necessary for the Holy Family to have passed through the whole of Egypt and left traces everywhere, so that although it is Muslim territory today, it may still be possible for the faithful to live in it as Christian territory, and it is necessary for Our Lady to appear and for the powerful protection of the saints to be tangible in the miraculous icons which heal the sick. Moreover, do not the great saints who are honored in the Muslim *mouleds* of Dessouqi, Tanta, Fayoum, Qena or Luxor also perform miracles? In similar fashion, it is easy to understand that the essential practices of the Christian life are formulated in a way parallel to the "Five Pillars of Islam": for the Christian, too, the profession of faith, prayer, fasting, almsgiving and pilgrimage is the axis of his life. And does not St. Paul recommend that a woman should be veiled? It is something admirable that monastic life finds fresh inspiration in its sources, in the ancient Apophthegmata of the desert fathers, making new use of these in the attempt to offer living models to the community. Anthony, the father of monasticism, for example, also gave practical and spiritual guidance to the patriarch Athanasius, Shenoute of Atripe made Coptic Christianity triumph. The hermit monk Mina, who was to become the patriarch Kyrillos VI, embodied these themes at the opportune moment when he was the community's charismatic guide at the time of the national leader Nasser. The Coptic monastery, even if initially this was the humble cell of the monk Mina, must be very visible and imposing. In spite of the risk of departing from its original ascetic ideals, the monastery's role is to draw universal attention to the presence of the Coptic community that would otherwise be drowned in the multitude of mosques. To outsiders the monastery embodies an affirmative presence while at the same time it reassures the Coptic community of its own vitality.

We shall not give further examples here of this complex process that is imposed on a minority that feels itself threatened in its very being, torn between the attachment to that which excludes it from the majority – since this is its very identity. Nevertheless, the necessity of living this way is in keeping with the majority of Islamic community's way of doing things, torn likewise between the search for an ideal identity in a necessarily exaggerated image of the past and the difficult transposition of the identity into modern conditions which are totally different. It would also be inappropriate, for one who is not actively involved in this process, to place special emphasis on some of its manifestations. Nonetheless, if I permit myself to take a position at the heart of the Coptic minority, it seems to me difficult to avoid one fundamental question concerning the role of monasticism as the resource providing the community with its identity, and of the monk as promotor and chief defender of this identity.

Let us recall the facts. The Coptic Church chooses its patriarch and its bishops from among the monks, to the exclusion of the married secular clergy. The patriarch is not only the representative, but the true head of his community, exercising a power that is in practice at his own discretion (within the limits of the ecclesiastical canons), since his synod and his council share in his power only to a small extent. It is he who chooses the bishops. These numbered 26 at the death of Kyrillos VI, but now number 70, since many new dioceses have been created in order to provide a better framework for the clergy and the laity. Thus, the structuring framework of the community is essentially monastic. Likewise, there has been a great increase in the number of lay men and women mobilized in the services of the church, since such services go far beyond the specifically religious needs, to include social activities grouped around the church (like the activities of the Muslims centered around the mosque). These laypeople are permeated with the monastic spirituality and are the primary transmitters of this spirituality in their own milieu, under the direction of the bishops.

Fundamentally, this spirituality implies a condemnation of the world and flight from it into the desert. The "world" so full of ambushes which the Christian community experiences today in its Islamic environment is a very specific reality. Is there not, therefore, a risk that the "world" condemned by the Gospel, the "world" from which the Christians must save themselves, may imperceptibly come to be identified with the contemporary world which rejects the Coptic believer? This would mean that the process of turning back to one's own identity would lead to a kind of emigration into the interior of the Christian community. In the same way, the monastery can be perceived as a kind of refuge. This danger has been clearly identified by some bishops, who insist on opening the Christian social services to all those who are in need, whatever religion they may belong to,[2] but it is not easy to break through the cordon of the community in either direction.

In turn, this kind of internal emigration back into the little Christian world of Egypt can only promote the tendency, which is already strong (for various reasons), to emigrate in reality to countries with a Christian civilization, where the numerous Coptic communities established in the USA, in Canada, in Australia and in Europe are "waiting for you." The sustained attention which Patriarch Shenouda III pays on his many journeys to safeguard these diaspora churches and their insertion into the canonical framework shows how important this movement is. In return, it is hoped that these brethren who enjoy freedom of speech and of action abroad will support the believers who remain at home.

Once again, one may note here that the same concern is shared by Copts and Muslims: to maintain the religious identity of their fellow believers who have emigrated abroad. It is too early to know whether this identity will prove equally resistant in both groups, or whether, on the contrary, the evolution of mentalities and the immersion of the Copts in another Christian universe will have an impact on the milieu from which they come.

## Notes

1. In precise terms, according to the censuses of the population, 6.7% in 1966 and 5.8% in 1986. Thus the absolute number of Copts would be about 3,600,000 – it is certainly below 4 million. On this disputed question, cf. Y. Courbage and P. Fargues, *Chrétiens et Juifs dans l'Islam arabe et turc*, Paris: Fayard, 1992, 283-286. Apart from the principal reason these authors give for the decrease of the

proportion between Copts and Muslims over the space of twenty years – namely a lower birthrate, due to a higher social status – I believe that one must add the influence of emigration: we have no figure that has been checked and shown to be correct, but members of the community speak of 400,000 Copts abroad. (*Ed.*: Some estimates are lower, see p. 31.)

2. See D. el-Khawaga, "L'affirmation d'une identité chrétienne copte", *Itinéraires d'Egypte*, Cairo 1992, 345-365, where three tendencies among the Copts are identified, represented respectively by Patriarch Shenouda III, the majority which I have set out in the greatest detail; by the Bishop of Beni Suef, who opens his social services to all, with the help to the Banat Maryam, a community of active nuns, and finally by the well-known monk Matta al-Miskin, for whom the monastic vocation, implying an exemplarily strict detachment, cannot lead to assuming ecclesiastical tasks.

Christiaan van Nispen tot Sevenaer

# Changes in Relations between Copts and Muslims (1952 – 1994) in the Light of the Historical Experience

"The Copts are not a minority, but an integral part of the human cultural mass of the Egyptian people": this is the title of a lively article written on 21 April 1994 by the famous Egyptian journalist, Muhammad Hasanayn Haykal. In the article, Haykal protests against the fact that a congress, to be held in Cairo, about the "rights of minorities in the Arab motherland and in the Middle East" had included the Copts among these minorities on the same level as the Kurds in Iraq or the Armenians in Lebanon.[1] A number of other writers and prominent personalities have followed Haykal in his protest, most notably Pope Shenouda III himself, the distinguished patriarch of the Coptic Orthodox Church.[2]

It is significant that the question of the rights of the Copts in Egypt should have been posed by the arrangers of a conference on the rights of minorities, since the news brought by the media about religious violence in Egypt leads many people to wonder what is happening to the Coptic Christians in this situation. Nevertheless, it is more significant still to see the virtual unanimity among Copts and Muslims in their straightforward refusal to see the Copts classified among the distinct and specific minorities which must lay claim to their proper rights separate from the rights of all citizens, no matter what real problems may in fact exist in Coptic-Muslim relationships. The Copts feel themselves – and are felt – to be primarily an integral part of Egypt, although the very fact that this is stated so insistently shows that a problem does exist.

The storm around this conference shows the complexity of the relationship between Copts and Muslims in Egypt today. Many things have changed in this relationship in the twentieth century, but if we are to understand this changing reality correctly, we must see it in the light of history.

# The historical experience of Muslims and Christians living together in Egypt

*Before Muhammad Ali*

If we take the reign of Muhammad `Ali, governor or viceroy of Egypt (1805-1848), as the point of demarcation between the pre-modern and the modern periods, this is because during his reign (coming soon after Bonaparte's expedition, which also left a profound mark on Egypt) modern society began to establish itself in Egypt, with consequent changes in the relations between Copts and Muslims. This is, therefore, the end of the pre-modern history which began with the Arab conquest of Egypt.

It is well known that the word "Copt" is the European form of the Arabic word *qibt*, derived from the Greek work *aigyptos* (="Egyptian"), used initially by the Arabs to denote the entire indigenous population of Egypt, which was wholly Christian at the time of the Arab conquest (639-642) and used the Coptic language (the final phase of the ancient Egyptian language).[3] This population, which had been bullied by Byzantium earlier on, experienced the apogee of its own culture in the first century after the Arab conquest.

The majority of this indigenous population passed gradually to Islam, which thus became the religion, not only of the conquerors, but of the majority even of the original Egyptian people (so that probably nearly 90% of the Muslims of Egypt could be called "Copts" from an ethnic point of view, in the sense of being descendants of the Copts who lived there at the time of the Arab conquest). It was probably in the ninth century that the Egyptian Christians made the transition from being a numerical majority to a minority (and it is in fact in this century that we find the last Coptic revolts).[4] At the same time, there was a gradual transition from the use of the Coptic language to the use of Arabic on the part of the entire population. The first Coptic author to write in Arabic was Sawirus Ibn al-Muqaffa`, bishop of Ashmunayn in the tenth century, and he explains this on the grounds that Christians are not able any longer to understand the Coptic language.[5] It is unclear how long Coptic managed to survive as a living language in some places. With the passage of time, the designation "Copts" has been reserved for the Christians of Egyptian stock, thus distinguishing them from both the Muslims and the Christians of non-Egyptian origin. It was probably during the Mameluke period (1250-1517) that the proportion of Copts to the population as a whole became fixed at broadly its modern level,[6] i.e. scarcely rising above 8% (today, closer to 6%).[7] It is above all in the center of Upper Egypt that the Copts have managed to survive, though we must not forget their numerous presence in the capital, too.

It is true that the Copts are above all centered in specific regions (especially the provinces of Assiyut and Minya), and even there sometimes in specific towns and villages – sometimes with their own quarter, but often also mixed with Muslims. Nevertheless, they are indeed the same as all Egyptians: they speak the same language, live in the same culture, practice more or less the same customs and traditions, and share the same feelings and reactions. Thus, Copts constitute the same human substance as other Egyptians, which includes other distinctions like that between "peasants" and "town-dwellers," "people from the north" and "people from the south." Hence, despite the clear distinction between Copts and Muslims in the religious sphere, there exists at the same time a mutual cultural interpenetration[8]. In fact, one can speak of a typically Egyptian Christianity and a typically Egyptian Islam – something that does not of itself diminish the "orthodoxy" of either group in its respective religion. This can be seen, for example, on the occasion of the pilgrimages and the local religious festivals (which have a large place in Egyptian religious life). Thus, the Coptic element and the Muslim element are in a certain sense a part of the identity of everyone, both Copts and Muslims.

Although the Copts have known periods of cultural effervescence in the course of their history, especially in the religious sphere (including that of theology), it cannot be denied that they have also suffered particularly harsh periods, especially during the Mameluke and Ottoman periods. Nevertheless, it is important at the same time to note that the most difficult periods for the Copts coincided in general with the periods of crisis for the entire Egyptian population.

*From Muhammad `Ali until 1952*

It is with the reign of Muhammad `Ali that modern Egypt takes form and Egyptian society undergoes important economic, political, social and cultural changes. The emancipation of the Copts took place in this context. In 1855, during the reign of Sa`id, the *jizya*, the head tax imposed on Christians and Jews, was abolished and Copts were enrolled in the army. In 1879, the Khedive Tawfiq proclaimed the equality of all Egyptians. A number of Copts were to occupy important positions as landowners, with important places in some public services as well, especially the banks and railways; they had a virtual monopoly on some of the free professions, above all as chemists and to a large extent as physicians.

Largely thanks to the increased societal importance of the laity, the Coptic Church had an important awakening in the second half of the nineteenth century. This awakening was especially inspired by Patriarch Kyrillos IV (1854-1861), who is therefore known as the "father of reform." A number of modern schools were opened, including the first school for girls; Egypt's second printing press (after the famous one at Boulaq) was imported, and important benevolent societies were founded. Laypeople, engaged in these endeavors, tried to get a say in the direction of church affairs, above all in the day-to-day workings and legal organization. They succeeded in obtaining the foundation of an advisory board, "the Communal Council" (al-Majlis al-Milli), composed of laypeople but with the patriarch as its president. The history of the relationship between this council and the hierarchy is full of tension, but its very existence indicates the role played by the laity in the renewal of the community.[9] Thanks also to the laity, the clergy began to be better educated, for they took the initiative in the foundation of a seminary at Cairo in 1893.

The laity of the Coptic Church which was renewed in this way succeeded also in playing a growing role in public and political life. One of the high points of this process was the nomination in 1908 of Boutros Ghali (grandfather of today's General Secretary of the United Nations) as prime minister of Egypt. Nevertheless, Boutros Ghali's assassination by a nationalist in 1910 sparked off a period marked by tensions, finding expression in the Coptic Congress of Assiyut and – as a response to this – the Islamic Congress of Heliopolis (1911).

The common resistance to the British occupation by Copts and Muslims in 1919, with the foundation of the *Wafd* party by Sa`d Zaghloul (1858-1927) as the nucleus of this resistance, allowed this tension to be forgotten and formed one of the peaks of national communion and of shared citizenship, with the combination of the crescent and the cross as its symbol and its slogan "Religion for God, and the motherland for everyone". At this period, the priest Qummus Sarjiyis (1883-1964) preached in the al-Azhar mosque, and Muslim sheikhs preached in the churches. Until the present day, the year 1919 has remained the great symbol to which reference is made when people speak of "national unity," the unity of the whole people of Egypt, Muslims and Christians. The national cause represented by the struggle for independence led to the confessional divisions being superseded to such an extent that a Christian, Makram `Ubayd (1889-1961), could be elected to parliament in a district that was almost entirely Muslim (the Sayyida Zaynab quarter in Cairo). It is in this context that the Copts themselves refused the British proposal, made in the course of the preparations of the projected constitution of an independent Egypt, that the Coptic minority should be given reserved seats and guarantees in parliament. The Copts wanted to be able to enter parliament as citizens, not as members of a minority.

Although the period between the two World Wars is the period of glory for specially Egyptian nationalism, in which the Copts took their own proper place, this same period nevertheless saw the birth of another strong movement which insisted on Islam as a factor of political identification. This is the Muslim Brotherhood, founded at Isma`iliyya in 1928 by Hasan al-Banna (1906-1949). This movement grew in an astonishing manner in the course of the 1930s. Although the Muslim Brothers wanted to propose the Islamic model as their political platform, Hasan al-Banna himself insisted forcefully that this movement did not in the least exclude the Copts as citizens; as symbol of this affirmation, he always had a Copt as a member of the Bureau of the Muslim Brothers (the nominee Wahib Doss).[10] It is striking to note that when Hasan al-Banna was assassinated in 1949, Makram `Ubayd was one of the principal personalities who took part in his funeral. Besides this, as early as the beginning of the century a well-known Copt, Wisa Wasif (1873-1931), had accepted within the framework of the Nationalist Party the idea of Islam as a political movement that could include the Copts (although Wisa Wasif was later to join the *Wafd* party). Nevertheless, the Islamist tendency, of which the Muslim Brothers are the most important expression, was always to be felt by the Copts as a threat to their juridical and de facto situation.

It was towards the close of this period, during the 1940s and the beginning of the 1950s, that the specifically religious renewal of the Coptic Church began, involving an admirable spiritual strengthening and an affirmation of the Coptic religious identity from within; at the same time, however, this led also to a turning back on oneself and a mental retreat by the Copts from society as a whole.

## The changing situation from the 1952 revolution onwards

*1952-1970: the period dominated by Gamal `Abd al-Nasir*
The period after the end of the World War II was very troubled and unstable for Egypt, with growing discontent at the intrigues of the political parties, a progressive disaffection in relation to the monarchy, and a keenly felt frustration at the defeat of the Egyptian army – of Arab armies as a whole – in Palestine in 1948. Thus there was no resistance to the revolution

of 23 July 1952, which was well received by the population as a whole, Copts and Muslims. Gamal `Abd al-Nasir, who was the moving force of the new regime from the outset, became the official leader in 1954 by assuming the office of President of the Egyptian Republic. He gave the republic its characteristics gradually, especially by strongly affirming Arab nationalism – rather at the expense of Egyptian nationalism – and by adopting some of the structures of socialism (creating what came to be called "Arab socialism").

Gradual agrarian reform was among his first measures, followed later by the nationalization of numerous societies and businesses. In themselves, these measures were not in the least aimed at the Copts as such, but were inspired purely by socioeconomic and political motives. Their effect, however, was to weaken the influential Coptic class, which had previously played an important role in political life; this also contributed to reducing the weight and role of the laity within the church itself. Some members of this upper class initiated the movement of emigration which was a completely new phenomenon for the Copts (and for all native Egyptians) and which was to become so important from the 1970s onwards. The fact that it was now the state that would make the appointments in the public sector, with the automatic appointments of all those who had diplomas from universities and secondary schools, meant the diminution of the importance of the Copts in sectors where they had previously been in the majority (as in the free professions). In the case of most other sectors, however, this system also had the opposite effect of guaranteeing the appointment of Copts, as well as of everyone else.

At the same time, the impact of the Coptic Orthodox on the education sector diminished because they felt themselves driven, above all for financial reasons, to transform almost all of their schools into so-called "subventional schools." These are schools run by the state, but privately owned; in practice, this transformation amounted to a nationalization.[11]

Thus, nationalism was to have serious consequences for the position of the Copts. As we have seen, they had been completely at home in Egyptian nationalism proper, which accentuated primarily the entire cultural patrimony, with the Pharaonic culture as its most sublime expression.[12] The emphasis given by the revolution to the Arab aspect of nationalism implied that a greater place was given to the Islamic component of this nationalism. Actually, Arab nationalism itself has frequently changed from a basically secular movement (maintaining itself initially by means of the "Islamic empire" that was the Ottoman realm), often initiated by Christians (especially Syro-Lebanese), to a more Islamic movement in the face of the

Western powers, which were looked on as Christian. Despite this, there was still a place for Christians within the Arab nationalism of Nasser, and the Christians themselves did not refuse this place at this period, although their sympathies were rather less attuned to it than were those of their Muslim compatriots.[13]

On the other hand, the 1950s and 1960s were to represent the great vigor of the specifically ecclesiastical renaissance of the Coptic Church. The Sunday schools, founded in 1953 and led by laypeople – in particular by university students (or graduates) – renewed and propagated religious culture by means of groups of students called families (*usar*).[14] The newfound vigor included also the strengthening of theological instruction, especially with the foundation of evening courses in theology addressing university students, many of whom were to become parish priests (who are always married) or monks. This resulted in an important rejuvenation of the clergy (above all in the towns) and of monasticism, which was to become the principal pole of Coptic life, and hence of the episcopate (the bishops are always monks, because they must live in celibacy). The nature of this renaissance involved a progressive strengthening of the ecclesiastical, indeed the clerical structure.[15] It must be noted that the environment providing the support to all these sectors of the Coptic ecclesiastical renaissance were principally the same circles supporting the revolution, i.e. the lower-middle and middle classes, the group that would profit most from the opening of the university to everyone when education became free.

The combination of all these factors explains a certain withdrawal of the Copts from public and above all political life in this period, although this remains within the framework of the traditional religious diversity, which (as we have noted) is the fundamental reality.

*The recent period: 1970-1994*
Gamal `Abd al-Nasir, the great symbol of the Egyptian revolution, of Arab nationalism and socialism, and of the role of Egypt in the liberation of the Third World, died on 28 September 1970, to be succeeded by Anwar al-Sadat, his vice-president and companion from the outset, who had a rather different orientation. Consequently, a new epoch commenced.

The change had in reality already begun in 1967. The defeat in the war against Israel in June 1967 had been felt as the failure of the ideals and the ideology of the revolution, of Nasser's model with all it implied. The liberation of Sinai, initiated by the war of October 1973, was to deliver Egypt from humiliation, but this did not at all imply a return to the pre-1967 model. From 1967 onward, the national platform represented by the revolution of

1952 (like that of 1919, although this was different in kind) has been lost. This has implied a progressive loss of national cohesion and a fragmentation of society on various levels.

At the same period, Egypt witnessed a rapid economic and social transformation. The villagers, who had virtually never moved, emigrated in large numbers to the towns and especially – after 1973 and the consequent enrichment of the countries producing oil – to the Persian Gulf and Iraq. This was to create profound transformations of the entire economic and social structure of the villages. Simultaneously these structures experienced a profound cultural change thanks to school education – begun by the revolution – and the arrival of electricity with television and video in its wake, introducing new cultural models which were very different from the traditional models. The population of the big cities (above all Cairo and Alexandria) increased drastically through emigration from the villages, creating new urban jungles which were to become centers of deep frustration.

All of these profound changes were to bring a progressive loss of the traditional structures of diversity, especially those between Muslims and Christians, who each had their own rites; rituals which were particularly manifest on the occasion of family events (births, marriages and deaths) and feasts. This strengthened the tendency for individual and family relationships to be replaced by relations between groups and confessional communities.

This loss of the national platform and of national cohesion, as well as the profound disturbance of the economic and social structures, with the transformation, indeed the crisis of cultural models, often meant that people lost their systems of reference and their places of identification. In this cultural tempest, the only structures which seemed to remain standing were the religious ones, and thus people increasingly turned to religion for support, reference and identification. This is true just as much of Christians as of Muslims. Thus, religious belonging increasingly becomes the unique or principal means of defining oneself, i.e. something that divides citizens rather than something that unites them.[16]

When, besides this, all these changes involve insecurity, inequalities and injustices, strengthened during the 1980s by the increasing economic crisis, then religion also becomes the place of utopia, of dreams of justice, of equality and security: "If 'God's law' prevailed, then we would not be in these difficulties." It is clear that this last element plays a greater role for the religious majority, the Muslims, because the minority would never be able to dream of imposing an economic and socio-political system in the name of the religion. This is why the minority spontaneously prefers a secular socio-political system, one not determined by religion, in order not to find itself marginalized even more.

These socio-cultural evolutions explain why, in the course of the last twenty-five years, more and more people are defining themselves as Muslims or Christians rather than as Egyptians and why there are more and more demands for the application of the *shari'a*, Islamic law, and slogans saying that "Islam is the solution," even if it is not at all clear what this means in concrete terms. This has a great utopian power, expressing the existing malaise and permitting the mobilization of people.

It is this constellation of evolutions that allows us to understand the rise of Islamism, i.e. the tendency to want Egypt governed by the *shari'a* and to be purified of everything that prevents society from living in accordance with the Islamic model. This is intensified even further when the authorities themselves seek to make use of this tendency to check the influence of Nasserism and of the Left (even if these authorities then become themselves the victims of what they have encouraged, as we see so clearly in the assassination of Anwar al-Sadat).

The influence of the Islamist movement will not be limited to the various Islamist groups. It will spread out through a growing Islamization of the general atmosphere of the country, even if the institutions of the state generally continue to function according to more secular models.

By necessity, the Christian community obeys the same sociological laws in general. Besides this, we have already noted the weakening of the laity's share in government and the strengthening of the role of the clergy in the Coptic Orthodox Church in the preceding period. This progressive clericalization of the church was to be continued vigorously with the reign of Pope Shenouda III (from November 1971). Thus, the clergy take on more and more the representation of the Christian group within Egyptian society, at all levels, local, regional, and national. The patriarch himself, Pope Shenouda, a very strong personality and one of the symbols of the Coptic renaissance, came increasingly to play a political role and to be seen not only as the representative, but as the real political leader of the Christians. President Anwar al-Sadat disliked this evolution of Coptic leadership; the resulting conflict climaxed in September 1981 when the patriarch was deposed by the president – i.e., the state withdrew its recognition of him – and Shenouda was put under house arrest in a monastery, precisely one month before Sadat's assassination (which some Copts took to be the divine punishment for this act of deposition). Furthermore, this conflict itself, in which those with the task of directing the church were accused of wanting to create a Coptic state, caused or intensified a certain rupture between Christians and Muslims in the national community.

When we find contemporary acts of terrorism which are aimed more particularly at Christians (though often also with the aim of creating difficulties for the state) and a certain augmentation of the level of discrimination, then it is easy for a feeling of persecution to spread, so that some despair of any real possibilities of a common citizenship and turn back on their own community in a ghetto mentality. Against this background, the phenomenon of Coptic emigration takes on increased importance (it is said that 200,000–300,000 Copts live abroad today). Some communities of emigrants (above all in the United States) play a very negative role, too, deepening the conflict and reinforcing the image of persecution.

Nevertheless, if the evolution of society from 1970 onwards has caused a fragmentation of society of which the religious rupture is the most visible expression, it must be noted that none of this has destroyed the traditional substratum of diversity which we pointed to at the beginning of this essay. It is important to remember this because the difficulties of the recent years risk obscuring this reality both for outside observers and for the Copts themselves. Copts and Muslims continue to live together, mixing with each other at school, at work, and in the whole of public life, living the same culture, confronted basically by the same problems, although with different accentuation. Together, they continue to form the people of Egypt.

Besides this, in the face of the rupture and the difficulties, we can also see the birth and growth on both sides of a clear and sincere affirmation of the will to live together, on the national level, the religious and the local levels.

An example of this will is the growing interest in the defence of human rights, the rights of every person irrespective of his religion or inclinations. This finds expression above all in the Egyptian Association for Human Rights, in which Muslims and Christians act to defend both Christians who are victims of terrorist acts and Muslims who are victims of injustice. One can also mention the Society for National Unity, where Christians and Muslims have come together to struggle to maintain their common citizenship. There is also the Association for Religious Brotherhood, very small in size but a place where Muslims and Christians come together on the basis of their faith in God, convinced that this can unite them despite the profound differences in faith. It is not only persons of a secular inclination who share this will to live together, but also persons of an Islamist inclination, especially among the Muslim Brotherhood. Thus, the last years have seen many initiatives to display communion (such as the organization of festive meals in common when the fast is broken on the evening of Ramadan) and to meet in order to reflect together on the future of society. All this expresses both a growing awareness of the problem and the will not to give up in face of it.

These examples of the will to live together concern primarily intellectuals (though their influence must not be underestimated), but one can find it on the popular level, too, expressed in a spontaneous and direct manner, refusing to abandon this centuries-old diversity which is so typical of Egyptian society.

## Challenges to relations between Copts and Muslims

We have seen that in today's situation, the maintenance of authentic and deep relations between Copts and Muslims is not an automatic matter that can look after itself. It presupposes an explicit will to maintain what is commonly called "national unity" despite the different societal models that are proposed.

The first of these models is the secular model, or actually "lay" model (some prefer to speak today of the "civil (*madani*) model of society, because of the pitfalls involved by the word "lay" (`*almani*) in a liberal or a socialist form). As we have noted, this model is the spontaneous preference of many Christians, because it gives them by definition a status of full equality.

The other model offering itself as an alternative, expressing the proper patrimony and bypassing the dilemma between capitalism and socialism, is the Islamic model, but this finds various expressions, as far as the place of the non-Muslims is concerned. Those who follow the teaching of Sayyid Qutb do not admit that the Christians have the right to full citizenship and to equality in the Muslim state, while others – and especially the majority of the Muslim Brothers – consider Christians to have full right to citizenship and equality with Muslims. They insist on the distinction between Islam as a religion and Islam as a civilization and a political platform, holding that nothing prevents Christians from assenting to the latter. Some of them even say that one could replace the term "Islamic principle" by "believing principle," in the sense that the important thing is that the societal foundation be based on transcendence and on the divine foundation of public morality, in order to free it from human arbitrariness. While recognizing the sincerity of those who defend this viewpoint, one can, however, ask serious questions about its coherence: to what extent is it logically possible to grant that non-Muslims not only enjoy their private freedom, but also can participate fully in decision-making, in the definition of the national principles? And who is going to determine the concrete contents of the *shari`a* that is to be applied, given the multiplicity of interpretations, at least some of which can only evoke fear in non-Muslims (and in a good number of Muslims)? All these questions do not compel the Christians to refuse this platform completely, but they can provide the context for a clear, fruitful and constructive dialogue that can help everyone to build together a future that is truly respectful of human diversity.

The only truly negative attitude on the part of the Christians, faced with these models, would be to turn back upon themselves and form a ghetto, retreating from the national community. This recalls the remark made one day by a professor of political sociology, himself a Muslim, to the directors of Christian schools: "I myself, like other Muslim intellectuals, am aware that the minority have problems. But first of all, do not forget that the majority have problems too. And above all, do not attempt to solve your own problems apart from the efforts that are being made to solve the problems of society as a whole."

All these perspectives show that the discussion we recalled at the beginning of this essay, on the occasion of the Congress about minorities in the Arab world (May 1994), to determine whether or not the Copts of Egypt are a "minority" in the socio-political sense, is far from being a purely theoretical discussion. It represents a choice that must be made anew at each period, both by the Muslims and by the Copts themselves: do all really want the Copts to be full citizens, an integral part of Egyptian society and of its culture, or is this refused in practice (whatever fine declarations may be made)? Each one has his own share of responsibility for the answer that is given.

## Conclusion

The experience of Copts and Muslims living together in Egypt, as we have sketched here briefly, is a unique experience of two communities who together form the national reality of the same country from the very beginning of the existence and the expansion of Islam. This experience includes challenges, tests and indeed sufferings, but it has been able to survive despite everything, and constitutes the very riches of Egypt. At the same time, it is never a fixed given, something automatically put into practice: at each period, and today more than ever, it must be refashioned and recreated in an original manner, on the very basis of the historical inheritance – common and distinct – which all have received together. This is the challenge addressed to the totality of Egyptian society today. It is also the lesson that other societies, each in its own way, can draw from this rich and unique experience of the co-habitation of Copts and Muslims in Egypt.

## Notes

1. *Al-Ahram*, April 21, 1994.
2. In the course of a press conference which Shenouda III gave on this occasion.
3. See artikel: "Copt" by Pierre du Bourguet SJ, in *The Coptic Encyclopedia* (Aziz Atiya ed., New York: Macmillan, 1991) Vol. 2, 599-601.
4. About how this change of situation is reflected by the *History of the Patriarchs*: M.P. Martin, "Une Lecture de l'Histoire des Patriarches d'Alexandrie", *Proche Orient Chrétien* 35 (1985), 15-36, esp. 19-22. Idem, "Note sur la Communauté Copte entre 1650 et 1850," *Annales Islamologiques* 18 (Institut Français d'Archéologie Orientale du Caire), 1982, 193-215, at 195.
5. M. Martin, "Note ...", 197.
6. Ibid., 198.
7. Ibid., 193 and 212; also Martin. "Une lecture ...," 36.
8. This cultural interpenetration can, for example, be observed in the preservation of the same ancient Egyptian elements, especially in some forms of behavior and traditions concerning the cult of the dead.
9. See Adel Azer Bestawros, "Community Council," *The Coptic Encyclopedia*, vol. 2, 580-582.
10. One must note that Sayyid Qutb, a thinker of the Muslim Brothers who was executed in 1966, a radicalizer of the ideology of the Brothers who was disowned by the Supreme Guide after his death, did not adopt this open and moderate attitude of Hasan al-Banna, and held that non-Muslims ought not to have the same rank as Muslims in the Muslim state. See: Olivier Carré, *Mystique et Politique*, Paris: Cerf, 1984, 105 and 122.
11. According to the statutes of the "subventional school," as promulgated by the state, the director and the teachers are appointed, and the entire program prescribed, so that the owner of the school retains only the property of the buildings, which he lends out to the state. One of the reasons for this change of status of the Coptic Orthodox schools is the loss of the agricultural revenues which permitted the great Coptic families to maintain these schools: this was no longer possible for them after the agrarian reform: Fadel Sidarouss, "Eglise Copte et Monde Moderne," Ph.D., Beirut: St. Joseph University, 1978, Vol.I, 25.
12. It is typically among the Christians that one finds Pharaonic names such as Ramses, Ahmos, Isis, and Osiris.
13. It must be recalled also that the secular aspect of nationalism remains strongly affirmed at the same period in parties like the Ba`th (in power in Syria and Iraq), one of whose founders was the Christian Michel Aflaq.
14. Sidarouss, "Eglise Copte," 23.
15. Sidarouss (ibid., 32-34) speaks of "a clergy retrieving its laity."
16. It can also be observed that this phenomenon occurs again within the Christian group, where – despite all the ecumenical efforts – it can be seen that the particular confessional identity is being strengthened. Here too, greater emphasis is laid on what differentiates the various Christian confessions from each other. On the Coptic Orthodox side, the act symbolizing this most clearly is the rebaptism required in the case of virtually all other Christians who, for example, wish to become Copts because of marriage.

Samuel Rubenson

# Tradition and Renewal in Coptic Theology

Egypt is not only the land of Christian monastic origins, but also of modern monastic revival. For more than three decades large numbers of young Copts have retreated into the desert reviving the ancient monasteries once founded in the fourth and fifth centuries. The monasteries have been enlarged and modernized by new monks who are usually well educated in modern schools and universities. Modern technology and modern means of communication have been introduced and some of the monasteries have close relations with churches and monasteries in Europe and North America. At the same time the old traditions are upheld and the spiritual writings of the early centuries, preserved in numerous manuscripts in the monastic libraries, remain standard reading.[1] Tradition is the heart of this renewal.

Although the monasteries are located in the desert they are today easily accessible, and large numbers of visitors from all areas and levels of the church pass through the gates. Many of the young bishops of the Coptic Orthodox Church are themselves products of this monastic revival. Through minor books and pamphlets as well as magazines they contribute in making the monastic tradition accessible. The influence from the monastic revival is especially manifest in youth work and among Coptic students at the universities. From one of the monasteries, St. Macarius, there is, moreover, a steady flow of articles and books on spiritual issues. There can be no doubt that the monastic revival has affected and does affect the Coptic Church at large.

At the same time theology in the Coptic Orthodox Church is taught at the Coptic theological seminaries, primarily the Coptic Orthodox Theological Seminary at Abbasiya and the Higher Institute for Coptic Studies, both attached to the patriarchate in Cairo. But while the renewal in the monasteries is nourished by patristic literature, especially the writings of the monastic fathers, preserved in the manuscripts, the seminaries rely on text-books shaped by the contact with Western academic theology, but for their content dependent upon a theological tradition deeply rooted in Medieval Arabic theological literature. Although there is a long history of co-existence between these two traditions and forms of theological literature, there are today signs of a growing tension, largely caused by the increasing contact with Western patristic and ecumenical theology. The purpose of this contribution is to look at this tension and the theology of the monastic revival in relation to the theological tradition of the Coptic Orthodox Church.

## Early developments in Coptic theology

Through Alexandria, the major center of Eastern Mediterranean intellectual life in Late Antiquity, Egypt was in touch with the development that shaped Christian theology in the first five centuries A.D. It was in Alexandria that the most far-reaching enculturation of the Gospel into Hellenistic philosophy took place, but also from Alexandria that some of the greatest defenders of the Christian faith came.[2] The great Alexandrian church fathers, however, wrote in Greek, and with the partition of the church after the Council of Chalcedon in 451 Alexandrian theology lost its prominence. The famous catechetical school was moved to Asia Minor and with the persecution of the Copts by the Byzantine emperors, the monasteries, in particular the monastery of St. Macarius, became centers of Coptic theology which led to a gradual transition from Greek to Coptic. Moreover, Egypt was cut off by the enduring schism from much of the subsequent theological developments in the Byzantine Church, especially after the Arab conquest in 642 A.D.[3]

In Egypt outside Alexandria Coptic literature was born in the fourth century with Anthony, Pachomius and the greatest of all Coptic authors, Shenoute of Atripe. Their writings, as well as much of the Greek writings translated into Coptic, were, however, less concerned with dogmatic theology and more with spiritual experiences and counseling. Of the major works of the Fathers of the fourth century very little was ever translated into Coptic. Even the Fathers of the Coptic Church, St. Athanasius, Theophilus of Alexandria, and St. Cyril are with minor exceptions only preserved in Coptic in collections of homilies and excerpts from polemical and dogmatic treatises transmitted as arguments for Coptic theology in larger anthologies.[4] The result is that Coptic theological literature in the early Middle Ages tended to become a very conservative and non-reflecting transmission of apologetic theological statements in addition to a much more vivid hagiographical, homiletic, hymnographic and pastoral literature.

The Arab conquest and the gradual acceptance of Arabic as the language of the Christians opened a new chapter in Coptic theology. In the late tenth century the need for Christian instruction in Arabic, due to the rapid decline of Coptic, was felt in Egypt and a Golden Age of Coptic Arabic literature began.[5] As part of this literature, Arabic translations of patristic texts were made, but again only an insignificant portion of the major patristic texts were translated, mainly moral, ascetical and canonical literature.[6] With Arabic as a lingua franca the Copts entered into a vital exchange with other Christians in the Middle East. Thus, they gained access to parts of their own spiritual traditions which had never been translated into Coptic.[7] The old Christological controversies were still alive and Arabic translations of the old texts were needed. The defense of Christianity against Muslim polemics also necessitated the spread of Arabic translations of patristic texts, a development originating with the Melkites of Palestine. Both factors contributed, however, to a concentration of translations of excerpts that could contribute to disputed Trinitarian and Christological terminology.[8] Although the Coptic Arabic literature began later than the Syrian Arabic, it has ended up being much more extensive and original. Some of the greatest medieval Christian Arabic authors were Copts.[9]

The theological output of the golden centuries in the Middle Ages shaped Christian Arabic thinking and has to a large degree determined the theology of the Coptic Orthodox Church since then.[10] Behind the theological renewal that came with the use of Arabic was the need to defend Christianity against Islam. The style and contents of many of these original works betray their background in the apologetic dialogue and discourse. The questions are put to the Christians who have to give a rational answer acceptable to the Muslim interrogator. Thus some of the most prominent subjects are the Trinity and the Incarnation. The common battleground is the Arabic language, already impressed by the influence of Islamic philosophy, and the Aristotelian philosophical heritage translated into Arabic by Syrian Christians. With a word borrowed from the West, much of the medieval Christian Arabic theology could be termed "scholastic."[11]

## The background of modern revival

After the end of the Golden Age in the fourteenth century Coptic theological writing almost ceased until the beginning of the nineteenth century.[12] With Muhammad `Ali, Egypt was suddenly opened up to the West. In addition to explorers, merchants, technical experts and secular teachers, missionaries of various Protestant and Catholic affiliations settled in the country in growing numbers. Many of them soon engaged in teaching activities aimed at the Coptic Orthodox, and especially the British missionaries from CMS hoped to influence the Coptic Church in the direction of the Reformation and its theology. Instead of establishing an Anglican church in Egypt they tried to work with the Orthodox. Numerous Copts who later became prominent in the church were educated in their schools.[13] With the enthronement of Patriarch Kyrillos IV, "*Abu al-Islah*" (the father of reform), their influence was at its peak. For a short time they even managed the first Coptic Orthodox Theological school.[14]

The latter part of the century saw a Coptic Orthodox reaction against Western Christian influence. Partly it was a reaction against some of the most radical reforms of Kyrillos IV, but mainly it was part of the growth of an Egyptian national consciousness strengthened by the British occupation in 1882. The church had by then accepted many of the methods of the missionaries in areas like education and distribution of literature. Now these were used against the missionaries by Copts educated in the modern schools. Thus, the late nineteenth century gave rise to a renewal of Coptic theological literature, but largely in a polemical form. The themes were again decided by the opponents, Catholic and Protestant, rather than Muslim, and the role of the Coptic theologians was largely apologetic. The exposure to missionary activity had, however, made a deep impact. It is within a Western, mainly Catholic, theological framework that the Copts defend the controversial issues.[15] Unfortunately the ecclesiastical conflicts between the reformers in the *Majlis al-Milli* and the hierarchy long prevented effective reforms of theological education.

An outgrowth of this defense of the Coptic Orthodox tradition against the proselytism of the missionaries, and one of the most important factors behind the revival that started in the 1940s, was the Sunday School Movement. Based on ideas largely taken from Protestant missions, it had been developed by some of the great Copts of the early 20th century, primarily Habib Girgis, and had become the major form of Coptic religious instruction in the growing cities, especially Cairo. Through these schools young Copts received a thorough religious training under enthusiastic young teachers. In them a new generation of lay leaders with modern secular education became devoted to the church. A large number of them later entered the desert monasteries, contributing to their revival.[16] But the schools were still dependent on the old "scholastic" tradition to which Western methods of religious instruction, in particular Bible reading and a systematic exposition of liturgy and sacraments, had been added.[17]

A very different impetus came out of the desert tradition itself, where radical hermits during the Second World War began to attract disciples. One of them was an uneducated Ethiopian monk, `Abd al-Masih al-Habashi.[18] Numerous young Egyptians were disappointed with the Egyptian kingdom and its dependence on the British. Muslims rallied in movements of Islamic revival, secularized soldiers in clandestine groups of Socialists and Copts in Coptic organizations.[19] Some left society behind and went into the desert. In the monasteries they found not only spiritual leaders, but also libraries with manuscripts containing their spiritual heritage, the writings of the radical monastic leaders of the first centuries, like St. Anthony, St. Macarius, and St. Isaac of Niniveh.[20] But some did not find the life in the monasteries radical enough and retreated further into the desert to be able to live the life of the desert fathers of the fourth century.

In 1959 the monastic revival received its most prominent supporter by the election of Kyrillos VI as patriarch of Alexandria. He was a well known hermit and preacher, who had studied the early spiritual fathers and for some time been the disciple of `Abd-al-Masih al-Habashi. As a strong spiritual leader without any bonds to the pre-revolution Coptic elite, Patriarch Kyrillos VI could cooperate well with Nasser and strengthen the position of the church in general and Coptic monasticism in particular. With his support, hermits and young enthusiastic monks undertook to rebuild and revive the old monasteries which then attracted young men from Cairo and elsewhere. Among them we find most of the prominent leaders of the Coptic Church of today, like Pope Shenouda, Bishop Athanasius of Beni Suef and Bishop Mousa of the Bishopric for Youth.

Many of these young monks were, however, soon picked out to become bishops, giving them limited possibilities to engage in theological research and reflection. Their theological production has thus mainly been aimed at elementary education of the Copts in general, primarily based on expositions of the Bible. In the monasteries the teachings from the Sunday schools were supplemented by the readings of the Church Fathers and especially the monastic fathers. The need for modern Arabic translations of the Greek fathers was clearly seen as well as the need for a theological training of a more patristic and less scholastic type. Thus, the educational center *Bait al-takris li-khidmat al-kiraza* started the Patristic Center of Cairo in 1982 with the explicit aim of translating patristic texts into Arabic and supporting higher theological education, especially in patristics, by sending young Coptic theologians abroad. Numerous works of especially St. Athanasius and St. Cyril, but also the homilies of St. Macarius, have been translated with the support of the center. The example of the *Bait al-takris li-khidmat al-kiraza* has spread widely, and there are numerous series of publications of Arabic translations and commentaries of patristic authors.[21] Although most of them have no scholarly ambition, but aim at the general audience, there are notable exceptions, the most important being the learned edition of the Arabic *Didascalia* with an extensive introduction by William Sulayman Qilada.[22]

Thus, the monastic revival has laid a basis for a patristic revival as well as a modern Coptic Orthodox theological literature grounded in early monastic theology, its most prominent and prolific representative being the abbot of the monastery of St. Macarius the Great, Father Matta al-Miskin. I will for that reason take his production as an example of what this revival means.

## The theological writings of Father Matta al-Miskin

Father Matta was born and grew up in Alexandria where he became a successful pharmacist before he turned a monk in 1948. He fully engaged himself in the reading of the early monastic fathers and soon began to write extensively on spiritual life, quoting the fathers, especially St. Isaac of Niniveh. In 1952 his major work *Hayat al-Salat al-Urthudhuksiya* (Orthodox Prayer Life) was printed in its first edition. It was later augmented and reprinted in several editions, the fifth printed in 1987. In the 1960s Matta al-Miskin refused to be enrolled in a monastery and decided to live with his disciples as hermits in Wadi Rayan. Here they established an ascetic life according to the tradition of the first monastic movement and continued to study the writings of the Fathers. In cooperation with the center in Cairo, *Bait al-Takris li-khidmat al-kiraza*, Matta al-Miskin continued his literary activity. In 1969 he and his disciples were asked to take over the almost ruined monastery of St. Macarius. Under his leadership the monastery was enlarged and completely renovated and soon attracted numerous young monks.

After settling in the monastery, Father Matta's theological production grew rapidly. Besides his Orthodox Prayer Life, by now a classic, his major works are *Al-Rahbana al-Qibtiya fi `Asr al-Qiddis Anba Maqar* (Coptic Monasticism in the Age of St. Macarius the Great) (1972), *Al-Afkharistiya wa al-Quddas*, vol. 1 (The Eucharist and the Mass) (1977), *Al-Qiddis Athanasiyus al-Rasuli* (St. Athanasius the Apostolic) (1981), *Al-Madkhal li-Sharah Injil al-Qiddis Yuhanna* (Introduction to a Commentary on the Gospel of St. John ) (1989), *Sharah Injil al-Qiddis Yuhanna* vols. 1-2 (A Commentary on the Gospel of St. John) (1990), *Al-Qiddis Bulus al-Rasul* (St. Paul, the Apostle) (1992), and

*Sharah Risalat al-Qiddis Bulus al-Rasuli ila Ahli Rumiya* (A Commentary on the Letter to the Romans) (1992). In contrast to much earlier Coptic theological literature, they are all based on solid studies of the patristic literature and show a growing knowledge of and critical discussion with Western theological research. Of scholarly interest is also an edition of the Arabic version of the Letters of St. Anthony,[23] as well as his significant contributions to ecclesiology and ecumenical theology.[24]

Among his minor works are a series of commentaries on the great feasts: *A`yad al-zuhur al-Ilahi. Al-Bishara – al-Milad – al-Khitan – al-Hurub ila Misr – al-Ghatas – `Urs Qana al-Jalil* (The Feasts of Divine Manifestation: Annunciation, Nativity, Circumcision, the Flight to Egypt, Epiphany, the Wedding in Kana), collected in one volume (1980), *Al-Sawm al-Arba`ini al-Muqaddas* (The Fast of the Holy Forty) (1970, revised 1976), *Ma`a al-Masih fi alamihi hatta al-Salib* (With the Lord in his Suffering until the Cross) (1961, revised 1965, revised 1976, revised 1981), *Al-Qiyama wa al-Su`ud* (The Resurrection and Ascension) (1982), and *Al-Ruh al-Quddus al-Rabb al-Muhyi* (The Holy Spirit, the Life-giving Lord) (1981). Other minor booklets deal with aspects of Christian Ethics, the traditions of the church, the Fathers, various theological topics and the church and society.[25] In addition to these books Matta al-Miskin has written innumerable articles in the journal of the monastery, *Murqus. Risalat al-Fikr al-Masihi li al-Shabab wa al-Khuddam* (St. Mark Monthly Review), which has been published in 10 editions a year since the end of the 1970s. Some of the minor books have been translated and published in an English volume,[26] and others in small pamphlets in English, French and German. Extracts from the book *Orthodox Prayer Life*, as well as the *Introduction to the Gospel of St. John*, have been printed in English translation in the monastery's journal.

It is, obviously, beyond the scope of this short article to provide an accurate characterization of Matta al-Miskin's entire authorship. Instead, three important features that seem to be characteristic of his writing will be highlighted: the Incarnation, prayer and communion. In addition, I will try to answer the question about the main factors directing the work of Matta al-Miskin: the experience of intense readings of the Bible, the influence of the patristic fathers and the ecumenical purpose.

As with many of the Eastern fathers, especially St. Athanasius and St. Cyril of Alexandria, two of Matta al-Miskin's favorite fathers, the Incarnation is central to Matta al-Miskin's theology. The Incarnation reconciles heaven and earth.[27] Through the Incarnation man is given the capacity to transform transcience of life into a history of salvation. Time has the power to kill, but the incarnation and resurrection of Christ deprives time of this power. Through the incarnation of Christ, material and transitory creation becomes sanctified. In his ethical writing this leads to a positive evaluation of how the body and sexuality might reflect spiritual riches.[28] Asceticism is thus a natural result of belief in the incarnate nature of Christ. Another important aspect of this emphasis on the Incarnation is Matta al-Miskin's view on the historical character of Christian faith. Especially in his ecumenical appeals Matta al-Miskin stresses the historical character of doctrine, which he maintains is part of the enculturation that is central to Christian faith as faith in the incarnate Son of God. The church is called not only to manifest Christian unity but to unite the world. This task presupposes a Christian unity which can only be achieved through a communion of saints, that is a communion based on repentance, humility, love and mercy.

Another key to the theology of Matta al-Miskin is the central place he gives to prayer. Although man is called to live an active as well as a contemplative life, it is clear that it is the contemplative life that is the most vital. It is this life in seclusion that prepares humans for eternal life in the presence of God and keeps them upright in active life. Thus, the most vital factor in transforming the human being is prayer. Ascetic practice is necessary as the means to prepare for and uphold a life in prayer. In his book *Orthodox Prayer Life*, Matta al-Miskin discusses the different levels of prayer and what is necessary to make progress. This discussion is close to the traditions of the spiritual fathers with their progress from natural contemplation to spiritual contemplation and then to vision. Here Matta al-Miskin sees a development from ecstasy to vision and then to union. Characteristic of Matta al-Miskin's text is his emphasis on the spiritual gifts received by contemplation, especially joy. He also gives a very optimistic view on the possibility of a true vision and knowledge of God, making a sharp distinction between what humans can achieve by nature and what is given by grace. His mysticism must thus be counted as a "mysticism of light" in contrast to that of St. Gregory of Nyssa and many Western mystics.[29]

A third feature of Matta al-Miskin's theology is the central place given to participation and communion. Man is created for communion with God, a perfect communion which can only be achieved on the basis of original likeness and through participation. Due to the fall the original communion is lost, but through Christ it can be regained. It is, however, not regained by faith alone or by baptism alone, it has to be regained by a living participation in Christ. Virtues gained in obedience to the commandments, righteousness achieved through humility, suffering, tears and prayer are nothing but participation in Christ by imitating his life and death. To accept pain and humiliation, to cancel one's own will and mind, is to participate in

Christ. Humility is, as in the *Sayings of the Desert Fathers*, the central virtue, and suffering is a natural part of spiritual life. Here it becomes clear how far Matta al-Miskin is removed from an exclusively Platonic tradition with its neglect for the body. One can find numerous parallels among later Byzantine writers in the hesychast tradition, like St. Symeon the new Theologian, or even St. Gregory Palamas. For Matta al-Miskin the body is central, for it is through the Incarnation that heaven is brought to mankind and it is through and in the body that man grasps what is spiritual. Asceticism and purification is not intended to kill the body but to prepare it for participation in the resurrection of Christ. The meaning of the cross is thus not only atonement, but participation. The suffering of Christ perfects the Incarnation by integrating human suffering, despair and death.[30] Through the Eucharist a person takes part in the death and resurrection, in atonement and sacrifice, and through this participation forgiveness is given.

## Conflicting traditions

Behind the theological revival here exemplified in the writings of Matta al-Miskin one can detect three major factors that are prominent in the theological discussion of the Coptic Orthodox Church of today and that generate some of the growing tensions between tradition and renewal. First there is the question of use and interpretation of the Bible. With the coming of the missionaries, and especially the Protestants, the Bible was spread and read to an extent unknown before. The authority of the Bible, taken for granted, became a growing problem with Protestants quoting key texts in their critique of Orthodox practice. Are they to be opposed by a defensive position using the Bible in much the same way to support tradition or by a very different approach to the Scriptures reviving the exegetical tradition of the Alexandrian fathers? The second factor is the use of the Eastern spiritual fathers of the first centuries, whose teachings are not always easy to harmonize with official church doctrine. Here the tensions in Egypt today are quite similar to those between the hesychasts and the hierarchy in medieval Byzantine tradition. Thirdly there is the ecumenical situation of today. Through Matta al-Miskin and the Patristic center of Cairo the theological revival has received a strong impetus from the Orthodox theologians of Europe and the USA, like Vladimir Lossky, John Meyendorff and John Zizioulas, but also to some extent from modern Catholic theologians.[31] Their radical theology, especially in the field of ecclesiology, is in itself a severe critique of some of the practices of Coptic religious tradition.[32]

Coptic theology today is marked by a knowledge and practical use of Scriptures uncommon in contemporary Western theology. In the writings of Pope Shenouda as well as in those of Father Matta al-Miskin, every page betrays a familiarity with the biblical writings. This is a result of a probably unique combination of an influence of Protestant emphasis and distribution of the Scriptures and the monastic tradition, and practice of repetitive reading and meditation on the Scriptures popularized in the movement of monastic renewal. The latter gives an emphasis to the Old Testament that is strange to most modern European Christians. Most prominent among the books of the Old Testament are the Psalms, which the monks learn by heart, but also the prophetic and historical writings of the OT are quoted extensively. The unity of the Old with the New Testament is central as well as the Christological and ecclesiological interpretation of the OT.[33]

The tension between renewal and tradition is primarily caused by different reactions to Western biblical criticism. Influenced by the Islamic understanding of the Qur'an as literally the Word of God and by Protestant emphasis on the simple meaning of the text, there is a strong tendency towards a literal and fundamentalist interpretation of the Bible in popular Coptic theology today. The apologetic character of many of the writings of Pope Shenouda, directed mainly at Protestant sects like the Plymouth brethren, and using almost exclusively biblical arguments, reinforces this tendency. This line of defense is, however, severely struck by modern biblical exegesis based on the tradition of historical criticism. Thus, the defense of the tradition leads to a total rejection of the results of biblical criticism and its scepticism concerning the literal historicity and literal meaning of much of the biblical material.

In his important exegetical works Matta al-Miskin takes another line, integrating some of the results of modern biblical scholarship.[34] This is made possible by relying on the patristic tradition and especially the allegorical exegesis and hermeneutical principles of the school of Alexandria. Scripture is always applied with an emphasis on its deeper meaning. What is essential is the spiritual message for the Christian today. The Bible is not to be investigated but experienced. Knowledge of God, which is the ultimate meaning of Scripture, has to start with humility and purity. The Bible cannot be understood unless there is a relationship and an obedience to what it gradually reveals. Scripture does not give arguments for doctrine or descriptions of faith, but authenticates what man has experienced in his own encounter with God and scriptural reading thus helps to regenerate and bring him back to his original creation.[35] Thus, Matta al-Miskin can remain undisturbed by Western biblical criticism with its roots in Renaissance Humanism and the Enlightenment.

Secondly, there is in the monastic theological renewal a strong dependence on the writings of the Eastern spiritual fathers of the first centuries. One of the most prominent among them is Isaac of Niniveh, a seventh-century Syrian author, whose work has made a deep impact on Orthodox spirituality. Although a Nestorian himself his writings were translated into Greek and included in the Greek Philokalia. Most probably Matta al-Miskin is here influenced by the later Patriarch Kyrillos VI, who had studied Isaac when he was still a hermit.[36] Through Isaac's writings, as well as the homilies attributed to Macarius the Great, Matta al-Miskin is deeply indebted to the Syrian ascetic tradition with its emphasis on the heart. Thus, the Origenist legacy evident in the writings of St. Anthony, Evagrius, John Cassian and others is counterbalanced by the less intellectual and philosophical Syrian tradition. Even in his commentary on the Letters of St. Anthony, Matta al-Miskin avoids a discussion on the most Origenistic features of the letters.[37] Common to both, and prominent in Matta al-Miskin's thought, is, however, the emphasis on man's original creation in the image and likeness of God and the optimistic view of man's spiritual capacity.

These texts, unaffected by the apologetics of the Coptic Church against Christological opponents (Chalcedonians and Nestorians), and unaffected by the influence of Arabic Muslim philosophy, belong to a very different theological tradition than the "scholastic" theology of the 19th century Coptic Church rooted in medieval Christian Arabic tradition and shaped by debates with Catholics and Protestants. Some of the most severe theological conflicts within the church during the last decades can most easily be explained by this difference. A first example is the debate on the presence of the Holy Spirit in the Christian, where Pope Shenouda has questioned some of Father Matta's statements that are based on the writings of the early fathers, in this case the homilies of Macarius the Great.[38] A second example is the conflict over the interpretation of atonement, where Pope Shenouda stands closer to the Western tradition of Anselm of Canterbury, also found in medieval Arabic writings, while the Coptic lay theologian Dr. George Bibawi relies on St. Athanasius and a Greek patristic tradition.[39]

Thirdly there is the very strong ecumenical drive visible in much of the monastic renewal. This is deeply rooted in the monastic theology of the early centuries.[40] The constant appeal to the Fathers in the works by Matta al-Miskin is to a great extent the result of an understanding of his tradition as part of the church universal, transcending the Coptic tradition.[41] There can be no doubt that the patristic heritage is the common ground Matta al-Miskin seeks to unite Christians of different traditions. Instead of entering into polemics with Western or Eastern "scholasticism," trying to defend specific Coptic traditions or trying to defend Christianity in concepts acceptable to Muslims, he retreats to the Church Fathers. In his urgent appeals for Christian unity he urges the churches to move from dogmatic self-righteousness to deeper levels of spirituality, love and mercy.

This sometimes very radical view of Christian unity, which does not start with dogmatic statements, but a unity in spiritual life, is also visible in some of the writings of other Coptic leaders such as Pope Shenouda or Bishop Gregorius. But here one gets the feeling that the structure of the ecumenical movement growing out of dialogues between various Protestant groups, and shaped by the shadow of the Reformation and ongoing dialogue with the Roman Catholic Church, leads to a certain "confessionalism" that does not exist in the monastic setting. The Coptic Church is perceived as a closed circle which can be entered into through baptism only. The Western ecumenical concept of a family of churches who share mutual responsibilities and are involved in a gradual process of fully recognizing each other is still alien to the Coptic Church.[42]

## Conclusion

In contemporary Coptic Orthodox theology, there is a clear tension between tradition and renewal. Unfortunately, this tension, which is present and probably necessary in all theological development, is negatively influenced by a history of polemics with Islam and with Western missionary activity. Since the deposition of the Alexandrian patriarch Dioscorus at the Council of Chalcedon, the Coptic Church has found itself in a position of defense. Thus, much of its theological history is characterized by polemics against the Chalcedonian definition, against Islamic criticism of the doctrines of the Trinity and the Incarnation, against Roman Catholic views on papal primacy and against the theology of missionaries often centered on doctrinal points, like purgatory or priesthood. Attempts at renewal have often been looked upon as undermining the lines of defense and thus apologetics have tended to harden the doctrinal positions. Thus, even the use of Western scholarship on the Fathers is sometimes met with great suspicion and rejected with the help of the medieval Arabic tradition in which they are represented only in excerpts aimed to prove the heresy of the Chalcedonian Christological position.

The renewal in the church is largely a result of the revival of desert monasticism. Here, from the depths of the tradition of the desert, the church has found new self-confidence. But unless this monastic renewal and its spirituality is reflected upon theologically and brought into dialogue with modern theological scholarship, Orthodox, Catholic and Protestant, it will hardly contribute to the development of Christian theology in a wider context. On the contrary, it easily becomes restricted to an emotional spirituality which leaves the doctrinal traditions unaffected, or even contributes to their becoming petrified, and thus even supports fanaticism and doctrinal self-glorification. With Matta al-Miskin, the Coptic Church has, however, a profound theologian who has been able to absorb and critically examine Western theological research without becoming apologetic. The task remains, however, to interpret his spiritual theology in the context of the intellectual dialogue between Western and Eastern Orthodox theology as well as between Christian and Muslim theology.

A specific context for this dialogue between the theological insights of the monastic renewal and Western tradition are the ecumenical dialogues between the Coptic Orthodox Church and other churches. The dialogues with other Orthodox churches have a longer history and have ended with a recognition of theological agreement, an agreement clearly manifest in cooperation in theological education.[43] The dialogue with the Catholic Church was resumed in 1988 after a break of nine years, and has reached an agreement on the central Christological issue. But there has been little progress on the traditional points of disagreement and few signs of any impact from the spiritual revival. An exception to this are some of the encounters arranged by the Catholic institute *Pro Oriente*.[44] Discussions are also going on with the Anglican Church and with the Church of Sweden. All hope the dialogues will be able to overcome the suspicions of previous encounters and open up a chapter of common study of the Fathers and of the different transformations of their legacy in Western as well as in Eastern "scholasticism."

Notes

1. The libraries of the monasteries are still only partly and, in many cases, unsatisfactorily catalogued. See i.a. Yassa `Abd al-Masih, *Kataluj Makhtutat Dair al-Anba Antuniyus bi-l-Bahr al-Ahmar* (typewritten without date). An exception is Ugo Zanetti, *Les Manuscriots de Dari Aba Maqar*, (*Cahiers d'Orientalisme* 11), Geneva, 1986. For a survey of the different collections see: *Bulletin d'Arabe Chrétien* vol. V (1981) 81-82. At the monastery of St. Menas a microfilming project is gradually collecting and cataloging films of manuscripts from private collections as well as from churches and monasteries.
2. The most prominent Alexandrian theologians are, on the one hand, Clement of Alexandria and Origen, on the other, St. Athanasius and St. Cyril.
3. The relations with Syria and Palestine remained strong, not only with the non-

Chalcedonian Syrian Church but also with Melkites and Nestorians who shared the Coptic experience of Arab Muslim rule. The theological exchange was, however, mainly in the field of ascetic and mystical theology emanating from the monasteries in Sinai, Palestine and Syria.

4. For Coptic translations of patristic texts see the assessment and references to the works of Leipoldt, O'Leary and Krause in Tito Orlandi, "Coptic Literature," *The Roots of Egyptian Christianity* (ed. by Birger A. Pearson and James E. Goehring), Philadelphia: Fortress Press, 1986, 51-81.
5. For the Coptic Arabic literature of this period see: Georg Graf, *Geschichte der christlichen arabischen Literatur* II, (Studi et Testi 133), Città del Vaticano, 1947, 294-475.
6. For the early patristic literature see: Khalil Samir, "Arabic Sources for Early Egyptian Christianity," *The Roots*, 82-97; for the monastic literature see: Samuel Rubenson, "Arabic Sources for the Theology of the Early Monastic Movement in Egypt," *Parole de l'Orient* XVI (1990a1991) 33-47.
7. These are mainly the Greek and Syrian authors translated into Arabic by Melkites and Syrians. Some of these writings, like the homilies attributed to St. Macarius the Great and the homilies of St. Isaac of Niniveh, are central to the modern monastic revival in Egypt. Other examples are the writings of St. Gregory of Nazianz, Dionysius the Areopagite, Maximus the Confessor and St. John the Ladder.
8. The most famous patristic anthologies in Arabic, the *I'tiraf al-Aba* (The Confession of the Fathers) and the *Durr al-Thamin fi idah al-din* (The Precious Pearl), are both rooted in Coptic traditions of anti-Chalcedonian polemic. For remarks on the translation of patristic literature into Arabic in Egypt see: Samuel Rubenson, "Translating the Tradition. Some Aspects of the Arabization of the Patristic Heritage in Medieval Egypt," to be published in *Medieval Encounters. Jewish, Christian and Muslim Culture in Confluence and Dialogue* 1 (1995).
9. Some of the most important being Sawirus ibn al-Muqaffa' (10th C.), Simon ibn Kalil ibn Maqara (ca. 1150-1210), Al-Rahid Abu-l-Khayr ibn al-Tayyib (ca. 1160-1245), Al-Safi Ibn al-`Assal (ca. 1180-1255), Al-As`ad abu al-Faraj Hibatallah ibn al-Assal (ca. 1190-1255), al-Mu`taman abu Ishaq Ibrahim ibn al-Assal (ca. 1200-1260) and Shams al-Ri'asa abu-al-Barakat ibn Kabar (ca. 1270-1324).
10. In the 1980s a debate on the medieval Christian defense of the Trinity by an "attribute-apology" engaged bishops and theologians and made the conflict between a patristic and a traditionalist approach manifest. See: Jurj Habib Bibawi, *Al-Qiddis Athanasiyus al-Rasuli fi Muwajaha al-Dini ghair al-Urthudhuksi*: Cairo, 1985.
11. There is a growing scholarly discussion on the philosophy and theology of the Christian Arabic medieval literature. See i.a. the series *Patrimoine d'arabe chrétien* and the volumes emanating from the International Conferences of Christian Arabic Studies published in *Orientalia Christiana Analecta* 218 (Rome 1982), and 226 (Rome 1986) and in *Parole de l'Orient* XVI (Kaslik, Lebanon 1990-1991).
12. See: Graf, *Geschichte der christichen arabischen Literatur* IV, 114a142.
13. An important example is the monk Andrew who became metropolitan of Ethiopia with the name Abune Selama.
14. See: B. Evetts, "Un prélat réformateur. Le patriarche copte Cyrille IV (1854 à 1861)," *Revue de l'Orient Chrétien* 17 (1912) 3-15, J. Heyworth-Dunne, "Education in Egypt and the Copts," *Bulletin de la Société d'Archéologie Copte* VI (1940) 91-108 and R. Strothmann, *Die koptische Kirche in der Neuzeit*. Reprint. Nendeln, Liechtenstein: Kraus Reprint LTD., 1966. The only biography of Kyrillos IV is unfortunately in Arabic: Girgis Filutha'us `Awad, *Al-Anba Kirillus al-Rabi'*, *Abu al-Islah al-Qibti*, Cairo, 1911.

15. See: Graf, *Geschichte*, 145-159. The most prominent representatives of this theological reform movement were Afram `Adad and Filitha'us Ibrahim.
16. One of these leaders was a young teacher at the Cairo university who later became a monk and in 1971 was elected patriarch as Shenouda III.
17. The literature on the movement is still very limited, but see: Wolfram Reiss, "Geschichte und Entwicklung der Sonntagsschulen in der Koptisch-Orthodoxen Kirche," *Der Christlichen Osten* 47 (1992).
18. On this strange solitary monk see Otto Meinardus, "Zeitgenössische Gottesnarren in den Wüsten Ägyptens," *Ostkirchliche Studien* 36 (1987) 302-306. Another important father of monastic revival was Dawud al-Maqari.
19. For this period and the reactions of young Egyptians against the national kingdom see: B.L. Carter, *The Copts in Egyptian Politics*, London: Croom Helm, 1986, and the auto-biography of Anwar al-Sadat.
20. For this revival see also Otto Meinardus, "Zur monastischen Erneuerung in der koptischen Kirche," *Oriens Christianus* 61 (1977) 59-70, and Gottfried Glaßner, "Erneuerung im Zeichen der Mönche," *Erbe und Auftrag* 66 (1990) 29-43.
21. The most important are the 32 volumes of translations in the *Nusus al-aba'* and the 4 volumes of studies in the *Darasat aba'iya* published by the Patristic Center, and the more than 20 volumes in the series *Aba' al-Kanisa* published under the auspices of the bishop of Alexandria.
22. *Ta`alim al-Rusul (al-Dasqaliya)*, ed. by Dr. William Sulayman Qilada, Cairo: Dar al-Thaqafa, 1989 (second edition).
23. *Rasa'il al-Qiddis Antuniyus*, Dair al-Qiddis Anba Maqar, 1979. See: Samuel Rubenson, *The Letters of St. Antony. Origenist Theology, Monastic Tradition and the Making of a Saint.* Lund: 1990, 20f.
24. *Al-Kanisa al-Khalidah* (The Everlasting Church) (1960, 1974, 1984), *Al-Wahda al-Masihiyah* (Christian Unity) (1965, 1978) (Eng. tr. One Christ and One Catholic Church, 1980; Christian Unity, 1982), *Al-Wahda al-Haqiqiya* (True Unity) (1988) (Eng. True Unity will Inspire the World, 1988). Although Matta has been critical of official ecumenical work he has made the monastery a center of ecumenical encounter and in his latest work he has come to a much more positive assessment of ecumenical discussions.
25. Although an ascetic of the desert, Matta al-Miskin has not avoided discussing political issues. In several articles he supported President Sadat, the October war, as well as his trip to Jerusalem, and president Mubarak. In a small booklet he gives his opinion on socialism, sectarianism and religious fanaticism: *Maqalat bain al-Siyasa wa al-Din* (Essays between Politics and Religion), 1977, 1980.
26. Matthew the Poor, *The Communion of Love*, Crestwood: St. Vladimir's Press, 1984.
27. See i.a. the small pamphlet *Al-Masih fi al-`Ahdayn* (Christ in the two Testaments), 1979 (Eng. translation in *The Communion of Love*, 39-51), and *Masih al-Tarikh. Masih Hayyun* (The Christ of History. A Living Christ), 1976 (Eng. translation in *The Communion of Love*, 53-63).
28. Noteworthy is his small booklet on Birth Control, *Ra'i fi Tahdid al-Nasl*, 1968 (Eng. translation: *A Viewpoint on Birth Control*, 1981), where he argues in favor of the programs of birth control on theological grounds.
29. Although Matta often censures Origen for his Platonic ideas, he comes rather close to the Origenist tradition in his positive view on the knowability of God. In spite of his extensive quotations from St. Augustine he clearly represents the Eastern tradition with its emphasis on deification as something experienced in mind and body.
30. In his emphasis on the suffering of Christ and the necessity of tears, Matta is deeply indebted to the Syrian spiritual fathers. Fine examples are given in his

collection on the Suffering of Christ mentioned above. Some articles from this book are translated into English as booklets: *The Passion of Jesus Christ in Our life*, 1982; *The Mystery of the Cross*, 1980, and some are included in *The Communion of Love*.

31. The first volume of studies in the Fathers published by the Patristic Center was a translation into Arabic of the book *Being as Communion*, by Metropolitan John Zizioulas.
32. The critique, especially of traditions concerning ritual and views on purity, comes from monastic reformers and patristic scholars, but also from the hierarchy, as is evident in some of the published replies of Pope Shenouda to various questions put to him before his weekly sermon in the cathedral. English translations of these are available under the title *So many years with the problems of people*, Vols. I-IV, Cairo 1988-1992 and later editions.
33. A good example of the use of the OT for ecclesiological themes is the booklet on priesthood by Pope Shenouda, where Christian priesthood is defended largely from inferences from the priesthood of the Old Testament.
34. Thus, there is in the introduction to the commentary on the gospel of St. John a discussion on the authorship of the book, revealing an open attitude towards biblical criticism which is not generally accepted in the Coptic Church..
35. By Father Matta there are, in addition to the recent commentaries on the Gospel of John and the Letter to the Romans, several small booklets dealing with the interpretation of Scripture; see i.a. his *Kaifa Taqra' al-Kitab al-Muqaddas* (How to Read the Bible), 1966, 1976 (Eng. translation in *Communion of Love*, 15-37).
36. In his *Orthodox Prayer Life*, Matta al-Miskin refers in his list of manuscripts in the first place to a manuscript containing the four books of St. Isaac transcribed from the copy belonging to the priest Mina al-Baramasi al-Mutawahhid (the anchorite), the later Patriarch Kyrillos VI.
37. See his *Al-Qiddis Antuniyus Nasik Injili* (St. Antony: An Evangelical Hermit), 1968, 1976, and his *Rasa'il al-Qiddis Antuniyus ma`a Talkhis al-Badi' al-Ruhiyah al-Hamah* (The Letters of St. Anthony with a Summary of the Main Spiritual Principles), 1979.
38. I have not been able to acquire a text with a direct attack on the views of Father Matta, but most probably some of the answers in volume four of the book *So Many Years with the Problems of People* are directed against his Pneumatology. See Question 17 which is a reply to someone who has read a book about Pentecost, probably the one by Father Matta al-Miskin. From here we can understand that the conflict has to do with the question of the indwelling of the Spirit and behind it the concept of deification, common to the Eastern fathers, but avoided by Pope Shenouda.
39. For a background see: Dr. Jurj Habib Bibawi, *Al-Qiddis Athanasiyus al-Rasuli fi Muwajaha al-Turath al-Dini ghair al-Urthudhuksi* (St. Athanasius the Apostolic versus the non-Orthodox Religious Legacy), Cairo, 1985. See also his "Atonement and Mercy. Islam between Athanasius and Anselm," (unpublished lecture, Lund 1994).
40. In writings like The Letters of St. Antony the idea of unity is central: God sent his Son to gather the dispersed humanity and bring it back to the communion of all spiritual nature, which is the Church. Cf. Samuel Rubenson, *The Letters of St. Antony*, 64-68.
41. His choice is by no means restricted to the Eastern monastic fathers, but includes most of the writers before 451 and also a choice from later authors, regardless if they are Chalcedonian or not. Even late Byzantine authors, like St. Gregory of Palamas, are quoted. A prominent place in his writings is given to St. Augustine,

which is rather uncommon among Orthodox theologians. In contrast Origen is strongly censured for his Platonic thinking and authors indebted to his legacy, like St. Gregory of Nyssa, Evagrius of Pontus and St. Maximus the Confessor, are almost absent.

42. See for example the statement by Bishop Gregorios, "The Recognition of the Sacraments of Other Churches by the Coptic Orthodox Church" presented at the Seventh International Congress of the Society for the Law of the Eastern Churches, Geneva 1985 (typescript).

43. The agreements from the first four unofficial consultations (1964, 1967, 1970 and 1971) were printed in *The Greek Orthodox Theological Review*. Important contributions from Eastern and Oriental Orthodox theologians were later collected in *Does Chalcedon Divide or Unite?* (ed. Paulos Gregorios, William H. Lazareth and Nikos A. Nissiotis), WCC, 1981. The more recent discussions are covered by *Irénikon*, and the documents published in *Dokumente wachsender Übereinstimmung. Sämtliche Berichte und Konsenstexte interkonfessioneller Gespräche auf Weltebene*, vol. 1-2, Paderborn & Frankfurt a.M.: Von Harding Meyer..., 1983, 1991.

44. The documents emanating from the earlier phase of this dialogue are published in English *(The Roman Catholic Church and the Coptic Orthodox Church. Documents (1973-1988))*, Vatican City: The Pontifical Council for Promoting Christian Unity, Information Service N. 76 (1991: I). For a Catholic analysis see: Johannes Madey, "Die ökumenischen Beziehungen zwischen der katholischen und der koptisch-orthodoxen Kirche seit 1973," *Catholica* 35 (1981) 141-153. Later developments are regularly commented upon in the journal *Irénikon*.

Mark Francis Gruber

# Coping with God: Coptic Monasticism in Egyptian Culture

One contemporary monk's version of a popular Coptic religious lesson was recounted to me in a monastery of the Wadi al-Natroun:

> In Egypt, religion is a simple matter understood by all the Copts from childhood. In fact, religion is as simple as the alphabet. [The word "alphabet" has some currency in Arabic-speaking Egypt due to centuries of Greek, French, and British influence.] "Alpha" is the sign of the eagle, the symbol of the Spirit of God's court, the transcendent, the realm of angels, and the saints. "Beta" is the sign of a house, the place of human habitation. It stands for the realm of the earthly and familiar. "Alpha and Beta" have been combined through Jesus Christ, and the Christian can speak about religion in one such simple term. The eagle has perched at the window of our house. God and all his hosts have come among us. Everywhere we see signs of their visit, and we are not surprised. In the West, the eagle has flown far above, more like a black dot in the sky than a bird in the house. So far away is the dot that many cannot even see it. But for us, there is little else to see. Religion is so simple, like the alphabet.

The old monk's story, whatever its origin, is illustrative of an essential character of Coptic cosmology: as a reflex of the central orthodox belief in the Incarnation, transcendence and immanence have merged. The conjunction of the divine and the human provides to the Copts a cipher for the resolution of the tensions and the pressures of their beleaguered ethnic existence. The cosmological center of Coptic society is exhibited wherever this cultural conjunction takes place. Beyond the Eucharistic liturgy itself, Coptic monasteries provide the contemporary locus for the immanent dwelling of a transcendent God, as they have for thousands of years. And, as the forces which challenge Coptic society change, the monasteries, in turn, adapt the cipher of transcendence made immanent in order to maintain their cultural function. How monasticism functions in Coptic culture (how it abides in the cosmology of the Coptic people), and how contemporary monasteries have adapted to the pressures of modern Egyptian society are the topics of the essay below. To appreciate these matters, the cosmology of the Coptic people must be considered more closely.[1]

Coptic life is permeated with all manner of transcendental presence. Angel guardians, archangels, heavenly hosts, patron saints, saint intercessors, saint occasional-defenders, and the Virgin Mary round out the constellation of divinely commissioned agents of God who pervade Coptic society. They are present as a consequence of the act of divine incarnation, as an elaboration of the immanence of God becoming man in Jesus Christ. The category of secularity has collapsed under the weight of heaven. Hence, the Copts are available to experiences of visions, locutions, inspired dreams, mystical apparitions, miracles and revelations. Copts experience such phenomena collectively much more often than religious devotees of the West (where these things occur rarely and then almost always privately) because the cosmology of the Copts—"alphabet"—is general currency, whose power and value are paradoxically reinforced and underwritten by the pressure of their minority status in the vast sea of Arab Islam. The Copts need their heavenly friends since their counterpoint—earthly enemies with religious zeal—abound.

All this is not to say that divine immanence is an undivided good for the Copts. While the incarnation of God is the glory of their religion and, by their account, the boast of the human race, it occasions rather significant problems. By definition, God is wholly perfect. A great collection of literature, the Bible, Coptic liturgical texts, hagiography, church canons, hymnody, etc., unanimously attest to God's unalloyed goodness and purity. So long as God remained only transcendent, his perfection would be a matter of detached admiration, much like the philosophical reflections of a neo-Platonist. But the all-perfect, all-mighty God who was first revealed as holy, i.e., separated from the forces which embroil the world, has condescended into the field of earthly forces by becoming a human being. His holy presence within the earthly realm throws into sharp relief the gross imperfections and corruptions of the world.

A cursory review of Coptic communal prayers reveals a profound sense of personal and collective unworthiness before the face of an all-too-near deity. For instance, as the priest approaches an incensation prior to the Coptic liturgy, he chants:

> Please accept this incense from our hands, from us the sinners. Accept [it] as the sweet-scented incense for the forgiveness of our sins, and the

sins of all Your people.[2]

The priest then incenses the sanctuary. Afterwards he intones a long prayer for the repose of the dead:

> And if they have been careless or negligent like all human beings who live in this world in flesh,
>
> Kindly, O Lord, forgive them, for You are good, and You are the Lover of Mankind. . . .
>
> For no one is free from sin even if his life is just a single day on earth. . . .
>
> To all of us, kindly, O Lord, grant us the Christian perfection which would be pleasing to You.[3]

The congregation responds:

> Grant, O Lord, to keep us throughout this day without sin. . . . Blessed are You, O Lord, make me understand Your righteousness, Your mercy is everlasting, O Lord; please cast not away the work of Your hands.[4]

Shortly thereafter the congregation recites the *Trisagion*, a basic prayer-component of Coptic ritual:

> Holy God, Holy Almighty, Holy Immortal, O You, Who were born of the Virgin, have mercy upon us.
>
> Holy God, Holy Almighty, Holy Immortal, O You, Who were crucified for our sake, have mercy upon us.
>
> Holy God, Holy Almighty, Holy Immortal, O You, Who arose from the dead and ascended to Heaven, have mercy upon us.
>
> Glory be to the Father, and to the Son, and to the Holy Spirit, now and forever and ever and to the ages of ages. Amen.
>
> O Holy Trinity, have mercy upon us. O Holy Trinity, have mercy upon us. O Holy Trinity, have mercy upon us.

Lord, forgive us our sins. Lord, forgive us our iniquities. Lord, forgive us our trespasses.

Lord, heal those who are sick among Your people; heal them for the sake of Your Holy Name. Give rest to the souls of our fathers and brothers who have departed.

O You Who are without sin, Lord, have mercy upon us. O You Who are without sin, Lord, help us and accept our supplications.

For Yours is the glory, and the honor, and the tri-holiness. Lord have mercy; Lord have mercy; Lord bless us. Amen.[5]

Such prayers would seem to a Westerner, religious or not, to be overly self-deprecating and morose, or even forced and dramatized. In Coptic worship, however, these prayers are animated by a communal perception of divine immanence which both energizes and validates the authenticity of such sentiments. The Copts experience a sense of relief to pray penitentially, for the display of compunction is a necessary aspect of any intuition of divine proximity. Only societies which no longer really perceive God's immanence (or his "otherness") can rather blandly conduct liturgical services without much reference to unworthiness, sin, or shame.

The Coptic monk is one who, above all, abides in the presence of God. Whereas, it may happen that a member of the laity might avoid renting a flat immediately next to a church because the constant reminder of divine immanence can become burdensome (e.g., when a husband and wife argue, or when a child needs to be disciplined), a Coptic monk is never far from the realization of God's encompassing nearness. Chapels abound in the monastery, as well as holy pictures, icons, candles, and shrines. The monk's body is enshrouded in holy garb; his face is—in contradistinction to almost all Coptic laymen—framed by a holy beard, as well as a hood. Beyond this, the desert is itself an immensely powerful arena of the enveloping divine presence. Heaven and hell converge there, and the monk never leaves it. No one is a better student of divine immanence than the Coptic monk.

When compunction is the consequence of the perception of divine immanence, the monk must therefore be constantly in the process of self-depreciation before God. The most contrite of Copts should be the monk. No surprise, then, that the most common designation of a monk in Egypt, "*rahib*," means literally "dreader" of God. The "dread" which essentially defines the vocation of a Coptic monk is not easy for the Western Christian to appreciate, much less so the secular social scientist or skeptic. Religions of dread and anxiety evoke the very worst of modern secular stereotypes of the mentality of the Dark Ages: superstition, scrupulosity, and the fear of demons, hell, and witches. All too often casual Western observers have tried to fit Coptic religion into a leftover framework supposed to fit the world view of early medieval Europe. Such a framework probably has more to do with modern Westerners' perceived need to repudiate their own foundational heritage than with either earlier Western historical epochs or present-day Coptic cosmology.

The "dread" in the Coptic *rahib* has much more to do with the Hebraic sense of "fear of the Lord" (and, therefore, a distant cousin of the Islamic notion of the same phrase), and represents the virtue of being always mindful of the world's most essential and overwhelming truth: "In Him we live and move and have our being."[6] The continuous awareness of this truth constitutes the central mission and special vocation of the Coptic monk. Any member of the Coptic Church may, of course, claim the same prerogative, both in its occasional frustrations, or in its blessed successes.

When a monk fails to abide in the awareness of God's immanence, he has reason to suspect his own infidelities, selfishness, and sins as the cause. These aspects of his soul are occasions of dread before the judgment of God. When a monk does perceive the divine presence, he is at the same time immediately and reflexively aware of his own creaturely contingency and moral finitude, and is therefore likewise in dread. For good reason, the monk is named *"rahib,"* for dread is the defining modality of his life in one way or the other.

In view of the Coptic understanding of the monastic vocation, much of the peculiarity of monasticism in Egypt can be better appreciated. Western observers of monks invariably notice the centrality of a rule in the formation of a monastery, or the soul of one of its members. The rule, such as the *Holy Rule of St. Benedict*, or the *Rule of St. Basil*, is a document which outlines all of the discipline of monastic observances and the organizational principles of a monastery. Coptic monasteries likewise frequently stress their "rule" of life. The outside observer might suspect that a special Coptic code is being referred to. St. Pachomius, founder of Coptic communal (cenobitic) monasticism, did in fact write a clear and orderly (paramilitary) code for his monastic foundations. Other foundational documents abound in Coptic monasticism: the *Life of St. Anthony*; the *Paradise of the Fathers*, as well as many others, written in Greek, Latin, Syriac and Coptic. However, one would be misled if one thought that any such document was in itself "the" rule of a Coptic monastery.

Rather, any such rule given from religious tradition is a supplement to the Coptic rule. For them, "the rule" is the constant realization of the divine presence. To that end, any number of disciplines, practices, devotions, liturgies, and monastic relationships are of proven worth and enjoy standard acceptance. But no formula could ever exhaustively contain the process of the realization of God's nearness. Rather, the essential component of the rule is always interior, and not subject to a general appraisal of external acts.

For this reason, the Coptic monastery places a much greater stress on the dynamic relationship of a monk to his spiritual father than it does on his mastery of a foundational text. A spiritual master can address the monk to the challenge of realizing God's presence in a way that private reading of a written rule cannot. Personal reflection on a document lends itself to the ordinary filters of rationalization and categorical reduction common to most minds. But the discourse between a soul and a spiritual father exercises the dynamics of mutuality which impel the monk to rise above private preoccupations and transcend internal forces until he stands in honesty before the divine interior presence. The spiritual master challenges the monk to acknowledge contritely the areas of his life where he has resisted the realization of divine presence, and conversely, the spiritual father supports the monk in the moment of the crushing realization of God's greater immanence. Moreover, the spiritual father reminds the monk in due time that yesterday's limited awareness of divine immanence cannot detain him from the journey toward greater immersion in the Holy Presence tomorrow.

Spiritual fatherhood is a part of all Christian monasticism. In Egypt it has never been subordinated to a formal text, save perhaps that of the Gospel—which itself has been rightly observed to be a relational word designed to proclaim to another soul a call unto immersion (baptism) into divine mutuality. But because spiritual fatherhood has not been subordinated to any particular monastic codification in Egypt, monasticism there is less standardized and routinized compared to its Western counterparts. Western rules, after all, regulate daily schedules (horariums) and personal routines down to the smallest details. Spiritual fatherhood concerns itself, by contrast, with one's manner of prayer, one's faith, and one's moral development and growth in holiness. In Western monasteries, a monk might be expected to attend all of the communal prayer services (the "Hours" of the Divine Office) in the church of his abbey. If he does not, especially on a regular basis, he is liable to be unfavorably judged by his superior, or at least suffer the social sanction of peer disapproval. For in Western monasteries, the Divine Office is canonically established, codified, and proscribed by the rule. In Egypt, by contrast, the Divine Office, which while certainly supported by the monastery as an aid to seeking holiness, does not necessarily draw each monk into attendance under pain of any sanction. It may well happen that any number of monks absent themselves from various or all of the Hours of the communal Office because their search for awareness of God does not warrant attendance at this point on their journey—as best discerned in dialogue with their spiritual father. (In Egypt at present, the abbot of most monasteries holds the position of spiritual father to most, if not all, of his monks.)

Indeed, the priority of establishing institutional formalities for monasticism, which is so prominent in the West, is secondary to the Copts. Individual holiness outstrips in importance communal integration. Hence in Egypt, the ideal of the monastic vocation is to arrive at the stage of eremitical (hermit) perfection, wherein the cultivated awareness of God's immanence blocks out all other social or natural concerns. The Coptic monk desires to be alone with the Alone, in such a way as to render as secondary all institutional and collective activity. Outside Egypt, monasteries often believe that the level of fraternal charity in the ranks and of hospitality to the guest are the best evidence of holiness in the lives of individual monks.

In Western monasteries, the labor of the monk is deemed to be a critical element of the abbey's good order. Western monasteries stress the value of self-supported (and traditionally, self-sufficient) communal life. The other value of disciplined labor is that surrender to routine work also delivers an aspect of the divine presence to the monk. In Egypt, this latter aspect alone is highly regarded. The Coptic monk does not have to be an economic asset to his cloister. If he earnestly pursues the presence of God in his life, he justifies his existence and is worthy of being supported by his brothers and by the alms of the whole church for the "service" he provides by growing in holiness.

Perambulation around the grounds of a monastery is a recreational and social pastime of the Western monk. Naturally, it is an occasion for private reflection and prayer as well. In Egypt, communal walking is not a highly regarded religious practice, but private excursions into the empty desert are considered ideal opportunities for immersion into God and the processing of all interior conflicts necessary to approach that end. Thus, the desert regions surrounding all of Egypt's monasteries are often dotted with the figures of black-robed monks in solitary contemplation. Such opportunities afforded by the desert are so highly prized by the Coptic monks that the desert is very nearly a normative element of their monastic ideal, as important to them as the Holy Rule is to Catholic Benedictines.

Asceticism, the practice of bodily and emotional mortification, is a part of monastic life everywhere. Outside Egypt, the rationale for asceticism is most likely to be expressed in terms of the need to gain personal mastery over the concupiscence of the flesh. Even when the word "concupiscence" is no longer employed, Western monks often share a profound suspicion (with the laity) of the unworthiness of the body. The body tends to be viewed somehow as beyond integration into holiness and, therefore, it must be suppressed habitually (asceticism) in order to release the person's more spiritual potential. More than a little Platonism has haunted the Western churches due to the strong and early Greek influence in the formation of Christian piety. Traditionally, Western and Orthodox monks of Europe fasted to dampen the animal appetite of hunger, were celibate to break the thralldom of sex, kept vigil through the night to keep the body from seduction in dreams. At times, some monks subjected their flesh to flagellation to master the temptations of creaturely comfort.

Coptic monks have also always practiced significant ascetical works. Indeed, at times in their history, they competed with each other in their mortifications, and excelled all other monastic traditions in the gravity of their practices. This fact, coupled with their profound sense of compunction, as discussed above, could easily persuade the outside observer that the Copts share a Platonic mistrust of the physical body, along with the rest of popular Christendom. In fact, if a Coptic monk is asked about the severity of his fasting or his vigils, humility might compel him to explain that his mortifications are necessary to rein in his disordered moral and spiritual life. But this answer would derive more from the reflex of humility than from a dualistic philosophy. Platonism and neo-Platonism are specifically Greco-Roman philosophical traditions, which undoubtedly influenced the Egyptian Church as well, but which were strongly resisted in the anti-academic monastic movements of the Coptic desert.

Instead of seeking philosophical systems for an explanation of Coptic asceticism, we might better examine the cosmological foundations of their ritual life. The Copts are the descendants of the aboriginal people of the Nile Valley and the Delta. They share a spiritual bond with the Semites of Palestine and the Bedouins of the Maghreb. Their attitudes about the flesh have much more to do with these people than with the speculations of the Greeks. Indeed, the emergence of the Coptic culture in late Roman times represents a certain repudiation of Greek ascendancy in Egypt. The re-emergence of an earlier attitude toward religion, albeit in Christian adaptation, granted the practices of asceticism a somewhat different basis for the Coptic monk than for his European counterpart. The Coptic monk experiences ascetic acts (following his Semitic/Hamitic heritage) more as participation in sacrifice than as an exercise of discipline.

Now, even in biblical records, the proper object of ritual sacrifice has never been the "second fruit," but the first. The shepherd was never to sacrifice the lame or the halt, but the unblemished and the strong, as directed in the Book of Leviticus:

> The Lord said to Moses, "Speak to Aaron and to his sons and to all the Israelites, and tell them: When anyone of the house of Israel, or any alien residing in Israel, who wishes to offer a sacrifice, brings a holocaust as a votive offering or as a free-will offering to the Lord, and if it is to be acceptable, the ox or sheep or goat that he offers must be an unblemished male. You shall not offer one that has any defect, for such a one would not be acceptable for you. When anyone presents a peace offering to the Lord from the herd or the flock in fulfillment of a vow, or as a free-will offering, if it is to find acceptance, it must be unblemished; it shall not have any defect. One that is blind or crippled or maimed, or one that has a running sore or mange or ringworm, you shall not offer to the Lord; do not put such an animal on the altar as an oblation to the Lord. An ox or a sheep that is in any way ill-proportioned or stunted you may indeed present as a free-will offering, but it will not be acceptable as a votive offering. One that has its testicles bruised or crushed or torn out or cut off you shall not offer to the Lord. You shall neither do this in your own land nor receive from a foreigner any such animals to offer up as the food of your God; since they will not be acceptable for you."
>
> The Lord said to Moses, "When an ox or a lamb or a goat is born, it shall remain with its mother for seven days; only on the eighth day onward will it be acceptable, to be offered as an oblation to the Lord. You shall not slaughter an ox or a sheep on one and the same day with its young. Whenever you offer a thanksgiving sacrifice to the Lord, so offer it that it may be acceptable for you; it must, therefore, be eaten on the same day; none of it shall be left over until the next day. I am the Lord."[7]

God did not need the finest fruits or the best offering, of course. Rather, Israel needed to give evidence—to itself—of the priority of its relationship to God (mutual presence) over the seductions of material securities and economic forces. The sacrificial destruction of the best gifts reinforced the Hebrews' investment in, and cultural appreciation of, something better, the immanence of the transcendent God in Israel, of his covenant with them.

The Coptic monk makes a sacrifice of his bodily comfort, of his procreational potential, and of his impulse to roam a wider world—not because he or his culture views these things as fundamentally bad or suspect—but, all to the contrary, because these experiences are esteemed as comprising much of what is best to offer to God. Such an attitude grants to Coptic asceticism a very different aspect than that of Western mortifications. A Western monk may call his mortifications sacrificial from time to time (much as a Catholic makes a "sacrifice" by giving up smoking in Lent, for instance), but since he suspects that what he is giving up is inherently unworthy of holiness, his intention is not sacrificial in the full Semitic meaning of the word. The

Coptic monk is not unaware that human sinfulness can affect (even chiefly affect) all that is highest in human aspirations (e.g., delight in creation, intimacy with others), but he still believes that limiting these expressions of self constitute the best sacrificial gifts he has to offer to God.

A small philological investigation could serve well here. The proper language of the Copts (Arabic) admits of two different words for what is translated into English as "sacrifice." One word, "*dahiya*," describes an act of self-denial whose intended effect is to rein in an appetite or passion to good or godly order. The offering of *dahiya* is a corrective to the laxity of the flesh and an effort to reform the character of the offerer.

A second word for "sacrifice" is "*dhabiha*", which denotes an object given over in a cultic ritual. Such a sacrificial gift can be destroyed by fire, cut by a knife, or emptied out in loss onto the earth. In any case, it is an offering of something prized whose loss hurts, and the process of giving it costs. Asceticism would seem to belong to the first term, and the Copts consider that the mortifications practiced by the laity are indeed *dahiya*. But when a monk practices mortification, the Copts employ the second term. Since a monk is defined in terms of his constant presence to God (*rahib*), his asceticism takes on the aspect of an offering on an altar. In this case, his offering is in reality his own life which is perceived in Coptic cosmology as one slow, lifelong, burning holocaust going up to heaven.

When this perception is appreciated, a great deal of the singularity of Coptic asceticism becomes comprehensible. Desert Father literature is full of anecdotes of monks whose acts of mortification were excessive from every known measure of spiritual prudence. They attempted to stand, hands outstretched, sleepless by the weeks. They reduced their diet to incredibly small and infrequent rations. They endured the shadeless Sahara heat, or the unblanketed cold of winter desert nights. They took grueling hikes into the unchartered desert and risked various degrees of dehydration. In all of this, the Westerner expects to find extreme penitential morosity, or even pathological self-loathing. He is surprised, instead, to discover simple joy and naive satisfaction.

For the monk conquered the limitations of the self not by self-absorbed punishments, but by an other-oriented self-giving. His whole attention was trained upon the One whose presence he alternately enjoyed and suffered. Even today, such an attitude pervades all aspects of monastic life and discipline in Egypt. Such a joyous attitude in apparent self-negation can only be predicated on the deeply convinced experience of divine immanence. Since Westerners culturally regard the very existence of God as a speculative matter, the existence of people whose lives make no sense except in relationship to God will always be categorically anomalous for them. But in Egypt, the monks are living embodiments of a cosmology of divine immanence, and their continued existence guarantees the extension of a divine covenant with their church. For an all-good God would not refuse gifts so total, nor orphan the people who supplied such sacrifice from their ranks. This is so in spite of the fact that an all-powerful God has no need of the gifts, and an all-just God knows the unworthiness of the people who offer them. In the Near East, sacrifices are more compelling than mere facts. Any mother who has graciously received a bundle of dandelions from her child knows the power in this intuition. She knows that, factually, the floral gift is simply worthless weeds. But the gift was perhaps all the child could just then offer to the one whose presence filled his heart. It was a relational gesture more than a botanical project. Maternal refusal was unthinkable. The Copts expect that their monks are similarly placed before God on their behalf.

When Copts visit the monastery of Al-Suriany in the Wadi al-Natroun today, they are led through a labyrinth of chapels, chambers, and halls hewn out of rock till they come to the cave of one of the first desert fathers. Suspended from the high vault of this little dark room dangles a metal wire to almost shoulder-level of the pilgrim. This wire, the pilgrim is informed, was tied to the hair of the ancient saint while he stood so that, should his head begin to bob in weariness, or his body slump in exhaustion, he would be immediately jerked back into his vigil of prayer. The rare pilgrim from the West hears this (perhaps apocryphal) account and is horrified. Such unhealthy extremism, such fundamentalistic excess! But the Coptic audience is invariably delighted. Here is a gesture which aspires to respond to God wholeheartedly; here is a sacrifice bound to win his favor.

In recent decades, as Islamist pressures on the Copts have increased, the desert monasteries have enjoyed greatly increased membership. In numbers and in spirit, the desert monasteries have revived, moving from a cosmological place-holding position for a vivid monastic hagiography to a vital segment of an ethnic community and minority church. In the process of revivification, the symbol of sacrifice has been adjusted to the contemporary idiom of careerism and self-promotion. The sacrifice much lauded in the contemporary Coptic monastery is the post-graduate vocation, from one who has worked very hard and has everything to lose. He is precisely the kind of man that Coptic society esteems when he "gives it all up" for God. The monastic vocation of the "doctor and the engineer"—two professions which obsess the imagination of Egyptian academe—is the stuff of contemporary Coptic oral hagiography. The much-discussed existence of such monastic candidates confirms the sacrificial modality of the desert cloister.

Coptic lay society may not have the vocation or the opportunity for continual awareness of God, but when they do have occasion to be mindful of divine immanence, they are all the more conscious of their failure to be truly or fully holy according to the monastic ideal which monopolizes the Coptic vision of committed spirituality. They recall the New Testament injunction to "pray constantly,"[8] and shrink within at their inability to do so. Indeed, much of the spiritual life seriously recommended to the laity seems designated to make them feel failures of faith.

Coptic custom dictates that all Copts must fast from all animal products (e.g., meat, eggs, milk, butter) during certain seasons of the year. These times include Lent, Advent, octaves of feasts of special saints, as well as the Wednesday and Friday of every week. All totaled, the lay Copt is obliged to fast over 200 days a year! Such a demand is frankly unrealistic for many Copts, but the obligation is held by the clergy. Pope Shenouda III recently told a large assembly that health concerns for the aged and the pregnant did not excuse anyone from the fast. Moreover, he reminded them that not even a mouthful of water could be swallowed by any Copt—no matter what the medical condition might be—on the day of Sunday until after Communion had been received. Since the liturgy itself is at least three hours in length, and may begin late in the morning, considerable discomfort would be suffered by many.

A discipline of daily prayer of extraordinary proportion is enjoined upon the Copts. A Western monk may hope to pray all of David's 150 Psalms in a week; the Coptic laity are asked to pray all of them in one day! The manual of Coptic prayer, the *Agbeya*, is rounded out with long prayers, hymns, and collects. Practically speaking, few Copts can hope to pray the required prayers on any one day in an ordinary lifetime. Such expectations for religious observance are well beyond any possible full compliance, yet given the Coptic intuition of God's nearness, such expectations are slight and simple after all.

Frustrated by the inability to match the visitation of God with the intensity of awareness that it requires, the Copt is relieved that the monk, in his stead, can supply the sacrifice of constant presence that is appropriate: the human hospitality of the divine. All the demands put on the Coptic laity serve to make their admiration of and devotion to the monks all the more profound. Herein lies the sociological function of such unrealistic demands.

Once again, the contemporary secular mind may not appreciate at once the communal dynamic at work in this process. The Westerner, with echoes of the Reformation still sounding in the background, might object that even if one grants all the immanence of God attested by the Copts, no one can expect that one person's appropriate response to that presence—no matter how intense—can serve to make anybody else more acceptable to God. The absolute sovereignty of the individual is asserted as if it were a universal commonplace.

Actually, the Western view of the individual as real while the communal is abstract, is a special stylization of philosophy almost unknown elsewhere. To the Egyptian, the community is real, much more real than the individual who takes his life and hope, language and learning, safety and security from it. While the participation of the individual is often required, and intensely so, no one is called into participation in life except through the dynamics of the kin, the village, and the religion.

Until today, the occurrence of the "blood feud" is very possible in Upper (more Coptic) Egypt. In such a feud, revenge for a wrong may strike any member of the family of the one who did the wrong. Hence, the guilty party, the individual offender, be he an extortionist, a vandal, a slanderer, a rapist, or simply an accidental destroyer of life or property, may by his status or distance be impossible to punish directly. Yet the offended party—through the agency of his kin loyalties—can re-balance the accounts of justice by proportionally afflicting an equivalent member of the offender's kin. Such an indirect redress is experienced by all concerned as understandable within the communal framework of social thought, even it is leads to an escalation of counter-strikes.[9]

The ideal of communal interconnectedness having concrete moral consequence and significance is certainly biblical. Recall the words of Saint Paul:

> But the gift is not like the transgression. For if by that one person's transgression the many died, how much more did the grace of God and the gracious gift of the one person Jesus Christ overflow for the many. And the gift is not like the result of the one person's sinning. For after one sin there was the judgment that brought condemnation; but the gift, after many transgressions, brought acquittal. For if, by the transgression of one person, death came to reign through that one, how much more will those who receive the abundance of grace and of the gift of justification come to reign in life through the one person Jesus Christ.
>
> In conclusion, just as through one transgression, condemnation came upon all, so through one righteous act acquittal and life came to all. For just as through the disobedience of one person the many were made sinners, so through the obedience of one the many will be made righteous. The law entered in so that transgression might increase but, where sin increased, grace overflowed all the more, so that, as sin reigned in death, grace also might reign through justification for eternal life through Jesus Christ our Lord.[10]

Christianity, with its notion of God becoming incarnate *in human nature*, and with its belief in *vicarious redemption*, as well as in mediation and intercession, is much more communally oriented than the Western individualist may care to admit. For the Copt, the church really *is* the Body of Christ, and the work of some of its members (desert contemplation and ascetical sacrifice) may redound to the benefit of all, especially if the latter renew their bonds of respect and almsgiving support to the former.

The Western observer is almost doomed by cultural prejudice to interpret such dynamics as religious elitism, clericalism, and the selling of divine blessings. The West is conditioned to view communal dynamics in terms of market and class. But the Copt is still innocent of such interpretive frameworks, and believes that what he cannot himself attain for the integrity of his spiritual life and salvation, he can nonetheless hope for by all the more assiduously belonging to the community that has members who can attain such things. A sense of belonging is the force which makes such belief operational, and a lack of such sense enfeebles the Westerner's efforts to understand it.

Coptic society, then, must be understood as a community whose membership blends into the heavenly communion of saints and fades into the earthly desert of the monk. And from such margins of heaven and desert, the dense concentrations of villagers and urbanite Copts hope to recover their collective orientation to God. The saints are, in fact, the sign that the community has already succeeded in part. The desert monk is a sign that the community is still functioning to receive the immanence of God into the heart of the people in a manner that accords honor to God and hope to the people. The monk's practice of holiness, his ascetic sacrifice, is, after all, a sacrifice on the community's behalf. Only the Westerner believes that a monk leaves the community in favor of personal perfection. The Copt believes that the monk simply leaves the surface of communal existence so that he may dwell in the desert heart of the people where his every spiritual act will ripple with consequence throughout his beleaguered church.

Finally, it is the conviction of this author that the burden of the Coptic cosmology, laden as it is with the weight of divine immanence, the reflexive sense of unworthiness and guilt, the demands of rigorous religious observance, intense communal dynamics, and an elaborated and complex liturgy, catechism and hagiography, is exactly the counterweight of spiritual and communal integration the Copts need in the face of their national alienation and persecuted religious status.

Neither their own religion nor their difference of religion from the Arab (Muslim) nation is easy for them to bear. But instead of both burdens doubling to crush them, the one relieves the pressure of the other. The nation has orphaned them, but God hems them in. The nation has let them twist slowly in the winds of Islamic fundamentalism, but God has raised up zealots of contemplation for them in the desert, from which breezes of consolation blow. The nation has isolated them from international assistance, but they feel that God has reserved them for a special purpose.

Christian monasticism was born in Egypt, and from the beginning it bore the stamp of a people who were never permitted a secular self-government. Rather, as a people, the Copts have survived on a spiritual consensus which draws much of its compelling power from the role of the desert monks.

## Notes

1. The primary readership of this article is assumed to be Western, and generally educated. Much of what is described about Coptic monasticism can be made more accessible to the Western reader if the material is contrasted with the better-known examples of European monasticism, Catholic or Orthodox. Such comparisons are made in this essay to help orient the information to the limitations and intuitions of the Eurocentric mind.
2. Ernest T. Abdel-Massih, Mikhail M. Melika, and Roufail S. Michail, *The Divine Liturgy of St. Basil the Great and The Evening and Morning Raising of Incense Prayers* (Troy, Mich., St. Mark Coptic Orthodox Church, 1982), 16-17.
3. *The Divine Liturgy of St. Basil the Great* (1982), 25.
4. *The Divine Liturgy of St. Basil the Great* (1982), 26, 27.
5. *The Divine Liturgy of St. Basil the Great* (1982), 36.
6. Acts 17:28. (All Scripture quotations are taken from the St. Joseph Edition of the *New American Bible*, New York: Catholic Publishing Co., c1987.)
7. Leviticus 22:17-30.
8. Ephesians 6:18
9. Edward W. Lane, *Manners and Customs of the Modern Egyptians*. 1836. Reprint. New York: E.P. Dutton & Co., 1954, 105-106
10. Romans 5:12, 15-21.

Mark Francis Gruber

# The Monastery as the Nexus of Coptic Cosmology

## Behavioral Embodiments of Value

The consequences of the special cosmology of the Copts, which orients their social life to divine transcendence-made-immanent, are nowhere more clearly evident than in the desert monasteries themselves. The "Other-in-this-worldly" orientation of Coptic religion ("Other" referring to God, as opposed to merely an "otherworldly" religion) expresses itself not only in religious rituals, sacraments, visions, miracles, and asceticism, but in the special modality of social relations and public personae peculiar to the monasteries of the desert. For Copts, the attitude and the interrelations of monks are perceived alternatively as the restoration of the Eden-like paradisiacal ideal, the mirror of angelic hosts in choral unison, the pure extension of the apostolic Church's primal glory as told in the New Testament hagiography of the Acts of the Apostles, or an anticipation of the perfection of human social life in the resurrection on the last day. Monks are thus perceived as new Adams, angels, apostles, or heavenly glorified beings. The realm of monks, the monastery, is the locus, therefore, of the cosmological ideals which undergird Coptic cultural identity. The cosmological and cultural role of the monk is laden with many layers of meaning. Such a role can be better appreciated by the analytic of social science provided by Erving Goffman. This analytic is by now a mainstay in the social study of central, cultural figures and essential cosmological roles. A short consideration of this analysis is helpful here.

Erving Goffman perceived that any general role in society proceeds from an ideal human type who embodies the role perfectly. Goffman calls efforts at establishing credibility in a role "performance." A person, in order to project a believable selfhood, must embody certain consistent patterns of behavior which are measured against the ideal human type. To the degree that a person approximates the ideal personal pattern, he or she accrues social weight and influence.[1] A person may be "taken in" by the role performed and may come to believe in the role being projected as though it were the essential self.[2] A considerable effort will need to be made to protect the image, which is intuitively perceived as fragile and vulnerable to damage, by the appearance of cross signals.[3]

For Goffman, there is no essential self, merely the dramatic effect of the performance inter-subjectively believed.[4] His conclusion seems to be an unnecessary excursion into epistemology. Suffice it to say that a coherent social perspective of a group depends upon consistent self-presentation.[5] For the Copts, the same insight holds. The credible performance, or self-presentation of the monks, yields an ethnic social perspective and reinforces the Coptic cosmology. The monk, therefore, has a different style of expressing openness toward social status. Because he has ostensibly rejected the prevailing social models of the secular world, and because he has based his social persona upon the sacrificial model of religious existence, the monk must not promote himself for leadership in the monastery in any direct way which would be immediately intelligible to the secular world. The monk must, in fact, eschew leadership and ambition in dramatic ways if he intends to pursue status ecclesiastically and spiritually.

As Simon Tugwell states: "What is, at first sight, surprising is that many of them [the monks] acquired a position of considerable authority and power. The explanation is, probably, that by their total renunciation . . . they came to represent a completely different kind of power, which can be used to challenge the political and economic power which is normally operative in our society."[6]

The social history of the Coptic monasteries shows the essential revolutionary spirit of the proto-monks. They rejected the oppression of the Copts under Imperial rule, and opted out of its social stranglehold over Egypt by taking to the desert and living a countercultural life. The credibility of their indictment of the Empire rested upon the idealism of their lifestyles in contradistinction to the mercenary and ambitious examples of the country's leaders. To that end, they repudiated secular power and the lust for power and, instead, honored the powerful symbol of self-denial and powerlessness.

The monks enlist the Gospel to support this strategy and recall Christ's words: "For everyone who exalts himself shall be humbled, while he who humbles himself shall be exalted."[7] They free themselves from the economic restraints of the secular world by renouncing personal marriage and families which would give them greater responsibilities for income and property, and put them more easily on the secular track of striving, earning, and ambition. Instead, they form counter-familial structures based on spiritual fatherhood and not on the carnal paternity which typifies the basis of the secular, social organization.

Such reversal of the secular order and the inversions of its values became essential hagiographical components of desert monasticism and defined it for centuries, even when other sociological facts indicated significant adaptation of monasticism to cooperation within its social milieu. The institution of monasticism seems, therefore, perfectly suited to hermeneutical deconstruction. For in its counterpoint to the world's symbolic order, monasticism affords the attentive observer a village-level inversion of the plural symbols of the complex state. This symbolic realm is projected into a small community setting.

Herein lies another reason for the preference of the desert wilderness in the establishment of monasteries. The desert is not only physically barren, but it is bereft of social markers or boundaries. By definition, the wilderness is without internal borders, properties, pathways, human associations, and historical references. The desert comes into social awareness as an undifferentiated whole. As such, the arid wilderness is an ideal blank screen onto which may be projected an inversion of the secular social order. Occupied lands present too many distortions coming from the ascendent social order for its inversion to be projected thereon. (When the Western church attempts to establish monasteries, it also prefers more sequestered regions. When that is not possible, special care is taken to consecrate sufficient "cloistered" zones within and around the monastery to create *terra incognita*, at least in the appraisal of the surrounding church.)

Monasticism presents a microcosmic inversion of the pluralistic values of the repudiated state on the more uniform stage of a desert community. The monastery is, then, a key to understanding a pluralistic and secular state (monasteries often occur in such environments). How monks attain to leadership may be a case in point.

The ritual for the installation of a Coptic patriarch contains a very revealing element, precisely for what it attempts to conceal. According to the rubrics, the patriarch-elect, a monk from the desert, is brought to the installation ceremony literally bound in chains.[8] Coptic history and hagiography abound with stories about contented hermits being forced out of their solitude by a church which needed their holiness and wisdom. So apparently unwilling were these hermits to submit to ecclesiastical position, that they had to be fettered in iron in order to be brought to their appointments. The frequency of this occurrence, the ritual suggests, was so great that eventually the chaining of the patriarch-elect became customary. The ritual also suggests that the patriarch-elect realizes that, by being in the desert, he is already in the spiritual heartland, the symbolic capital of his ethnic church, and that he does not want to be "exiled" to the merely functional ecclesiastical center of the church.

Curiously, no one has suggested that the social function of these fetters outstrips in importance any alleged historical antecedents for their use. Yet no one could believe that the office of patriarch in the Coptic Church has been consistently occupied by a series of unwilling popes. In point of fact, the Sacrament of Holy Priesthood and the consecration to the episcopacy can only be conferred upon a willing recipient. Such canons are held universally in apostolic churches. Moreover, should an unwilling monk still somehow be made patriarch, once installed, he would be the ultimate authority in his church and, therefore, free to express his unwillingness without further contradiction. He would return at once to the desert! Finally, should he be forced, somehow, to remain in office unwillingly, he would make life difficult precisely for those who forced him from retirement. This response would inhibit the ecclesiastical apparatus from ever choosing such a monk to begin with.

The rubric of restraining a monk-to-be-patriarch and the hagiography of the unwilling hermit seized by a spirit-directed electoral body are extremely successful symbols in the Coptic Church, with analogues in other churches as well. They are symbols of power eschewed. For power unsought and a position evaded are the hallmarks of credibility for monastic leadership. A monk cannot be ostensibly an ambitious man, for this appearance would obviate the statement of his own lifestyle. Should he become a leader, he does so, as it were, unwillingly. Of course, he does not really assume leadership unwillingly, else it would not be done, but he accepts the leadership with a proper attention and respect to the inversion of secular ambition to which he has pledged his life, that is, to humility. Moreover, the charisma of the power he holds is a type which would be dissipated were he to grasp that power too deliberately. The delicacy of the monk's position in relationship to power is safely secured in the hagiography and rubrics of the Coptic Church.

Thus, a patriarch-elect need not himself wish to evade his new office, nor need his predecessors have wished to do so. He needs only to cooperate with the custom of appearing not to want the position during the proper ceremony. He thereby preserves a ritual innocence toward ambition, and the church articulates his crucial importance in its internal life. The function of this particular patriarchal ritual serves as an example of monastic leadership models in general.

## Desert Poetics

In the desert today, many monks circulate stories about the manner of ordination to the priesthood. Each one tells about how the patriarch or another bishop called the monk to serve as a deacon assistant in the liturgy and that, in place of a simple blessing during the liturgy, the bishop imposed his hands on the head of the unsuspecting monk, making him a priest.

Now this story is more often told about other priest-monks than claimed about oneself by a priest-monk, but both cases exist in some numbers. The story has similarities with the ritual of the patriarch-elect in chains. In both cases, imputed unwillingness to pursue ecclesiastical promotion serves as the guarantee of a monk's purity of intention. The private intentionality of a monk in legitimating his authority is perhaps of greater importance than for other kinds of leaders who more directly pursue power. Admixtures of zeal and ambition are regularly expected of secular leaders. But a monk is expected to have renounced personal ambition, so that its reappearance in him would not only indict his present image of disinterested service, but would also undermine the basic identity which his role as monk projects.

The projection of an appropriate personal image which corresponds to one's role is more than a private concern. Culture itself supplies the proportions of a persona to which individuals attempt to conform.[9] Coptic culture is no exception in regard to the role of the monk. Hagiography supplies much of that proportion and suggests the rules for inverting the secular social order in particular monastic lives and examples. But even without hagiography, the inherent logic of secular-value-inversion would itself direct individual monks to embody the particular ideals proper to their special calling.

Following Goffman, Herzfeld has elaborated on the process of projecting a personal image into social roles. He calls that process "poetics," which at once recognizes the set structure of certain roles and the individual's performance skills at giving content to that form. Poetics is that performance of an individual designed to evoke archetypal categories which would identify an actor with "ideological propositions and historical antecedents."[10] Hence, there are certain stylized behavior patterns which supply actors with a full repertoire of activities proper to their personae and incorporate them into an historical movement, giving them the power to embody a tradition and recapitulate an ideal.

Coptic monasticism has its own poetics in this sense. The Coptic monk has a repertoire of behavior which allows him to reflect hagiographical ideals and to dramatically invert the secular values of his day. He invests himself by stylized speech, garb, food, and gestures with the power of the Copt's ancient desert heroes from an age of giants.

There will always be a certain question of credibility in the appropriation of such heroic roles and the projecting of such lofty ideals. People will remember the earlier lives of the monks and recall their human frailties. They will notice the aspects of a monk which do not conform to the ideals he projects. Once again, the distance a monk takes from the world is critical in this regard. Distance is not just a geographical matter. The monk must not be a familiar of the world, just as the desert is not familiar to the world. He must be distant in the sense of detachment from casual human commerce. In such a distance, the incongruities of his life and role will not be too apparent. Such incongruities would be the personal shortcomings, past failings, or temporal ambitions in a man which would contrast with monastic sensibilities. Herzfeld notes that an actor of poetics must take care to suppress any sense of incongruity which is inevitably created by projecting roles of "grandiose implications."[11]

Nothing could be more "grandiose" than for a human being to claim to live the life of an angel. Yet the monk claims just such a life in Egypt. The secular and Islamic detractors of this role will be numerous and forceful; hence, the Coptic affirmation of it will be serious and intense. Therefore, the Coptic monk does not typically employ humor in his analysis of monastic life. When humor is evidenced, it is marginal to the essential aspects of a monk's daily activity and life. Humor supplies just that sense of perspective which the truly grandiose does not require, and cannot abide. What is truly heroic does not need to be, indeed, ought not be, diminished by irreverent or mundane associations. Distance and humorlessness of a certain kind, then, typify the poetics of monks in relationship to the world and to the laity.

What of the poetics of the monks in relationship to one another? How do they present themselves to each other in terms of leadership and respect? How do they suppress the incongruities in one another which they perceive at close range?

As noted above, a monk recommends himself for authority and position by deliberately making counter-indications of these interests. Such counter-indications have evolved into patterns of behavior which are recognizable, although not necessarily consciously employed or explicitly understood. Such behavior is, nevertheless, symbolically communicative within the social matrix of the monastery and the Coptic Church.

Self-deprecation is one such counter-indicative behavior practiced in many forms in the monastery. For the monk to present himself properly for notice and esteem, he must verbally negate himself in whatever area he is particularly tending to pursue. "Books are too burdensome for me to concern myself with. They belong to brilliant people who can better appreciate them than I can." Such are the expressed sentiments of one monk candidate in the Wadi al-Natroun who was once a head librarian.

Self-deprecation is not to be confused with self-effacement. The latter is tending toward the background and anonymity, while the former is directed toward advertisement. True self-effacement occurs in the monastery perhaps very much, but by its very nature is not a social act readily given to analysis, unless one is determined to interpret it as a refinement of self-deprecation.

Monks frequently express deprecatory remarks not only about their competencies, but also about their holiness. "I am really just a beginner in matters of the spirit," is an oft-stated sentiment. "I am a weak man who needs the monastic life because of my weakness with temptation," said one monk living a celibate life for over twenty years. "Theological talk is beyond me. I cannot understand deep matters of religion," is another common declaration. But the quickest way to gauge the social meaning of such sentiments is to simply agree with them when they are voiced. The reaction to literal agreement is consternation and silence. The reaction intended by the behavior, therefore, was not agreement, but contradiction, or, at least, tacit disbelief.

Alter-adulation is another method of self-promotion in the monastery. Monks frequently extol the talents and holiness of each other, especially when the other is present: "Abuna (Father) Sylvanus is a visionary. Bishop Amoun, the saint, has appeared to him and instructed him."

"No, no, Abuna Meshack, you are the visionary. You are pure of heart, and God's holy light shines on you."

"Abuna Sylvanus, you are too humble. You must not hide your light under a basket." The conversation can go on at length and be modulated for pilgrims in attention, or for fellow monks where it is somewhat more subtle. The dynamic of the dialogue is more powerful than self-deprecation by itself. The dialogue permits deprecation to be explicitly contradicted, and contractually engages the monks in mutual endorsements. Yet at no time does the monk explicitly boast. He retains a formal humility.

Self-abasing gestures are an important conventionalized form of role-defining behavior for the monk. Monks customarily greet each other by a stylized kissing of each other's hands. They slide their palms over the other's in an abbreviated motion of grasping the other's hand, and then take their own hand to their lips with a kiss, which represents a symbolic kiss of the other's which they had been holding. Thus, in principle, by this gesture, two monks can kiss each other's hand simultaneously without awkwardness. But, frequently, monks will attempt to kiss the other's hand actually, and not just figuratively. One will attempt to grasp the other's hand while he is unsuspecting, and quickly press it to his lips before the monk can resist. The implication is: "You are holier, for I take my blessing from your hand. We are not equals, for I have honored you first, and I am therefore subordinated to you."

Of course, the other monk cannot allow this to occur too often. If he does, it will be apparent that he is in danger of permitting personal aggrandizement and, by that very appearance, he will in reality lose credibility. He would not be embodying the poetics of monastic humility, but evidencing the prestige-seeking behavior of the secular world. Therefore, he tries to grasp the hands of the approaching confrere, even as that one tries to grasp his. Often, then, the monks can be seen in a tug-of-war over who will be abased before the other. The intention of expressing abasement is even clearer when the ritual is extended. A monk will try to touch the feet of another monk and then take his own hand to his lips in a symbolic kiss of the feet he has just touched. Or he will touch the ground on the place where the other has walked and kiss his hand as if to say, "I kiss the ground on which you walk."

The social meaning is well conveyed: real monks are humble, and humility is the only possible meaning of such gestures. The paradox is that over-expressing humility exalts oneself, to one's own detriment. The struggle is unresolvable and unending. Significantly, monks who engage each other in such public acts are much more often members of the same informal intra-monastic polity, rather than monks from less familiarly associated groups in the monastery. Reinforcement of the group seems to derive from their mutual reinforcement of each other.

Self-deprecation, alter-adulation, self-abasement are dramatizations of communicative behavior. They are gestures which are intentionally evocative, and they define much of the social field of the monastery and its internal divisions. The gestures are sheer oppositions to self-promoting behavior in the world. In secular Egyptian society, as in so much of the world, a man tends to directly articulate his strengths, denigrate the weaknesses of his rivals, and posture himself to his fullest advantage in his business dealings.

The credibility of the monastic community rests on its oppositions to secular views and symbols. One might object that this opposition has been nullified by the above analysis, and that any oppositions in the monastery to secularity are only strategic appearances. But this is not the case. The monks do not "deploy" their behavior. The project of any human society entails the inter-positioning of each of its members. Social coherence requires strategy, even as individuals have renounced it as their primary interest. The monastery simply exhibits the irreducible social imperatives of humanity, even if it ostensibly repudiates one particular cultural configuration of those imperatives. The monks' repudiation of one culture's expression of social positioning did, in fact, serve to condition their own new countercultural expression of social positioning. That the monks have not transcended humanity altogether is hardly a matter of duplicity or guile. Rather, their behavior is an articulation, albeit a tortured one, of essential social forms.

Still, for the symbolic work of the monastery to be accomplished in Coptic society, it is often necessary for the rather limited transcendence of monastic "anti-strategies" to be dramatized as full transcendence from a fallen human condition. Hence, exaggerated claims about the lives of the monks, their fasts, their silences, their mysticism, etc., are frequently made by one monk about another, or by the laity. Exaggerations, however, are inlaid on pre-existent lines of reality, and often call attention to important lines of counterculture which might otherwise be missed.

The behavior of the monks among each other, their distance from the world, and their relentless, serious concern about who they are constitutes much of the poetics of their monastery. Poetics, as the word connotes, implies drama. A monk is a dramatic, heroic persona, even if his own character is actually rather ordinary. The great claims of a religious order are better served by heroes than by doctrines. The Copts, who depend upon their religion for ethnic survival, will discern or impute heroic ideals in their monks because to do so invests their religion with greater symbolic power and social efficacy.[12] The monk must provide the dramatic persona onto which a religious counterculture can be safely projected. If he embodies those ideals well, so much the better. A living saint may be perceived to add present vitality to their voluminous hagiography. Even if he does not perfectly embody these ideals, the public presentation of monastic poetics will serve to keep custody of the ideals which grant the Copts ethnic viability.

Finally, there are a number of monks within the monastery who generally fail to exhibit the strategic, social behavior described above. They are self-effacing, rather than self-deprecating. Their desert walks are not calculated to be noticed by conspicuous departures or returns. They do not belong, or belong exclusively, to any intra-monastic polity. They are not in line to greet the abbot on his return from a trip, or the patriarch from his visit. They do not conspicuously seek a desert cell or cave, although they are reclusive enough within their own cell. Indeed, these monks are to the monastery what the monastery attempts to be for the world. They grant a kind of legitimacy to the monastery, and form, not its margins, but its silent heart. If other monks do not quite embody the special qualities of monastic transcendence, they can be comforted that the whole monastery is not so undermined. But some do embody these ideals, at least well enough to grant the whole community sufficient orientation to continue its cultural course. These latter monks derive no visible social benefit for their service which, if it were publicly noted, would be an undesired indictment of the rest of the monastery. Thus, their monastic lives seem to be, in reality, something of the sacrificial act that all monks' lives are projected to be.

## The Monastic Regimen

Nothing might appear to be a more straightforward matter than the daily routine and diet of the monks. Westerners expect that monks, above all people, have achieved a regularity in their schedules and a uniformity in their practice. This may once have been the case in most Western monasteries, and still is true in some, but Egypt's monasteries are quite different. Here, regularity and uniformity do not obtain.

Following upon what was said above about their sense of a monastic "rule," Coptic monks follow a course of daily life which is idiorhythmic, that is, they practice a form of monasticism found more typically in the Eastern churches, which permits a great range of individual variation. Part of the reason that the idiorhythmic model is prominent in Egypt is that the most important social relationship in the monastery is dyadic, between the spiritual father and each monk. Collective relations receive little stress. The ideal of the eremitical life is somewhat maintained by this arrangement.

There are no community meetings or common recreations, no shared retreats or general conferences in most Coptic monasteries. A community exists in the monastery as an accidental consequence of the aggregate of so many individual monks clustered around their spiritual father. The aggregate community is important in some respects, for it provides a base upon which the monk can more successfully live his private vocation, and it serves as a collective dramatization of monastic sacrifice which might be more obscure were only individuals given to project that symbol. And, of course, the collectivity of a monastic institution is more capable of ecclesiastical interplay than that of isolated ascetics.

Still, the Coptic monk retains the primary sense of his own individuality. There is little which is hard and fast for the consecrated monk which cannot be negotiated with his spiritual father. The progress of personal growth for the monk is very much a process of privatization of religious practice. The hours of prayer performed standing upright in the church among fellow monastic candidates is soon translated into private devotions in his cell, once he receives the full monastic habit. Daily Mass and Communion give way to occasional liturgical celebrations, for instance, when it is the "turn" of the monk-priest to officiate. Austere common meals give way to private meals prepared in one's own cell. With so much private practice of the monastic life, advertised schedules of daily religious activity in the monastery are somewhat obfuscating.

In spite of the enormous range of individual practice and the impossibility of knowing the range of privatized devotions, the monks of most desert cloisters readily supply the pilgrim with a "horarium," that is, an hourly schedule of the monastery. A rigorous schedule of the hours of a monk's day has more value as yet another symbol of the sacrifice of monastic asceticism than as a predictive device for where the monks may be at any given time. Nevertheless, such a schedule is fairly indicative of at least the whereabouts and activities of the monastic candidates, as well as some of the monks who may occasionally participate in collective activities again. An idealized schedule of a Coptic monastery is presented below, therefore, as much a partial description of the behavior of some monks as an artifact which describes the ascetical ideal held by all monks:

| | |
|---|---|
| 3:00 a.m. to 6:00 a.m. | Morning Psalmody and Incense in common |
| 6:00 a.m. to 9:00 a.m. | Liturgy in common |
| 9:00 a.m. to 1:00 p.m. | Work projects |
| 2:00 p.m. | First meal in common |
| 3:00 p.m. to 5:00 p.m. | Spiritual reading; meditation |
| 5:00 p.m. to 6:00 p.m. | Evening prayer in common |
| 7:00 p.m. to 8:00 p.m. | Evening meal in common |
| Midnight | Private monastic prayers; prostrations |

Some commentary on this regimen may be helpful. The spiritual exercises of the morning, which last from 3:00 a.m. to 9:00 a.m., are performed with the monks standing on their feet almost the whole time. These six hours of standing are the great ascetical work of most monks for, as candidates, they were performing this feat daily. The monks stand in two small antiphonal scholas during the endless psalmody and incensing. The melismatic chant, the aching legs and back, the heavy acrid smoke, and the dullness of light are all conducive to a kind of minor hypnosis, which the monks are more ready to regard as an inducement to prayer than might a bystander.

The morning exercises are the most poorly attended common events in the monastery. The monk-candidates and the monks who are newly consecrated, but have not yet been ordained to the priesthood, are well represented. The ubiquitous blind cantor[13] is escorted to the church by one of the monastic candidates. At 6:00 a.m. the priest in charge of the monk-recruits arrives and notes those in attendance. He is acknowledged in a deferential ritual greeting by all who preceded him. He then begins the hour-long prayers of praise which initiate every liturgy. While he does so, a few priests arrive and are vested for the liturgy. Just as one taper may light several candles, several Masses may be celebrated from the same beginning of praise prayer by this group. A priest who arrives at 6:30 a.m. may join the prayers at this stage, and then go off to another altar (*haikal*) within the sanctuary to begin a separate liturgy.

Various lay employees of the monastery also arrive at this point and, with the monks who have come earlier, are apportioned out as diaconal liturgical assistants to the officiating priests. By the chanting of the Gospel around 7:30 a.m. (the last possible moment a concelebrating priest or monk-communicant may arrive), the number of monks involved in the morning exercises may reach twenty-five. After this point, the monks disappear behind a curtain in the wall of the sanctuary and participate in the core of the liturgy as a distinct body, separated from the others in attendance; i.e., the pilgrims, retreatants, employees, etc. Unseen by the others, they may be seated on the sanctuary floor, making prostrations during the high points of the ritual. The monks explain that they have a reserved space in the liturgy closer to the altar because their life of sacrifice makes them more united with the sacrifice of the altar. In the Coptic religious view, what happens in the sanctuary is heavenly, and those who serve there commute from earth to heaven. The monk is such a man.

The first meal at 2:00 p.m. in the monastery is communal and is well attended. It consists mainly of rice and falafel beans called *"ful."* The monks are seated in a U-shaped configuration of connecting tables with the abbot at the middle. At his left is the youngest (i.e., the newest) monk in the monastery, and at his right is the oldest—mirroring the supposed seating arrangement of Christ at the Last Supper where John, the youngest apostle, and Peter, the senior, sat on either side of Jesus. The monastic community fans out in a proper order from these anchored positions, with the consecration date of each monk establishing his place on the bench. During the meal, a monk reads from the ancient desert literature to the silent, eating assembly.

Not all monks attend the meal. Some may be fasting or eating alone. Most monks have some provisions stored in their rooms, with hot plates on which to prepare the food. The evening meal is more likely to be eaten in this way, as this communal meal has less structure: no presiding superior, and no secondary dishes, except for rice and beans. (Secondary dishes include tomatoes, oranges, lettuce, leeks, lentils, olives, and carrots.) Barley-bread cakes are served at every meal.

As fasting foods, the items above contain no animal products in their preparation or serving. Fast days in the popular Coptic calendar account for over 200 days of the year when no animal products are to be eaten. The average Copt might only fast on the more important of such days, for instance, in Lent, or in August before the feast of Saint Mary's ascent to heaven, but the monk is supposed to honor all fast days. Monks are generally believed by the Copts to be vegetarian, and many are. Nevertheless, on Sundays and major feasts, hard-boiled eggs, milk, butter, cheese, fish, chicken, and lamb may appear on the communal table.

There are seven structural parts to the daily prayer routine of the monks. These parts are called "Hours" (*Agbeya*), much as in Western monasticism. For the Copts, each Hour commemorates a critical event in Christ's saving work; most, therefore, are associated with the Cross. The praying of the *Agbeya* incorporates each day of the monk's life into the timeless mystery of Christ's passion, further uniting the monks to his sacrificial role.

Evening prayer is actually a combination of several Hours of the Divine Office. Each segment contains substantial clusters of psalms, petitions, readings, and collects. Nevertheless, the whole prayer lasts less than a half hour, even though the number of psalms alone would ordinarily take several hours to recite or chant. The psalms are distributed, one per monk, in order to pray all of them simultaneously. This expedites the prayer very quickly. The monks explain that if one prays a psalm in faith, all enjoy its benefit, and that owing to the unity of faith, all claim it in the mystical economy of the Body of Christ. Attendance at this prayer may increase to half of the monks.

Around midnight, each monk is to wake from sleep to begin an hour of private prayer in the inner room of his cell.[14] These series of prayers are designed to sanctify the night, a time which is thought to be dangerous to the purity of a monk's imagination and body. During this time, he spends the excessive energy of his body in a series of one hundred and fifty or more prostrations. These profound bows, called *"metanoia,"* which bring his body flat upon the floor, are said to sublimate passion into prayer, or, at least, to exhaust bodily restlessness. The very privacy of these prayers and the delicacy of their significance make them impossible to satisfactorily monitor. The manner in which each monk enacts the prayer is conditioned by the advice given by his spiritual father, but the difference between the ideal of the private mortification and its particular enactments by each monk (i.e., the number and degree of prostrations) cannot be observed.

The *Agbeya* explicitly presents the monk in the role which he otherwise portrays by his "poetic" behavior as discussed above. The monk is perceived by the Copts as one who continually offers up the prayers of the *Agbeya*, and he is thereby invested with the fullness of its associated meanings. The performance of these daily prayers somewhat resembles the traditional expectations afforded Western clergy, who have been ideally characterized in the constant recitation of their breviary. The monastic regimen described above does not proscribe seven separate interludes of prayer. The Coptic monk, like his Western counterparts, conflates these seven separate moments into more inclusive prayer times in the morning and in the evening.

The Coptic laity are encouraged to pray the *Agbeya* whenever possible, and pilgrims to the monastery are often quite prepared to join in the monastic prayer. There is, however, a special "eighth hour" of prayer which is reserved for the monks alone. This prayer, called "the veil" (*"sitar"*), is prayed in conjunction with the monks' common evening prayer, after the sequence of the regular Hours. The word for "veil" (*sitar*) is used because it recalls the modesty of Mary, the mother of Jesus, who is pictured in the Near-Eastern imagination as veiled. A monk "veils" himself in prayer as he anticipates sleep, for sleep is considered to be a potential threat to modesty and purity.

The Gospel read during the *sitar*, that of Saint John 6:15-23, concerns the desire of the crowds to make Jesus their king. Jesus must flee from them, alone, into the wilderness to evade their plans. Interestingly, then, the *sitar* "veils" the monks most explicitly from the temptation of ambition. Lust, sloth, and gluttony are less proximate to their religious role and are less likely to arise out of desert poetics than the desire to gain social and symbolic advantage.

## Conclusion

The constellation of behavioral and cultural features peculiar to monasticism reveals it to be a critical component of Coptic society. As an arena of cosmological performance on the desert stage of Egypt, the monastery dramatically links a beleaguered minority[15] to their divine judge and protector. The monks conjoin the angelic ideals and heavenly values of the Copts into a concrete embodiment of humanity, and thereby guarantee the coincidence of an ethnic population with an ecclesiastical communion. The monks anchor a people into a church. The unique survival of Coptic Christianity in an endless sea of Islam may be accounted in some significant part to its special investment in the monastic ideal. Indeed, most Copts explicitly state that they could not perdure without the monks. If this is so, the monks are a central nexus of Coptic social and cultural life, a vital link of ethnic aspiration and spiritual survival.

## Notes

1. Erving Goffman, *The Presentation of Self in Everyday Life*, Garden City, N.Y.: Doubleday, 1959, 252.
2. Ibid., 17.
3. ibid., 141.
4. Ibid., 253.
5. Ibid., 253.
6. Simon Tugwell, *Ways of Imperfection: An Exploration of Christian Spirituality*, Springfield, Ill.: Templegate, 1985, 15.
7. Gospel of St. Luke, 18:14. *The New American Bible*, St. Joseph Edition, New York: Catholic Book Publishing Co., c1987.
8. O.H.E. Burmester, *The Rite of Consecration of the Patriarch of Alexandria*, Cairo, 1960. Unpaged.
9. Goffman, *Presentation*.
10. Michael Herzfeld, *The Poetics of Manhood: Contest and Identity in a Cretan Mountain Village*, Princeton, N.J.: Princeton University Press, 1985, 10.
11. Ibid., 10.
12. Ibid., XIV.
13. Congenital blindness, and blindness induced by poor diet, sanitation, and disease, is fairly common throughout the Third World and in Egypt. The Copts have long since educed cultural meaning from the tragedy by assigning the ministry of cantor in the Church to the sightless. A blind boy is strongly encouraged to begin the process of sacred musical formation until he has memorized the tomes of Coptic liturgical hymnody by adulthood.
14. The modern cells of the typical Coptic monks are fairly standardized, most having been built around the same time. The greater part of the cell is a circular affair, with a bed and a desk placed beneath a high-domed roof, five meters in diameter. The bed is little more than an elevated wooden mat. In this room, each

monk is free to choose furnishings and decorations. Typically, there are icons, lamps, extra chairs, small tables, and shelves, but no modern appliances. All the floors are carpeted with throw rugs. Beside this larger room, the cell has an added smaller rectangular "prayer room," two by four meters, and less than two meters in height. The site allows the monk to pray without the distraction of his personal effects or bed in view. A monk may store the Bible there along with some other spiritual books. The "inner cell" is where a monk ideally spends his time, unless he is walking alone in the desert.

The external facade of the cell is made from limestone blocks which are used everywhere in monastery buildings. There are no eye-level windows. For light and ventilation, the cells have narrow vertical slits in the area were the vaulted roof connects to the wall. The inner wall is plastered. In addition to the numerous individual cell units, some monasteries include a building of common cells. Its cells have analogous space and functions as do the others; it may house as many as forty monks. All monks, whether in private units or a common building, usually share common sanitation and lavatory facilities, although some monasteries have provided them for each monk.

15. Shawky F. Karas, *The Copts since the Arab Invasion: Strangers in their Land*, Jersey City, N.J.: American, Canadian and Australian C. Coptic Associations, 1985, 92-121.

Nelly van Doorn-Harder

# Discovering New Roles: Coptic Nuns and Church Revival

"Our community[1] was set up to find a synthesis between the rules and examples of the early church and modern life. We had to start something like this because before women stayed inside the houses and only the men went out to work in the churches. And, as our bishop has taught us, with the help of the Holy Spirit, we can start to discover ourselves and our own potentials."[2]

"Discovering" seems to be the most appropriate word to characterize the current process Coptic religious women are going through in order to reassess their new role in a revitalizing church. At the moment there are three different groups of religious women: contemplative nuns, active nuns and consecrated women (*mukarrasat*) who eventually hope to become officially recognized deaconesses.[3]

The Coptic Church has known contemplative nunneries since the start of communal monasticism by Pachomius (292-346). The new community for active nuns, the Daughters of St. Mary (*Banat Maryam*) in Beni Suef, started in 1965 as a community for women who wanted to live a monastic life of active service. At present the sisters work in the educational and medical fields and initiate projects for community development. The community had the blessing of Patriarch Kyrillos (1959-1971), but as yet has not been officially recognized by the church authorities. The existence of the active community brought to light that the Coptic Church needed to create a structure that served to incorporate active lay women into the church system. To address this need, the institute of "consecrated women" was initiated by the present patriarch, Shenouda III, at the end of the 1970s. Although the status of the "consecrated women" is still far from ideal, they obtained official church recognition in 1992.[4]

These three groups mentioned are trying to discover new rules, themes and models from the Bible and tradition that can be applied to modern life. Each group also strives to reintroduce or reapply themes from the tradition in order to create a synthesis between the models and the rules of old and contemporary life.

Nowadays, an increasing number of young Coptic women are interested in the monastic profession. The number of nuns has increased manifold compared to a count of around 150 in 1973. In the contemplative nunneries the acceptance of new candidates has been brought to a halt because their abbeys are cramped. At the time of this writing the Coptic Church roughly counts 450 contemplative nuns, 90 active nuns and 500 consecrated women.

The majority of the new candidates has a much higher education than their mostly illiterate forebears. The new educational level also stimulated nuns to research their own heritage. Few models are available for these new nuns. Some are mentioned in the Bible, and a few women are quoted in an anthology of stories from the desert fathers and mothers. These holy mothers do not distinguish themselves from the fathers through the use of womanly language or by addressing specific female problems. This reality, however, does not seem to bother the present-day nuns. Coptic nuns are neither looking for a specific type of discourse for women, as, for example, one developed by feminist theologians, nor are they after a degree of emancipation that would allow them active participation in the administration and hierarchy of their church. What the nuns are trying to do is develop a role for themselves that sufficiently complies with the expectations of their surroundings, that is, the Coptic Church and community, and Egyptian society. Coptic nuns realize that antagonistic behavior would hamper their cause and limit their potential to operate within the Coptic system. By discovering and using themes of the tradition to develop their position and tasks, the nuns have powerful allies, such as holy fathers, mothers and saints, that can not be contradicted.

This article attempts to show some ways the contemplative and the active nuns use to accommodate Coptic tradition to their current needs. I will pay little attention to the consecrated women, because they do not live in organized communities but perform different services in the bishoprics to which they are connected.[5] To date a systematic study about their ministry is lacking. About the lives of the contemporary nuns I have written more extensively elsewhere.[6] This article will focus on some of the areas where the reapplication of themes and ideas drawn from the tradition is most prominent. These are: 1. ways of finding a synthesis between the ideal models and reality, 2. some visible markers that express adherence to traditional patterns, such as dress and buildings, 3. the adaptation of the convents' rule, and finally 4. a sample of the modes through which the tradition is being lived out.[7]

## Synthesis between reality and the ideal

During one of his public Bible studies (May 5, 1989), Patriarch Shenouda III was asked how a potential candidate for the monastic life could prepare herself or himself while still living "in the world." The answer was: "Read the sayings and stories of the desert fathers, mothers and saints. Learn the psalms by heart, throw bad books out of your house and try to get used to living without amusement and worldly distractions."

The gist of this answer means an unconditional mental and physical removal from the world. Although nowadays monastic candidates are required to have some years of professional experience before entering, they have to prepare themselves for the ancient ideal of a hermit's life. This eremitic ideal was most prominent in the early centuries of Christianity and hence can be learned best from the stories about this time. Most of these stories deal with men; apart from biblical women such as St. Mary and Eve, only four female ascetics are quoted in the monastic handbook *Bustan al-Ruhban* (the Garden of the Monks) that is used by Coptic monastics. Throughout Coptic history female holy models are scarce, which means that the contemporary nuns have to decide for themselves which male or female examples to follow.

*Contemplative nuns*
The contemplative nuns strive to follow the early models as closely as possible. Their attempts toward this goal are expressed in the fastidious performance of prescribed and extra prayers, acts of worship, fasting and a staunch effort to ward off the world outside the convent by controlling the contact between the nuns and external influences such as visitors and newspapers. The average visitor to a convent seldom meets face to face with any of the nuns apart from the mother superior or the nun who is appointed to take care of the guests.

Excessive fasting as the desert fathers used to practice is a point of constant discussion among the monastics. During the frequent days of fasting, monastics limit their ration to one meal a day, mostly taken around noon. This is the practice as recommended by the early fathers. Rigorous diets of one meal a week were practiced only by a select company of ascetic zealots.[8] Nevertheless, there is a constant striving among present-day monastics to excel in fasting. Since contemplative nuns do not have active duties outside the convents, they consider themselves as the best candidates for following more severe regimes than active nuns, laypeople and even monks. Also, the Coptic community regards them as the group that adheres most strictly to the early ideals and thus represents them. One finds this attitude expressed in (most probably fictive) stories like the one about Mother Irini (born 1940), the mother superior of the Convent of Abu Saifein in Old Cairo, who is said at times to live on half a zucchini and some salt a day.

The disregard for bodily needs in fact reflects some of the ideals of the monastic life: to reach the state of an "angel on earth" and to suffer diseases, caused by the lack of proper food, that can lead to holiness brought about by suffering patiently. The supreme goal of a monastic is to leave the world behind so that nothing earthly and temporal matters anymore. The initiation rite into monasticism, during which the prayer for the dead is pronounced over the monastic candidate, intensifies this image of a person who is already halfway to heaven, albeit still alive. Someone whose life evolves between heaven and earth in fact has neither time nor interest for earthly business, such as social work or caring for the needy. Hence, the contemplative nun also follows the models from the Coptic tradition who spent a lifetime praying on behalf of the Coptic community. Needless to say, due to her status between here and above, the contemplative nun is in an excellent position to pursue this responsibility.

*Active nuns and consecrated women*
The tendency to highlight the most rigorous examples from the tradition greatly influences the Coptic attitude towards women who live an active form of religious life; the Banat Maryam and the consecrated women. Due to their work, these women have fewer hours to spend in prayer. Moreover, austere fasting would interfere with their physical duties. Also, the fact that they have to move around in normal society induces the Coptic community to consider them as spiritually less elevated than the contemplative nuns.

The Banat Maryam themselves defend their position by pointing out that "Our Lord Jesus did not just stay inside the sanctuary but went around to meet with the people." They are weary of over-zealous asceticism because, according to them, "the middle way saves more [souls]." Bishop Athanasius, their abbot, likes to encourage them to "be natural, be simple, be peaceful. This is Jesus Christ, this is Incarnation. He did not remain in the sky and say 'come up here'."

Nevertheless, as do contemplative nuns, the Banat Maryam try to follow the tradition and remain close to its ideals, albeit with concessions to present-day life. With the rest of the Copts they agree that every church worker must have a solid knowledge of the Coptic tradition and know the writings and sayings of the early fathers. They realize, however, that contemporary human beings have different needs and capacities than the heroes of the old days. For example, fasting too rigorously can lead to physical problems that in the long run will become impediments to the performance of the sisters' duties.

Although their duties are in the world outside the convent, the sisters and consecrated women try to withdraw from secular influences by practicing the Jesus prayer or continuous prayer.[9] This spiritual exercise prevents them from being drawn too much into the flow of ordinary life. Continuous prayer is the preeminent occupation of monastics. While contemplative nuns try to limit their chores and work to activities that will not interfere with their work of continuous prayer, the active nuns also try hard to remain inside the monastic tradition via their prayer life.

## Markers of tradition

Trying to live out the Coptic tradition is expressed in a variety of visible signs such as clothing, ancient abbeys and producing Coptic art.

*Clothing*
Before the revival, the contemplative nuns dressed in an outfit similar to the conventional dress of other Egyptian women. Nowadays, they have added subtle variations to their habit so that it can no longer be mistaken for ordinary dress. Their headgear, or *qalansuwa,* is the most prominent symbol of revived Coptic monasticism. It is a skull cap that is divided in two halves with six crosses embroidered on each half. According to the tradition, it was first used by the father of monasticism, St. Anthony (251-356). During one of his numerous struggles with the devil, Anthony's cap was torn in two halves when the evil one tried to rip it off his head. While still being an ordinary monk, the present Patriarch Shenouda III reshaped and reintroduced the use of the *qalansuwa* because monks and nuns had grown lax in using it.[10]

*Buildings*
The origins of the contemplatives' abbeys, or at least their premises, are all historic Coptic sites. Some of these can be traced back to locations where, according to the legend, the Holy Family passed through during the flight in Egypt.[11] Most of the convents in Cairo were once connected to the patriarch's see, while the convent of Sitt Dimyanah (N.E. Delta) is built next to the shrine of its patron saint, St. Dimyanah.

The ancientness of monastic buildings in itself is considered a source of daily inspiration. The monastic literally walks in the footsteps of saints who lived during the period that Copts perceive as the zenith of Christian, that is pre-Muslim, life. The benefits of the saints' presence are not limited to monastics but encompass the entire Coptic community. As such, the whole community has a vested interest in maintaining the saints' influences. This includes conserving the saints' places which are mostly monasteries and convents.

Some monastic groups, however, are not satisfied with the degree of ancientness of current monasteries and convents. They insist on reaching for the roots of monastic life and strive to establish monastic buildings in the ultimate monastic place: the desert. Bishop Ammonius (of Luxor, Esna and Armant) is one of the initiators of a project involving nuns that aims to restore and re-inhabit what used to be monasteries in the desert of Upper Egypt. According to him the contemplative convents in Cairo are "just modern buildings in the middle of a big city." He considers the newly built mother house of the community in Beni Suef as "a hotel that misses the old spirit; the spirit of orthodoxy."[12] This remark stresses the fact that not even the oldest abbey in Cairo (that supposedly stems from around the eighth or ninth century) is considered sufficiently authentic when judged by the most ideal criteria of Coptic tradition.

Behind the disapproval of abbeys built near populated areas, we can detect the old monastic warning as expressed by one of the founding fathers of monasticism, St. Macarius the Great (c. A.D. 300-390). He urged his disciples, at the first appearance of non-monastic settlements in the desert, to "take up your sheep-skins, and go away."[13]

*Art*

The contemplative abbeys are decorated with icons and murals that convey the traditional stories. Mostly they depict the patron saint, or saints, whose relics are kept in the convent. Icons are ubiquitous among the Copts, in churches, convents, monasteries and homes. In the convents icons give lay Copts an opportunity to become more acquainted with their favorite saints and with the Coptic heritage. Producing icons through different mediums, such as painting, embroidery, woodcarving or in mosaic, has in fact become a major source of income for the contemplative nuns. Several convents have an enormous mural of their patron saint at their entrance that leaves no doubt about the nuns' affiliation. The icons also provide an opportunity to accommodate tradition to the nuns' own ideas. In one of the convents, for example, one finds a mural of the Virgin Mary with long flowing hair. Normally she is depicted with her head covered by a modest head gear. The nuns now reason that in the early icons St. Mary used to be painted with her hair uncovered and that the covering of the head is due to Muslim influences.

Apart from depicting their patron saints on icons, some of the contemplative nuns have capitalized on the Coptic respect for the saints by furthering the cult around relics kept in their convents. Mother Martha (1900-1988) of the Convent of Amir Tadrus in Harat al-Rum started this trend in the 1950s when she renovated her convent and expanded its property with an adjoining church. Nowadays, several convents hold elaborate celebrations to commemorate the day their patron saint was martyred, when his or her relics were brought to the convent, or when the church that bears the saint's name was consecrated. Because of the occasional miracle, visitors feel encouraged to visit the convent frequently in order to "greet their saint."[14] Certain convents provide trinkets, like pendants, keyhangers or headscarves with the saint's picture. These are worn by Coptic believers who derive strength and consolation from the "presence" of their favorite saint. Such accessories also serve as symbols of Coptic identity.

## The Rule

Another field for discovering the tradition was the monastic rule.[15] For centuries, monastic lessons had been transmitted orally. Increasing numbers of candidates, however, forced the ruling abbesses to look for more coherent systems. Traditionally, Coptic monasticism does not know a detailed system of rules and regulations as can be found in Catholic monasticism. The members of a monastic community used to follow the so-called idiorythmic system: different patterns of religious life, such as hermits or cenobitics, lived together in the same monastery. The monastery was kept together by the spiritual guide who directed each monastic concerning his or her program.

Mother Irini, the superior of the Convent of Abu Saifein, wished to break with this convention and decided that contemplative nuns should live a structured, communal life. She introduced a system in her abbey that is based on the precepts that Pachomius (292-346) drew up for his communities.[16] In accordance with common practice, Mother Irini herself has taught her nuns the new system orally during weekly sessions with the whole community.

When nuns from Irini's convent became superiors elsewhere, they applied the system that she designed, so that most of the present convents claim to follow the Pachomian system, rather than the conventional idiorythmic system of the monks. By searching the tradition, contemplative nuns found a way to differentiate their system from the one still used by most monks.[17]

From the picture presented so far, it becomes clear that active nuns and consecrated women do not have a prominent role in this process of rediscovering and using symbols of the Coptic heritage. The office of deaconess already existed in the early church and is mentioned in the New Testament. But in the Coptic frame of mind the responsibilities of a deaconess or an active nun belong to the realm of contemporary life. This means that they are not regarded as authentically Coptic. Especially the community in Beni Suef ardently tries to highlight possible references to the tradition. A drawback in their attempts is the fact that the Coptic community is much less informed about biblical and early Christian women who worked in active church service than it is about the eremitic models. The Coptic community still has to get used to women in active church service.

The prime biblical female model for the monastic life is St. Mary, the Mother of Christ. She is the patron saint of the active community, where the nuns like to point out that Mary was quick to visit her cousin Elizabeth upon learning that Elizabeth was pregnant in spite of her advanced age (Luke 1:39). Mary's wish to serve in obedience remains the active community's inspiration.

Nevertheless, Mary remains the prime model for the eremitic life. She is believed to have lived a life of prayer and seclusion after the Ascension. In Coptic circles it is not uncommon to find the comparison between a particularly virtuous, contemplative nun and St. Mary. The biographers of Mother Martha, for example, stretched their imagination to find parallels between her and St. Mary. Both women were called 'the chaste one', and are believed to have lived a life of prayer and devotion from their earliest childhood.[18]

## Modes of living out themes from the tradition

In the Coptic framework it is sometimes hard to discern whether strains from tradition have entered into everyday life by chance, or by deliberate imitation. Many aspects of regular conduct hold elements from the tradition that is ingrained in Coptic behavior during the course of many centuries.[19] In this article we will look at two aspects of this vast field of interaction: the transmission of knowledge and the way nuns are guided in the process of making decisions.

*The transmission of knowledge*
Both contemplative and active nuns play an important role in communicating religious knowledge to the Coptic community. In a broad sense, this knowledge also includes the practice of spiritual and practical counseling. According to Patriarch Shenouda III, "teaching and preaching is the church's first responsibility. All the great church fathers taught their community."[20] The patriarch himself follows this tradition through his numerous publications and by giving a weekly public Bible study. While the words of the ancient fathers were transmitted orally, the teachings of the current patriarch are recorded in writing and on cassette in order to be distributed among the Coptic community. The same procedure is followed by the bishops in their diocesan meetings and by the superiors of convents.

The Sisters of Mary, for example, seldom miss a public Bible study given by their abbot Bishop Athanasius. They avidly take notes of what is being said in order to discuss the lessons among themselves. Apart from the study of the Bible and the *Bustan al-Ruhban*, studies given by the superiors form the core of the nuns' monastic education. This method seems to come naturally to a society where reading still is not a popular activity. Writings and ideas are explained orally by a figure of authority in order to be handed down to other members of the Coptic community. Authority is derived from one's position, as is the case with the patriarch and the bishops, or it is ascribed to a person on the basis of charismatic leadership. The position of mother superior is sufficient to provide a superior with authority in relation to the nuns in her convent. The words of a mother with strong charisma, however, are accepted by the Coptic community at large as well.

The lessons of such a key figure are manifold; she/he explains texts from the Bible, and discusses questions concerning daily life. It is the figure with authority who is believed to have acquired an insight based on a life of prayer and contemplation. According to the Copts, the Holy Spirit guided the patriarchs from the Old Testament and the leaders of the early church, and equally guides the present charismatic leaders. They are thus qualified to address and translate issues brought about by modern life and give advice as to how the believer can be a good Christian and live according to the tradition at the end of the twentieth century.

Within this system, Western ways of conveying knowledge, such as workshops or seminars, are virtually unknown. Only the sisters in Beni Suef try to have discussions about their vocational and monastic life. Once I attended such a seminar led by Sister Emmanuelle, a Catholic nun who is well-known for her community development work among Cairo's garbage collectors. What I experienced as fascinating and powerful lectures, several of the younger nuns considered a waste of time. "Let us go back to work or say some prayers," was one of the frequent comments.[21] Only some of the sisters who had studied abroad, showed a sincere interest in the different sessions. Nevertheless, their prevalent opinion was that they "preferred to listen to the bishop's teachings."

The fact that the majority of the sisters reject the (for them) unconventional teaching methods can not simply be ascribed to their unfamiliarity. Their skeptical attitude has to be connected with the ultimate basis for the system of transmitting knowledge. This system goes back to the relation between the holy father in the desert and his pupils. The father was visited and asked to explain questions about numerous topics. Thus, he became the pivot for a community of followers who would disseminate these ideas and try to live according to them. In the case of famous fathers and mothers, like Anthony, Pachomius or Syncletica, their words were cast in writing and are still used today as sources of guidance and inspiration.

For contemplative nuns religious counseling is one of the foremost ways to convey stories and wisdom from the tradition to lay Copts. For example, a visitor who visits the Convent of Mari Girgis in Old Cairo will be received by an elderly nun who is especially appointed to minister to visitors who come for advice or encouragement. The nun sits in the chapel of Mari Girgis that adjoins the convent and holds the so-called chain of martyrs and some relics of the saint. The chain is believed to possess miraculous powers because it was used to torture martyrs during the early Christian centuries. While the nun discusses the visitor's problem, she will frequently refer to biblical stories, quote desert fathers, encourage the visitor to hold the container with the saint's relics against the body, or she will put the chain of the martyrs around the visitor's neck.

Mixed in with this performance of words and ritual is (according to Coptic understanding) sound social or psychological advice. For example, a woman who is maltreated by her husband is encouraged to be patient and, if need be, to bear the suffering since, so the Copts reason, patience and longsuffering are among the prime Christian virtues. Furthermore, Copts consider suffering patiently in a difficult marriage to be one of the roads that can lead to sainthood. This approach can be interpreted as a last resort in a reality where pursuing a divorce is not allowed. After having discussed the woman's problem, the nun puts the chain around the woman's neck and prays that she may be strengthened. After this, the woman's hand is put on the cylinder with the relics. The nun prays that Mari Girgis will pray for the couple. She also reminds the woman about the great sufferings Mari Girgis himself had to go through before he received "the crown of martyrdom."

Before she leaves the convent, the woman receives a tiny bottle with holy oil from the saint's sanctuary that she can rub on her forehead whenever she feels "weak". After this more or less ritualistic procedure, the nun advises the woman to read the Bible and frequently pray together with her husband. Finally, the nun also suggests that the woman undertake a serious effort to find out whether there is something that is bothering her husband, or why he has problems understanding his wife.

A session like the one described above can frequently be witnessed in any one of the contemplative convents. Myriad problems are brought to the nuns' attention: what study to choose, how to pass an exam, find the right partner to marry, educate one's children, problems at work and so on. It provides the nuns with ample opportunity to advance their role as upholders of Coptic tradition and to convey its stories in a form that is adapted to the contemporary context. The original paradigm is again the one of the desert father or mother with their followers. In this case, the mother superior of a convent is the one whose counsel is most valued. But since the nuns are perceived as representatives of the mother superior who convey her ideas, their advice is deemed acceptable as well.

Active sisters and consecrated women hand down stories from the Bible and tradition during the Bible studies that they teach to children, adolescent girls, women and the elderly. In order to strengthen their own authority the sisters and consecrated women use the lessons they themselves received from their spiritual guide. For example, one consecrated woman from Alexandria told me that she always used the stories and interpretations of the Bible she had learned from her confessor, the famous saintly priest Abuna Bishoy Kamil (1931-1979). And the sisters in Beni Suef like to draw from the many stories and explanations they heard from Bishop Athanasius.

*Living the Tradition*

The way contemplatives undertake decision making and seek advice themselves is strikingly similar to the conduct of the desert fathers and mothers. For example, in *The Life of Shenoute by Besa*, Shenoute (died around 466), the Coptic monk par excellence, regularly holds conversations with Jesus Christ.[22] Besa writes as if it concerns two old friends meeting: "One day, our father and our Lord Jesus were sitting down talking together."[23]

The Lord Jesus also proved a useful ally in projects Shenoute was about to undertake: "Before they had yet built the church, our Lord Jesus Christ appeared to our father apa Shenoute and said: 'Arise, and measure out the church and the foundation of the monastery, and build a sanctuary in my name and yours'."[24] When Shenoute protests against this plan because he lacks the money for such a project, he is sent into the desert where he finds a "small leather bag [of gold]....Thereupon, our Lord Jesus Christ came to our father, and they went off together and laid out the foundation of the sanctuary."[25]

The last story prompts the recollection of an incident that happened in 1959 at the Convent of Amir Tadrus in Harat al-Rum. The superior at that time, Mother Martha, was working out plans to build a new church adjoining her convent when she was visited by two men. One of them showed her the plan of the projected church and told her that it was to have three *haikal* (altars). According to her biography, the utterly terrified and amazed Martha asked the men who they were and suddenly understood "You are the Lord!" (*al-Sayyid al-Rabb*).[26]

As was the case in the lives of the early fathers and mothers, in the Coptic universe intervention of saints on behalf of the struggling humans is considered a common affair. Apart from support from above, saintly interventions underscore the degree of holiness of the still living person. They substantiate the fact that he or she is friends with the saints. Hence stories in which saints help the nuns abound in convents with a superior who is considered saintly. After Mother Martha, Mother Irini has become such a figure. One especially finds numerous miraculous stories connected with the convent's ambitious building projects that are in constant danger of being thwarted by bureaucratic regulations.

One such story about the construction of the farm of Abu Saifein's convent contains several elements one can find as regularly recurring in Coptic tradition.[27] One of the nuns told the story as follows:

> The number of nuns grew more and more, so we started to build extra cells in our abbey in Old Cairo. Furthermore, big rooms were divided into two and the end of each corridor was transformed into a small cell. We also had to reject many potential novices. We understood that we needed an extra house, but how could we find such a place? We are contemplatives and can not go out to look for it. So our superior [Mother Irini] decided that special prayers should be devoted to this project. She told us to pray for extra space at certain times a week, but not to give it any further thought. She did not allow us to undertake any action ourselves to find something, and forbade us to mention the project to our relatives.
>
> Exactly one year later, during the time of these special prayers, Abuna Tekla, a priest from Alexandria, came with his wife to the convent. His wife had three times a vision of St. Abu Saifein. The first time this happened, Abuna Tekla and his wife thought it had been a dream. When Abu Saifein appeared again they decided to pray about this. The third time the saint instructed them to donate to the convent in Cairo a piece of land that Abuna had purchased recently to build a community house for his church.
>
> Ummina Irini and the priest went to see the land. They inspected it for two hours and the moment it was agreed that the land suited the convent's needs, doves without wings appeared and flew over their heads.

The story concurs with the discourse that is used to convey some of the stories from the tradition. An active search by the nuns themselves seems out of the question, they are not even allowed to find a place through the network of family and friends. The prime excuse is that they can not leave the abbey. A few years later, however, when the farm is under construction and the grounds around it have to be cultivated, nuns regularly travel between the convent and the farm. They also have to move around in order to buy materials for building the farm and tilling its grounds. By choosing the way of passive waiting, combined with utter secrecy, the way is opened for a true miracle to occur. Considering Mother Irini's reputation as a saintly nun, nothing less than a miraculous event is to be expected. Her behavior fits the stories from the Coptic tradition where miracles were such a common part of the lives of church leaders, desert fathers and mothers and saintly monastics, that absolutely nothing could amaze them.[28]

Nevertheless, the miraculous event has to be scrutinized since it could be a trick of the devil. This is dutifully done by Abuna Tekla and his wife. When the final pact is concluded, doves appear. They are considered the ultimate symbols of saintly presence and miraculous occurrences. For example, the presence of the popular St. Dimyanah is always accompanied by the appearance of a dove that can only be seen by a chosen few. In order to be adequately weaponed against cynics who might call the presence of the doves a mere coincidence, the point is made that the birds are without wings.

This incident is only the beginning. During the whole process of building and acquiring the appropriate permits, there are tales of intervention of the saints. Especially St. Abu Saifein is active to further the cause of the nuns from "his" convent. According to the stories told by the nuns, he intervenes when cases against the nuns come to court. For example, when their title to the ground was disputed, he simply destroyed the papers concerned. While the farm is being built, the saint regularly appears both to Muslims and Copts. Thus, the Muslim construction workers become convinced of the legitimacy of the nuns' claim to the land. Coptic believers are reassured by the fact that the saint's working is not limited to Cairo only.

The ultimate proof of legitimacy comes during a mass that is attended by the superiors and abbots in the farm's new chapel. Those who are present during the celebration of the Eucharist suddenly behold several of the popular Coptic saints inside the sanctuary. According to the nun who related the story, saints Abu Saifein, Mari Girgis, Mari Mina, Mary the Mother of Jesus and the former patriarch, Kyrillos VI, all appeared inside the sanctuary. Again in the *Life of Shenoute* we can find similar occurrences.

For example, one day a person "dressed in a royal robe and very beautiful in form" joined the worship of Shenoute's monks.[29] After the stranger recited some of the lessons for the brothers he "walked into the sanctuary and disappeared."[30] Hereupon Shenoute revealed to the brothers that it was the prophet David who had joined them.

Through behavior that is familiar to the Coptic frame of mind, the nuns obtain a seal of authenticity. This enables them to give spiritual counseling and to work as intermediates between the Coptic believers and the saints. At the same time it allows them to become independent of outside assistance and undertake their own work.

Within the nucleus of the convent the numerous miraculous events confirm the charismatic authority of the superior, Ummina Irini. The same happened after David's visit to Shenoute's monastery; the monks were "all amazed at the way in which God had glorified the holy and great prophet, our father apa Shenoute."[31] David's visit served Shenoute's position as saintly abbot.

At the same time, this kind of apparition helped the nuns and monks forget that life under Shenoute's administration could be harsh. For example, there is a record about disobedient nuns who were punished with ten to forty blows on the soles of their feet.[32] Nowadays, monastic life can be equally oppressive for nuns who do not entirely fit into the system. Sometimes there is no way out, either from the system or from a tyrannical superior. When in such a case a miraculous event asserts the superior as a chosen leader, a harsh regime can be accepted as being in accord with the will of God.

It is this universe full of mystery and miracles that the active community contradicts and complies with at the same time. Although all the nuns are firmly rooted in Coptic faith and tradition, they try to seek the miraculous more in day-to-day events. Albeit, the sisters have their favorite saints and some of them can relate an incidental apparition or miracle. But reaching into the outer world while still alive is not their main goal. According to them, "the biggest miracle of all is the true conversion of a sinner."

## Conclusion

In order to emerge from an existence of obscurity, and to be able to operate within the complex system of the Coptic Church, the contemplative nuns have sought to re-introduce and re-apply themes from the Coptic tradition.

In doing this they have heavily capitalized on the Coptic penchant for seeking the intercession of the saints. Furthermore, the contemplative nuns developed the image of being true followers of the tradition who uphold its ancient values and customs. Concurrently, however, contemporary life forces them to explore new paths to comply with modern needs and values.

The active sisters (and following in their footsteps the consecrated women) could be considered as a product of new trends and needs within the Coptic Church. They are a new phenomenon within the Coptic context. Rather than re-applying tradition, the community of active sisters probes the tradition for recognizable figures in order to convince the Coptic public that their claim to authenticity is legitimate. In other words, they try to convey the message that the institution of active nuns is a truly Coptic phenomenon and not something introduced by 'others,' such as the Catholic Church.

Regardless of their vocation, be it active or contemplative, Coptic women seem to need a tool to justify their activities to the Coptic community. In order to achieve this goal, the Coptic tradition is useful to the nuns in discovering and developing a new identity that fits the developments that are taking place within the Coptic Church today.

## Notes

1. The Daughters of St. Mary in Beni Suef.
2. Sister Aghape, head of the Banat Maryam in Beni Suef, a community for active nuns, and Bishop Athanasius, Metropolitan of Beni Suef and Bahnasa, Jan. 9, 1992.
3. For more information about the process that precedes full consecration as a deaconess in the Coptic Church, see in this volume: Dina El Khawaga, "The Laity at the Heart of the Coptic Clerical Reform", 142-168.
4. It is not clear why the Coptic Church did not maintain the position of deaconess after the first centuries of Christianity. So far, I have only heard speculations about this topic, such as that after the tenth century the prevailing Muslim environment did not allow women to move around freely. The office of deaconess, however, is already mentioned in the Bible. For example, at the end of his letter to the Romans, St. Paul greets several female helpers whom the Copts today consider to be deaconesses (Rom. 16)
5. Although the consecrated women are scattered all over Egypt, the Coptic Church is trying to develop a center where they can gather for retreats and the like at the premises of the contemplative convent of St.Dimyanah.
6. For more comprehensive information about Coptic nuns see: Pieternella van Doorn-Harder, *Contemporary Coptic Nuns*, Columbia, SC: The University of South Carolina Press, 1995.
7. This article mainly draws from information obtained during interviews and observations made between 1987 and 1990.

8. Lucien Regnault, *La Vie Quotidienne des Pères du Désert en Egypte au IV Siècle*, Mesnil-sur-l'Estrée: Hachette, 1990, 77.
9. This prayer is originally based on the prayer of the tax collector in Luke 18: "God, be merciful to me, a sinner!" (v.18). The prayer, or its variations, should be repeated silently as much as possible. (translation according to the *Bible, New Revised Standard Version*, New York, Oxford: Oxford University Press, 1989.
10. Anba Mata'us, *Sumuw al-Rahbana* (The Excellence of Monasticism), Cairo: Viktur Kirillos, 1990, 154.
11. According to the tradition, these are the convents of Mari Girgis and Abu Saifein in Old Cairo, and the convents of Mari Girgis and Al-`Adhra' in Harat Zuweilah.
12. Interview February 15, 1989.
13. Benedicta Ward (transl.), *The Sayings of the Desert Fathers*, London & Oxford: Mowbray, 2nd. ed. 1984, 128.
14. Cf. Doorn van, N. "The Importance of Greeting the Saints; the Appreciation of Coptic Art by Laymen and Clergy." in Hondelink, H. (ed.) *Coptic Art and Culture*. Cairo: Shouhdy Publishing House (1990) 101-119.
15. Also see: van Doorn-Harder, *Contemporary Coptic Nuns*, 51-60.
16. Pachomius is considered the founder of the communal or cenobitic system of monasticism.
17. Some monasteries have tried to implement the Pachomian system. Most of these experiments failed, but the monks in the monastery of St. Menas (Mari Mina) still live according to the Pachomian system.
18. Rahibat Dair al-Amir Tadrus bi Harat al-Rum, *Al-Umm Martha*, Cairo: Viktur Kirillos, 1989, 41, 46-47.
19. An example of this phenomenon is the cult that stems from the veneration of saints. For parallels between the veneration of saints today, in the pharaonic times and the early Christian centuries, see: Baumeister, T., *Martyr Invictus*, Münster: Verlag Regensberg, 1972.
20. Interview January 23, 1992.
21. This seminar led by Soeur Emmanuelle took place during the second week of August 1989.
22. David N. Bell, Introduction, Translation and Notes, *The Life of Shenoute by Besa*, Kalamazoo, Michigan: Cistercian Publications, 1983.
23. ibid., 62.
24. Ibid., 51.
25. Ibid., 52.
26. *Al-Umm Martha*, 25.
27. The farm is situated west of Alexandria, on the road to Marsah Matrouh.
28. See a.o. the *Bustan al-Ruhban*, for a concrete example see *The Life of Shenoute*, 81,82.
29. *The Life of Shenoute*, 68.
30. Ibid., 69.
31. Ibid.
32. Ibid., 10.

Anitra Bingham-Kolenkow
# Talking through the Saints[1]

A spiritual son questions. The spiritual father tells a story of a biblical patriarch, a desert father or a modern holy one; all are saints; their story illustrates a point. The son knows what the father wants, but the story leaves space for the son's own interpretation; the criticism is not direct. The world of Coptic spirituality is built on stories of saints: stories of the Bible (patriarchs are called saints), of the desert fathers, apocryphal stories of saints made for modern ears and stories of everyday holy ones or of one's own spiritual father or mother.

The stories offer a kaleidoscope of uses. A spiritual father talks to his son through the Bible and the son may argue back through the Bible; stories of the Bible also may be used to show the complexity of a situation. In modern Egypt, parables may be used for conversation over difficult issues (as Nathan talks to David).[2] A monk said he could not talk about certain topics with others – and shortly thereafter he told how his bishop said that people would not listen to certain similar points so the bishop used a story to raise the issues. The monk also said that stories were like cowboy movies; the actions stood for good and evil, showed you how you had sinned and could make you aware of problems relatively fast. In a variety of ways stories can depict an ideal or criticize a situation. They enable a monk to picture himself in a certain situation. Modern monks live their lives not only according to the Bible, but use desert saints as their models. Psychologically, stories of saints encourage and actualize the possibilities of the ascetic life.[3]

A story was also good to stop fights because monks started to listen. A joke or laughter-producing story calm an angry situation; "I can only talk to Father N. with jokes." Or the story was good to console; one monk told how he had known that a person was upset and just went and told Bible stories to comfort the sad mind. As families have their own stories and jokes, so do the monastic communities. One keeps monastic tradition alive by telling stories of "what your spiritual father (or mother) did." Stories of ancient hardship serve to relativize modern difficulties; monks also tell stories of modern fathers who only eat one meal a day and give much of that to a cat. ("I could not do that," said the monk. "I still need my sugar.") And you hear how monks tell admiringly of a father who put them in a room with rats running through to test them.

In recent days, miracle stories become important as encouragement in dark times or to justify one's actions. Stories are also written apocryphally to express a point of view. Revelations are put in ancient mouths or new exegesis is given of ancient biblical prophecy.

Stories of saints, ancient or modern, do not always depict ideal behavior. One of the monks said to another, "We can not translate all the stories of the *Forty News* because others will get a bad idea of us."[4] A bishop said to a priest, "Do not translate certain parts of the story of Pachomius (290-346); it will give people bad ideas." But to tell of reality is, of course, the crucial point of ancient story or modern. Fictitious names and locations enable one to talk about real problems and give a new perspective. In fact, because the stories talk about commonplace difficulties of monastic life, stories become good vehicles for talking about its problems. One can ask, "is it like the story of 'x'?" and the monk can say that it is more like 'y.' If heroes have problems, then we can have problems, too. If David sinned, we can sin. David's family gives examples of sins. Job complains and one can use his words. Even great saints have leadership problems. If Pachomius tries to deal with thousands and sometimes succeeds and sometimes fails, so can present leaders. Ancient writers told stories of Pachomius's problems about succession and modern monks may talk about leadership by means of talking about Pachomius.

Or one can talk about severity (using St. Shenoute, d. ca. 450) or stories about favoritism (using Pachomius). And the *Forty News* warns old and young monks that they can be in danger of falling any day; "I could have fallen just like that father;" the test is not over until the end. The readers of John Climacus (570-645) see old men asking about their fate, and John Climacus recognizes that these men may be more holy than he (even if they are sinners).

Leaders need to be transmitters of tradition through story. Leaders must also have stories of their own life, both to remain humble and to show that they understand (as did St. Pachomius). A monk was talking to a young man who felt caught trying to decide between religious and scientific ideas of life. The monk said,"I was like that young man." When a young monk heard this, he was much relieved that a father whom he admired had had the same problems as he.

In an Orthodox hierarchical society, obedience is stressed and the spiritual father expects to be listened to by the son. But a high value needs to be placed on stories which also enable the father to listen— to hear how leaders listened or how leaders can get into trouble. Modern pseudepigrapha enable modern monks and leaders to speak about present issues of what a monk should be like. Stories facilitate a kind of internal negotiation where people put themselves in the situation of parables of past teachers. The stories are not necessarily from Coptic stock. Modern stories or tales of Tolstoy will spread through a monastery like wildfire and every one will quote them to you. Stories, though quite pointed, are a permissible medium to convey criticism, complaints and other negative feelings. The mind loves stories. The remainder of this paper will give several extended examples of the spectrum of stories monks tell.

## The Bible

Scripture is the major resource for talking in the monastery. Monastic spirituality is built on deep reading of (meditation on ) scripture. The Bible is read attentively in liturgy and recited in the daily "praises." Monasteries have programs of reading the whole Bible in the fast preceding Easter as well as the normal reading of the Gospels and Revelation (with many other passages) during Holy Week. A monk or bishop will regularly cite stories, and also ask about stories or passages which fit a certain situation. For example, a nun will show the importance of Christian women by pointing out the three women receiving the spirit in a Pentecost icon.

The use of a citation may be very simple. A bishop may say an Old Testament saint's life illustrates faith. Abraham illustrates faith and obedience. Be like Isaac – obedient to your father without questioning. In this, the bishop's group of examples may be like the book of Hebrews with its list of those who lived by faith. Simple stories or parables may be used to end an argument. A monk is meant to be trusting of his father regardless of circumstance, like Abraham when told he would be the father of many peoples.[5] The monk is asked to be like Isaac, trusting his father although his father seems ready to kill him.[6] Or the monk is to be like Jesus, obedient unto death.

Major problems in the monastery have their Bible story: unwillingness to get rid of wealth – the rich young ruler as in Luke 18:18; different roles and skills – John the Baptist and Jesus or Peter and Paul (married and unmarried, both died in Rome); cruel laughter or exclusion – disciples exclude the little children, the elder son, the unmerciful servant.[7] A bishop may say, "If you love the New Testament you cannot sin. If you cannot do this it is because you rely too much on yourself." On the other hand, he may recognize the difficulty of living with the Bible and tell the story of a monk who said, "I cannot live with the commands of the Bible. Tell me what I should do." The saint replied, "Take a basket and put it in the Nile and get it out all day and come to me in the evening and tell me what you have done." When evening came, the monk said, "I spent the day putting the basket in the Nile and the water spilled out." Then the saint asked him, "Do you find the basket cleaner than when you put it in at the beginning?"

A monk may be told gently when he has received the patriarch's or bishop's blessing for a project, "Your struggles, like Jacob's, may not be over when you get the blessing." The ambiguity and blessing of an overly fond mother like Rebecca (or an overly fond father like Jacob, who gave favor to Joseph), who enables you to triumph over your brother, set up the struggles you may have with other people and angels. Your life may be like a succession of struggle stories where God and your supposed allies keep testing you, but keep on asking, like the woman in the New Testament who kept bothering the judge to obtain justice.[8] God may grant your request but it may not be good for you.

Bible stories especially illustrate complexity. A monk will say, "Who would want a friend like Joab?" (the army leader of David), but another monk would chime in, "But Joab took the hard deeds on himself, and David was very good at leaving hard deeds to Solomon, too. What would you do with a son like Absalom who was leading a revolt against you and whom you love?" The telling of such stories prepares young monks to become priest-preachers and talk to communities. The Coptic monk knows the Bible. He will bring up Joab with a slight smile. The monk knows people in the monastery like Joab – useful but ambitious, whose aims may be good for you but who will somehow harm those close to your heart. The ancient world would know David as a man of blood, but David is also seen as one who does not allow himself to take vengeance; Joab and then Solomon become David's agents.[9] There is enough ambiguity.

A bishop may say, "The Bible says 'Obey your leaders'." And you realize that in this situation the story needed is that of Nathan and David's willingness to hear Nathan. "We need to be like David listening to Nathan and not like the Pharisees who did not listen to Jesus as to a prophet." Then what do you do with prophets who forecast ills against you, like Micaiah, son of Imleh, who never prophesied "anything favorable..., but only disaster?"[10] And what do you do with prophets that God sends to mislead kings? One monk, identifying with those prophets, said, "They know I am always going to be in opposition." And what do you do to encourage leaders in difficulties, or those who become suffering servants, as in Isaiah 40ff.?

A bishop also said, "Father and son both need to listen. People must tell their difficulties; Elisha must ask what is wrong. Not all of us are like Daniel, able to know others' thoughts. The Bible tells us we must hear everyone; Jesus hears the cries of people; he comforts them not only by hearing but by practical work" (healing). The same person told the story of the saint who was walking and came upon people who needed food to live. He had nothing but his Bible; he gave them the Bible to be sold.

David's Psalms also provide language for praise in spite of difficulties, or to talk to God in horror and faith, as Ps. 22, "My God, my God, why have you forsaken me....I am like water ... You who fear God, praise."[11] Thus, we can realize how much more in difficulty Jesus was when he used the psalm. Monks (as Jews did in the past) use psalms to fight demons and exorcise them. The book of Proverbs gives a language of balance; do not reprove one who made you, but the wise man will love you. Proverbs also presents two women calling from the road: Wisdom who argues for prudence (8) and the noisy foolish woman (9:13-19). Both talk to the simple.

Job and other sufferers give stories and language for complaint. Job's helpers are like those who justify a leader when he has allowed his advisors to do wrong things to a virtuous monk to test the monk. But, said one monk, "You will face God and difficulty; the fathers said 'Practice God in difficulty.'"

The monks especially love the Song of Songs. As in Gregory of Nyssa's time (330-395), it is interpreted as the language of Jesus' love for the monk or Christian. The sixty cassettes of the priest Father Ibrahim about the Song of Songs tell how Christ cannot refuse the Christian anything.

Monks like allusions from the Bible or the saints to give encouragement to one who is caught in a difficult situation – saying for example, "I will die before you will and will ask St. Peter at the gate to let you be with me in heaven." Or, "I will ask that the cloud of St. Paul (the hermit) travel with you on your journey." The good will of the monk is transferred in the saying through allusions to a whole complex of thoughts (heaven, St. Peter and community); a monk talks to God and asks for a cloud to help now as God helped St. Paul in the past – half serious, half family joke. Monks by the name of Suriel were delighted to hear that an ancient version of the Bible (Targum Neofiti) named Suriel the angel who struggled with Jacob and furnished the ladder (giving rise to new iconography).

Monks actualize themselves through allusions. A monk will say, "We are like Moses, having left Egypt (Cairo) for the monastery." Or a monk will say, "I am like Peter. I am not sure. I will not deny under pressure." A monk will make a story or liturgy immediate by interpretive participation with the young men in the fire (Dan. 3):

> Say to yourself, take off your sins and mistakes, what you love; Take new heart; what fire makes of an old man, cleans him, gives him purity. The three young men are me; come young men, praise! Keep me from the devil. My Lord, I am your servant, do not remember my mistakes because I want you to speak with them. I say I am your servant; I follow you with all my heart; do not refuse me. Ask the three young men to remember me in front of God (during the marching song of the saints). Jesus Christ, how he takes flesh, how he comes with Mary. How the Lord is happy to take him back. Please when you come again, do not say 'I do not know you,' but put me with the good people. I want to listen.

As in the time of the desert fathers, a monk will be counselled, justifying an internal struggle by the saying of going the second mile, so now a monk will use the "second mile" saying as a basis for his life. As in the time of Evagrius Ponticus' (346-399) *Antirrhetica*, biblical sayings still get used as remedies for particular sins.

Jesus is an important person to actualize. The monks say that they must share suffering with Jesus. They must use present difficulties to be a witness to others by their own lives. They see monks who suffer as suffering like Jesus and by their suffering enabling miracles for others. On the other hand, the desire for humility makes them say, "I cannot be like Jesus." So you have to work around that by saying, "Do what Jesus or Paul *said* to do." If they say, "We are only little children," you reply, "Jesus said that we all are to be as little children." Spiritual direction takes place by dialogue, and knowing the Bible and the Fathers is the way the dialogue takes places.

Dialogue is not only for the present but also to interpret scripture to know the future. As in the past, people use the visions of Daniel to speak to present and future. This is a time of apocalypse for Egypt. The expectation of the end is strong. Where a bishop may once have said, "A monk needs to think about his own salvation and not about the end of history," he now sees the book of Daniel as giving an exact forecast of what will come to pass. There is worry about terrorists who may bomb the mosque-temple in Jerusalem and earthshaking wars that will be a prelude to the endtime. "Therefore we must move the temple; ask the scientists." There is a very careful reckoning of Danielic times and other images from scripture producing a forecast of an earthquake in Jerusalem in the near future with the need to rebuild the temple – and many kinds of improvement of relations between parties, with the second coming of Christ in 2001. The Coptic interpretation of the endtime makes it into one of those good miracles which bring people together, like the appearance of St. Mary in Helwan and Zeitun (in 1968 and 1986). There is also an anti-Christ who was born in 1969 and will be crowned in 1998, and a forecast of a limited nuclear war.

Another bishop once said, "It is the wisdom of God for each generation to have people who believe that the end has come." But now he says, "You are too optimistic if you think this will not take place." Or, "We need to live as though the end were present" (as did Jesus and his disciples) and actualize the possibilities of good community together. As St. Anthony (ca. 251-356) said, live as though each day was your first and last – and do not fear (for fear is a sign of demons).

## Ancient desert fathers and modern city saints

The stories of the desert fathers (as well as the modern city saints) also depict a way of life. One monk said, "They lived a life according to the Bible; they teach us how to live according to the Bible." Indeed, St. Anthony uses biblical heroes (Job, Moses) again and again.

The *Paradise of the Monks* (translated into Arabic from western editions in 1967) tells stories of the fathers listed according to monastic virtues. This is an ancient way of organizing the fathers' lessons. Modern spiritual fathers tell their sons to read and use the stories as part of spiritual direction. A monk once asked me to approach a study of monastic life through a listing of monastic virtues and vices, because, according to him, "This is the way of the fathers." Monks may tell the story of St. Anthony having a monk cover himself with meat – and be attacked by dogs and birds – to speak about poverty.[12] A monk of the Monastery of the Syrians wrote a book about the way of life of ancient monks; it speaks to modern monks about the lack of possessions.

A monk will say a spiritual father needs to be patient and gradually change a monk to another way of life, as in the story of the former criminal turned saint, Moses the Black. The fathers put Moses (who was very large) on a balance with a great tree trunk. As the trunk dried out, Moses slowly lost weight. Or, a monk remembered, "The bishop said, 'Do you want me to be harsh like the one who had a tree for beating monks in the Syrian monastery?'" Or a monk will tell the story of St. Anthony's reply to a hunter who saw the monks playing and commented on the fact that they were not in prayer: "If we stretch the brethren beyond measure, they will soon break."[13] Or a monk will compare Father Matta al-Miskin's method of spiritual direction[14] (seeing what the soul will become and admiring and shaping it) with Anthony's saying that the monk needs to decide what virtue he will forge.

As in the time of Pachomius, older fathers tend not to listen to leaders or to want to call down apocalyptic judgment on people (as in the Testament of Abraham, read on the Feast of the Three Patriarchs in September).

John of the Ladder (Climacus) is another recommended author. Monks may use his book, *The Ladder of Paradise,* to highlight the ambiguities of monastic life. *The Ladder* gives monastic characteristics as rungs of a ladder. The icon of the ladder shows monks falling off this ladder. John tells that fasting may indeed lead to bad temper, or a demon may harden hearts, which John calls a "bitter joke played on us by demons."[15] John says we may see irritable people who are practicing vigils, fasting and stillness.[16] At the same time, John tells admiring stories of the Shepherd who makes his monks live lives of great humility (more than any monk would do in this age, according to a contemporary monk).[17] Step 5 especially tells of a prison where severely punished people actually live lives which seem more ideal than those of "good" monks.[18] John also realizes that a superior who reveals his own failings engenders distrust and hence John speaks indirectly, "I have seen" and talks of different situations, telling of different possibilities and the care the surgeon must take in applying the right medicine to the situation.[19] As one monk said, "Discernment by a father is like diagnosis by a doctor." According to him, "Trust in God is like life insurance when the diagnosis fails." Monks will contrast this discernment with the attempt by some leaders to use one law and regulation for all.

Monks use sayings of the fathers as encouragement after bad dreams; as Anthony said, the dreams are given by God if they give you joy; it is demons that make you fear.[20] Fear is considered "some sort of sin, call on the name of Jesus." (Or for worry at night) "Do not hesitate to go late at night to those places where you usually feel afraid; have care and concern about the best path, but do not fear."

Monks have their favorite father's sayings on the wall, but at the same time realize: "I try to live them, but it is above me." John Saba (the old man), is a particular favorite on Coptic walls. So are Isaiah of Sketis, as well as Pachomius and the *Paradise of Monks*. The late Bishop Theophilis gave the Westerner Thomas a Kempis (with the *Paradise* and John Climacus) for new monks to read.

The monastic custom of naming monks after a saint makes the monk (or nun) the carrier of stories of that saint, in fact a reincarnation of that saint for each community to keep the ideal alive in the carrier of a name. There are also stories about relationships between monks and women. As the book of Proverbs presented two women (or two ways of wisdom and folly), so the icon of St. Samuel shows him with two women: St. Mary giving blessing and another woman tied to St. Samuel to make him give up his vow of chastity. Monks compare someone to Hilaria, the daughter of a king who put on male dress to live with the monks, or they talk of Melania, who lived with monks and founded monasteries with Jerome (392-420) in Palestine. The nuns take ancient female martyr names and research their namesakes. They relate that Mother Irini (the mother superior of the Convent of Abu Saifein) talks with St. Mercurius (as St. Shenoute used to talk with Jesus and Old Testament figures). Monks tell the stories of Theodore (Tadrus) and Archilides and their mothers to justify not seeing their families, or they will tell of Maximus and Domadius to speak of close relationships with brothers or friends. As in the ancient world, Arsenius and Moses the Black are used as examples of isolation and hospitality, and Cassian (360-435) is quoted when discussing refusal to see bishops and women.

Monks love stories about animals and nature. As John Climacus says, "The cat keeps hold of her mouse and the hesychast holds his spiritual mouse." So a monk will say: "a good monk is like a turtle, which is quiet and stays in its house."[21] Or a monk will tell of Abuna Justus, a holy monk from the Monastery of St. Anthony (1910-1976), who gave his meat to a cat. Monks also love to hear the story about an engineer living in Cairo who eats once a day and gives his cat better food than himself. Monks also quote the famous saying of St. Anthony about a monk being like a fish out of water if leaving the desert.[22] Or they may remind you of John Climacus' saying that a plant may grow well with the virtues of the world and wither in the desert.

Monks also tell of or compare the saints to ordinary people. For example, they tell how an outsider made them aware that something they did might be misinterpreted. Or as an example of sacrifice, a monk will tell of a monk who heard of another needing a desk and gave his own desk (although he might never get another one).

Copts also tell stories of canonized modern saints.[23] Anba Abraham (the saintly bishop of Fayoum, 1829-1914) is known for his love of the poor and his willingness to help them. But his hagiography includes a negative miracle story where a man (having plotted with a friend to deceive the bishop) asks for money to bury his friend. The man returns and finds the friend dead. A bishop said, "We warn people of sin."

There are wonderful stories, especially from Upper Egypt, of contemporary lay persons who live holy lives; their spiritual children become tellers of stories about these images of humility and power on earth: Of a young man who came and planted flowers in an old monastery and said, "I do not have to be a monk." Or, in Bagoura a man had a vision and started to gather plots of land, money, artists and helpers to build a church. After the death of a man who had been helper of all the youth of Luxor for years, his children tell of miracles and how even at the time of his death he was thinking of those who were in need of help. They also tell of his having made complete plans for a hospital.

Sometimes laypeople tell their own miracle story to show that God still helps. There are many stories of how God showed them a vision of a particular monastery (and thus justified their going there). Visions and dreams become the basis of radical change, as when a Muslim gives his patrimony to a monastery in Upper Egypt because its patron saint appeared to him. There are many varieties of a story where a late night visitor to a church, with possible bad intentions, is grasped by a bony hand from a saint's casket in the church and must stay until morning when the monks come and pray for him. The story becomes protection for the church against robbery or misbehavior.

## Modern spiritual stories

In *The Forty News* there are many stories which were written in comparatively recent times to talk to the present through stories of seemingly past fathers. Monks warn, however, "They were not written in ancient times and may not be true." The first story tells of the goodness of a monk – and then tells how Satan keeps after the monk and the monk falls into sin even at the end of his life. Thus, the story is not really blaming the monk, but asking the audience to beware of facing temptation (it will always continue) and falling. The stories show how Satan can lash the monk or change shapes, clothes and character. The monk must not only be gentle as a dove but wise as a serpent to judge Satan disguised as an ascetic monk or as a person who wants directions.

A book that became immensely popular among the Copts was Father Ishaiah Bibawy's *Robe of Uncle Daniel*.[24] It uses the ancient story form of one who comes from the dead, telling about what he saw and learned. The contents of the revelation are taken from the Bible and, like any apophthegm, the story gives a living context to the revelation. The niece Ruth runs to the door, recognizes and proclaims her uncle, who is clothed in a white robe. Uncle Daniel is placed back in the life of his friend, Simeon the elder, who anointed Emmanuel and used to talk to Anna (Luke 2:25-38). The whole story uses biblical quotations both for description and speech. Uncle Daniel describes the other world, the promise of the coming of the Lord and the general resurrection. He covers many theological points such as Hades, free will, souls and bodies after death. Uncle Daniel visits St. Mary and the sick. His main task is to preach preparation for eternal life. He talks of prayers of the dead for the living. Then uncle Daniel departs for heaven. The robe becomes a basis of healing, carried by Ruth, handed to Irene and worn by St. Peter at his martyrdom. The robe is defined as faith and belief in the power of the Lord.

I can only conclude by echoing the last verse of John's gospel: if all the stories I have been told were written, there would be no easy end.

## Notes

1. Talking through stories is an ancient method. The Hebrew world used and changed ancient myths. The N.T. used the O.T., the church fathers used both N.T. and O.T. to talk to their readers. A few examples: The prophets refer to God's care in Egypt or in the wilderness (Hos. 11:1-5, Jer. 2:2). Reformers in the time of Josiah use rewritten ancient law (like Deuteronomy) to speak to their time. Is. 51 refers to Abraham, Sarah, and a wilderness like Eden as well as the Lord's fight with the cosmic dragon (a common Near Eastern motif). The rabbis argue through midrash of biblical passages to present their theological viewpoints (Midrash Rabba and Talmud). Like the stories cited from the Coptic world, the Jewish world also built pseudepigraphic prophecy from O.T. texts to speak to its audience (e.g. 4 Ezra and 2 Baruch).

    The N.T. shows Jesus talking about Sodom and Gomorrah (Matt. 10:15) or the prophet Jonah and the people who came to hear Solomon (Matt. 12:39-42). Matt. 24 par. is reinterpreting Daniel and other prophecies. The passion narrative is full of explicit fulfillment passages and many allusions to the O.T. (as the three days in the tomb; cf. any good gospel commentary). The parallels to the O.T. show how the life of Jesus was seen fulfilling-building on the O.T. (Matt. 21:4-5). Jesus also uses the words of the O.T. (Matth. 21:16, 42; 24:38-39). Of course, the gospel parables are the best place to see Jesus talking through stories of everyday life.

    Church fathers like Ignatius often make allusions to N.T. stories. Barnabas regularly quotes O.T.(as 4:7-8 (Moses) or 11:6-7 (Ps. 1)) as well as alluding to the relation of Jesus and the OT (as 7:3-11). Augustine's and Chrysostom's sermons (like those of any good preacher) address their audience through preaching on scripture. Bishop Theophilus (of the Syrien Monastery) liked the Syrian Philoxenus (440-523) who used scripture to make monastically useful points.

    I was delighted to find Coptic monks and bishops doing likewise, as recognizing such conversations in the ancient world has been one theme of my scholarly life: e.g. talking to community through writing prophecy; "Introduction to 2 Bar 53, 56-74," (Harvard, Ph.D. Thesis, 1971), "The Testament of Abraham as a Testament," in: *Studies on the Testament of Abraham*, G. Nickelsburg (ed.), Missoula, Mont.: Scholars Press (1976) 135-152, and "Alternative Myths in a Gnostic World," *ANRW* 2:22.1.
2. See: 2 Sam. 11-12.
3. H. de Wit, *Contemplative Psychology*, Pittsburgh: Duquesne, 1991, 133-4 and Bruno Bettelheim, *Uses of Enchantment*, New York: Knopf, 1976, 61ff.

4. The *Forty News* is a collection of monastic stories and sayings that recently was "discovered" in one of the Coptic monasteries. Its authenticity is highly questionable and monks warn against believing these stories too readily.
5. Gen. 18:17ff.
6. Gen. 22.
7. Mark 10:13ff., Luke 15:25ff., Mat. 18:23ff.
8. Luke 18:1ff.
9. For Joab see: 1 Sam. 25:32-33, 26:9, 2 Sam.1:16, 3:27-29, 4:4-12, 14, 18:9-33, for David to Solomon, see: 1 Ki. 2-5-9.
10. 1 Ki. 22:8.
11. Also: Mark 15:34.
12. Benedicta Ward (transl.) *The Sayings of the Desert Fathers*, London & Oxford: Mowbray, 1984, 5 (Sayings of St. Anthony no. 20).
13. Ibid., 3 (Saying no. 13).
14. Father Matta al-Miskin is the prior and spiritual father of the St. Macarius Monastery.
15. St. John Climacus, *The Ladder of Divine Ascent* (revised ed.), Boston, Mass.: Holy Trinity Monastery, 1978, 7:48.
16. Ibid., 8:21.
17. Ibid., step 4.
18. Medieval monks had a penitential canon of eight odes in honor of the "holy criminals" plus illustrations cf. J.R. Martin *The Illustration of the Heavenly Ladder of John Climacus* (Princeton University Press: Princeton, 1954, 128ff.) who suggests that the example of the holy criminals was to move "to a spirit of more profound contrition," 148.
19. Climacus, *Ladder*, 4:39, also see: 8:18 where John tells stories of the monastery and the different advice given to different people.
20. Athanasius, *The Life of Antony and The Letter to Marcellinus*, (Robert C.Gregg, transl. and intro.), New York, Ramsey, Toronto: Paulist Press, 1980, 57. Also see: Climacus, *Ladder*, 21:12.
21. Climacus, *Ladder*, 27:7.
22. Ward, *Sayings*, 3 (saying no. 10).
23. In the Coptic Church the official process of canonization by the Holy Synod can take place 50 years after a saint has passed away. After a saint is officially recognized by the Church, his or her name will be added to the Synaxarium, the official list with saints.
24. Cairo, 1990 (no editor).

Kari Vogt

# The Coptic Practice of the Jesus Prayer: A Tradition Revived

"Prayer is a language" (*al-salah lughah*), says the mother superior of one of Cairo's contemplative nunneries. This is how she defines prayer, the most important activity for the one hundred or so women who live within the nunnery's walls. It is an activity which occupies about eight hours of the nuns' day – or even more! For what is involved is not only the divine office, the long liturgical prayers, or private prayer alone in one's cell. The ideal is "the unceasing prayer" (*al-salat al-da`ima*), a term that not only indicates a state of unceasing adoration, but can also be applied to the so-called Jesus Prayer.[1]

This article is based on conversations with two Coptic bishops and with monks and nuns from different monasteries. I also had a number of conversations with active nuns and with *mukarrasat*, consecrated women.[2] The theme of these conversations was the so-called Jesus Prayer (*al-salah Yasu'*) as it is practiced among monastics in the Coptic Church in Egypt today.

An early form of the Jesus Prayer was probably known and practiced in Egypt as early as the eighth or ninth century A.D.; this at any rate is what recent studies have sought to demonstrate.[3] But this history is little known among the Copts, most of whom look on the Jesus Prayer exclusively in the light of the post-1950 religious revival, closely linked to the Sunday School Movement.

We can thus ask: when and how was this form introduced? Can we speak of a revival of an originally Egyptian tradition of prayer? Or is the Jesus Prayer testimony to a renewed contact with the Greco-Russian Orthodox Church, where this very prayer is an important part of monastic spirituality?[4]

The French sociologist Marcel Mauss wrote in 1909 that prayer is the least investigated of all religious phenomena, and this assertion still retains its validity.[5] There are exceedingly few studies that shed any light on the praxis of prayer, and the Jesus Prayer with its rich tradition is no exception. Other questions touched on here are: how widespread is the use of the Jesus

Prayer in the Coptic Church today? What instruction does the individual receive, and how and why is the Prayer practiced?

## The Prayer-formula

The Jesus Prayer, as it is practiced by the Copts, can run as follows:
"Ya Rabbi Yasu' al-Masih irhamni."
"Ya Rabbi Yasu' al-Masih a'inni."
"Ya Rabbi Yasu' al-Masih khallisni."

Which means:
"Oh my Lord Jesus Christ, have mercy on me."
"Oh my Lord Jesus Christ, help me."
"Oh my Lord Jesus Christ, deliver me."[6]

But variants exist; some informants, for example, supply the following formula:
"Ya Rabb Yasu' al-Masih ibn Allah irhamni, ana al-khati`a."
"Ya Rabb Yasu' al-Masih ibn Allah a'inni."
"Ya Rabb Yasu' al-Masih ibn Allah usabbihukah," or
"Ya Rabb Yasu' al-Masih ibn Allah usabbihu ismaka al-quddus."

Which means:
"Oh Lord Jesus Christ, Son of God, have mercy on me, a sinner."
"Oh Lord Jesus Christ, Son of God, help me."
"Oh Lord Jesus Christ, Son of God, I praise you," or
"Oh Lord Jesus Christ, Son of God, I praise your Holy Name."

This is somewhat reminiscent of the fourfold formula in Coptic manuscripts of the ninth and tenth centuries, which E. Lanne calls "the Jesus Prayer in its 'Macarian form'."[7] Thus, the Coptic formula can deviate to some extent from the simpler Greek-Russian variant:

"Lord Jesus Christ, Son of God, have mercy upon me, a sinner," or, when the Prayer is recited in common: "Lord Jesus Christ, Son of God, have mercy upon us."

It is, however, this short formula which is mentioned by a few Coptic informants, and which is also quoted by Patriarch Shenouda in the foreword to the Arabic edition of *The Power of the Name*. The same formula is also found in other Arabic translations of texts about the Jesus Prayer.[8]

In the fully developed hesychastic tradition, the Jesus Prayer can be combined with carefully controlled breathing. This is recommended by many well-known spiritual fathers in the contemporary Greco-Russian Orthodox Church.[9] These breathing exercises are known to the Copts and are mentioned by several informants, who, however, emphasize that this is not practised in the Coptic Church. On the other hand, some monastics will make use of the Jesus Prayer together with prostrations, *metaniyat*, which are carried out daily in one's cell.[10] But only one of the monks in my sample practiced the Jesus Prayer in this way. He added that the customary practice is to say "kyrie eleison" during the *metaniyat*.

In addition to the Jesus Prayer in the form of a settled formula, the informants also mention the repetition of the name of Jesus alone and short prayers, so-called "arrow prayers" (*sahmyat*), as a characteristic Coptic form of prayer.

Although the material presented here is limited, we can assume that the Jesus Prayer is widespread today in the Coptic Church. In the course of one of his popular Bible studies (on Wednesday evenings in Cairo), Patriarch Shenouda emphasized that the Jesus Prayer is well-known and recommended to all Copts, but that it is at home primarily in monastic circles.[11] This is confirmed and supported with further details by all my informants.

## The introduction of the Jesus Prayer

The two bishops who were asked about this topic stressed the publication of two books as the most important reason for the Jesus Prayer becoming known in contemporary Coptic Egypt. The Russian classic, *The Way of a Pilgrim*, was translated into Arabic during the late 1950s, and Father Matta al-Miskin's *Orthodox Prayer Life* was published in 1952.[12] This book contains a chapter on the Jesus Prayer and reproduces long sections from the first part of the Pilgrim's story. These two books speedily became very popular and inspired many young people who were later to become important actors in the Coptic revival. Bishop A. belongs to this first generation. He says:

> "I read *The Way of a Pilgrim* as a young man and became so enthusiastic precisely because it makes one know what to do: It gives a direction to the free prayer, and contains all the necessary elements. Later I have asked: 'Why exactly these words, why limit oneself to these particular words?'."

The bishop's spiritual guide at that time was Patriarch Kyrillos VI. Bishop A. relates that "the only time I mentioned the Jesus Prayer was when

I asked his permission to practise it. Kyrillos gave his permission at once. Bishop A. later worked to spread the knowledge of the Jesus Prayer through the Sunday schools: "not to impose, but to encourage." His view is that "the Jesus Prayer may help the monk during the first period of monastic life, but later, when he becomes more experienced, he might wish to express himself with more freedom. The monk has to be careful not to neglect 'short calls'." The bishop points to a story in the *Bustan al-Ruhban* about a monk who weaves a basket and lifts his eyes from his work at regular intervals. A novice asks what this means, and the reply is that this is how prayer and work are combined. "The monk is like the student who leads a disciplined life and works hard in order to master a large amount of knowledge. The monk must first acquire prayer; later, he can practise it in freedom – just as the student does after his examination when he practises his profession."

Bishop A. is one of the few who see the Jesus Prayer in an historical perspective:

> "The Jesus Prayer is a part of the Egyptian tradition that goes back to the first Christian centuries. The first monks were expected to practise *al-salat al-da`ima*, the unceasing prayer. This was, however, not what we call the Jesus Prayer today, but a formula like 'Oh Lord, help me,' 'Kyrie eleison,' 'Forgive me, Oh Lord, I am a sinner,' – what we call 'arrow prayers' (*sahmyat*). These short prayers are easy to combine with all kinds of work; making baskets or other handwork. The Coptic Church has no rules [concerning the prayer]: We admire the strict rules of others – they admire our freedom." The bishop adds: "Continuous prayer can be attained in various ways, and some monastics have advanced very far; I remember once recommending an elderly nun to take breaks in her work in order to pray. She replied in surprise: 'I do not need any breaks, why should I talk to Jesus about anything else [apart from the work]? I talk with him all the time!'"

Many women who were involved in the first phase of the Sunday School Movement later chose to begin active service in the Coptic Church. Sister A. belongs to the first generation of active nuns. She says:

> "I got to know the Jesus prayer when I was about fifteen years old and active in the Sunday school. At that time I learned the divine offices and the Psalmody; I was also taught to pay attention to feelings and thoughts during prayer, a form of introspection. I read *The Way of a Pilgrim* in an Arabic translation and learned the Jesus Prayer. Many years later, I was invited to England and also stayed in Father Sophrony's monastery.[13] There I witnessed how the Prayer was practiced in common; an experience I valued greatly."

*Instruction*
Sister A., who is responsible for the instruction of the active sisters, relates: "I teach the sisters the Jesus Prayer, and emphasize that this is Coptic tradition. I also tried to introduce the recitation of the Jesus Prayer in common, as in Father Sophrony's monastery, but this was not successful." She further tells:

> "There is a quiet period in one's cell every day, and then we recite our prayers and the Jesus Prayer. We also attach great emphasis to the name of Jesus. Some sisters are illiterate, but all learn a large number of prayers by heart; most of the prayers are linked to the name of Jesus and are handed on from one generation to the next."

Sister D., one of the consecrated women (*mukarrasat*), relates how Bishop Bimen of Mallawi (d. 1986) gave her instruction in the Jesus Prayer:

> "I received instruction in the Jesus Prayer from Bishop Bimen, and this is how I practice the Prayer: I sit before an icon of Christ in my cell. I sit completely still, sing a song of praise and think of the good things God has done for me before I begin to recite the Prayer. When I am alone, I pray aloud. Bishop Bimen told me: 'You must say the Prayer slowly and attentively, because the devil wages war against us, and we are continuously exposed to his assaults. This Prayer is like an arrow that goes directly to the Father's heart, and the Son has mercy on you and sends the Holy Spirit into your heart."

Thus the Jesus Prayer can form part of the instruction of novices, but lay people, too, can be exhorted to recite the Prayer. Sister D. is responsible for a group of women students in Cairo and relates that she attempts to encourage them to pray the Jesus Prayer ten times a day. Two priests tell that they recommend the Jesus Prayer to their spiritual sons and daughters who live "in the world."

In the Greco-Russian Church, a prayer rope or rosary (*komvoschinion; tochtki*), normally with a hundred knots, is often employed in conjunction with the Prayer, not primarily in order to count the number of times it is repeated, but rather as an aid to concentration and the establishment of a regular rhythm.[14]

*The prayer rope*
An Egyptian Jesuit novice relates that he went on pilgrimage to the Monastery of Abu Mina, where he asked a well-known Coptic monk to bless his rosary.[15] The monk replied: "It is not necessary to bless a rosary. You are born with a rosary, namely your fingers, and all you need is them. Count the individual fingers and use your thumb when you count."

This points to an established praxis in the Middle East when prayers (and prostrations) are counted; something well-known among both Christians and Muslims. Prayer ropes are also popular today; they are made in many Coptic monasteries and can often be found in the small shops that sell pious souvenirs. They are also given as gifts, and the recipients include laypeople. It is probable that their use has grown in popularity in recent decades. Sister A. says,

> "When I was young, I was told that the prayer rope was Catholic, and that I therefore should not use it. I learned to count on the fingers of my left hand – one makes the sign of the cross with the right hand. Now I possess a prayer rope, but I no longer use it. If it is necessary to count, I use my fingers."

Today, Sister A.'s community themselves make their prayer ropes. During the olive harvest, all the sisters assemble in the kitchen to prepare pickles, and the olive stones are cleaned and threaded on a strong thread. This is customary also among contemplative nuns and in the monasteries of monks.

Many monks bear the characteristic Greek *komvoschinion* on their persons; a Greek monk who visited the Monastery of St. Anthony taught Abuna M. to knot woollen prayer ropes of this kind. Now he always has one in his pocket. The monastery's abbot shows his own *komvoschinion* with one hundred knots. Abuna M. says that this is a part of Coptic tradition, pointing at one of the monastery's icons from the eighteenth century which shows St. Anthony with a prayer rope in his hand. He also tells how St. Pachomius used a prayer rope in order to count kyrie eleisons: "But Satan untied the prayer rope to prevent St. Pachomius from completing his prayers. Then St. Pachomius tied the thread cross-shaped, and Satan had to give up his attacks."

A young monk at the Monastery of St. Bishoy uses an ordinary Catholic rosary of wood when he prays the Jesus Prayer, and says: "The prayer rope is useful when you want to concentrate. It involves the senses, in this case the sense of touch, which is important." The Muslim *misbaha* is also used; Abuna I., one of the oldest monks in the Monastery of St. Bishoy, is very familiar with the Jesus Prayer and uses a *misbaha* with 33 beads.[16] According to Abuna I., this number refers to the fact that Jesus lived to the age of 33 years. Some Copts use a regular *misbaha* because they are easy to get hold of. But most doubtless still make use of their fingers.

## The Jesus Prayer: Coptic or foreign?

Bishop S. in Cairo, who himself began to practice the Jesus Prayer as a young man, says that this is a case of "Russian influence." He is unaware of any roots the Jesus Prayer might have in Egypt. Abuna B. in the Monastery of St. Anthony began to practise the Jesus Prayer in 1992, after reading *The Way of a Pilgrim* and a selection from the *Philokalia* on the Prayer of the Heart. First he sought permission from his spiritual father, who, however, observed that the Jesus Prayer was "foreign" (*ajnab*). His friend Abuna M. does not practise the Prayer "because it is not Coptic." According to Abuna B.: "There is no complete agreement. Some fathers in the Monastery of St. Anthony say that the Jesus Prayer forms no part of Coptic tradition, and reject it for this reason, while others have written it on the walls of their cells. I have also noted that some fathers in the Monastery of the Syrians have had the Jesus Prayer printed on small cards that they hand out to their penitents after confession."

Thus, opinions are divided. Those who themselves do not practice the Prayer because they consider it "foreign" do not reject the practice of others. Indeed, some can add that the Jesus Prayer is in keeping with Coptic spirituality.

*Why do people choose the Jesus Prayer?*
Three statements are often heard: "The Jesus Prayer is an arrow to the heart of God," "The Jesus Prayer gives protection against the attacks of the devil," and "The Jesus Prayer deepens other kinds of prayer."
   Abuna B. says that praying the Jesus Prayer has helped him greatly, and he teaches the Prayer to all his spiritual sons and daughters. But he cannot tell his friend Abuna M. about all its blessings: everything that concerns one's personal prayer life is strictly private and may not be revealed to anyone other than one's own spiritual father. Many also emphasize that it is not customary to discuss the personal practice of prayer in the monasteries. Sister D. observes: "This Prayer is very secret and personal, and cannot be shared with other people or with your community."
   Sister A. says: "The Jesus Prayer is for busy people. It gives control over thoughts and feelings and can be practiced without attracting notice – it is discreet, and we are surrounded by Muslims."
   A novice in the Monastery of St. Bishoy summarizes what many monastics say about the Prayer, while at the same time clarifying the reasons for his own personal choice of the Prayer:

I make use of the Jesus Prayer while I am working, or when I would otherwise have lost time that could have been used for prayer, for example, when I am waiting. The Prayer has proved its usefulness in many situations, for example, when I go around the monastery and notice the work that has not been done – then the Jesus Prayer helps me to avoid condemning others, and makes it possible for me to divert my thoughts from things that do not concern me. The Jesus Prayer can also be employed in situations of conflict, if some kind of confrontation arises. It is a defense against the assaults of the devil, and ensures purity of thoughts. I find this Prayer so effective precisely because my attention is directed to my own situation: I am a sinner in need of mercy.

*The texts*
*Bustan al-Ruhban* (The Garden of the Monks), which has a central place today in the instruction of all Coptic monastics, often refers to the "unceasing prayer" (*salat al-da`ima*). This book can indirectly encourage the individual to choose the Jesus Prayer. Formulae that are similar to the Jesus Prayer are also found in the Psalter.[17] One can thus find a good basis in the classical texts; but as far as contemporary praxis is concerned, it can scarcely be doubted that Father Matta al-Miskin's book *Orthodox Prayer Life*, and the translation of *The Way of a Pilgrim*, have been decisive.

## Conclusion

The fact that the Jesus Prayer is widespread in the contemporary Coptic Church must be seen primarily in the light of the theological and monastic revival from 1950 onwards, where great emphasis is laid on the individual's spiritual life. It is striking how the Jesus Prayer has been integrated into the praxis of prayer. It has become part of the instruction of novices in several monastic communities.

This praxis is not wholly uncontroversial, but the fact that the foremost representatives of the Coptic Church can speak in 1991 of the Jesus Prayer as "important in the Egyptian past," and "in the center of the church's praxis of prayer," is a clear expression of official acceptance.[18] Patriarch Shenouda asserts that the Jesus Prayer has been practiced in Egypt from the time of St. Anthony and St. Paul until the twentieth century. Moreover, he describes Abuna Bishoy Kamil as the perfect representative of this tradition of prayer.[19]

When the Jesus Prayer is practised today, however, this is not a direct continuation of the classical Egyptian Christian patrimony, but must primarily be seen as an inspiration from the Greco-Russian tradition.

As well as the official rapprochements between the Coptic Church and the Greco-Russian Church in the 1980s, there had already been established a more direct and informal contact, and the Jesus Prayer can be seen as a concrete testimony to a renewed contact between the Eastern churches.[20] Naturally, the growth in the Coptic diaspora churches in the U.S.A., Australia and Western Europe can also have had its significance in this process of mediation.

In the Egyptian context, we can also see the official justification for the praxis of the Jesus Prayer as yet another interesting expression of the wish to promote the specifically Coptic character and identity while at the same time emphasizing that Coptic spirituality is a part of the patrimony of all Christians.

## Notes

1. The "unceasing prayer" belongs to the terminology of *Al-Bustan al-Ruhban* (The Garden of the Monks, Mutraniya Beni Suef, ed. and publ., Beni Suef, 1968), the collection of sayings of the Fathers, used by all monastics in the Coptic Orthodox Church. The two more precise term are *salat Yasu'* (Jesus prayer), and *salat al-qalb* (prayer of the heart).
2. These conversations were held in Egypt in August and September 1992, and in April and May 1993. Sixteen persons were involved: two bishops, seven monks, several contemplative nuns and active sisters, one *mukarrasa* and one layman ordained to the diaconate. The various categories of Coptic nuns are described in N. van Doorn-Harder's article: "Discovering New Roles: Coptic Nuns and Church Revival," in this volume.
3. See: A. Guillaumont, "La Prière de Jésus chez les Moines d'Egypte," in: *Aux Origines du Monachisme Chrétien. Pour une Phénoménologie du Monachisme*: Bégrolle en Mauge, Abbaye de Bellefontaine, 1979, 178. This article was first published in English in *Eastern Churches Review* 6, 1974, (66-71). Emmanuel Lanne, "La 'Prière de Jésus' dans la Tradition Egyptienne. Témoignage des Psallies et des Inscriptions," *Irènikon* 50, 1977, (162-203).
4. For the history of the Jesus Prayer in the Greco-Russian Church, see: *The Jesus Prayer, by a Monk of the Eastern Church* (Lev Gillet), New York: St. Vladimir's Seminary Press, 1987, 23-79. Also see: Bishop Kallistos of Diokleia (Kallistos Ware), *The Power of the Name. The Jesus Prayer in Orthodox Spirituality*, Oxford: SLG Press, 1974, 3rd ed. 1991.
5. Quoted by M. Bertrand in: *Pratique de la Prière dans la France contemporaine*, Paris: Editions du Cerf, 1993, 8.
6. P. van Doorn-Harder, *Contemporary Coptic Nuns*, Columbia: University of South Carolina Press, 1995, 150.
7. E. Lanne, "La Prière de Jésus," 210.
8. Patriarch Shenouda supplies this formula in his foreword to the Arabic translation of Kallistos Ware's *The Power of the Name* (*Quwat al-Ism. Salat al-Yasu' fi al-Ruhaniya al-Urthudhuksiya*), Cairo: Matba'at al-Anba Ruweis, 1991, 10.
9. Archimandrite Sophrony, *His Life is Mine*, London and Oxford: Mowbray, 1977, 114.

10. P. van Doorn-Harder, *Coptic Nuns*, 150.
11. August 12, 1992.
12. The Arabic edition of *The Way of a Pilgrim*, (*Sa`ih Rusi 'ala Durub al-Rabb*), does not give the year of publication.
13. The reference here is to Archimandrite Sophrony (d. 1993) and the Stavropegic Monastery of St. John the Baptist, (Tolleshunt Knights, England) that the sister visited in 1984.
14. Bishop Kallistos of Diokleia, *The Power of the Name*, 7.
15. Conversation with a novice in the scholasticate of the Jesuits at Shoubra, Cairo, April 1993.
16. The Muslim rosary, *misbaha*, or *subhah*, is made up of 99 beads, the number of the Names of God. The most common subdivision is into three sections, each of 33 beads. The *misbaha* is on sale everywhere in Egypt and easily available to the Copts.
17. One sister copied out parts of Monday's psalter by hand to show me the similarities. See also E. Lanne, *La Prière de Jésus*, 172-174.
18. *Quwat al-ism*, 19.
19. Published by St. George Church in Sporting, Alexandria. In keeping with this, many of the most widely read texts about the Jesus Prayer in the Greco-Russian Church were translated into Arabic after 1950. These are found in many monastic libraries today. Abuna Bishoy Kamil (1931-1979) in Alexandria gave the impetus to the translation of a significant number of these texts, not only of *The Way of a Pilgrim*, but also of selections from the *Philokalia on the Prayer of the Heart* (1973) and *The Jesus Prayer* by "A monk of the Eastern Church." Abuna Bishoy Kamil himself wrote a small book called *Salat Yasu'*.

    Among others, Tito Colliander's book *The Way of the Ascetics* (which contains a short chapter on the Jesus Prayer), texts on the Jesus Prayer by Bishop Ignatius Brianchaninov and – not least – texts by Theophanes the Recluse, are often mentioned in conversations in Coptic monasteries. Some monks and nuns read English, and thus know several of Archimandrite Sophrony's books.
20. In 1990, at Chambésy, the Coptic Orthodox Church took part in the annulment of the mutual excommunications which for centuries separated the Chalcedonian and the Non-Chalcedonian churches. See: P.M Martin, C. van Nispen tot Sevenaer and F. Sidarouss, "Les nouveaux courants dans la communauté Copte Orthodoxe," *Proche Orient Chrétien* 40 (1990) 251. Also see Samuel Rubenson's article on Coptic theology in this volume.

Saphinaz-Amal Naguib

# The Era of Martyrs: Texts and Contexts of Religious Memory[1]

"Through the centuries, before and after Diocletian, the annals of the Coptic Church history have been filled with accounts of martyrdom and persecution. With the celebration of the feast of the Martyrs this year, the Coptic Church starts its fourth year under the latest Islamic and government-directed persecution." (Coptic Church Review 5/3 (1984) 74)

## Construction of history: written texts and memory of people

The ways by which the present reconstructs the past and the past fashions the present are incorporated in the recording, memorization, transmission and commemoration of events that are viewed as significant. History is created both as it happens and retrospectively; time and memory are pliable and selective instruments of cognition. They structure different kinds of communication and reveal manifold dimensions of reality and truth. Concepts of time and the remembrance of events are culturally constructed, hence also religiously. Different calendars and a multiplicity of histories may co-exist in the same geographical area or nation. The history of the minorities in an area, be they ethnic or religious or both, is more often than not submerged in the larger history of the majority.[2] Minorities may therefore appear 'history-less' and 'event-less'; their history goes unrecorded except to themselves in their memories.[3] However, dissimilarities between 'history' and 'history of minorities' may be exacerbated when circumstances change and the trigger of events is pulled.

Copts constitute the religious minority of Egypt. Their 'otherness' does not rest upon linguistic or socio-cultural differences. Rather, it pertains to their shared religion which is fundamental to their sense of identity, of 'pure' Egyptianess.[4] While taking part in the historical process of the nation of Egypt in particular and the Middle-East in general, Copts also experience another historical reality based upon their experience as a religious minority. This is anchored in their religious memory where events tend to occur in recurrent cycles, and parallels are drawn between the past and the present. Stories of persecution, suffering and, at the mildest, discrimination, encompass a span of time stretching from the Roman Empire to the present. These narratives have been remembered and kept alive because they are relevant for the lives of continuing generations of Copts.

All histories are grounded in structures, systematic orderings of contingent circumstances. In their turn, such structures become manifest only through historical events where past and present meet. However, not all events survive in memory. For events to become part of history they have to be, or to have been, experienced as important. They are recorded and defined as *events* by their significance in terms of a particular system, be it religious, political or social.[5] Rather than causing each other, conceptual and material realities are simultaneous. Discourse and reality, memory and history often intermingle; they merge in order to (re)construct a specific identity.[6]

In his studies on social memory and collective memory, Halbwachs argued that memory is both action and representation.[7] It is structured by group identities and relies on specific written or oral texts that should be considered cognitively as avenues of ideas. The religious memory of a group reproduces the past not only through myths but also through the commemoration of specific events where the past is reified in different ways. Remembering and commemorating involve a specific kind of participation where behavior, decorum, space and time are the main elements.[8] Nora, who introduced the notion of *lieux de mémoire* (sites of memory) and *milieux de mémoire* (environments of memory), posits that sites of memory are *topoi*, that is, both places and topics, where memories merge, crystallize, conflict and delineate relationships between past, present and future. These sites of memory can be abstract or concrete. They can be conveyed through rituals, commemorations, behavior or consolidated in material objects, like archives, landscapes, monuments and museums. There are sites of memory, says Nora, because there are no longer environments of memory.[9] For Halbwachs, as well as for Nora, written history kills memory. Memory, for these two authors, stiffens once it has been recorded in writing. This is not always the case.[10] Like memory, history can be fashioned in various ways. History is a palimpsest on which layers bearing different versions of the same event have been inscribed. It is constructed, re-constructed, de-constructed. It is even 'invented' in the double sense of the word, 'discovered' and 'imagined,' to suit time, circumstances and the group that uses it.[11] Memory is inherent in orality/aurality and writing. But to survive the passage of time it has to rely on history. Memory represents the inner writing of history.

Conversely, history, the texts and the contexts act as the supports of memory, religious memory included.[12] As phrased by Hastrup:

> The story of the past is a selective accounting of the actual history. The selection is not accidental – it is the corollary of a structured memory.[13]

To reflect upon history and religious memory involves considering sets of flexible boundaries of which intertextuality is an aspect. Intertextuality presupposes investigating relations between various kinds of texts. It opens ways of 'reading between texts' to suggest new insights to a given body of material culture. In the present essay I focus primarily on the intertwinement between history and religious memory and on how texts and contexts not only evolve together but also modify each other.[14] Religion is here viewed as an 'unbound category,' both a way of life and an abstraction preconceived by culture and maintained by various lived experiences.[15] The type of religious memory I shall address is of a more temporal than theological kind. It is tied to the rememberance of martyrs and pertains to the identity of the Copts as a distinct autochthonous Egyptian religious community. Using Coptic and Copto-Arabic hagiographies and martyrologies, in particular texts relating the passion of Victor, son of Romanos, I first examine the significance of the appelation 'Era of Martyrs' by which Copts reckon their calendar, and analyse the image of the martyr. I then explain how Coptic religious memory is tied to a definite geographical territory and how the passage from one language to another has helped to keep this memory alive. Finally, I discuss the viability of intertextuality in the study of history and religious memory.

## Conceptualizing time: the era of martyrs

All calendars denote the presence of the past in the present. While certainly implicated in the larger progressive historical time of Egypt, the Middle East and the world in general, Copts also live in a different time. This time is defined not only by the elements which express the realities of the natural environment of Egypt, and of the political and economic life of the country, but also, perhaps even to a greater extent, by their religious memory. Time is conceptualized, represented, symbolized and constructed in accordance to the context. Different conceptions of time entail a manifoldness of histories. They recognize various cognitive systems which organize different kinds of communication. They are connected with power and economic dependencies, and often state religious membership. They serve to mark the borders between *us* and *the others* who also live within the same geographical space. As a bridge between *our* time and *their* time, one often recurs to a third *neutral* time perspective.

In today's Egypt, where three different calendars are used concurrently, there is more than one *time*. Each of these different times conveys its own specific body of meaning, of knowledge and of tradition. They also define interreligious relations between Muslims and Copts. In the modern Egyptian context we find the secularized, global common calendar related to the rest of the world; the Gregorian calendar, the Muslim lunar calendar that is tied to the *Hijra* (the Prophet Muhammad's flight to Medina in 632 A.D.) and the Coptic calendar, also known as the Era of Martyrs. That is a solar calendar based on the ancient Egyptian one where the rhythm of the Nile determined the agricultural and economic life of the country. Months have kept their ancient Egyptian names denoting the seasons.[16]

Although the great persecutions against the Christians actually broke out in 303 A.D., the Coptic Church calendar computes its years from September 11 (or 12 on leap years) of the year 284 A.D.. This was the year of Diocletian's accession to the throne of the Roman Empire. To the Copts Diocletian epitomizes the oppressor. By emphasizing that event the Coptic Church humanized its calendar and tied it to the experience of persecution and martyrdom. Martyrs are conceived of as the 'protagonists of time'; their actions still define the chronology of the Copts, so much so that the Coptic Church has also been known as 'the Church of Martyrs.' By combining linear historical time, tied to the acts of its martyrs, with nature's cyclical time, the Coptic calendar testifies concurrently to its deep Egyptian roots and to its place in the general history of Christianity.

## The image of the martyr

In recent times a resurgence of the notion of martyr has been observed in different parts of the world. The incipit of the present essay indicates that Copts today still identify with the martyrs of their church. What does an Egyptian Copt exposed to attacks by Muslim extremists, or to other less obvious degrees of official prejudice, have in common with an Iranian soldier who died in the Iran-Iraq war (1980-1988), or with a Chinese student killed during the uprising of students in Peking in 1989?

Before going further it is necessary to define the concept of martyr. According to Webster's Dictionary of the English Language, a martyr is: a) "a person who chooses to suffer or die rather than to give up his faith or his principles; a person tortured or killed because of his beliefs," b) "a person who suffers great pain or misery for a long time." Martyrdom entails also witnessing. It is an act during which the martyr seals his/her testimony with his/her blood. By testifying their attachment to their faith, Copts have often been the victims of various forms of discrimination, a situation which has kept reminding them of the Era of Martyrs. To elaborate on the sociopolitical conditions of the Copts today would largely exceed the scope of this paper. My aim is to offer a theoretical framework in order to provide a better understanding of the articulation of the Coptic religious memory.

Martyr is here understood in its original meaning of 'witness.' The idea of martyrdom in early Christianity combines self-sacrifice with the act of witnessing an event. The act of the martyr is voluntary, public and is performed in times of persecution. To illustrate the image of the Coptic martyr, I shall, in the following, give a synthesis of the traditions of Victor, son of Romanos. These traditions belong to the cycle of Basilides, also known as the cycle of Diocletian.[17]

Like the majority of Coptic martyrs, in particular those who were originally foreigners, Victor, son of Romanos, belonged to the social elite of his time. He was born in Antioch; he lived and died under the reign of Diocletian. We are told that his mother, Martha, was a pious noble Christian lady and that his father, Romanos, was Diocletian's highly trusted vizier. Martha and Romanos had been married for thirty years without having children. However, after years of prayers and devotion Martha was granted a son by the Virgin Mary, and in due time she gave birth to Victor. The child was baptized by the archibishop Theodore, and big festivities were held for the occasion. It is said that Victor combined the qualities of a devout Christian and ascetic with those of a born leader and courageous soldier. He occupied the third highest position in the empire at the age of 20. That was when Diocletian imposed the worship of idols. We are told that when Victor's turn came to fulfill the emperor's orders and to sacrifice to the gods, the young man refused to comply. In spite of his father's and Diocletian's efforts to convince him, Victor remained steadfast and true to his Christian faith. Exasperated, Diocletian ordered that Victor should be send to Egypt and put to death there. Before leaving, Victor was publicly humiliated in his home town, Antioch. He was nevertheless granted permission to say goodbye to his mother. Victor implored her not to forget his plight and to bring his body back to Antioch for a decent burial. In Egypt, Victor, son of Romanos, was submitted to three martyrdoms. All in vain; our martyr was adamant. The first martyrdom took place in Alexandria, the second one in Upper Egypt. After that, Victor was exiled to Heraklion, a deserted military camp in the desert, where he had a vision of Jesus. A year after this, Victor, son of Romanos, endured his fourth and last martyrdom. At this moment, a young woman called Stephanou, who had been watching Victor's ordeal, declared that she saw the crown of martyrs above Victor's head. Inspired by Victor's example, Stephanou proclaimed herself Christian and as a consequence of her conversion she was tortured and put to death. Victor, son of Romanos, was finally decapitated. A soldier named Horion gathered the severed body of the martyr and embalmed it. He then hid the mummified body of Victor in the ruins of the camp and afterwards left for Antioch. There, he handed over to Martha the sword that had been used to behead her son. Three years later, true to her promise, Martha, led by Horion, made her voyage to Egypt. She sailed up the Nile to where Victor's body was hidden. With the help of Horion and her companion and niece Thephasia, sister of the martyr Claudius, Martha brought the body of Victor back to Antioch, where she gave it a burial worthy of her son's status.[18] In my discussion of the interplay of texts and contexts I show how details mirroring the Egyptian context and others of the Arab-Islamic environment are interwoven in order to make the narratives accessible to the public.

By offering his/her life for a cause, the martyr, in our case study Victor, son of Romanos, places an ideology before physical survival. He consciously challenges the authority and legitimacy of those in power, thus debasing the supremacy of their rule. The gesture of the martyr tends to unite and legalize the oppressed group, as well as to provide the community of which the martyr is both the champion and the scapegoat with a symbol of rightfulness. Furthermore, the act of the martyr has a proselytizing effect. The martyr serves as an exemplar and a motive; for this he has to be remembered, revered and emulated.

## The 'Egyptianness' of Copts

Aziz Atiya asserted in his preface to *The Coptic Encyclopedia* that: "Copts are the purest descendants of the ancient Egyptians."[19] Copts regard themselves as the "true sons of the pharaohs." Pharaoh is used as a metonymy for "authentic" Egypt. It evokes an autonomous, glorious Egypt ruled by indigenous kings and not by foreigners. This was Egypt before the Ptolemaic and Roman period, Egypt before Byzantium and Constantinople, Egypt before the Arab invasion and Islamic hegemony.

The name Copt derives probably from the Arabic rendering of the Greek *Aigyptos/Aigyptioi*, i.e. Egypt/Egyptians.[20] In Arabic, *Aigyptos* was by analogy transcribed as a broken plural *'aqbat* which was reduced to a root of three consonants *qbt*. In Arabic administrative documents *qibti* defined the native inhabitants of Egypt, most of whom were Christians. With the arabization and islamization of Egypt, *qbt* served to characterize Egyptian Christians, thus underlining both religious membership and ethnicity. To be a Copt is therefore deeply entwined with a well-defined territory as well as related to a specific Middle Eastern Church. In addition, Coptic identity is also tied to language and religious memory.

Coptic oral tradition presents Egypt as a holy land to which Abraham, Joseph and Moses had come. Even Mohammad has been linked to Egypt since the Prophet's only son Ibrahim was born from his Egyptian concubine, Maryam the Copt. Egypt is, according to that tradition, the only country outside of Palestine that has been visited by the Incarnated Word.

The origins of Christianity in Egypt are obscure. The Gospel of Matthew (2:13-20) relates that the Holy Family sought refuge in Egypt and Coptic tradition specifies that Mary, Joseph, the infant Jesus and the nurse Salome lived in Egypt for three years (nine according to Muslim tradition). During that time they travelled widely throughout the country and Jesus accomplished many miracles. He began preaching in the Egyptian vernacular (i.e. Coptic) at a tender age and was initiated into the ancient Egyptian wisdom texts. These, it is believed, influenced his later teachings. An Arabic tradition recorded by Muhammed al-Baqir (676-731) tells us that Jesus was able to explain the meaning of the letters of the Arabic alphabet. Yet, an Arabic manuscript from the 17th century, now in the Bibliothèque Nationale in Paris, states that the Holy Spirit, thus implying also Jesus, spoke Coptic many times.[21] The text, which pertains to the polemical literature, relates the life and sayings of Samuel of Qalamun.[22] In the passage in question the saint laments the fact that so many Christians abandon the use of Coptic, the language of Egypt, in favour of Arabic, a foreign language. It is noteworthy that George Onsy, who illustrated Meinardus' book *The Holy Family in Egypt*, took his lead from the Coptic tradition. His drawing represents Jesus as a baby explaining the meaning of the Coptic alphabet.[23]

Coptic tradition maintains that Christianity was introduced to Egypt by the Apostle Mark, who also became the founder of the Church of Alexandria, its first bishop and its first martyr. This story can be traced back to the second century and was first transmitted by Eusebius who wrote: "They say that this Mark was the first to be sent to preach in Egypt the Gospel which he had also put into writing, and he was the first to establish churches in Alexandria itself."[24]

The introductory statement "they say" indicates that Eusebius had relied on an already existing oral tradition. Although the historicity of this tradition is uncertain it should not be rejected altogether.[25] Mark had probably visited Egypt and had become acquainted with the Jewish Greek-speaking community of Alexandria. It was in that environment that Christianity spread, probably from the middle of the first century A.D.. Texts were translated into the Egyptian vernacular at a later stage and thus, from being a 'Greek-speaking' religion, Christianity was made accessible to Egyptians living in the hinterland.[26]

It is significant that during the Graeco-Roman and Byzantine periods, the capital of Egypt, *Alexandria ad Aegyptum,* was not considered an integral part of the country. It was called 'Alexandria near Egypt,' and had developed into a cosmopolitan center of Hellenistic thought and scholarship where Greek was the main language. Egypt was the hinterland that lay behind lake Mareotis.[27] From the third century B.C. Egypt had been dominated by foreign rule, where Greeks and Romans formed a privileged category. Apart from the limited sphere of the court, magistrates and higher class city dwellers, Hellenistic influences did not penetrate to such an extent that they took root in Egypt. A constant tension existed between native Egyptian tradition and the Hellenistic and later Byzantine culture represented by the gymnasia in Fayum and Oxyrhynchus and mostly by the capital, Alexandria.[28] To the Graeco-Roman and Byzantine world, Egypt was an exotic country, the home of old wisdom and knowledge, the land of secrets and mysteries. Nevertheless, in spite of its antiquity, the indigeneous inhabitants were viewed with contempt. They were represented as a 'primitive' people who lacked the refined manners and intellect of Greeks and Romans. Reciprocally, Egyptian documents of the period reflect distrust and even hate towards their foreign rulers.[29] This does not imply, however, that the different communities were completely ignorant of each other's customs and ways of thought. In fact, cohabitation meant that they knew a great deal about each other, notwithstanding the distorted images they had.

The estrangement of Egyptians from their rulers has been a characteristic of the country's political situation from Antiquity until modern times. By the 10th century, confronted with the spread of Islam, Christians of Egypt had become the autochthonous ethnic and religious minority of the country. As such, they felt more estranged from those in authority then the rest of the Muslim population. Coptic and Copto-Arabic hagiographies emphasize this alienation and present it as a cause for their sufferings. The figure of Diocletian as it is remembered in Coptic and Copto-Arabic narratives illustrates well that feeling. Diocletian is said to be originally a Christian. Some texts tell us that he was an Egyptian goatherd, others that he was a person of low birth who resided in Egypt for a long time. However, once he became emperor, Diocletian turned against his former religious brethern and countrymen, savagely persecuting them. The reasons given for Diocletian's apostasy and persecutions are varied. According to Coptic religious memory they were caused by the betrayal of the patriarch of Antioch[30].

## Language shift, a medium for religious memory

Memory is not only structured by collectively held ideas and by experiences shared with others but also by language. The major languages of Egypt during the Hellenistic, Roman and Byzantine periods were Egyptian, Greek and Latin. Egyptian remained the language of the majority of the people. Many documents were bilingual, written in Egyptian (hieroglyphs and demotic) and Greek.[31] Greek was the official intellectual written language in Egypt because of the status of Alexandria in the Hellenistic and Byzantine world. It was the administrative language and the tongue of the intelligentsia. Latin was not much used in Egypt before the reign of Diocletian (284-305 A.D.), and was mostly restricted to the army and the administration.[32] From about the third century A.D., Egyptians wrote their language in Coptic, a script consisting of the 24 letters of the Greek alphabet to which they added a few demotic characters. Coptic represents the last stage of ancient Egyptian in its spoken form, and the number of dialects in which it was written account for its basic orality. The spread of Christianity from the second century onwards found a powerful medium of expression in the developing Coptic language and script. Contemporary documents attest to a relatively high degree of literacy which was widespread in different levels of society during the first centuries A.D., even in provincial Egypt.[33] The consistent use of Egyptian vernacular became a major tool in the transmission of religious memory, as it not only brought to surface ideologies of cultural identity among the native Egyptians but also promoted the diffusion of Christianity throughout the whole country.[34]

Diglossia, that is, the use of different languages in distinctive connections, was attached to ethnic and social bonds. This, in my view, was an important factor which led to the distancing of the vast majority of Egyptians from their rulers. However, the social and linguistic distinctions separating the Greek, the Roman and later the Arab and the Turkic populations from native Egyptians did not mean that people with different cultural backgrounds were unable to communicate. As mentioned above, in Antiquity and Late-Antiquity official documents were often drawn up in two or more languages and scripts. Recent research has demonstrated that, already in the Late Period, a number of Egyptians and Greek intellectuals were bilingual and even trilingual. Egyptian religious thought was not unknown to Greek philosophers and, reciprocally, Egyptians were not ignorant of Greek philosophy. This helped familiarize the Greek intelligentsia with the Egyptian world-view and vice-versa.

The situation did not alter with the Christianization of Egypt, and leading Egyptian Christian figures like Pachomius, Athanasius, Anthony, Shenoute and Besa knew two languages. Without being necessarily equally fluent in both Egyptian and Greek, they were probably capable of making themselves understood by different types of followers and adversaries.[35] The use of two languages was still in practice after Egypt came under Arab rulership in 642 A.D., and there were no drastic changes even after a decree in 706 A.D. established Arabic as the official administrative language of Egypt. Many bilingual and even trilingual documents indicate that the passage from a plurality of languages to the adoption of a single language did not happen overnight.[36] Nevertheless, the Coptic language was losing ground and was being replaced by Arabic, as disclosed by the polemics attributed to Samuel of Qalamun referred to earlier.[37] Coptic remained the liturgical idiom of the Church. Yet, elevated to the rank of sacred language, Coptic ossified and gradually became a dead language.[38] From the 10th century onward a steadily increasing number of texts originally in Coptic were translated into Arabic or were directly written in Arabic.[39] Among these texts, hagiographies form an important body of material. Coptic cycles relating the acts of martyrs were produced from the 9th to the 12th century and the last Coptic hagiographies were composed during this period. I have argued elsewhere that martyrdom narratives, like those belonging to the traditions of Victor, son of Romanos, give evidence of a long chain of manuscript transmission. Texts evoke other older texts, they create a "genealogy of texts" where authority relies on authenticity of age. They were re-written, re-interpreted and combined with other independent texts to form new texts. These sources were translated from one language to another, thus attesting that the continuous interaction between languages provided a stable ground in keeping Coptic religious memory alive.[40]

## The church of martyrs and its followers
## – native and nationalistic

The Coptic Church has often been labelled as 'native Egyptian and nationalistic.' Smith has presented Copts as a 'demotic community' and 'vertical *ethnie*,' meaning that Copts constitute an autochthonous subject group defined by its religious affiliation.[41]

There are many forms of nationalism, each reaffirming a different cultural attachment. It is therefore important to understand, to quote Louis Dumont, the various 'cartographies mentales' and to examine each case separately.[42] One should be careful in using terms like nation and nationalism when dealing with pre-modern times. A sense of citizenship, of an identity tied to a specific territory and to its boundaries, is not invariably related to the concept of the modern nation-state or 'imagined communities' as they have been envisioned by modern theoriticians of politics.[43] Nation means also 'people,' 'race.' The term covers the inhabitants of a more or less well determined region who share common history and customs, and often speak the same or related language(s).[44] In the case of Egypt, documents prove that a sense of bond to the territory existed already in early pharaonic times. Egyptians identified with their country and on several occasions rebelled against foreign domination, as indicated by the texts describing their struggle against the Hyksos, the Persians, and the Ptolemies.

In his detailed study of early Christianity in Egypt, Griggs argues that during the three first centuries Christianity was not nationalistic but rather divided into the bishopric of Alexandria and the many independent churches and monasteries of Egypt.

> The third century was one of conflict in Egyptian Christianity, for the growing ecclesiastical authority of the Alexandrian bishop met with various kinds of resistance in the long-established churches and local groups of Christians scattered throughout Egypt.[45]

According to Jones, regional theological deviations from the main church are not to be considered nationalistic, as they did not pursue any political, social or national aim.[46] During the first centuries the bishops of Alexandria, from Demetrios (189-231 A.D.) to Dionysios (247-264 A.D.), strove to establish themselves as the arbiters of church doctrine in defining orthodoxy and heresy. They also undertook the responsibility of ecclesiastical education. The catechetical school of Alexandria was gradually absorbed by the bishopric and placed under the direct control of the patriarch of Alexandria. Moreover, the authority of the Church of Alexandria was reinforced by taking charge of the appointment of bishops in different parts of Egypt, including the Thebaid.[47] Monasticism, 'the gift of Egyptian Christianity to the world,' grew rapidly during the third and fourth centuries and many sought refuge and comfort in newly established monasteries. They brought with them their riches, which they donated to the monastery they joined. Thus, much of the land which was not in secular control fell into the hands of the monasteries. These were determined to defend their possessions jealously and to remain free from any binding allegiance with the bishopric of Alexandria.[48]

The authority of the Church of Alexandria was strengthened by Athanasius I (326-373), who managed to curtail the autonomy of the monasteries and bring them increasingly under the rule of the patriarch of Alexandria.[49] This political step combined with the increasing tensions between Alexandria, which was steadily loosing its primacy as an ecclesiastical center, and Constantinople in addition to the outcome of the Council of Chalcedon in 451; all contributed to reinforce the feeling of religious national identity of Egyptian Christians.[50]

The Council of Chalcedon was the decisive event that marks the turning point in the history of the Coptic Church and of Alexandria as an ecclesiastical center. Egyptians who adhered to the so-called monophysite doctrine were labelled as schismatics as far as Rome and Constantinople were concerned. Ever since Chalcedon, the Coptic Church has felt rejected from mainstream Western and Eastern Christianity and has withdrawn into itself.[51] Furthermore, the Council of Chalcedon established the see of Constantinople at the second rank after Rome. Antioch was placed at the third rank, and Alexandria lost its prestige for centuries to come. The doctrines of the Council of Chalcedon were accepted by the Byzantine Church, also known as Melchite. Moreover, the see of Constantinople was given jurisdictional primacy in Asia Minor and northern Greece. In Egypt the emperor imposed a Melchite patriarch in Alexandria, while the native monophysite line had its own patriarch, also in Alexandria. According to Atiya, the division of the bishopric of Alexandria into one 'foreign' and one 'local' line, intensified Egyptian religious nationalism and contributed greatly to the establishment of a unified native church.[52] From that time, the imperial power was severely weakened and Egypt gradually 'de-hellinized.'[53]

A wave of persecutions against Egyptian monophysites extended from 451 to 641, that is, until the Arab conquest. Historical documents indicate that the native Church of Egypt had been favorable to the Arabs in their war against the Byzantines because Egyptian Christians saw an opportunity to free themselves from the domination of the Byzantines.[54] In 641 `Amr ibn al-`As defeated the Byzantine forces at Babylon, and in 642 Alexandria was surrendered to him by treaty.

Once Egypt became part of the Islamic world, the authority lay in the hands of the Muslim rulers. Christian and Jewish rights and obligations were clearly defined in the Qur'an and *Shari`a* as 'people of the Book' (*ahl al-kitab*). They were tolerated as *dhimmis* (protected people) and were allowed to practice their own forms of worship as long as they accepted Muslim rulership and paid special poll and land taxes. The situation of these religious communities, however, depended largely on the whims of their rulers. Times of crisis endangered their position and left them exposed to various types of discriminations (like being refused high posts in the administration, having to wear distinctive clothes, the prohibition of carrying arms and riding horses). In reality, the plight of native Egyptians was not much different than during other foreign domination. One major difference, however, was that an Egyptian could hope to move upwards in the social strata once he became Muslim. As a Muslim he would be able to retain all his privileges and be fully integrated in the society. Conversions to Islam were numerous, and by the 10th century the majority of the population in Egypt was Muslim.[55] The intrusion of the Crusades did nothing to improve the status of the Christians in Egypt and other parts of the Middle East. On the contrary, it caused a backlash and made them into suspicious elements, this despite the fact that to the Latin Church all Eastern Christians were schismatics, if not heretics.[56]

Regardless of the turmoils that have punctuated their history, Copts have remained fervently attached to their country. In modern times their religious nationalism has blended with newer concepts of secular nationalism pertaining to the nation-state. Copts have been among the most active elements in the Egyptian struggle for independence.

## The interplay between texts and contexts

Coptic religious memory is primarily textual. It relies on the *lieux de mémoire*, whether they are written words or images, architecture, iconography, landscapes, commemorations or the person.[57] These *lieux de mémoire* are more often than not preserved by the *milieux de mémoire*, that is, by those who remember and transmit their knowledge. Religious memory, like memory in general, is an active search for meaning and its transmission involves conceptualization. Conceptualization requires adaptation of details to fit the present. Unless a group possesses the means to freeze time, the natural tendency of religious memory is to forego what is not meaningful in the collective memories and insert what seems more appropriate to the particular requirements of the moment.[58]

Stories of martyrs were recycled, incorporated into what Baumeister has called the *'koptischen Konsens,'* and adapted to different tastes and mentalities.[59] Taking the narratives of the martyrdoms of Victor, son of Romanos, as an example we notice details that reflect the Egyptian context. To name a few, we remark that the names of the months are Egyptian and that Victor's body was mummified. Martha's journey on the Nile in search of Victor's remains evokes the quest of Isis. Like Isis, Martha was not alone in her search. She was accompanied by Thephasia and by the faithful Horion, who had embalmed the martyr's body and hid it in a safe place. The wailing rituals accomplished by Martha and Thephasia, the constant presence of Horion, and the reburial of Victor remind us of the legend of Osiris and of the roles played by Isis, Nephthys and Anubis.[60] Entwined in the Egyptian setting, Copto-Arabic texts display features from their Islamic surroundings. We observe in the traditions of Victor, son of Romanos, that the hard, male dominated, military Roman background of Coptic traditions is gradually transformed into a more cushioned 'oriental' environment, dominated by intrigues worthy of a Thousand and One Nights in Copto-Arabic traditions.[61] The narratives are composed of several interlaced tales, like the ones of the martyrs Claudius, and Cosma and Damien. The style of Copto-Arabic texts alternates between formal and gossipy tones. We are given details of Diocletian's origins, of his marriage and of his entourage. Incessant palace strifes and intrigues of the harem are disclosed. We discover that the father of Victor, Romanos, was originally a Christian, that he held a high position in the army and that he was the king's trusted vizier and confidant. Arabic documents specify that Victor's mother was called Martha, and Victor is often called the "son of Martha." According to some sources Martha left her husband, Romanos, after he took an active part in the persecutions of Christians. We read about the lavish festivities given by Victor's parents and their generosity towards the poor at the occasion of his birth and of his baptism. The queen, who in the texts is always accompanied by her sister, is depicted as wicked, greedy and sterile. It is said that, unable to contain her jealousy during the baptism of Victor, son of Romanos, she tried to kill the baby. Fortunately, Victor was saved in extremis by the Virgin Mary. The baptism ceremony must have been quite an eventful celebration. Not only was the baby's life endangered, but under the influence of his nagging wife, Diocletian tried to steal the gold veil that God had sent down and in which the baby Victor was wrapped. Similar to the deus ex machina, however, an angel descended from the sky, snatched the veil away and flew up into the air with it. It is said that Victor, son of Romanos, grew up to be a very handsome youth and that women could not take their eyes off him. Information on kinship is another aspect of the Copto-Arabic versions. We learn, for example, that the martyr Claudius was the paternal cousin and bosom friend of Victor; he is also said to be the son of the king. Martha was the paternal aunt of the martyr Theodor the Oriental, and her female companion was Thephasia, the sister of Claudius.[62]

## The flexibility of textual boundaries

"There is" – observes Bakhtin – "neither a first nor a last word." Hence, past meanings are never final and forgotten. Contextual meanings are incessantly being re-discovered, modified and renewed. For Bakhtin: "Nothing is absolutely dead: every meaning will have its homecoming festival."[63]

In his introduction to *The Invention of Tradition*, Hobsbawm develops the same line of thought and explicates the premises on which the notion of unbroken continuity with the past is built. He remarks that continuity relies on the act of forgetting and that at the heart of all meaning there is an absence. It is this absence, the act of forgetting, which engenders a renewal and a sense of continuity. To remember does not mean to copy the past, but rather to re-live a past event and set it in a new frame. When the event has taken on the patina of myth it is freed from the constraints of exactitude and authenticity and may be re-fashioned in various ways. Stories are retained by transferring them into new contexts. However, this transposition from one context to another entails a displacement of reality and a reinterpretation of the original text. The themes remain similar in substance but the connotations vary. Accordingly, a changing political and social perspective gives rise to recontextualization. This dynamic process of repeated (re)interpretation and (re)contextualization creates a set of changes within memory itself. The remembrance of martyrs exemplifies the articulation of the Coptic religious memory and the stories of their suffering and sacrifice are revived in times of crisis.

The mnemonic maps of Copts consist of written words, iconographic texts and oral narratives. Texts conserve the memory of events through the medium of words written and spoken, monuments and images. Coptic hagiographies, martyrologies, encomia and panegyrics represent many-layered narratives which originally had been elaborated in the monastic milieu. They are still read aloud or retold to a wider mixed congregation on the martyr's day. I consider these texts as *milieux de mémoire*, where knowledge is transmitted both orally and in writing. They testify to the way religious memory is being actively reinterpreted and incorporated in a process of constant restructuring and construction. The narratives serve not only to preserve historical events for posterity, but also to express religious, political and social ideals, as well as public and individual ethics. They act as avenues of ideas and actions between different categories of believers. The fields of reference used in the texts encompass a wide range of associations in order to reach the different levels of understanding in a mixed congregation. Orality and literacy are not mutually exclusive. Both illiterate, semi-literate and literate persons are capable of appreciating the same text, although not in the same way.[64] In their writings, Barthes and Foucault have expounded that texts do not exist independently from their contexts.[65] Creating a text does not merely involve writing. Reading a text, listening to it, and in the case of iconographical material, seeing it, are active generative processes where meaning is produced by the encounter between texts, readers and contexts. Texts are performative mediators of knowledge; they are neither direct expressions of reality nor are they completely estranged from it. In the continuous interaction between text and context, the context becomes the essence of religious memory and not merely its background.

The tales of martyrs were, and still are, used not only to keep the memory of past events alive but also to help understand the present. Events are grouped around the characters and these embody meanings. Symbolic patterns have been elaborated in order to reflect the reality of successive historical periods. Metonymic logic, words and situations evoking current events permit the reader and the audience to transform the texts. The narratives signify something beyond the texts and become relevant for the present. An example taken from the Copto-Arabic tradition of the passion of Victor, son of Romanos, serves to illustrate the open boundaries of Bakhtin's ideological texts.[66] The passage that interests us here mentions that 'in those days' everybody in the kingdom was Christian, including the king, Diocletian. The father of Victor, Romanos, was the trusted vizier and confidant of the king. After some tribulations, Diocletian decided to introduce idolatry in the kingdom. However, his scheme was stopped by the patriarch of Antioch, Theodore, who, according to our document, was the upholder of the Church's teachings. Diocletian and Romanos plotted against the patriarch and had him killed. Having got rid of their main obstacle, the two men enforced the worship of idols throughout the empire, and those who did not comply were tortured and sentenced to death. Most were too scared to challenge the 'evil pagan king' and his acolytes, many abandoned Christianity and embraced the king's religion. The removal by force of the head of the church and the problem of apostasy are recurrent events in the history of the Egyptian Church, which Coptic religious memory kept in store for centuries.[67] Yet, whatever the setting, the martyr, in our case study Victor, son of Romanos, stands steadfast against the enemies of his religion, and the suppressive ruling power reified by Diocletian is being continuously "re-historized."[68] In the narratives, the martyr is similar to the prophet of Ardener who gives voice to a recent epoch while he himself is situated in a much more ancient time.[69] Like the prophet, the stories of his/her acts warn of realities to come before they have been registered and assimilated by the collective memory.

Let us remember.....

Without the commemoration of suffering and sacrifice, people would, as put forth by Amato, lose their own specific stories and be reduced to the role of uninvolved spectators.[70] The history of a particular community would drown in the more encompassing history of the majority of the population. The remembrance of martyrs allows the Copts to constantly (re)actualize their historical religious narrative. Commemoration involves more than revival. It entails regeneration. History and religious memory are the threads that are interwoven to pattern the tapestry of the Coptic religious memory; the Era of Martyrs is deeply anchored in that memory.

## Notes

1. The present article is part of a wider study, "The Martyr as Witness. Coptic Oral and Written Traditions and the Transmission of Texts as Mediators of Religious Memory," in which I examine different levels and ways of expression of Coptic religious memory. The research has been made possible thanks to a post-doctoral fellowship at the University of Oslo, Faculty of Arts. I am grateful to Nancy Frank, Chief librarian at the Institute and Museum of Anthropology, University of Oslo, for reading a first draft of this paper and for acting as language consultant.
2. To discuss different theories on minorities and ethnicity would largely exceed the limits of the present article. The minority I am considering here is a minority in number as well as in 'voice.' In this paper I argue that Copts do not form a distinctive ethnic group in Egypt and that they stress their identity as Egyptians. As for treating the complex question of minorities, I have mostly relied on the

different articles found in *The Social Psychology of Minorities, Minority Right Group, Report no. 38*, 1978, and in the special issue on minorities of the *UNESCO Courier*, June 1993. Among the arguments put forth by the various authors the following points seem relevant when examining the position of Copts:
1) Minorities constitute subordinate segments of complex state societies.
2) Minorities are self-conscious units bound together by the idiosyncrasies which their members share and by the special disabilities which these bring.
3) "In a context of persecution or discrimination, it is likely that minority members themselves will be led to experience whatever defines them as "different" as the key element, perhaps the only pertinent one, in their social identity." (D. Meindel, "What is a Minority?" *Courier*, 13)

3. P. Connerton, *How Societies Remember*, Cambridge, 1989, 19; E.M. Tonkin, M. McDonald & M. Chapman, *History and Ethnicity*, ASA Monographs, London: Routledge, 1989, 7f.
4. A.S. Atiya, *History of Eastern Christianity*, New York: Millwood, 1980, 16.
5. Connerton, *How Societies Remember*, 42f.; K. Hastrup, *Other Histories*, London: Routledge, 1992, 7f.
6. E. Ardener, "The Construction of History: Vestiges of Creation" in: Tonkin, McDonald & Chapman, *History*, 6; Hastrup, *Other Histories*, 11 and E.J. Hobsbawm, "Introduction: Inventing Traditions," in: E.J. Hobsbawm & T. Ranger (ed.) *The Invention of Tradition*, Cambridge: Cambridge University Press, 1983, 2.
7. M. Halbwachs, *La Mémoire Collective*, Paris, 1950, and *Les Cadres Sociaux de la Mémoire*, Paris: PUF, 1976.
8. Halbwachs, *Les Cadres*, 178f., 187f.
9. P. Nora, "Entre Mémoire et Histoire. La Problématique des Lieux de Mémoire," in: P. Nora et al. (eds) *Les Lieux de Mémoire*, vol. I: La République: XVII-XLII, Paris: Gallimard, 1984, XVII.
10. S.-A. Naguib, *Mirroirs du Passé*, Genève: Cahiers de la Société d'Egyptologie, 1993, 11f., 57.
11. A. Blok, "Reflections on 'Making History,'" in Hastrup, *Other Histories*, 121f. and Hobsbawm, "Introduction," 2.
12. Ardener, "Construction," Hastrup, *Other Histories*, 8f.; M. Kilani, *La Construction de la Mémoire*, Genève: Labor et Fides, 1992, 36f. & 297f.; Naguib, *Mirroirs*, 11f., 57.
13. K. Hastrup, "The Prophetic Condition," in E. Ardener, *The Voice of Prophecy and Other Essays*, Oxford: Blackwell, 1989, 227.
14. Hastrup, *Other Histories*, 11.
15. B. Saler, *Conceptualizing Religion. Immanent Anthropologists, Transcendent Natives, and Unbounded Categories*, Leiden: Brill, 1993, 212f.
16. A great number of festivities are tied to the country's ecology and evoke those celebrated in the pharaonic past, see a.o.: Naguib, *Mirroirs*, 9f.; C. Wissa-Wassef, *Pratiques Rituelles et Alimentaires des Coptes*, Cairo: IFAO, 1972, 23f.
17. S.-A. Naguib, "Martyr and Apostate: Victor son of Romanos and Diocletian. A Case of Intertextuality in Coptic Religious Memory," *Temenos* 29 (1994) 102.
18. Forget, 1912: 92f.; Nakhla, 1951: 115f, also see: S.-A Naguib, "The Martyr as Witness. Coptic and Copto-Arabic Hagiographies as Mediators of Religious Memory," *Numen* (1995).
19. A.S. Atiya, *The Coptic Encyclopedia*, vol. 1, New York: Macmillan Publ. Co., 1991, LXI. Copts are not alone in claiming their origins from a glorious past. Other religious minorities in the Middle East use that same argument as a proof of their authenticity. For example, the Maronites in Lebanon maintain that their ancestors were the Phoenicians, and the Assyrians in Iraq say they descend from the Assyrians.

20. *Aigyptos* derived probably from the ancient Egyptian *Het-ka-Ptah*, that is "The House of Ptah's Ka" which was the name of the god Ptah's temple in Memphis. The Coptic name for Egypt was *Keme* in Saïdic, *Xemi* in Bohaïric. It stems from the ancient Egyptian *Kemet*, meaning 'The Black Land', which was the name for Egypt in pharaonic times. *Kemet* was actually used to describe the Nile Valley, while *Desheret*, or 'Red Land', designated the desert.
21. Bibliothèque Nationale Paris (BNP) Ms. Arabe 150, fol. 75v-77r.; J. Ziadeh, "Apocalypse de Samuel, Supérieur de Deir el-Qalamoun," *Revue de l'Orient chrétien* (1915-17) 394f.
22. D.W. Johnson S.J., "Anti-Chalcedonian Polemics in Coptic Texts, 451-641," in B.A. Pearson & J.E. Goehring (eds.) *The Roots of Egyptian Christianity*, Philadelphia: Fortress Press, 1986, 220f.; L.S.B. MacCoull, "Three Cultures under Arab Rule: The Fate of Coptic," *Bulletin de la Société d'Archéologie Copte* (1985) 66.
23. O. Meinardus, *The Holy Family in Egypt*, Cairo: A.U.C. Press, 1986, 46.
24. Eusebius, *Historia Ecclesiastica*, translated by J.E.L. Oulson, *Eusebius, The Ecclesiastical History*, London, 1964, vol. II, 16, 1.
25. B.A. Pearson, "Earliest Christianity in Egypt: Some Observations," in Pearson & Goehring, *The Roots*, 137f.
26. C.W. Griggs, *Early Egyptian Christianity. From its Origins to 451 C.E.*, Leiden: Brill, 1993, 15f.
27. H.I. Bell, "Alexandria ad Aegyptum," *JRS* 36 (1946) 130-132, Favard-Meeks & D. Meeks, "L'héritière du Delta" in: *Alexandrie IIIe Siècle av. J.C.*, Paris: Autrement, 1992, 25f.
28. A.K. Bowman, *Egypt after the Pharaohs, 332 BC – AD 642 from Alexander to the Arab Conquest*, Oxford: Oxford University Press, 1990, 29f, 122f.
29. Bowman, *Egypt*, 122f.; H. Green, "The Socio-Economic Background of Christianity in Egypt," in Pearson & Goehring, *The Roots*, 101f.
30. Naguib, "Martyr and Apostate," 108.
31. Hieroglyphs or "sacred letters", were special for important or ceremonial purposes. Hieratic or "priestly writing", was used by priests to record religious texts. Demotic, or "popular writing", was the script of daily life resorted to for all sorts of administrative and legal documents as well as private affairs and commercial transactions.
32. Bowman, *Egypt after the Pharaohs*, 158.
33. C.H. Roberts, *Manuscript, Society and Belief in Early Christian Egypt*, London: Oxford University Press, 1979.
34. D.W. Johnson, "Polemics," 226f.
35. Johnson, "Polemics," 226f.; C. Kannengiesser, "Athanasius of Alexandria vs. Arius: The Alexandrian Crisis," in Pearson & Goehring, *The Roots*, 211f.
36. MacCoull, "Three Cultures," 62f., and: "The Strange Death of Coptic Culture," *Coptic Church Review* 10 (1989) 36f.
37. BNP Ms. Arabe 150, fols. 75v-77r.
38. C. Cannuyer, *Les Coptes*, Turnhout: Brepol, 1990, 41.
39. See the articles: "Literature, Copto-Arabic" (Atiya), and "Islamization of Egypt" (S.I. Gellens), in *The Coptic Encyclopedia*.
40. Naguib, "Martyr and Apostate," 102f., 108f. Also see: "The Martyr as Witness."
41. A.D. Smith, *National Identity*, Penguin Books, 1991, 62.
42. I am thankful to Daniel de Coppet, Director of the École des Hautes Études des Sciences Sociales (EHESS) in Paris, for inviting me to take part in the seminar led by Louis Dumont on the topic "Nation, souveraineté et monarchie," November 1992.
43. B. Anderson, *Imagined Communities. Reflections on the Origins and Spread of Nation-*

*alism*, London: Verso, 1992, 5f.; E.J. Hobsbawm, *Nations and Nationalism since 1780. Programme, Myth, Reality*, Cambridge: Cambridge University Press, 1991, 3f.; E. Renan, "Qu'est-ce qu'une nation?" *Oeuvres Complètes*, Paris: Calmann-Lévy (vol.I) 1947, 887f.; A.D. Smith, *The Ethnic Origin of Nations*, Oxford: Basil Blackwell, 1986, 6f.
44. Smith, *Ethnic Origins*, 8f.
45. Griggs, *Early Egyptian Christianity*, 106.
46. A.H.M. Jones, "Were Ancient Herecies National or Social Movements in Disguise?" *The Journal of Theological Studies* X (1959) 280-298. For an insightful study of contemporary religious nationalism see: Mark Juergensmeyer, *The New Cold War? Religious Nationalism Confronts the Secular State*, Berkeley: University of California Press, 1993.
47. Griggs, *Early Egyptian Christianity*, 102.
48. Ibid., 100f.
49. Ibid., 148.
50. Ibid., 215.
51. For an interesting geographical and political presentation of the spread of monophysite churches in the "Byzantine commonwealth" see: Garth Fowden *Empire to Commonwealth. Consequences of Monotheism in Late Antiquity*, Princeton: Princeton University Press, 1993, 101f.
It is noteworthy that although Diocletian's capital was Nicomedia, Coptic and Copto-Arabic hagiographies place it in Antioch. By blaming the archbishop of Antioch for the sufferings endured by Christians, Coptic religious memory kept alive the perfidy of the Antiochenes at the Council of Chalcedon.
52. Atiya, *History*, 70f.
53. Griggs, *Early Egyptian Christianity*, 210, and the article "Egypt, Roman and Byzantine Rule," (H. Henein) in *The Coptic Encyclopedia*.
54. See: article "Crusades," (A.S. Atiya) in *The Coptic Encyclopedia*.
55. See: article "Egypt, Islamization of," (S.I. Gellens) *The Coptic Encyclopedia*.
56. P. Hitti, "The Impact of the Crusades on Eastern Christianity," in: S.A. Hanna (ed.) *Medieval and Middle Eastern Studies in Honor of Aziz Suryal Atiya*, Leiden: Brill, 1972, 211f.
57. A.o.: Naguib, *Mirroirs*, 11f., 57.
58. Kilani, *Construction*, 45f., 297f.
59. T. Baumeister, *Martyr Invictus. Der Märtyrer als Sinnbild der Erlösung in der Legende und im Kult der frühen Koptischen Kirche*, Münster: Verlag Regensberg, 1972.
60. BNP Arabe 131 fol. 49v., 64v; BNP Arabe 212, fol. 151v-154r, 197v-198r; BNP Arabe 4879, fols. 107r-108v; BNP Arabe 4782, fols. 68v-75r; BNP Arabe 4793, fols. 159r-162v, 229v.; Naguib, *Mirroirs*, 28f., 54, and: "Martyr and Apostate," 104.
61. Naguib, "Martyr and Apostate," 103.
62. Naguib, "Martyr and Apostate," 103f., also see: BNP, Arabe 131, fols. 65r-65v, Arabe 212, 156r, 159r.
63. M. Bakhtin, *Speech Genres and Other Late Essays*, ed. by C. Emerson & M. Holmquist, Austin: University of Texas Press, 1986, 170.
64. Naguib, "Martyr and Apostate," 109.
65. R. Barthes, *Le Degré Zéro de l'Écriture*, Paris: Éditions du Seuil, 1953, *Essais Critiques*, Paris: Éditions du Seuil, 1964 and *L'Empire des Signes*, Genève: Albert Skira, 1970, M. Foucault, *Les Mots et les Choses*, Paris: Galllimard, 1967 and *L'Archéologie du Savoir*, Paris: Gallimard, 1972.
66. BNP Arabe 212, fols. 157v-158r.
67. Naguib, "Martyr and Apostate," 108.

68. Ibid., 104f.
69. E. Ardener, *The Voice of Prophecy and Other Essays*, Oxford: Basil Blackwell, 1989, 135f.
70. J.A. Amato, *Victims and Values: A History and a Theory of Suffering*, Contributions in Philosophy 42, New York: Greenwood Press, 1990, 210.

Dina el-Khawaga

# The Laity at the Heart of the Coptic Clerical Reform

The massive institutionalization of the clerical body is indisputably the most spectacular example of the Coptic renewal from the end of the 1960s onwards. After many decades, indeed centuries, in which the Coptic faith manifested itself principally through the maintenance of the cultural and mystical patrimony far from institutional involvements, the clerical consolidation has become the decisive trait of the religious awakening. This reform is intimately linked to the arrival of a new profile of clergy within the Coptic Church: young, educated, modernized and concerned for the social and political status of the faithful as a whole. The new clerical generation which begins its vocation at the end of the 1940s has nothing in common with the profile of its traditionalist predecessors, who were illiterate and shuttered within a mystical piety which was inherited and transmitted as it stood.

Despite this obvious shift within the clergy, it is not so much the modernization of the ecclesiastical structures that is at the heart of the demands made by the new generation: it is rather the return to the sources, following the example of the early church, and the purging of the canonical, clerical, monastic and pastoral literature of the relics of a tradition of very unequal value, that expresses the project of the new clergy who preach the Coptic renewal. The attachment to the original foundations and precepts is, however, experienced in a spirit, and according to forms, largely impregnated by modern rationality. On the other hand, according to those involved personally, this attachment is not only a religious goal in itself, but also a means of binding all Copts to the example of the glorious past they had in the first four centuries.

There is no shortage of examples to shed light on this spirit which gives expression to a rigorous ethics, pastoral care and a growing rationalization: the redrawing of diocesan boundaries in view of a better service, the nomination of auxiliary bishops to help the diocesan bishops or the patriarch in person, the increase by two or three in the number of general episcopal offices,[1] are only the first level of this ecclesiastical restructuring. The second level of the process is represented by the expansion of the order of the presbyterate, the redefinition of its responsibilities and of the profile required, and the centralization of its training; last but not least, the third sector of this institutional restructuring is the reform of the minor orders, such as the diaconate, the subdiaconate and the archdiaconate, the new value given to the pastoral and pedagogical vocation of the early church by mobilizing tens of thousands of young people to "serve" in the parishes.

This immense process of institutionalization requires the observer to ask what it all means. Is this a "straightforward" effect of modernization on the clerical sphere and its functioning? Or is what we are seeing rather a deliberate process, chosen and intended by these new agents to bring together religious commitment, modernization and political consciousness? If this is in reality the case, do the initiators of this project aim more at the insertion of their flock in a world "without guide posts," or the religious consolidation of a whole community which has been subject for a long period to double assaults by "religious others," whether non-Coptic Christians or Muslims? Does the visible aspect of the "institutionalization" conceal other, equally profound transformations on the level of the relations between the church and the laity, or between communities?

## A clerical or a collective institution?

All the changes introduced by the agents of the renewal, with the patriarch at their head, to institutionalize the clerical body, differentiate it and make it give better service, could become part of the collective concerns of the community only if their implementation went beyond the intra-clerical projects[2] and took on importance vis-a-vis a large public: the laity of the renewal. This sustained attention to make the institutional, administrative and collective restructuring a collective endeavor was generated by the fact that the process of institutionalization risked slackening the close links between the laity and the clergy and creating a disparity between the interests and concerns of the clerical pole and those of the public as a whole, who were exposed to other types of problems (social, economic, or simple religious questions).

Thus, in order to prevent this relationship from hardening into something merely formal, it was necessary to accompany the restructuring of the clerical body with a presentation of this restructuring as a vital, collective undertaking which must be given priority. This operation was more or less successful, because all the clerical agents made use in their reform measures (as in their internal disputes) of themes dear to the Coptic consciousness, themes dear to the Copts. They always presented the actions which were taken as the straightforward path to rekindle the original church into life, to purify the religious literature and the institution which incarnated orthodoxy, to reactivate a tradition which had been interrupted, or finally to serve those laity who lacked means (symbolic or material).

The debates about the decrees of the patriarch or the decisions of the synod are never (or scarcely ever) presented as debates among specialists, or as merely administrative reforms. Every new measure was accompanied by an emotional salvo (even when all that was involved was the opening of a new local seminary, or the transformation of the Mass on the fortieth day after death into a simple prayer), as if the starting of a clerical institution was not something sufficiently justified in itself. But these explicit affirmations were also accompanied by an implicit argument: The importance of constructing an "institution" which represents and unites the community. In point of fact, the provocations carried out by Islamists from the beginning of the 1970s onwards, the polemic against the church and the state bodies concerning the application of the *shari`a* at the same period,[3] and the extreme hostility shown by President Sadat to the Coptic patriarch confirmed the importance of possessing an institution whose competence and representative quality could not be called into question.

But neither this mobilization of "collective emotion" nor this situation of tension could guarantee a new, permanent and stable identification between the laity and the "clerical institution" of the same type as that which characterized the relationship between the laity and their original church. This was a popular church, with only an elementary hierarchical system, in step with the community in its condition of rudimentary knowledge, mysterious piety, absence of theological vision, and the like. The voluntary efforts and show of triumph which were strongly present in the institutionalization were certainly seductive for the Copts as a whole, but they did not succeed in hiding the other effects of the process which had been initiated, namely the sheer weight of the clerical body, and the more effective means of bringing pressure to bear, of sanction or of exclusion. These final aspects (once they were felt) greatly risked replacing the previous osmosis by a situation like that found in political parties or militant groups as far as their internal organization was concerned.

It is in this perspective that the agents of the renewal have had recourse to forms of action aimed at binding the Coptic public to these new clerical configurations, leading the public to identify with them and make them a collective project. Obviously, these forms of action were varied, and did not all have the same effectiveness. Nevertheless, they shared the same aim, namely to transmit to every Copt the conviction that he/she is, by definition, a member in solidarity with a collective institution. This is the new slogan that interests us here, for it goes beyond the concept of *ecclesia* (where all the faithful are by definition members in a total sense) while at the same time refraining from stating its aims in institutional or clerical terms (for this would make visible a cleavage between the clergy and the members of the community).

In order to study them, one can separate these actions as a whole into two groups of unequal distribution and unequal societal impact. These are: 1. the dissemination of proposals coming from the church hierarchy; actions addressed to the totality of the laity in order to bind them to the restructuring and to the daily life of the clerical institution, and to involve them as full-time partners in a project of institutional reform. Then we have: 2. the creation of clerical structures; actions aiming at a stable and structural transformation of certain old or new communal or religious activities, so that these become part of the clergy's work.

## The dissemination of proposals from the church hierarchy

The incorporation of the whole laity in the Coptic Church is an extremely difficult task.[4] This is why, on this level, the agents of the renewal seem to seek a simple dissemination of their ideas of restructuring, rather than a genuine integration of the body of the laity into the clerical or para-clerical networks. Thus, debates about the clerical reform that are open to the public, meetings with the patriarch on the occasion of the nominations of priests, or an appeal for the pastoral activities in the parishes to be carried out in a collective manner seem to be the principal contexts for the distribution of this new logic, aiming to make the laity more aware of the details of the institutional restructuring. It is, however, noteworthy that the inclusion of the laity does not extent to all the levels of the institutionalization. The mobilization which has been put into practice encourages a participation on the local level, without ever appealing to the laity to make known their views either on the process as a whole or on the changes that take place at the top of the hierarchy. Rather, it is a question of establishing new direct vertical relationships between the laity and the leaders of the clerical body. Thus, these new modes of involvement and of participation open the way to a double communication between the center and the clergy on the one hand, and the center and the "clericalized" laity on the other hand.

Although these new relationships are always established in the name of democratization of the running of the local churches and of the commitment of "the Coptic people," one cannot avoid observing the strongly centralizing implications of the way these relationships function. The commitment does indeed promote an intensification of the relationships between the laity and the center, but thereby weakens the cohesion and the unity at the local level. The following examples will further illustrate these remarks.

## The pastoral reform: a transparent debate

One of the clearest manifestations of the "clericalization" and its implementation is the inauguration in the patriarchal periodical (*al-Kiraza*) of two new sections dealing with the functioning of the local churches, 1. "Pastoral suggestions" (*Afkar ra`awiya*) and 2. "The page of the ordained fathers" (*safhat al-aba' al-kahana*). These are meant to maintain a permanent and open debate on the functioning of the local churches, the practice of the priests and the relationships among the various orders within the parishes. It happens fairly often that the church leaders make recommendations (or even warnings) to the priests through the medium of these two sections. For example, on the application of new laws or concerning the response they must make to new communal questions.[5] We must note that this openness, which characterizes the dialogue between the top and the local is carried out in the presence of, and with, the layperson. Indeed, this dialogue mobilizes the laity, because one of these two sections is based in part on readers' letters and suggestions. On the other hand, it involves the reader as an active partner in the process of the reform of the parishes, by giving information but above all by making the reader an onlooker and a guarantor of the good functioning of the parishes. This spirit is seen in those issues of *al-Kiraza* where the laity openly criticize the activities or the indifference of the local priests, or even suggest new measures to be taken. These issues are an obvious example of the prototype of the "clericalized layperson" whom the agents of the renewal promote, with the aim of making this a general rule for the laity.

The following sample, taken from *al-Kiraza* (1989), illustrates this process well: on June 9, a layperson sends the column *Afkar ra'wiya* some lines criticizing the large budgets devoted to the restoration of local churches (decoration, furniture), adding that at least some of this money could have been distributed to the needy among the faithful. The periodical replies to this letter, approving of the criticism and adding that in fact the patriarch is preparing a patriarchal decree specifying the details of the budgetary administration of the local churches, the percentage of social help to be given, and the patriarchate's supervision of how the system will function. In January 1989, the same periodical speaks of the conditions necessary for the priest to succeed in his pastoral visits. Under the heading *Ziyara aw Iftiqad* (visit, or pastoral visit), the periodical criticizes the practice of some priests who, far from centering their visits on spiritual instruction, slide off into secular subjects and cultivate social friendship instead of bringing spiritual help. On 21 April 1989, the same column takes the priest's role in family conflicts as its topic for debate, commending numerous specific instructions, forbidding the priest to take sides and reminding the laity of the importance of this neutrality. These samples show to what extent the layperson finds himself each week, not only integrated into the intra-clerical debate, but also given a position as "witness" to the proper functioning and the application of the directives which the heads of the clergy have defined.

## The reform of the parishes: a democratic administration

In the same spirit as the "appeal to the participation of the Coptic people", one finds a second measure that is equally successful in binding the layperson to the daily life of his or her local clerical institution. This concerns the reform of what the Copts call the *Majlis al-Kanisa* (Church Council).[6] This is an old structure, originally linked to the laity's attempts to modernize the Coptic Church at the beginning of this century, but it had lost its effectiveness and its real existence in the course of time. It was given new life by the agents of the church reform ("which ensures both the democratization of the administration and its practical effectiveness," we are told) through the strategy of a massive encouragement to participation. The council is enlarged; the entry of new members representing young people, civil servants and women is assured; the maintenance of an active rhythm in the holding of meetings and the issuing of recommendations is often encouraged by the patriarch in person. This restructuring of the council does not, however, signify a simple revival of old structures. In practice, it is more like an attempt to bring the laity closer to the center of the church and more particularly to the patriarch. The vitality of any specific council does not in fact depend on the prerogatives granted to it, but on the relative closeness of its members to the patriarch, and the opposite is true, too: namely, that a relationship of conflict between the members and the patriarch can completely block the action of the council. This democratizing initiative, encouraging the integration of laypersons who favor the changes that have been introduced and who are ready to unite with the head of the church, thus appears to be a clerical strategy well suited to control a good number of "independent" or hostile spheres in the dioceses.

In the case of neutral places (i.e.,places characterized neither by an affinity nor by a hostility vis-a-vis the patriarch), the members of the council must give direct proof of their cooperation. This means that they must take the initiative of submitting periodically to the representatives of the hierarchy the list of new candidates for the priesthood, the evaluation of the priests who exercise the ministry, in terms of their clerical activities, their financial management and the environment of the community. Besides this, where there are local tensions they must supply an account setting out the respective positions of the different parties.[7] It is at this stage that laypeople involved in this process take on the full role of "mediators" between the institution and the public, making a report as complete as possible of all the points of view, the suggestions and the implicit criticism of the local population.[8] We should note that this democrato-clericalizing reform, saturated with mutual surveillance on all levels, is viewed very negatively by those clergy and monks who dislike centralization. They often quote it as an example of the patriarchal "manipulation" of the local elites who are looking for a role to play in the project of renewal.

## Activities in the parishes: a conscious confusion of tasks

Apart from these two instances, the agents of the renewal have revived practices which consciously confuse the missions of the priest and of the committed laypeople. Without ever placing these on the same footing, the highest authority in the church nevertheless appeals to both to carry out the same kind of task. The most striking example is *al-iftiqad*, i.e. the regular pastoral visits to the faithful (following the categories of locality, gender or age) to encourage or to check their religious and communal practices:[9] weekly masses, meetings, individual and collective reading of the Gospel, daily private prayers, etc. In fact, neither the writings nor the proposals of the agents of the renewal make it clear whether these pastoral visits are the work of the priest, the deacon, the volunteer, or of the simply committed layman or woman. All are called to do this, without exception; and when they do so, all are representatives of the clerical institution.[10] What is true of the *iftiqad* holds also of most of the daily activities of the parishes: the creation of new publishing activities, the organization of preaching in the services of worship and the meetings, the starting of a choir or a local paper in the name of the church or the diocese. In all these cases, there is a mingling of tasks and authorization, and it is only the episcopal or patriarchal power that can play the role of judge among these protagonists, who henceforth perceive themselves as equals.

We can learn much from the ideas of Naguib, a thirty-year-old former Sunday school teacher at Fagallah (north of Cairo):

> I cannot say that the whole church is against the initiatives of young laypeople. That depends on the priest of the parish. Mine was too authoritarian, but that is not often the case. One could not make even the slightest innovation without meeting his opposition; one could not decide to hold a meeting, unless it was his idea. Even on the level of daily living, he had to agree in advance about the songs and the lesson I was going to teach the children. Let us not even mention the pastoral visits. Although we had the authorization, at least in relation to one's friends and people one knew, to give spiritual instruction in informal meetings, the priest felt that we were encroaching on his territory. He asked us to tell him, so that he could go to visit the person in need. This curtailed the service too much. You know, the patriarch does not share such ideas. In his weekly instructions, he calls on everybody to act and to serve. It is true that he defends respect for the clerical body, but he does not ask to lose our own personalities...

*The attention given to the families of the clergy as a part of the institution*
The final context for identifying the laity with the clerical institution is the launching of a new tradition[11] of organizing meetings, formation sessions and gatherings with the wives and the children of the priests.[12] Indeed, sometimes when it is a question of a late ordination, the church can designate a bishop or an old priest to have a series of personal meetings with the family of the recently ordained priest, with the aim of preparing the family as a whole for this social, religious and spiritual transformation brought about by the ordination.

George, a twenty-eight-year-old practicing Christian, experienced this when his father, a pensioner, decided to be ordained as a priest. George thought that this decision had no consequences for the rest of the family, at least for the children (who were 22 and 24 years old at that time), but he admits that he was wrong:

> I had not the least idea that my life would be completely turned upside-down after the ordination of my father. I played in a music group, but I had to stop, because the son of a priest has to give a good example. I used to go sometimes to the town center at evening with my friends, but I had to stop for the same reason .... During the first months, a priest who prepared us for the change of status visited us many times. I am still not prepared, six years after the ordination of my father and ultimately ... I do not believe I will ever really be fully involved in my father's ordination.

It is probable that the course recommended for George's family is the same as that laid down in the course of the collective meetings.[13] The important point here seems to be the clerical interventionism in the form of taking charge of the family or seeing to its "conscientization." The pride accompanying this fact is as strong on the side of the hierarchy as on the side of the family.[14] The wives of priests have the impression of belonging to the institution more than other laypeople. As for the central bodies, they speak of this collective initiation as the high point of the institutional restructuring. In this way, the dissemination of the clericalizing thought is ensured through the policy of the participation or involvement in the clerical functions through matrimonial and family bonds.

## The clericalizing structures: retrieval and innovation

Unlike the preceding examples, the clericalizing structures endeavor to "make concrete" the new mode of active involvement and are concerned only with certain sectors of the Coptic community, attempting to change their religious or communal activities into structures linked to the clerical institution (in a dependence that is not only religious, but also institutional, financial or even symbolic in relation to the church). This is why this branch of the clericalizing action is concentrating on activities which flourish, but which escape clerical control or stand outside the aegis of the clergy, in order to bind them institutionally to the clerical hierarchy. The examples here are the Communal Council (*Majlis Milli*) in its new version, the centralization of Coptic youth activities by the establishment of a general episcopal office for youth, and finally the network of the "consecrated virgins," converted into an order of deaconesses. These three examples illustrate three different modes of lay participation. Despite their diversity, the fate of all these networks has been the same, for all have been transformed in the course of the last twenty years into organizations with a clerical significance (although the degree differs from case to case).

The restructuring of the Communal Council (*Majlis Milli*) is perceived, at least initially, as the revenge of the agents of the renewal against the anticlerical wing of the laity and the government which supports it and tries to reactivate its communal representative function.

The establishment of an episcopal function to centralize youth activities is based on a completely different argument: it is considered both as a defence against a potential "protestantization" of Coptic youth, or at least the danger of any kinds of contacts young people might have with structures external to the community, and as a measure to ward off a hypothetical challenge that could be provoked by young people who were too zealous.

The conversion of the consecrated virgins into deaconesses is perceived from a different angle, since it is presented as an action in the campaign against the breakdown of the networks and groups in the community, something that offers pastoral services to its members.

Thus, the annexation is presented as the solution to multiple external or internal problems, organizational or pastoral, political or purely religious. Besides this, the clericalization is presented in all these cases as the absolutely essential means of defense for the survival of the group, not as an institutional end in itself or a clerical offensive. According to the agents of the renewal, the primary concern is the preservation of unity, even if this unity risks converting the religious bond into a clerical bond, with the consequent deformation of the ecclesiastical and the communal spheres.

*The Communal Council: the "remake"*
The relations between the agents of the renewal and the *Majlis Milli* from 1973 onwards reveal the capacity of the clerical hierarchy to reinsert into their organization structures which, historically speaking, had a lay nature. It was the state that called elections for the *Majlis* in 1973 in order to create again a pole parallel to the mobilizing bishops and the patriarch. This was a poor calculation, since it failed to take account of the profound transformations that had occurred within the Coptic community.[15]

Conscious of the objectives of the political power, the church did not oppose it, but succeeded by various stages in neutralizing the effects of this interference. The series of the measures taken tells us a great deal about the "domestication" undertaken by the patriarch to meet the offensive by the political power (or the lay wing). It shows to what extent the clericalization in some cases slips into an affirmation of the representative political character of the ecclesial agents against those who historically represented the elite of the "Coptic people," or against the state which has always manipulated the political representation of the community.

The initial action vis-a-vis the ministerial decree calling the elections can be considered the first stage of the process we are calling "reinsertion." The clerical body launches a press campaign tracing the history of the *Majlis Milli*, a campaign marked by waves of polemic between the *Majlis* and the members of the clergy.[16] In this way the clergy succeeded from the outset in influencing a large part of the Coptic public by insinuating that the *Majlis* has historically been a source of conflicts. A second message then replaces the first, insisting on the patriarch's good intentions, his will to cooperate with the new council and his expectation about the electoral results.[17] This message is completely credible, because in this period (1972-1973) the patriarch has a tense relationship with the synod[18] on the subject of divorce and second marriage, and does not yet have sufficient alliances to impose the projects he wishes. Thus, the new *Majlis* finds itself from the start obliged to follow a politics of conciliation, since every tension with the patriarch would risk confirming its destabilizing and malicious aspect in the eyes of the Coptic electors.

Besides this, the head of the clerical body does not fail to make use at the same time of more classical methods to give orientation to the votes of the electors on the national and the diocesan levels: the support of certain candidates, the distribution by word of mouth of a precise list, and above all accounts in the patriarchal periodical *al-Kiraza* of the visits made by certain laypersons to the patriarch.[19] The preferences of the church circulate in a semi-official manner at each electoral campaign, supporting almost exclusively names from the "lay wing of renewal," i.e. persons who have had the same type of formation, career and ideological orientation as the new clergy, or who at least have ended up by admitting the ecclesiastical guardianship over the whole community. The influential Coptic upper-middle class and the landed proprietors are replaced by a new profile of candidates: lawyers, doctors or university professors. Most of these come originally from the Coptic middle classes, having left the countryside in order to study in the modern educational networks; they have attended the Sunday schools and have sometimes even followed the same clerical studies. Thus, it is not enough to be attentive to the clerical aspirations, if one wishes to be elected: one must also give proof of fidelity over a long period to the ecclesiastical magisterium and to its representative character.

The second stage of this process is even more revelatory of the clericalizing strategy. In the course of the first meeting of the *Majlis* after the election,[20] the patriarch ordained all the members to the diaconate, an unprecedented measure through which Shenouda III gave a new meaning to the lay participation and ended with one stroke the classical antagonism between the *Majlis* and the clerical hierarchy. What we find is no longer a rivalry, nor even a complementarity, but a hierarchization into which the laity are inserted. This hierarchization confirms for the first time the unanimous recognition of the clerical guardianship by the Copts as a whole. Thus, the transformation of the *Majlis* from a communal into a communal-clerical structure is the most striking example of the clericalizing transformation which has been undertaken.

After the election, the agents of the renewal had to redefine the breadth of competency of the *Majlis* that had been elected. This had been the historical substance of the old antagonism between the *Majlis Milli* and the clergy from the end of the 19th century until the movement of the Free Officers in 1952. The successive limitations imposed by the Nasser regime on the competencies of the Council[21] ultimately left no reason for the controversy. A reformulation of the competencies was therefore indispensable.

From the very meetings, the patriarch (who is always present as the chairman) drew up a long list of his expectations of the *Majlis*. The length of this list confirms the church's intention to cooperate; it shows, however, that this structure, in its new functions, resembles a department of the church rather than an autonomous communal organization. According to the new directives of the patriarch, the *Majlis* is confined to purely administrative tasks, such as the supervision of the working conditions of the clergy and of the teaching of the Coptic religion, the census of Copts (by means of registration of baptisms, marriages and deaths), the organization of young people, etc.[22] In keeping with this, very few functions concern the juridical domain: modifications of the law about the election of the patriarch, the juridical remodelling of the statutes of the *Majlis* and of the church councils (*majalis al-kana'is*). We should, however, note that these competencies remain basically insignificant, and that the vast domain of legislation, especially as far as it concerns the personal status of the Copts (which was the real point of struggle between church and state in the 1970s), remains the jurisdiction of the clerical agents.[23]

Besides this, when Sadat ventured to strip the patriarch of his functions and banished him to his original monastery in 1981, the political authorities – always insensitive to the balance of forces within the community – tried to reinforce the *Majlis* and re-establish it as a communal authority. This failed because it sufficed for the patriarch to oppose this from the monastery: the laypersons abstained from participation, thus confirming not only the unity of the community behind its patriarch, but also the loyalty of a clerical structure to its hierarchy.[24]

*The episcopal office for youth: clericalization as a prophylactic measure*
While the clericalization of the *Majlis Milli* can be interpreted as a simple action of clerical revenge, or as a political calculation, the foundation of a clerical structure to give a framework for the activities of Coptic youth is all the more revelatory of the strong aspiration to clericalize the faithful. The divergence of political aims which conditioned the relations between clergy and laity in the preceding example does not apply, as far as the young

people are concerned. From the end of the 1960s onwards, the young people seem to be more closely bound than ever to their church, accepting its religious and political guardianship. The church, on its side, has inaugurated a strategy of mobilization and help in regard to the youth. In other words, the situation of the 1960s was a successful example of cooperation and rapprochement. Given the absence of any tension and the existence de facto of efficient channels of communication, the centralization of the activities of Coptic youth under an episcopal office for youth seems superfluous.

*Coptic youth: from university cells to a general episcopal office*
The episcopal office for youth (the last general bishopric founded by Shenouda III) was set up only in 1980. Before this, from the 1960s on, the links between the young Copts and the church show an undeniable growth, finding full expression through an assiduous presence of young people at the spiritual "meetings" and clerical studies, and through a committed involvement in the pastoral services organized by the church.[25] University students were the pivot of the religious mobilization throughout this period. The weekly instructions of Shenouda III (inaugurated in 1962) are addressed primarily to them. Each Wednesday, there are many more than six or seven thousand persons present.[26] The number of well-disposed volunteers does not cease to increase, and the same is true of the entry of holders of university degrees into monasteries and parishes.

This massive presence expresses the prevailing uneasiness, especially from the military defeat of 1967 onwards, of Egyptian youth (here, the Copts) in search of a meaning for their life and of a feeling of unity. The collapse of the socialist and modernizing dream, the impossibility for the new educated generations to get higher in society and rise in the political sphere, the decomposition of the Egyptian army, which was the symbol of the strength and the modernization of the nation, and finally the total discredit of the organs of the state after the defeat, open the way to a massive depoliticization of the "disappointed" young people. It is primarily in a perspective of compensation that these young people, especially from 1968 onwards, throw themselves into the sphere of action which opens up alongside the political realm, viz. the ecclesiastical sphere.

This recourse to the church and religious values is not the first signal of distress emitted by young people in the 1960s and 1970s. Already at the end of the 1950s, some university students began to organize clandestine Coptic university cells (*Usar jami'yyah qibtiya*) within each department. The initial model was conceived at the medical department in Cairo. Its founder was a Coptic professor of medicine, Shafiq `Abd al-Malak, who had encouraged his students to organize themselves in order to reserve seats in the auditoria,[27] distribute stencilled notes, organize excursions, and hold collective prayers.[28] This model, which gradually became general in the other departments, too, permitted the Coptic students not only to help one another, but also to come closer to each other and so to organize collective activities proper to Copts.

The overlapping between religious practices within the church on the one hand and communal activities within the university on the other hand is typical of the profile of Coptic youth until the mid-1970s, a vital turning-point, for it was at this time that Islamist groups made their appearance not only in the universities, but also in the student housing. The appearance of Islamists meant that the Coptic students could no longer pursue their activities as they had done previously: they were, in a sense, obliged to go over either to open conflict or to a clandestine existence. This tension became more serious in the student apartments where the Islamists mobilized the residents for prayer five times a day, never passing up a chance to come to blows with those who did not take part in these prayers.[29] From the new situation of "re-Islamization of university life" onwards, it was no longer possible to maintain the detachment between the communal student environment and the religious environment within the church. In order to avoid clashes with these intransigent new activists, it was necessary to have recourse to protection from outside the university. The students turned to the patriarchate, which decided for the first time to build residences for male and female Coptic students (for example in Assiyut). Young people are also given financial support, so that they can get hold of photocopies and can organize study groups outside the Islamist networks.[30] Thus, it is the "style of action" of the Islamist groups that is the basis of the rapprochement of the Coptic students with their church.

The Coptic clergy who took charge of all the needs of these young people between 1975 and 1980 do not seem to find these new tasks and expenditures an excessive burden. In fact, this constellation allows the church not only to exercise its spiritual function, but also its status as a communal body, by protecting the young Copts who lack financial means and helping them to confirm their religious and social identity. Besides this, the university students who attend the church mostly end up involved in other activities within it.

It is precisely because of this ability to assimilate the young people into the clerical sphere that the reform introduced five years later (i.e., the foundation of the general bishopric for youth in 1980) seems at first sight not to add anything new. On the other hand, the creation of such a bishopric exposes the agents of the renewal to a variety of canonical, administrative and religious criticisms, since it introduces a new criterion into the institutionalizing reform, that of age, justifying the establishing of a specific episcopal office.[31]

*The episcopate as a means of controlling expression*
It is only by means of the daily details and the dissensions covered up by the "Coptic clerical opacity" that it has been possible to discern behind the hierarchy's official, triumphal version, which emphasizes the homogeneity of the young people, a second reality which constitutes the obverse of what is said by the priests (and bishops). This version takes into account the consequences of the massive involvement of the young people in the church and of the tensions which these provoked before the bishopric was set up.

Organizing themselves initially in a non-hierarchical framework which was fairly autonomous, the young people opted for forms of action which the hierarchy could not always tolerate. They tended to take initiatives about the nature and the substance of the pastoral services which were entrusted to them, trying out new ways of reading the Gospel, the church fathers or Canon Law, without the supervision of the spiritual fathers. Besides this, they expressed their often critical views openly about the canonical or pastoral reforms of Shenouda III or of the synod.

The fact of being directly exposed to the Islamists and subject to social frustrations gives them also a particular position that permits them both to express their own vision of things and to justify their activism. It is clear that these expressions in themselves are not anti-clerical, nor radical (in the religious or confessional sense). They are constitutive of the attitude "in perpetual negotiation" found in these young people who are located at the point where several fields of conflict intersect.[32] It is, in fact, this attitude that poses a problem for the agents of the renewal, who base their authority exclusively on the binary logic of church/laity, and look askance at every demand of the "corporate" type, every claim to mediation between church and laity, or between the community and that which lies "outside it."

We must also note that some young people showed themselves very critical of the hierarchy in these five years (1975-1980). Confronted by a great tension in terms of society, of politics, and of identity, and anxious to find a solution in religion to their double crisis, it was difficult for them to admit that the church, too, could turn against them or reprove their zeal to acquire knowledge and to act.[33] On the basis of this disappointment, the 1970s and 1980s teem with "non-declared" stories of excommunications, of schisms, of the consecration of secret churches among private groups, making the official hierarchy irrelevant, or of publications discrediting the agents of the renewal.[34] It is these cases of opposition and of religious revolts that lie behind the establishment of the bishopric for the young Copts. Is it aimed at channelling their expression, keeping their different position far away from the rest of the young people, who offered no revolt? Or was it an attempt at prophylactic isolation of a pocket of resistance? We will never know this, since all these problems are considered "state secrets" which must be dissimulated in general, and in particular in the case of the non-Coptic researcher.

*The clericalization of the young people: legitimation or centralization?*
Unlike the example of the *Majlis Milli*, the clericalization of the activities of the young people was not carried out by stages. The messages and modalities transmitted within the new bishopric are produced in one single move. They seek initially to correspond to two criteria: to provide religious legitimation to the decision to found the bishopric and to trace the guidelines of the substance and the meaning of the new activities, so that these may be granted the same status as the other general bishoprics (of social services, clerical education and scientific research). Thus, a whole new distinct sector of preaching and of publication is appearing under the name of sermons and publications for young people *(Wa`z wa ta'lif shababi)*, which is beginning to develop both on the level of the bishopric and also in many local churches. New themes and many patristic quotations are found in these new sermons and books, addressing the problems and concerns of youth. These efforts at religious legitimation (which the church call *Ta'sil kanasi*) seek to give this field of activities a dimension of clerical, indeed of historical legitimacy which the institution owes it to itself to take over and direct. Anba Moussa, the bishop with general responsibility for youth – with solid support from the patriarch – is not content with this dimension. He adds a second, very modern dimension of socialization, of constant dialogue with specialist scientists and of fairly free debates:[35] a step that tends to attract well-educated young people to him, to mobilize them and to persuade them to invest their energies completely in establishing the new network.

A central metaphor of the service of young people emerges from this double profile: the conception of the world as constituted by two complementary poles, the volunteers (servers: *khadim*) and the served *(makhdum)*. Among Coptic young people as a whole, those who belong to the bishopric are the former group, while the rest form the second group. The unity presupposed by the fact of belonging to the same generation is broken down by this binary vision of the world. On the level of this relationship and its management, the entire bishopric (bishop, clergy and young laypeople) have as their central and daily work the elaboration of the many rules that must be followed. The meetings, sermons, visitations, and the episcopal publications only serve to develop this spirit of a "distinct and exemplary body" both in relation to the world of youth and to the more general field of pastoral work.[36]

Thus, the specialized volunteers in the youth sector find themselves led on the one hand to commit themselves actively more than anyone else in the field of patristic and ecclesiastical knowledge for the sake of giving their pastoral conception a solid foundation and, on the other hand, to look differently on their friends, brothers, sisters and neighbors. These are no longer companions or people identical to themselves, but "served persons" who have to be taken charge of, given a practical framework in their activities, and be shown the right path. In this way, each *khadim* sees himself or herself more as expressing the will of the church than as belonging to a given social and geographical environment. The formation of the young volunteers thus consists in producing mediators between the clerical institution and the young laity, and in putting in position a structure that will prevent any potential crystallization of a movement in the name of Coptic youth. This production/prevention, which aims at generating a "clericalized" youth with the label of "servants of youth," also serves to provide new defenders of the clerical institution with the same views as their elders.

## From consecrated virgins to deaconesses: an intraclerical conflict

The final example of the structures clericalized by the agents of the renewal concerns the pastoral service by women called consecrated virgins (*al-mukarrasat*). This structure emerged at the beginning of the 1960s, beginning in the diocese of Beni Suef where several young and older women had expressed the wish to make a vow of celibacy, not in order to live a contemplative life as nuns, but in order to serve the community. They were initially supported by some diocesan and general bishops with "ecumenical" leanings, but these women lived a form of active life that went beyond the directives of the synod both in the period of Kyrillos VI and in that of Shenouda III.

It was difficult for this new orientation to find its place in the already existing categories within the Coptic Church, where women had only one church vocation, that of contemplative nuns. It was only in 1965, at the end of two years of an elementary form of organization, that this community was recognized by the patriarch Kyrillos VI as a "community of active nuns."[37] The recognition did not want to give this model a general validity, but only to bless an effective group which already existed. This is why Kyrillos VI emphasized, when he consecrated the community and performed the rites of initiation, that this was a unique form combining ministry and the life of nuns.

In the course of time, the service of the consecrated women of the *Banat Maryam* (the name of this community in Beni Suef) has grown in scope. Its members have built schools, a clinic and a home for mentally retarded children. The success of their various projects has permitted them also to become self-financing. It must be noted that the consecrated women of the *Banat Maryam* did not aim to spread their model to the other dioceses, nor to extend it where they were. Their main aim was to confirm their vocation as active nuns, and to get themselves accepted as such by the local and national community.

But after this success, several dioceses admired this model and promoted the foundation of new local groups of consecrated virgins in the 1970s and 1980s. Each group inaugurated an official sector of service as consecrated women, in keeping with the charism of its bishop, its pastoral sensitivity and quality of the women who wished to devote themselves to this type of service. This free and experimental application meant considerable differences between one place and the next. The consecrated women were sometimes virgins, sometimes widows. They lived sometimes in community, sometimes in a monastery close to the town, sometimes in their families. Sometimes they had religious names and habits; in other cases, they could not be distinguished from the rest of the faithful.[38] One thing, however, remained constant: the consecrated women gave an irreplaceable service to their locality. From the spiritual and the social perspectives, their presence gradually became something unquestionable. Their activities extended to sectors never served before (drug addicts, unmarried mothers) and included peripheral areas deprived of pastoral assistance (schools in villages and slums, literacy classes for adults, and medical care in the villages).[39]

Through this organization, this diversity and this liberty of the form adopted, the consecrated women have unintentionally been a sign from the 1970s onwards of a new orientation which it was probable the church would take. In reality, their success posed a more fundamental problem to the nascent clerical institution than the simple maintenance of an existing community or communities, namely that of the choice between institutionalization and centralization as potential modes of action to develop pastoral care, on the one hand, and the integration of initiatives in a diversified movement, on the other hand. A substantial dissension became visible between those who gave priority to vocation and dedication to service, and those who were increasingly concerned with the restructuring of the church in its various orders and grades. Those who did not favor centralization wanted to hold up the consecrated women as a counter-example. Through the protection they gave these women, they sought to reawaken the *ecclesia* in the modern context, in the face of the massive organizational formalization of all the fields of service begun by the patriarch and the young bishops.

*The first deaconesses as counter-example (1981-1988)*
The patriarch's customary course, defending the centralization, has attempted to shackle the development of the movement of the consecrated women by replacing it with an equivalent model: the order of deaconesses. This new structure, established in 1981, has to carry out the same services in reality as the consecrated women, but in the purely clerical framework of the female diaconate.

Drawing on a category which already existed in the early church,[40] but which had ceased to exist a thousand years previously, the agents of the renewal mobilize the sacred principle of the return to the origins in order to convert the cleft between centralization and decentralization into another cleft, namely the renewed value given to the early church as against adherence to the principle of "the church in the world." Apart from this, this creation had practical advantages. If one compares it to the "vague" status of the consecrated women, which depended until then exclusively on the diocesan bishop's will to support (or not to support) this form of service, the female diaconate is a clearly defined function in the hierarchy (i.e., carrying a salary and social advantages). Finally, in an oriental country where women's movement and activities are a constant preoccupation, the creation of the order of deaconess supplies both the respect due to every member of the clergy and the professional and social guarantees enjoyed by the male deacons.[41]

Using these arguments, the patriarch ordained 180 deaconesses in 1981 and declared that, from then on, the convent of St. Dimyanah would be their fixed national center. The average age of these deaconesses is higher than that of the consecrated women, in order to give the new order more credibility and seriousness. On the basis of this measure, the patriarch implicitly encourages the bishops to follow his example. In the course of this period, several bishops close to him have in fact ordained new deaconesses. Thus, two structures with a different nature, but carrying out the same activities, have coexisted for some years. This cohabitation is the most palpable example of the existence of two orientations in the whole church, the one centralist and the other appealing for tolerance of diversity of action within the church (in keeping with contemporary ecclesiastical experiences, or in the name of the non-centralized dimension of the early church).

*The consecrated women as subdeaconesses, or the victory of the clericalizing policy*
It was not until 1989-1991 that the diaconate of women was confirmed, and the synod decided to "reform" the groups of consecrated women. The result of the lengthy discussion of this measure in the synod, after a year's negotiation, was a synodal decree organizing the service of the consecrated women. The proposed reform consists in defining the status, the competencies, the formation, the prayer life, the spiritual framework, the promotion of this category, and the sanctions relevant to it. The new element consists in the change of the very meaning of the term "consecrated." The decree makes it clear that the service of the consecrated women is a preparatory phase before the female diaconate, and is no longer a religious form of service parallel to the order of deaconesses. The virgin or widow who wishes to consecrate herself to the "diaconal" service passes first through a phase of one year where she is called "one who desires consecration" (*taliba takris*). After this first year, the candidate for service becomes "assistant of the consecrated woman" (*musa`ida mukarrasa*). Then she goes on to a superior stage of formation where she is called "novice" (*mubtadi`a*) for two years. Thus, it is only at the end of the three years that she is declared "consecrated." She will then require five more years of praxis before receiving her first promotion to "sub-deaconess" (*musa`ida shammasa*), and five years more will be necessary before she finally becomes a "deaconess" (*shammasa*). This is an official consecration, a rite of initiation, but she will be required to provide numerous testimonies and evidence about her formation, her service, her spirituality, etc., before she can be admitted to this.

Thus the new reform demands eighteen years of uninterrupted service within this framework before a woman can be definitively admitted to the diaconate. Despite the complexity of the synodal project, the aim is clear. On the one hand, the service of women is from now on centralized, given a structure, and fundamentally clerical;[42] on the other hand, the various groups other than consecrated women no longer have any official legitimacy within the church.[43] Consequently, they cannot receive any help or recognition. It is possible that the deaconesses, after their status has been stabilized, and in view of the financial[44] and moral support they receive, will come to accomplish their mission just as well as the consecrated virgins once did, that they will have the same enthusiasm and dynamism that were characteristic of those who preceded them. Nevertheless, one distinctive trait will remain visible: their membership, official and included in Canon Law, in a clerical institution.

## Conclusion

The various facets of the process of clericalization show that it is not a simple project of the assimilation of the laity into the clerical institution. It is the institution itself which is transforming itself, both on the level of its structuring and on the level of the foundations of its authority. The average place of the "committed" laity presents one of the major problems for this extension of the ecclesiastic dimension to the daily life of the Copts. The frontiers separating the clerical body from the laity become doubly fluctuating in this situation, with its blend of pastoral reawakening, project of renewal and increasing demands for participation.

Neither the persistent use of the slogan of the return to the origins nor the process of clerical institutionalization can succeed in dissimulating the growing dimensions of tension, of diversity and of an overflowing of the boundaries, things that challenge the aspiration to homogenization and centralization. The recourse to new modes of legitimation, persuasion and insertion of persons within the church framework appears inescapable, if the clerical institution is to be guaranteed its function of channelling expectations and modes of expression. But the diversification of the foundations of authority in turn changes the laypeople's perceptions of what the function of their clergy is, and what it ought to be. More than the accelerated renewal of this church, more than the dizzying extension of its ecclesiastic sphere, we must emphasize its aptitude to manage at the same time the mobilization of the laity, a fundamentalist ethics and the rationalization of its functioning, as well as its capacity to set itself up as the ultimate authority of clerical and para-clerical regulation: this bears witness both to its success and to the narrowness of its margins of manoeuvre to maintain unity in an exceedingly difficult context within the community and between communities.

## Notes

1. In 1962, there were two general bishoprics, one for social service and ecumenical relations, the other for clerical education. Three others were added later: the first for scientific research, the second for youth, the third for the direction of the Coptic churches in France, which do not have the status of a diocese.
2. As well as the intra-clerical antagonisms which exist between the patriarch and certain ecumenical or eremitical tendencies.
3. For more details on this polemic about the partial or total application of the *Shari`a* and the successive tensions between church and state between 1972 and 1979, see N. Abdel Fattah, *Al Mushaf wa al-Saif* (The Koran and the Sword), Cairo: Madbouli, 1984.
4. This difficulty comes both from the heterogeneity of the laity and of the places involved, and also from all the factors mentioned above (a situation of crisis affecting religion, politics and society, in which the Coptic layperson lives).
5. See the examples of this debate in *al-Kiraza* : June 16, 1989, Nov. 25, 1989 and Dec. 2, 1989.
6. The church council was founded by the initiators of the *Majlis Milli* at the beginning of the twentieth century on the level of the big local churches, with a view to reforming their financial management, religious formation and the liturgical celebration of each church. This council originally consisted of the leaders of the community, the local priests and archdeacons. (Conversation with professor Milad Hanna, 18-12-1988.)
7. The function of "connection" carried out by the members of the church council is done in a consistent manner, either in the framework of direct meetings with the patriarch, or by means of a process of voting (in secret and by writing).
8. This organization of the tasks of the representatives of the churches, and above all of the members of each council, is promoted by the journalists of the patriarchal journal, who regularly report the meetings of the members of the councils with the patriarch, expressing congratulations at the good functioning of this organization: cf., *al Kiraza*, 16-6-1989.
9. This *iftiqad* has to be further defined: the visitor must also ascertain the spiritual life of the couple, the respect for the religion in the family, the absence of conflicts between father and mother, parents and children, etc. It should be noted that whenever family problems arise, the help or advice given is based on a religious vision, not on a societal logic.
10. A tape recording (made for sale) of a meeting held by Anba Moussa (the bishop for youth) shows how the young people are prepared for the *iftiqad*. In the course of this meeting, the bishop imparts the guidelines for the action of the volunteers (*khadim*) in their "informal meetings" with other young people, when confronted with the following cases: a young person who stops practicing his religion despite the warnings of the volunteer, a bond of love between a Copt and a non-Copt, the involvement of some young people in alcoholism, drugs or theft. In all these cases, the bishop advises the volunteer to make a first attempt at persuasion and, if this fails, to inform the priest so that he can take over. This hierarchical vision of things, typical of the bishopric for youth, is, however, not the only way of organizing the distribution of tasks.
11. Tradition here is understood in the sense of a norm that was established relatively late, but is presented by the group as an ancient or central value. On this sense of the word, see: B. Anderson, *Imagined Communities. Reflections on the Origin and Spread of Nationalism*, London: Verso, 1983.

12. On the organization of the formation meetings for the wives of priests at the monastery of Anba Bishoi at Wadi al-Natroun, see C. Chaillot's interview with Patriarch Shenouda III in 1988: "Comment vit la femme copte aujourd'hui au sein de l'Eglise," in: *Le Monde Copte* 16 (1988) 66-73.
13. Apart from the testimony of the patriarch (cf. ibid.), I have not been able to obtain any information about the contents of these collective meetings in the monasteries or with the bishops. All that the news columns of *al-Kiraza* contained were the dates. However, my interview with George shows us the pattern of the ritual of this initiation, where the whole family finds itself involved.
14. In the course of the interview with C. Chaillot in *Le monde Copte* (note 11 above), the patriarch recalls with pride his meetings at the monastery of Anba Bishoy with 70 priests' wives. He explains at length how the church prepares them to take their place, their service, their spirituality and the potential role they can have in the church.
15. This description was made by professor Milad Hanna in an interview, 18-12-1988.
16. See *Watani*, 20-12-1973.
17. See *Watani*, 20-6-1973.
18. During this period, some members of the synod had publicly criticized the patriarch for taking a number of measures without the consent of the synod, concerning divorce and second marriages, see: *Proche Orient Chrétien* 22 (1972) 188-190.
19. The naming of those who visit the patriarch signifies an agreement between host and guest, implying that this is a candidate who has the hierarchy's blessing.
20. This meeting was held on 30-8-1973.
21. Nasser's regime had suppressed the juridical competencies of the *Majlis* in the reform of 1955. It had also placed under its protection, in the same period, all the religious endowments; *waqfs* (Muslim and Copt): this was the major point of conflict between the *Majlis* and the clergy.
22. On the redefinition of the functions of the *Majlis*, see *Watani*, 19-8-1973 and 2-9-1973, as well as *Proche Orient Chrétien* 23 (1973) 357-359.
23. See: *Proche Orient Chrétien* 24 (1974) 68, and 35 (1985), 92-93.
24. The new elections were held only after the return of the patriarch, following the same rules. We should note that the majority of the candidates supported by the political power, and the majority of the members of the old Coptic bourgeoisie, were not elected.
25. It was even said sometimes that the only basis of the popularity and charisma of the patriarch was the young Copts' support and admiration of him.
26. Shenouda's instructions were held every Friday in the 1960s, and every Wednesday after his enthronement, always at 5 p.m. Now these instructions are made available for sale on tape recordings, and his books republished two or three times each year (in editions of 10 to 20.000).
27. Each of the medical departments in Egypt has 3000 to 5000 students, and auditoria constructed much earlier on, can hold only a fifth of this number. Thus the reservation of a place is a daily battle for the students. The same problem is found in the polytechnical and legal departments.
28. Interview with R. Habib, 8-5-1990.
29. This observation, which may appear very stereotyped, has marked many young Copts who live in student housing. Following a method of "encouragement to practice religion", the Islamists knocked on the door of every room at the time of prayer, to mobilize the students. Thus the Coptic students – and also the Marxists and (non-practicing) communists – ran the risk of friction with the Islamic militants five times a day.

30. The eviction of the Coptic university cells was compensated for in its entirety by clerical support: they made available rooms for the groups revising for examinations, photocopying machines, assistant teachers who went through the university course with the students, but also excursions and visits to the monasteries for the purpose of relaxation and of receiving a blessing before and after the examinations, and the offer of pastoral and spiritual services to meet more successfully the challenge of the university world which was undergoing the process of Islamization.
31. On the organizational level, this creation demanded to be justified by a new pastoral and canonical argumentation. The competencies and duties of the various general bishoprics had also to be redefined in virtue of this new situation.
32. Albert, a volunteer of the bishopric for social services, explained to us the particularly difficult place of the young Copts in society as a whole: "We are at one and the same time young people, believers, we have our duty as members of the community, we are all looking for work and a place to live, etc. The church has a special interest in our problems, and our daily life is made up of all these elements simultaneously." This description seems to me revelatory of the existence of a logic proper to the young people both within society and within the church.
33. On these protest groups, sometimes going so far as to disqualify the existing hierarchy, see R. Habib, *Al-Ihtijaj al-Dini wa al-Sira` al-Tabaqi fi Misr* (The religious protest and the class struggle in Egypt), Cairo: Dar Sina, 1989, 171-192.
34. In fact, the very tense relationship between young people and the clergy would never have been discovered if it had not been for the publication of R. Habib's book. Since he is a psychologist, a Protestant Copt and deeply involved in the social services offered by the Protestants, he enjoyed a position which I do not have at all. One must note that his scientific good intention has been called into question. Nevertheless, the information he gives appears entirely true and well-founded.
35. E.g., round tables and colloquia, the regular invitation of lay specialists, readings of American books on psychology and sociology.
36. In this perspective, a whole new literature is developing, aimed at the young *khadim* of the bishopric: the risks of emotional links in the relationship between the volunteers (servers) and the served (*khadim/makhdum*), the management of generation conflicts within the service of youth, and also the service of youth in the light of the early church, pastoral work as a central mission of the Orthodox Church, etc. These examples represent the principal themes taken up by the various channels of communication.
37. To understand better the differences between the active nuns and the contemplative nuns, cf. P. van Doorn-Harder, *Contemporary Coptic Nuns*, Columbia: University of South Carolina Press, 1995.
38. In order to discern the differences, an enquiry was carried out in 1989-1990 among two deaconesses at Assiyut, three consecrated virgins at Minya and one consecrated woman in Old Cairo. P. van Doorn-Harder and C. Chaillot have given me invaluable help in this.
39. For the various fields of service of the consecrated women in several dioceses, see C. Chaillot, "The Diaconate of Women in the Coptic Orthodox Church," *Orthodox Outlook* 3 (June 1990), 15-16.
40. Names like Olympia, Phoebe and Anastasia (the first deaconesses in the early church) were familiar to many clergy and laity, and were highly esteemed by every Copt who was anxious to see the glory of the first church shine forth anew.

41. It is the patriarch in person who evoked this problem of the service of women in his interview with C. Chaillot in *Le Monde Copte* 16 (1988) 66-73.
42. The details of this reform were not made public until 25-5-1991.
43. The group of *Banat Maryam* is the only one to remain legitimate in clerical eyes, because these women were consecrated by Kyrillos VI as "active nuns."
44. The salaries are fixed for each stage, as well as social security and the conditions for retirement.

Berit Thorbjørnsrud

# Born in the Wrong Age; Coptic Women in a Changing Society

"About my church, my service and my spiritual life, these are the only things which are sweet in my life and keep me alive. I can not imagine my life without God and the church": Neshrin.[1]

Neshrin is twenty-five years old, and belongs to a respectable middle-class family. She is the first of them to take a university degree, which will ensure her a good job, and she is now nearing the end of this study. Apparently, the future holds good possibilities for Neshrin. At the same time, she claims that the only valuable thing in her life is her relationship to God and her own service in the church *(khidma)*. Sometimes she adds sadly that she feels as if she was "born in the wrong age." Neshrin is a pious, religiously active young woman, which makes one wonder why she experiences the rest of her life as so frustrating and sad. Why does she feel that she is "born in the wrong age?"

In the literature about women in the Middle East in the 1980s, there has been a tendency to portray them as secure and well anchored in their identity as women. This has been a counterpart to the earlier trend of analyses of misery which attempted to show the oppression to which these women are exposed. As such, important things have been said, but the danger is that one simply tips the balance over from a negative stereotyping to a positive stereotyping. In order to understand Neshrin's frustration, I would claim that one must look more closely at the transitions taking place in Egypt and the consequences these have for young people in general and for young women in particular. For these are transitions that lead to new and more intense discussions of what and how a woman is to be, and how to face the uncertainty and frustration in relation to how one is to realize oneself as a woman – and in the case of Neshrin, as a Coptic woman.

In this article, I shall look more closely at this frustration, at what is involved in Neshrin's experience of being "born in the wrong age," and at the strategies she chooses to find a new meaning, a new identity, in a confusing situation.

Neshrin belongs to St. Dimyanah church in al-Salihiyya (both names are pseudonyms), which is a part of Greater Cairo. This is a lower-class area, and as such typical. While the Copts are spread over the entire range of classes in Egypt, most of them (like most of the Egyptian population in general) belong to the lower classes (working class and lower-middle class). In this respect, the processes one can observe in al-Salihiyya are relatively representative of processes in Egyptian society in general, and in Cairo in particular.[2]

## The St. Dimyanah church in the district of al-Salihiyya

Al-Salihiyya is a neighborhood marked by industry, the railway, highways and unfinished dwelling areas. There are no parks, restaurants or department stores here. Everything is small, narrow and humble. The area has a low status among the population of Cairo in general. Culturally speaking, it is marked by strong traditions. It is dominated by Muslims, and there is a prominent group of Muslim fundamentalists. But it also contains a sizeable group of Copts, who belong to three churches. The central church leadership of the area, with Bishop Raphael (a pseudonym) at its head, is in St. Dimyanah, and this church forms a kind of center for the Christian inhabitants.

St. Dimyanah has a large number of activities, such as a nursery, a children's home, a clinic, social projects for children and adolescents. Apart from these, there are the religious activities, such as worship, Sunday schools and meetings. The church has a number of salaried workers and an even larger group of volunteers, men and women, who do unpaid, voluntary service (*khidma*) in addition to their studies or other regular jobs. I shall concentrate on the women in this group of volunteers.

The volunteers (*khuddam* which literally means 'servants') carry out diverse tasks, but most often function as the church's representatives, e.g. in the religious education in the Sunday school, or in concretizing the church's message, for example in social work. Unlike those who have salaried posts, the volunteers have an extensive religious training and are given a relatively large responsibility. The activities of the various individuals vary, but it is not uncommon for them to spend three to five afternoons or evenings in the church: or, as one of them says, "We unmarried female volunteers spend 90% of our free time in the church, and only 10% at home." This statement is in contrast with the traditional expectations that children and young people spend virtually all of their free time at home. It can therefore be useful to start by asking how these young female volunteers experience their situation at home.

## New gaps between the generations

The family is the basis of Egyptian society, both ideologically and in practice. Nevertheless, Coptic young people often express frustration about their home situation.[3]
Typical statements are:
"My parents do not understand me."
"My parents cannot help me with my problems. I want to get out, it is too boring to be at home."
"What am I to do at home?"
Or, as Neshrin puts it: "My mother is kind, but she is so ignorant. She doesn't know anything about my things... I can't ask my mother, she doesn't have any experience, because she never leaves the house... They [the parents] don't know how to handle all the things I have to handle. Sometimes I feel like I have to find out everything for myself...."

The parents are traditionally expected to function as models and authorities for their children, but the statements above communicate a lack of correspondence between the map and the terrain. And this creates an uneasiness which leads young people to seek new authorities *inter alia* in the church.

Both the Muslim and the Coptic family are built up around two axes: gender and age. Men and women have complementary roles, and their age and knowledge mean that they are given authority vis-a-vis their children. Women have the main responsibility for the upbringing of children who are expected to model their future roles on the father and mother respectively. Traditionally, this has ensured a high degree of continuity. But because of the rapid changes in Egyptian society, many children grow up in a world different from that in which their parents grew up, and generation gaps are formed today much more than before. If one looks at Neshrin and her mother (who are typical in this context), one sees the following striking differences: the mother cannot read, and was married when she was 15 years old. When she was 25 (Neshrin's age today), she had already been married for ten years and had seven children. Her life was, and is, house and family, and it is only rarely that she goes outside the neighborhood. The world of her experience is that which lies close at hand, that which is traditional. Neshrin, on the other hand, is nearing the end of a university education, she is neither married nor engaged, she is a volunteer in the church, and she travels daily across the metropolis of Cairo. This gives her experiences and confronts her with challenges which are totally unknown to her mother (and to her father, a small merchant who can read only a little). And this makes it difficult for them to understand and to help Neshrin with her needs.

Traditionally, mothers and daughters have spent most of their time together, and there has been a continuous process of learning and copying. This has now broken down, in part, primarily because school, education, and, later on, paid work bring the children out of their home, away from their mother and into the charge of other "teachers."

In general, education is a high ideal in Egypt, conferring both prestige and middle-class status. It has long been something that the upper classes take for granted. For the lower classes, it represents something new, involving unforeseen consequences. For while they desire higher education, also for their daughters, they expect that they will maintain a traditional family ideology: they will help their mothers, learn to be good housewives, obey traditional rules of chastity, etc. And, as I shall show, these expectations are not entirely fulfilled.

## Consequences of education

Neshrin says: "It is clear that the ones who get the most education are the ones who go most to church. I see that among my friends in the college, among the Sunday school teachers here in St. Dimyanah, and in the monasteries." "It is important to be connected to the church, because that makes you relaxed. You feel encouraged and become happy, and when you go home, you study hard. If I stay away for a long period, I become worried and study badly." To understand the connection between studies and church activity, one must look more closely at the challenges young people encounter in the education system.

### *Focus on the individual*
The traditional family functions as a collective. Individual needs are subordinate to the common good. This generates a collectivist understanding of the personality. In antithesis to this stands the school system that focuses on individual achievements. Pupils and students compete against each other; the goal is the examination, in which the individual must rely totally on his or her own self. This antithesis between the family's collectivist system of

values and the school's focus on the individual creates uneasiness and confusion, and for many this can be assuaged only through a religious search.[4]

It is an enormous undertaking for lower-class families to get their children through higher education. It is obvious that resources are scant when a family has seven or eight children, and education is often possible only when several of the oldest children are working and help pay for books and school uniforms. Since the school system is overburdened, expensive private tuition is often necessary. A higher education will therefore frequently represent the united endeavor of the collective. In other words, the collective counts on improving its prestige and its shared reputation through the individual achievements of one of its members. At the same time, the collective has little or no experience of what is demanded of the individual to whom this task is assigned, and this can be a hard burden for the student. An illustration to this point is Huda's story.

Huda, fifth of eight children, was a brilliant pupil in school. When she began the last year of secondary school, the family decided together that Huda should try to get a place to study medicine (the study which demands the best marks and gives the highest prestige). For a period, the family spent around 20% of its income on extra tuition for Huda. She was freed from her usual duties, which were transferred to her siblings. The whole family, ten persons living in a space of 50 square meters, organized its life around Huda's studies. This means that they all tried to be quiet so that she could study, and everyone reminded her continually of her lessons, extra tuition, television educational programs, etc. Huda was at first happy to have this chance, but she soon began to have continuous headaches, lived under stress and became nervous, and her marks went down. It was hard to bear her siblings' jealousy, the stress, and the lack of understanding of the work she was supposed to do. In the preliminary examination, she had the worst results in her life. The family became depressed and everyone sought an explanation. Within the world view of the family, where academic success was due to intelligence plus many extra hours of tuition – which they had obtained for her – this was incomprehensible – or else they must explain it by saying that Huda was not intelligent after all, or that she had been lazy. For Huda herself, this was unacceptable, and she said instead: "I tried so hard, but I did not succeed. Every time I opened the books, I became dizzy. Whenever I have had problems with reading before, I took out the Bible and prayed to God. But it did not work this time. I did not manage to pray, and I still cannot pray. The only explanation can be that the devil is blocking my path. And I do not believe that I can study again, until I get away from the devil and come back to God."

This explanation entirely concurs with what she learned in Sunday school. It is hammered into children from their very earliest years that "the devil is smart" and is watching them all the time, to divert them from the right path – in this case, her homework. It is an unpleasant explanation for a young girl, but it makes sense: it excuses her partly from responsibility, while at the same time setting her individual defeat in a larger cosmic context, viz. the continuous conflict between God and the devil. This makes it understandable. Moreover, the religious explanation opens the door to other accessible strategies leading out of the disaster – to seek God through prayer and reading the Bible.

*In sha' Allah – If God wills*
There is a strong focus on examinations in the Egyptian school system, resulting in students' nervousness. School work is done in overly full, ill-equipped classrooms. Homework is done in narrow flats where the noise level can be high, or where the whole family tries to "keep quiet" so that the student will be able to read. This is, of course, no easy task, and it is then that many turn to the church, in order to "be encouraged" and "become relaxed" as Neshrin puts it.

It is customary for students to come and "receive *baraka*" (blessing) from the bishop, priests or monks before important examinations. For example, two students sat up for half the night before a big examination, so that they could follow a certain monk home. His presence, or his prayer, had a soothing function on their tender nerves. Others make an agreement with some specially beloved saint and promise that if he or she helps them, they will repay this by performing certain services. No one believes, however, that prayer alone is sufficient. God helps those who deserve it, i.e. those who study hard. But at the same time, nothing is possible without God's help. And God can perform miracles, if God wills it. In order to attain this, one must develop a humble and pious disposition, and/or carry out spiritual work or services in the church. To follow a monk home through dark streets at night can be one way of showing the correct disposition and thus deserving help.

The individual must make a contribution, but ultimately, everything depends on God's will, and the human's task is to show that one has understood this by laying everything in God's hands. Thus, the responsibility for success or failure is transferred, at least in part, from the individual to God, for even bad results can be understood as God's will. Neshrin, for example, failed an examination and was very unhappy. Her parents were furious and said that she had spent too much time in the church. She herself went to a monastery for a few days, to seek God and discover why she had failed. When she came back, she was calmer and said that she had now understood that God wanted to try her, to put her active commitment and her humility to the test. And her recipe for future success was to be more active in the church. She took her parents' rage to be an expression of their lack of piety, which prevented them from understanding that the fiasco was a part of God's plan for her spiritual development. Thus, even her failure took on a meaning within a religious framework. Through her humble acceptance of God's will and her subsequent intensified search for God, she appeared as pious in her own and other's religious eyes. This allowed her to rescue at any rate her religious honor, and she was once again a part of something larger than herself. This can make individual responsibility easier to bear.

## Pressure for Islamization

Egypt is a Muslim country, and the school system is defined within Muslim parameters. This sets its mark on many disciplines: for example, instruction in Arabic is carried out with the use of the Qur'an, history lessons emphasize Islamic history, etc. The Coptic element is nearly ignored. Coptic pupils react to this: the focus on Islam makes them aware of their own Coptic identity. Because Arabic is linked to Islam, they perceive it as the language of the Muslims and therefore not their own. Because history is the Muslims' history, not theirs, they begin to inquire about their own history. This means that they need to find their own language, their own history etc, and the church offers this through courses in Coptic and other subjects.

The strong fundamentalist tendency in Egypt finds expression in an increasing pressure. For example, an increasing number of Muslim women teachers wear the so-called *hijab* (a scarf that covers the head and the neck) and try to persuade their female pupils to do the same. This is not limited to the Muslim girls, but applies to the Christians, too. *Hijab* is perceived exclusively as a Muslim symbol, and this is interpreted accordingly as an attempt to convert the Christian girls or perhaps to force them to hide the fact that they are not Muslims.

The Copts also claim that they are discriminated against in the admissions to some educational institutions, when grants are given, and at examinations.[5] There are countless stories in Coptic milieux of students who, faced with Muslim fundamentalists as their examining board, were forced to state their religious affiliation, and ended up with poor results.[6] There are also stories about Christian examiners who assess Christian students too strictly, because they are afraid of being accused of favoritism towards those who share their faith. Both types of story can, of course, be used to explain away one's own failure, but it seems nevertheless certain that such discrimination does exist. Familiarity with such stories – whether or not they are true – serves also to create fear and apprehension. They also serve to make the young people aware of themselves as Copts, so that their religious identity becomes relevant to them and the need for Coptic solutions and help on Coptic premises is created. At many universities, for example, there exist clubs which are entirely Copt and where a Coptic emphasis is attached to all that is done. They pray, read the Bible, go on excursions together, etc. This contributes to the strengthening of the members' individual Coptic identity and to their sense of belonging to a different group than the Muslims. When they are confronted with a continually increasing Islamization, which threatens to make them invisible as Christians, participation in such groups can be a strategy of resistance which once again makes them visible.

*Out of home*

The school and studies take children out of the home for large parts of the day. This gives them new experiences and contact with those of the same age. Thus, the school is a place for play and for greater development for these children who live in narrow, overly full flats. After schooltime, they are kept indoors – when they are small. This is because it is shameful (`eib) for children to play in the street, and it is considered shameful for girls to go out when they are older.

School may be thought boring and frustrating, but when the school holidays come around, many nevertheless express their frustration at having to be at home all the time. The young students cannot meet their friends as usual, the girls must help at home, and all this makes the days long and dull. In other words, school tends to create the need for other activities than those offered by the home. For children in more prosperous districts, holiday time and free time can be filled with activities in clubs, travel, etc. This is not possible for children in al-Salihiyya. Poverty and a lack of organized activities for free time mean that there are no other alternatives. For respectable children and young people in general, and especially for girls, it is only the church that has something acceptable to offer.

## Women in the public sphere

Education is an ideal that applies to women, too, because it contributes to the raising of the status, not only of the woman herself, but of the whole family. Education, however, also represents a challenge to the traditional ideology of modesty, because it compels young women to move alone in the public sphere. Traditionally, women from the lower social stratum have spent little time out on their own. Male relatives have had the responsibility for protecting their reputation, and this has meant that they have escorted the women on necessary errands outside the neighborhood. This role as protector and guardian of women has been one of the most important criteria of masculinity. But now women are forced to go out alone. Men can no longer follow women daily back and forth, and women must learn to take responsibility for their own reputation. Men, too, must learn how to deal with women in the public sphere, and to hand over a large part of the responsibility for their female relatives to the women themselves. This is certainly not without problems, and women are exposed to a number of pressures from various sides. They must go out, and they want to go out. The family wants them to succeed outside. But at the same time everyone is afraid that something may happen that could compromise the reputation of the women, and thereby of their family.

It is acceptable that women go out to receive an education, and education is seen by definition as something that makes people well-bred and respectable (*mu'addab*). But at the same time, everyone looks closely at a woman who is out alone, and it is easy for her to become the subject of talk. This kind of talk among people is a force that can build or ruin reputations. Women know this, and they also know that they themselves do not necessarily need to do anything wrong: what other people (first and foremost, men) do in relation to them can be enough – even the suspicion that something has happened. Young women often say that people talk irrespective of what happens: "As long as I myself know, as long as my family knows, and most important of all, as long as God knows that I do not do anything wrong, then I cannot pay attention to such people!" Despite these brave words, women use a great deal of energy to preserve their reputation, i.e. to reassure that they are chaste even though they mix among men outside their own family group.

This situation is complicated by the fact that they are no longer able or willing to wear the traditional clothes that safeguard their modesty (black coat-dresses, scarves, etc.). Such clothes are seen as traditional, provincial (*baladi*), or quite simply lower-class, and they can no longer be used by women who aim to present an educated appearance, i.e. as modern and middle-class. These women wear frocks, dresses, blouses and similar clothes which make them more exposed, and, therefore, more vulnerable to gossip. As a number of researchers have shown, it is in this situation that groups of Muslim women put on the so-called Muslim costume, to signalize their own modesty.[7] But because this new costume (a long, wide dress and head-covering) is identified as Muslim, it cannot be used by Christian women in the same situation. They do not wish to present the appearance of being Muslims, and they must therefore find new ways of marking their Christian identity. They use Christian accessories, religious jewelry, put religious stickers on bags, books, handkerchiefs, or use keyrings with religious motifs and the like. The Copts have traditionally tattooed a cross on the inside of their wrist. Ceres Wissa Wassef claimed in 1971 that this custom was in the process of disappearing, but this seems to have been reversed in the 1980s. The majority have this kind of tattoo and great importance is attached to it.

These symbols of Christian identity are always discreet and flexible: they can be emphasized, or hidden at a moment's notice, for Coptic women must in general be careful not to offend Muslims with a display of Christian symbols, and they must be able to hide them quickly if anyone reacts.[8] Obviously, such symbols do not function as effectively as, for example, the Muslim veil. Marks of Christian identity function best when they are at the same time linked to specifically Christian work, i.e. activity in the church. But this in turn is an activity that is acknowledged only by those who know the woman in question, i.e. her family, friends and neighbors; only in relation to them does such behavior function. These people know where a woman in the public sphere comes from and where she is going, and they know that this is a woman who spends her free time in the church. This functions because it is known that the church does not accept just anyone, and thus the church's acceptance functions as a kind of stamp of approval.

The use of Christian symbols and activity in the church are not the only strategy for maintaining an unblemished reputation, but they are adopted by a growing number of Coptic women.

## Coptic women and paid work

In general, it is the husband who provides for the family in Egypt. This is defined as a very important criterion of masculinity. Women from the highest classes do have some tradition of work that brings income.[9] Women from the lowest classes have some tradition of informal economic activity.[10]

Beyond this, women's paid work has been seen as a threat both to masculinity and to femininity, and therefore as something shameful. Women (and men) continue to have a very ambivalent attitude to women's paid work.[11] But two factors contribute to the increase in the number of lower-class women who now go out to paid work: economic necessity and education. Education means that women can attain respectable work, such as that of a civil servant (*muwazzafa*). This can confer prestige as long as it is not presented as economically necessary. It is usual for women who work outside the home to emphasize that it is the men in the family who pay for everything: they themselves only buy things for themselves, or else they bring things "they find along the way" back to the house. It is a publicly known secret that these apparently inconspicuous purchases may be necessary contributions to the household. But it is in the interest both of men and of women to keep up this pretence.

Women's paid work is thus a threat to the traditional pattern of gender roles. And since, like education, it brings women out of the home and into contact with men who are not their relatives, it is a potential threat to the ideology of modesty. For Coptic women, this will mean that they continue with the strategies of identity which they developed in their time as students.

*Work-Meaning-Identity*
In the 1960s, a reform introduced by President Nasser meant that all who obtained a university education had an automatic right to employment by the state. This was meant as an incentive for people to undertake studies, but it worked so well that the apparatus of the state is now overflowing with employees who often have very little to do. In the case of many of these people, this functions as a form of "paid unemployment," something that has a number of consequences both for the state as an institution and for the individual employees. The state considers the stream of applications a problem, and tries to put a stop to it through various measures. This conflicts with the newly qualified person's desire for a job. For those who already have a job, this situation ensues in low salaries and apparent problems in finding meaning in "days empty of work."

To create a positive identity, one requires something with which to create it. One needs to be important in relation to something, and if this does not exist naturally, i.e. at work, one can be forced to create one's own identity, at work or somewhere else.[12] The feeling of being insignificant in their job, seems to be very widespread among civil servants, which most of the female volunteers in St. Dimyanah are. Naturally, this "paid unemployment" is frustrating for women who have given proof of an intelligence, an energy and a commitment far superior to the average, in that they have come through university education at all.

Irrespective of whether they are employed in the public or the private sector, their job has seldom any connection with their education. Access to study is decided initially on the basis of their grades in secondary school, and there is an automatic relationship between the grades and the type of study. Personal interest is scarcely relevant. New employees are given a place in the public sector where there is a vacant post. Thus, to take one example, Soheir, who had studied psychology, was given a post in the water supply ministry. The interest in such work tends to be minimal and is seldom mentioned as a reason for working outside the home. People take what they can get, as long as it is a good job that confers prestige and does not pose any threat to one's reputation. And it is naturally important for women who plan marriage and a family to have a safe job that gives rights in the form of maternity leave and the like, and that is not too demanding to be combined with a house and children. The motives for working which these women give are the need to get out, to meet people, and to earn money. Several investigations have shown that many Egyptian women spend their working day just drinking tea and talking with friends.[13] Although women continually complain about how tiring their job is, they can also admit individually that they perhaps work for as little as half an hour in the course of a working day. Public transport in Cairo is totally overburdened, and it is arduous to have to take public busses. Since jobs are assigned irrespective of where the employee lives, commuting two hours a day is common. This in itself is both tiring and time-consuming; and the journeys present a constant danger that the women may be harassed by men who take advantage of the anonymity of the crowd. This may partly explain the women's claim that their work makes them so tired. But there does seem to be a lack of proportion between the degree of exhaustion they indicate and the slow tempo of work that they themselves tell about. Therefore, these statements must be seen rather as attempts to play down the meaninglessness in their days, and instead to suggest that their jobs are important.

This work situation offers few tasks, little responsibility, and little to supervise. The work does indeed confer prestige, but otherwise appears to provide little stimulation for the development of a positive identity. Little is said about this, but one woman who herself had an interesting and demanding position was explicit about the depressing effect this had on people: "Look at all the people who travel back and forth every day to a work where they have nothing to do – day after day, week after week. What does this do to them? What kind of self-respect does this give them? I know many who get depressed because of this." At the same time, everyone knows that the authorities see the number of state employees as a problem, and that they are trying to cut down the number of new employees. In other words, it is said in public that they are superfluous and that their presence is a problem.

In general, their jobs seem to mean little to the women volunteers in St. Dimyanah, and the typical positions in the bureaucracy had few consequences for their activity in the church. For these young women, the ambivalence surrounding paid work results in a stronger emphasis on religiosity, so that they can present themselves as modest. And it is possible that the "work-free working days" are one explanation for the intensive activity in the church. The question remains: what do these women get in the church that they do not find anywhere else?

For most Coptic women, marriage and family represent life's goal and meaning. But this, too, is surrounded by frustration and apprehension today, and it can be useful to look more closely at the problems concerning marriage before we finally direct our attention to the church.

## Problematic marriage

A Coptic woman can choose between two ways of life: either to become a contemplative or active nun (*rahiba*), a deaconess (*mukarrasa*) or to get married. Although an increasing number of women become nuns, the great majority opt for marriage and family life.[14] In the past, the families arranged marriages for their sons and daughters. Today, the choice is increasingly left to the young people themselves. Engagement and marriage must still be approved by the parents, but in keeping with contemporary ideas of romantic love, young people are supposed to find partners by themselves. But this is not without difficulty in a district like al-Salihiyya, which is still dominated by strong rules concerning modesty: this poses limitations on where and how unmarried men and women can meet. In general, this happens when a man "sees" a woman, makes enquiries about her through neighbors and acquaintances, or the local priest, and then asks permission to visit her parents. This means that unmarried women are continuously "on display," and they must take care to look their best. At the same time, this must be balanced against the demand for modesty, i.e. they must present themselves as good, Christian, inaccessible women. One young woman described this balancing act as walking on the edge of a knife, i.e. a balancing act that demands a good and active cultural competence.

Economic problems, unemployment, lack of a place to live, and other factors make it difficult for young people to get married. This is problematic for the men, who are expected to bear the chief economic responsibility – i.e., to find an income, an apartment and most of the furniture. Nor is it easy for the father of several daughters to find the money for what is expected of a woman (bedroom furniture, general moveable goods, and a new wardrobe). Although young women themselves often help pay, the sums involved are considerable. This is why the age of marriage has become much higher. Men are seldom ready for marriage before they are thirty, and often much older. Women should be married before they are twenty-seven or twenty-eight, but it is not uncommon among the volunteers in St. Dimyanah to be about thirty before they marry. And more and more are still unmarried after they have passed their thirtieth birthday.

This means that marriage is surrounded by uncertainty and fear. It is still a shame to be unmarried, and it also means that one does not have access to the life one wishes for oneself, nor can one realize oneself in terms of the upbringing one has had. This again is a very serious threat to one's identity. Who is one as an adult, unmarried girl?[15] And what kind of future does one have? No one is tempted by a life spent at home as a daughter, as an assistant to one's mother.

*Mixed marriage*
According to Muslim rules, it is forbidden for Christian men to marry Muslim women, but allowed for Christian women to marry Muslim men. Among Christians, however, such mixed marriages are not accepted, but are considered shameful both to the girl herself and to her family. Christians are not allowed to conduct missionary work, so the only basis for recruitment is their own children. This means that a Christian woman who marries a Muslim represents not only the loss of one individual member, but also the loss of future Coptic children. This is a double reason to be afraid that young girls may come in contact with Muslim men. At the same time, everyone is familiar with young girls' fear of not getting married. A number of stories circulate in Coptic milieux about how Muslims try to ensnare women by using marriage as bait. This is experienced as a real threat, with the result that people are continually on guard concerning young girls' relations with Muslims. Perhaps this is the explanation of many young girls' markedly hostile attitude to the Muslims: more than any other group, they seem to express negative feelings about the Muslims. They often express a

distaste for all that is Muslim and claim that they wish no form of contact beyond that which is strictly necessary. But perhaps these should be interpreted more as statements about their own modesty, their own Coptic identity, than about their relationship to the Muslims. What they say can probably be understood to mean: "I am a good Christian girl, you do not need to be afraid that I will marry a Muslim man." In any case, such statements are perceived as expressions of a strong Coptic identity, and serve accordingly to calm potential suspicions, thereby ensuring one's good reputation.

## Coptic women and church service

According to Father Malaty, the church ought to be like a "loving mother for sinners."[16] Here all ought to be welcomed and cared for in keeping with their needs. All the representatives of the church in St. Dimyanah do their utmost to make this a reality. They try to empathize with all the problems of their parishioners, and also to be accessible in order to help them with these problems. They have a great belief in the value of personal relationships. This refers first of all to confession, but they are also available in a more general sense.

Confession in the Coptic Church involves a continuing personal relationship between priest and penitent. Confession focuses primarily on spiritual direction, but in practice this is defined very broadly, so that virtually all problems and needs are discussed. For example, the priests can have important functions in negotiations about marriage: a man who has seen a suitable woman can apply to her confessor for more information, he can perhaps get the priest to ask the woman if she is interested, and to organize the initial meetings. This means that the priests can take over a part of the family's role. Women who have transgressed against the rules of modesty can also find help to conceal this from their parents, and to find various solutions to the problem in which they have landed. The education of the priests, their experience of life, their authority and their insight make it easier to confide in them than in one's parents. Since the priests are bound by the church's law to be a "loving mother for sinners," they have a forgiving attitude which often goes further than that of the family. The family correctly feels that its own reputation and position are put at risk if one of its members transgresses traditional boundaries, and it can react with severe punishments. The priests, on the other hand, focus more on forgiveness and direction.

The priests do not accept the young people's breaking of boundaries, but their goal is to bring them to repentance, for as Father Matta al-Miskin says,

"Repentance is but a fall into the hands of God."[17] Their chief goal is to inspire the church members to seek closeness to God, and they believe that this is best done by meeting people with understanding and counsel. Besides this, their perspective is the parish, not the individual family. Peace in the parish is a goal for them, and they will do much to settle problems quietly.

This attitude often leads young people to go to the priests rather than to their parents. The priest's religious insight also makes him a greater authority in many fields than the parents. Thus, strong links are forged between priests and young people who have been looking for new models more in keeping with the modern age. This pastoral care directed towards persons indirectly serves to weaken the family's control over its members and to help young people to maintain a form of private life vis-a-vis their family. At the same time, they emphasize their individual existence by focusing on the importance of the relationship between the individual and God (via the priest). For the priest's pastoral care naturally depends all the time on the willingness of those who ask for help to accept the spiritual work imposed on them. Thus, the young people are bound more closely to the church.

*Recruitment – reputation and prestige*
The Coptic Church wants to have many volunteers, but does not accept just anyone. It makes a selection and keeps those chosen under continual supervision. It wants to have the "best" as its volunteers, and this is defined in accordance with specific criteria:

1) They must have a university education, or be in the process of such education. Some specially intelligent and keen persons can begin already while they are at secondary school, but the majority are older. This means that they belong to the best-educated elite of the district.

2) They must be known to the church's leaders, which means that they should have been to Sunday school when they were growing up, or have been often present on church occasions. They must have letters of recommendation from their own confessors, guaranteeing that they go to confession regularly. They must have the ability to treat all kinds of people with politeness and friendliness, and they must be able to tackle frustrations without becoming either nervous or angry. They must be obedient and show respect for their superiors. In relation to others they must be able to display firmness and determination. They also must know the difference between right and wrong, and be able to reject all temptations. In short, one must be unshakable and demonstrate this convincingly.

3) The church's course for volunteers is obligatory for them. This includes both instruction in the church's doctrine and a certain amount of

instruction in being a volunteer. The students are required to submit written work, and the course concludes with an examination. If the requirements are not fulfilled, the course has to be repeated.

The leaders' strategy in associating the volunteers with themselves is to develop their religious life. The requirements for being accepted are so strict, however, that the church has difficulty in recruiting enough volunteers.

This selectivity means that a certain prestige is attached to being a volunteer. In fact, in St. Dimyanah the demands are so high that only a minority is eligible. If one is accepted, this sends a signal that one is up to the mark both in a spiritual and a secular sense. The church's acceptance puts a stamp of quality on them and gives an indirect guarantee of their reputation. This is a very important point for women who depend on maintaining their reputation unblemished. Service is an important element in their reputation management, but it also helps the construction of their identity in other ways.

## Being a young person – church service and identity

*Identity*
Many young women live in a kind of cultural vacuum. Unexpectedly, they have been confronted with adolescence, without knowing how long this will last, something that they have not wanted. Unlike the situation in Western countries, no autonomous cultural value is attached to this period: rather, it is characterized as a preparatory stage before "real" life begins with marriage or, for the few, the transition to life in a convent. Since this period as a young person is something new, and because no value worth mentioning is attributed to it as yet, it has not been made the object of cultural elaboration. One consequence of this is that it contributes little to the creation of identity.

*What does service contribute?*
Magda is twenty-three years old, unmarried, well educated, and holds a job where she has virtually nothing to do. In the church, on the other hand, she is one of the leaders of the choir, of a children's club, and also a teacher in the Sunday school. Magda flies like the wind through her various activities, always busy, a thousand things in her thoughts. There always is some business that needs her attention. In the Sunday school, she is to teach her pupils correct Christianity. She is to inspire them to spiritual development and regular ritual practice. Theological ideas are to be interpreted and translated

into rules that can be applied in practice. She is to be a link between her pupils, the church, the school, and their families. A Sunday school teacher is to be a friend to the pupils, a person who through her own example and her pastoral care guides them into a correct way of life. Thus, she can become a kind of extra mother. Many teachers call the pupils their "spiritual daughters" (*banat al-ruhyin*). This relationship is based on spiritual values which are to serve the spiritual development of both partners. In the church, this is seen as the fundamental aspect of life, and great importance is attached to such matters as Magda's responsibility vis-a-vis her "spiritual daughters."

Mariam lives at home and helps her mother. At work she is in fact not very necessary, but in the church she is an active and very important person. She has responsibility for all courses in language and computing. The teachers are appointed in part by Mariam. All pupils must have her approval before they can begin at the school, and everything, great and small, is submitted to her supervision. Mariam is the church's representative vis-a-vis pupils and teachers, and as such she works very closely with the church's leaders. This gives her automatic access to Bishop Raphael whenever she wishes. In St. Dimyanah, where the bishop's word is virtually law, this is a very important source of power. Mariam's intensive activity in St. Dimyanah has also introduced her to church work at a higher level; among others, she is involved in the project of a new Christian institute. This gives her access to even more contacts and increases her importance further.

As social workers, Sunday school teachers or administrators, these women all have responsibilities which the church, they themselves, and the participants see as important. Everyone in the parish is proud of the activity in St. Dimyanah and see this as something indispensable: "Copts must look after Copts, because no one else cares". Indeed, the only mistake is that not more is done.

The volunteers are not independent in relation to their tasks: all take their place in a hierarchy led by Bishop Raphael. The organization of the various undertakings is determined at a level higher than most of the volunteers, but, like Mariam, they can work their way up in the hierarchy so that they are involved in making decisions. Apart from this, there are minor decisions that must be taken by the volunteers who carry out the work. It is Magda herself who decides how she will take up the various topics with her "spiritual daughters." She herself chooses the strategy vis-a-vis the girls' problems. She decides when the class can reward itself with an excursion. Within the framework laid down by the church and its highest leadership, the volunteers have a large measure of control over the tasks they are set to perform, and they appear as authorities in the eyes of those they help.

Everyone knows that the priests are higher in rank than Magda, but this does not change the fact that it is Magda who models the church's teaching for them.

The volunteers' tasks make them familiar with the church's administration. The higher they come in the hierarchy, the more access they have to the use of the church's offices. They have easier access to the leaders, and not least to information. All this shows who is inside and who is outside.

All the volunteers have a right to respect. They are addressed as "miss" or "Madame" (the men are addressed as *ustadh*, "monsieur"), and their pupils and clients treat them with great politeness. The higher up one is in the hierarchy, or the more inside, the more respect one has. Church service thus gives good possibilities for realizing oneself as a necessary and important person, and so provides material for the construction of one's identity. A volunteer can be anonymous, but he or she can also be, like Mariam, a person whom almost the whole parish knows and respects. Within this system, one can maximize power and importance through increased activity. Church service is not the object of the same cultural elaboration as marriage, and cannot equal it in weight, but it nevertheless compensates for something one fails to get as an unmarried person. One does significant work, one meets people and makes friends, and one is important to large groups of people. This means that one can have a larger sphere of work, greater power, and, if not greater social satisfaction, at any rate a different kind of social satisfaction than would be the case if one married. And this has a clear function of creating identity, at least within the church. Another function is the power of this social and religious system to include those people on the outside: the lapsed, the women who never marry, or otherwise the ones without a definite cultural identity.

*Old maid – disgrace or God's will?*
Mariam, who is thirty-five and unmarried, has an express wish to marry and have children, but as a good Christian she holds that it is up to God to decide this. Her primary obligation is to do what God wills, and perhaps God wants her to continue her service in the church. If God really wants her to marry, then she believes that God will show this by sending her a man who meets her requirements.

Although she is far beyond the age of marriage, she received two proposals. The first was from a colleague at work. Since she had great doubts, she went several times to a particular monastery to seek God's help. Being in doubt, she declined the proposal, first because she had not received any decisive sign from God that this man was God's choice for her, and secondly for economic reasons. Mariam is employed by the state, as was this man, but the problem was that he had no economic resources beyond his salary, so that they would have been obliged to live with her parents. Confronted with this situation she declined the proposal.

A few months later, she received an offer communicated by friends. She was interested, but became skeptical when she heard that the man smoked. Smoking is looked on as wrong in such a religious milieu. Some men smoke nevertheless, and most women would see this as a small problem: "Nobody is perfect, and every house has its problems." But Mariam became skeptical. She sought God once again, but this time, too, no decisive answer came. Besides this, new possibilities of work turned up. She was offered a job in a Christian charitable organization in another town. This would have meant commuting, something that is not seen as compatible with marriage.

Mariam expresses an obvious wish to marry. Nevertheless, she is not willing to accept just anybody. It must be a man who satisfies her requirements, which are much stricter than those posed by most women. In view of her age, it is not in the least impossible that this was her last chance; but she is willing to take this risk. It cannot therefore be decisively important to her to be married. She finds so much satisfaction in the life she leads now, and the possibilities it contains, that this has her priority.[18] Thanks to her service, she is an important person. If she married, she would have to give this up, because it would be incompatible with house and family, and because she herself believes that married women ought to be at home. She herself claims that she would stop her work as a volunteer and, if possible, she would stop working at her job too. For her, marriage means abandoning everything that she has built up over the past fifteen years.

Mariam is now at an age when her parents let her come and go as she wishes. She has built up a life around her own activity and her own strength. If she married, she would be able to continue with very little of this. "A woman should obey her husband," says Mariam. But it is difficult to picture a less submissive person than her. And she continues to go her own way.

Mariam has had difficult times because she is not married, but the service seems to have compensated for this and enabled her to build up another type of existence. Her fundamental faith in God's will has made this meaningful. Because, ultimately, everything is governed by God, she must try to make the best of everything. Such a view frees her from a feeling of personal shame because of being unmarried: on the contrary, in her own eyes she is obeying God's command. Others, who harass her, show thereby that they themselves do not obey God. In the church, the highest ideal is to serve God, the church and the parish, the more the better. The question of whether one is married or unmarried is less important. It remains important for individuals, and it remains important in the world around the church. But within the framework of the church's ideals and systems of prestige, marriage is less important. Most of the volunteers are unmarried, and marriage has a tendency to mean much less activity. The Coptic Church does not wish to end up with groups of elderly unmarried volunteers, but, in fact, marriage is a hindrance to the work it wishes to have carried out.

Mariam's alternative has been so successful that she now has a great deal to lose, so much that she is unwilling to give it up "for just anybody." She has developed a new role within the Coptic universe, a role that comes into conflict at many points not only with the traditional elaboration of women's role, but also with Mariam's own definition. She defines this so differently from the role she herself has realized that it would involve an enormous displacement for her to "change roles." And perhaps it is precisely in this gap between the two roles, as she sees them, that one must seek the explanation of her rejection of what might be her last possibilities of marrying and establishing her own family.

Groups of women, like Mariam, remain unmarried, whether they wish this or not. Irrespective of their individual desperation, they are compelled to create their own alternative. Education, access to paid work, and especially the possibilities of being active in the church, constitute alternatives for self realization. Many young women are gathered in the church. All must take a stand with regard to marriage, and the great majority are afraid of not getting married. Their frustration, however, is assuaged by the certainty that everything is and will be as God has decided. Desperation and suffering can well be a part of His ordering of things. The path to salvation is not necessarily strewn with roses; on the contrary, it is often experienced as a harsh process of purification. In this perspective, shame becomes irrelevant.

## "Born in the wrong age"

Educated Coptic young people are in a situation where the map and the terrain correspond badly. Brought up to see their parents as models and authorities, they experience now their inadequacy, and they look for new models and authorities. Brought up in the family's collectivist system of values, they are confronted with the school system's focus on the individual. Women are encouraged to pursue higher education, and later paid work.

This represents a challenge to traditional gender roles. Women must themselves take responsibility for their own reputations and discover strategies that allow them to appear as modest; also within men's domain. Marriage is no longer an entrance to adult life that is taken for granted. And the increasing pressure for Islamization creates fear and apprehension. In other words, the level of frustration is high. With this in mind, it becomes easier to understand what Neshrin means when she claims that she is "born in the wrong age."

At the same time, this is an expression of a general process in Egyptian society. In other words, Muslim young people are confronted with many of the same dilemmas and frustrations. But the problem is intensified for the Copts by the fact that they form a minority. The pressure from the Muslim majority in general, and from the Muslim fundamentalists in particular, makes the situation even more difficult. Their understanding of the situation, and their strategies for facing it, are also shaped within a Coptic universe of meaning. They turn to the Bible, and to its Coptic interpretation, in order to discover a meaning. This intensifies their Coptic identity, and this in turn has consequences for their manner of elaborating their identity in other contexts. For example, the generation gap between them and their parents is increased through the rejection by religiously active young people of a number of customs (*taqalid*) which their parents venerate. At the same time, the younger generation intensifies what it perceives to be religiously correct, such as fasting, prayer and church activities. They often accuse their parents of being religiously lukewarm, and take on a role as religious "textbook" in the home. Thus, the traditional roles are reversed.

General transformations in Egyptian society contribute to Coptic young people turning to the church. This makes it possible for the church to intensify its activity, and recruit even more people. This means that something happens to the church, too. While it is true that theological immutability is an important element in the church's self-image, this is more of an ideal than a reality. New circumstances and new volunteers with new needs dictate a new agenda, and shed new light on old truths. These transformations must form the topic of another study. I shall content myself with stating here that the Coptic Church today seems to be increasing in strength, and that it is changing along with general transformations in the country. These changes are also being propelled forwards by young women like Neshrin, who experiences herself as being born "in the wrong age," by young women who try to find new "maps" that correspond better to the "terrain" in which they live in reality.

## Notes

1. Quotations originally in English.
2. The material for this study is based on field work carried out during ten months in 1986 and nine months in 1992-93. Parts of the material can be found in my thesis, "Messias' Piker. En Analyse av Koptisk-ortodoks Revitalisering i et Identitetsperspektiv." Ph.D. thesis, University of Oslo, 1989.
3. Much of what follows is also characteristic of the Egyptian family in general.
4. See also: Mervet Hatem, "Toward the Study of the Psychodynamics of Mothering and Gender in Egyptian Families," *International Journal of Middle East Studies* 19 (1987).
5. See among others: Åge Holter, "Kristne under Islams Trykk," *Tidsskrift for Teologi og Kirke 4* (1983), and Kari Vogt, "Religious Revival and Political Mobilization," in Laanatza, Mejdell, Stagh Vogt & Wistrand (ed.), *Egypt under Pressure*, Uppsala: The Institute for African Studies, 1986.
6. Religious affiliation can be determined through names. A student's own name may be religiously neutral, but if the examiner asks the name of the father or grandfather, the religious background will be revealed sooner or later. Such questioning is not permitted, but, according to a number of informants, does take place.
7. See, among others: Fadwa el-Guindi, "Veiling Infitah with Muslim Ethic: Egypt's Contemporary Islamic Movement," *Social Problems* 28/4 (1981), and Arlene Elowe Macleod, *Accomodating Protest. Working Women, the New Veiling, and Change in Cairo*, New York: Columbia University Press, 1991.
8. It is, for example, not uncommon for Christian women wearing a cross to be called 'infidels' (*kafira*).
9. See: Safia K. Mohsen, "New Images, Old Reflections: Working Middle-Class Women in Egypt," in Elizabeth W. Fernea (ed.), *Women and the Family in the Middle East. New Voices of Change*, Austin: Texas University Press, 1985.
10. See: Evelyn Early, *Baladi Women of Cairo. Playing with and Egg and a Stone.* Boulder & London: Lynne Rienner Publishers, 1993.
11. See also: Andrea Rugh, *Family in Contemporary Egypt.* Cairo: A.U.C. Press, 1985.
12. The anthropologist Hans Christian Sørhaug says, for example, that in the development of the identity, it is necessary "that there exist objects which the individual can control, both individually and together with others, i.e. be a subject in relation to establishing boundaries between "I" and "you," "we" and "they," "me" and "you," "us" and "them," etc." in: "Identitet, Grenser, Autonomi og Avhengighet," *A1-dok.11 Arbeidsforskningsinstituttet*: Oslo, 1983.
13. See: Mohsen, "New Images."
14. See: Pieternella van Doorn-Harder, *Contemporary Coptic Nuns*, Columbia: University of South Carolina Press, 1995.
15. In Egypt, one is considered a girl (*bint*) until marriage when one becomes a women (*sitt*). An unmarried female is called a girl as long as she is unmarried, no matter how old she is. Anything else would be a terrible insult.
16. Tadros Malaty, *The Coptic-Orthodox Church as an Ascetic Church*, Alexandria: St. George Coptic Orthodox Church, Sporting, 1986.
17. Matta al-Miskin, "Our Heavenly Life of Struggle and Love," *St. Mark*, Egypt (1986) 10.
18. For a discussion of Miriam's church work see above.

Nora Stene

# Becoming a Copt: The Integration of Coptic Children into the Church Community

> "The revival of the Coptic Church has been so successful because, from the very beginning, the pattern was set that children should form the nucleus of the revival".[1]

The patriarch of the Coptic Orthodox Church has made strong statements about the importance of including children in the church community. The quotation above needs to be seen in the light of the activities the Coptic Church today offers its youngest members and the importance that is given to these activities.

During the last few decades, the Coptic Church has endeavored to reach laypeople and engage them more fully in church activities. Youths and children have been amongst the most important target groups in the outreach of the church. This must be seen in connection with the fact that the Coptic Orthodox Church recruits new members exclusively from the offspring of Coptic couples. Christian missionary activity is strictly prohibited in Egypt and there are but a handful of converts from the Muslim population. Each community tends to be endogamous. If a Christian woman marries a Muslim, her children are considered Muslim. Christian men cannot marry Muslim women without converting to Islam. These restrictions on recruitment have led the church to focus its attention on ensuring that those born into the community remain there.

Children are seen as particularly vulnerable to the influences of the non-Christian environment, especially at school, where knowledge of Islam and the Qur'an is part of the curriculum. Although classes are segregated for religious education, Christian schoolchildren are nevertheless exposed to Islam; some would argue that this exposure has increased in recent years.[2] In an interview, a Sunday school teacher in Cairo expressed the following sentiment:

"Before, the church was for the old. Now, the focus is the children because Muslims are attacking our children so hard. They learn to write 'I am a Muslim, Islam is my religion' in their Arabic lessons in school. So we must teach them differently in our Sunday schools."[3]

Although most Coptic children gain a degree of familiarity with the church by participating in family events, the leaders of the Coptic Church do not consider home education to be sufficient in the present situation. They wish to actively integrate children into the church life and to supervise their religious socialization.

The child-related church activities enjoy high prestige within the community. The patriarch himself is the head of the Sunday school movement. Furthermore, priests are encouraged to provide facilities in local churches for religious education and to administer rituals involving the participation of children.

This chapter sets out to show how Coptic families and the church seek to strengthen their children's bonds to the Coptic community by way of ritual activities and religious education. It also looks at the ideals and beliefs concerning children and childhood that underpin these activities.

## Integration through ritual activities

A variety of rituals form an integral part of Coptic religious praxis.[4] Of these, the seven sacraments are seen as the most important. For children, there are special *rituals of initiation* into the community, as well as *rituals of protection*. This section looks first at rituals that are performed for children by their parents or the church; then at rituals where children are themselves active participants.

### Integration and Protection

Born of Coptic parents in Egypt, a child is officially considered a Copt from birth. Nonetheless, parents usually feel it necessary for the child to undergo several rituals of initiation to begin integrating it into the family and the church community.

The first of these rituals is usually the cluster of celebrations known in Arabic as the *subu`* or seventh day feast. The *subu`* is celebrated by Muslims and Christians alike on the seventh day after the birth of a child, to offer the child protection and good luck. Most families make an occasion of the *subu`*, though there are religious and social differences in the way the feast is celebrated.

By the seventh day, the child should have received its name. It is now considered ready to be presented to a wider circle of relatives, friends and neighbors. Dressed for the first time in its own white clothes, the baby is carried by its mother to meet the invited guests. On this day the baby ceases to be a nameless infant, and becomes a real member of the family. A procession of children, holding candles and singing special *subu`* songs, greets the child. The songs ask God to grant the child a long life. Through exchanges of food and gifts, ties of obligation are established between the child and those present. The seventh day feast may include Christian components, if the parents wish. Crosses may adorn objects used during the *subu`*, and the small presents that are handed out to leaving guests may include pictures of saints.

More specifically Coptic is the ritual called *salawat al-tisht* or prayers over the wash-basin. In the *salawat al-tisht* ritual, a priest gives the child her/his first bath. It is usually performed around the seventh day, sometimes as part of the *subu`*. The priest may add salt and oil to the water in the shape of a cross as an additional blessing, or anoint the child after the bath. The salt is believed to chase away evil spirits, and to recall Jesus' description of His disciples as the salt of the earth. Passages from the Bible are recited and prayers are read over the child.[5]

Lay people and the clergy offer a variety of reasons for the performance of the wash-basin prayers. Amongst them is gratitude to God for the new child and a wish to give the child its first blessing from the church. Some people may see the *salawat al-tisht* as a preliminary substitute for baptism; this view is strongly rejected by priests who stress the importance of sacramental baptism. From the priests' point of view, *salawat al-tisht* is offered by the church to acknowledge the newborn and support the family during a period of transition. It is also seen as a substitute for the Jewish temple rite that Jesus participated in when He was eight days old.

There are indications that the *salawat al-tisht* ritual has increased in popularity in recent years, especially with a section of the urban educated classes.[6] For some Copts, the ritual is an opportunity to affirm a Christian identity. They may integrate the prayers into the *subu`* or substitute them for the traditional Egyptian seventh day feast. In this respect, the frequent performance of the ritual may best be understood in light of the Coptic religious revival.

Circumcision (*tuhara* or *khitan*) may form a part of early childhood rituals. It is performed by most Egyptian families. All Coptic boys and probably the majority of Coptic girls are circumcised.[7] In the past, circumcision had religious connotations; this can be seen in the church canon laws concerning baptism and in the popular traditions of having (male) circumcision performed at saints' festivals.[8] Today, the operation is generally viewed as necessary in the interests of hygiene and, for girls, also as a measure of social control. Since almost all Egyptians have had the operation, circumcision can also be understood as a physical sign of group membership. When Copts in Egypt circumcise their children, they demonstrate that they are adhering to society's hygienic and social customs. The practice of circumcision points to the fact that Coptic parents seek to integrate their children on several levels, both as Christian Copts, and as members of the Egyptian society.

From the Coptic Church's point of view, the most important rite of initiation is baptism, performed on infants by full immersion. Following the common orthodox and oriental tradition, baptism is immediately followed by confirmation and communion. It is baptism that truly initiates the child into the Christian Orthodox community. Just as the *subu`* changes the infant's status from unnamed newborn to family member, baptism changes its status from mere creature to Christian. Prior to baptism, the child is barred from communion and is considered a non-Christian. According to Coptic theologians, the unbaptized cannot reach paradise. Even so, the Coptic Church does not teach damnation for deceased, unbaptized children; it merely withholds judgement as to their fate in the afterlife. The importance of baptism is stressed, but seldom with reference to children as sinful beings. On the contrary, children are often referred to as "holy ones." As one Coptic priest put it: "Children are holy. They are born in holy matrimony. Isn't it written that the woman makes the man holy and the man makes a woman holy?"

Although small children cannot themselves express faith, they are baptized on the faith of their parents who promise to bring them up as Christians. To withhold baptism or communion from infants is seen as unjustifiable. Bishop Ammonius of Luxor elaborated on this as follows:[9]

> "Son of a rich man, is he not rich from birth? Doesn't everything belong to him? In the same way, we give all our riches to the children: baptism, confirmation, communion, everything. None of the blessings of the church shall be withheld from children."

Large groups of children are often baptized together.[10] Acutely aware of their minority situation in Egyptian society, Copts regard the gathering together of children for baptism as an event for affirmation and rejoicing. The newly baptized are dressed in new, white clothes. Sometimes, boys will wear miniature copies of priestly liturgical hats and girls will wear bridal veils. The children are carried by their mothers in procession around the church, receiving the congregation's acclamation of their baptism. The elaborate baptismal ritual is concluded with a speech by the priest, in which he reminds the mothers that the children need to be taken to church for communion and be taught how to live as Christians.

The baptismal ritual may be said to reflect and celebrate a close interconnection between child and mother. The child's baptism usually coincides with the mother's re-entry ritual into the church after childbirth and the mother is usually chosen as the child's sole godparent (*ishbina*), with the responsibility of bringing up the child as a Coptic Christian. In the period between birth and baptism, neither the child nor the mother takes part in the sacramental fellowship of the church, the child because of its unbaptized state and the mother because she is considered ritually unclean for 40 or 80 days after childbirth.[11] Although baptism can take place at any time, it is usually postponed until the mother can be present. This celebration of mother-child interconnection may be an explanation for baptismal fonts of modern Coptic churches being located in the women's section of the church and not at the entrance, as was customary previously.[12]

Priests strive to ensure that all Coptic children are baptized, the earlier the better. Recently, steps have been taken to remove obstacles that may hinder families from bringing their children to baptism. Fees are no longer taken for the services of the priest, and the white baptismal clothes that are required for the child may be given out free after the baptism. In their sermons, priests talk about the importance of baptism and, on visits to remote villages, they encourage parents to visit the nearest church with their unbaptized children. As a result of these efforts, there seems to be a tendency today for Coptic children to be baptized younger than they used to be, and for more families to have baptism carried out, including those of little means and those who live in rural areas.

Egypt is a country with high child mortality and parents naturally wish to protect their children against misfortune. The rituals offered by the church, such as the sacraments, are viewed as protective, as, too, are a number of smaller rituals often performed outside the church. Church leaders may be dismissive of what they see as *taqalid* or "folk-traditions," but these traditions nevertheless form an integral part of the religious life of many Copts. By bringing their children to *mawalid* (festivals for saints), providing them with amulets or entrusting them in prayer to particular saints, the families make available to their children the perceived protective powers of Coptic ritual life.

Children that are considered especially vulnerable might be the focus of a holy promise *(nadhr)* made by their parents. Such children are likened to Samuel, who was born after his mother Hannah had made a holy promise to God. Today, promises to honor a saint, feed the poor or give money to the church are usually fulfilled when the child reaches a certain age or is ready to have its first haircut. A cut in the shape of a cross may then be made in the child's hair. Some children wear distinctive clothes until the promise has been honored. One tradition known as *rahbin al-walad* (literally "making the child a monk") involves the child wearing a brown cassock, resembling that of a Franciscan monk or a desert father like St. Anthony.[13]

To spend the first years of one's life as a "child of promise" is a relatively rare occurrence. However, to be marked by the sign of the cross, in the form of a tattoo on the wrist, is a common thing for most Coptic children. The practice of tattooing crosses probably has roots in early Egyptian Christianity.[14] It is seen today as a sign of protection against evil spirits as well as a sign of Christian identity. Infants are tattooed at the request of their parents and young children will often renew their tattoos, of their own accord, when they reach school age. Both urban and rural Copts use tattoos and the practice does not seem to be in decline.[15] Families of high social standing may refrain from using tattoos and instead provide their children with gold crosses on chains.

The tattooed cross is a visible reminder of the child's identity. In the company of strangers, the child may be recognized, for better or for worse, as a Copt. The cross is usually quite small (approximately 1cm by 1cm), located on the wrist near the palm of the right hand. This gives the child the option to reveal or conceal it, according to the circumstances. Early on, she or he will learn that revealing a Christian identity can be problematic, and that what is valued inside the family or in the church may be rejected at school or in society at large. Within the church community, though, the tattooed cross is seen as a sign of honor. A well-known Coptic children's song starts with the following lines:

"I am a Christian, a Christian/
(Look at) The tattoo on my hand!"

*Active Participation*
Throughout childhood, most Coptic children take part in a variety of rituals that ensure their general socialization as Copts. The pattern is such that, whenever adults carry out ritual activities, children are there and participate as family members.

One of the most important aspects of Coptic religious life is the veneration of saints. The saints are seen as models to imitate. They are believed to have power to intercede and bring about miracles. The benevolence of a saint is activated through the development of a personal relationship with him or her; this is brought about by the believer approaching the saint through prayer. Children are believed to need the help of saints as much as adults and are therefore introduced to the cult of saints early on. Though there are hundreds of known saints, only a few are the focus of common veneration. Children usually favor the same saints as adults. There are saints who are themselves children; some of these child saints are amongst the most popular saints today.

Children are introduced to the saints by participating in their veneration, be it by greeting the icons, visiting pilgrimage sites, touching the caskets of relics or celebrating the saints' feast days. They are taught that they honor the saints by mentioning the saints' names, by asking for their intercession or retelling stories of miracles that the saints have performed. Objects connected to the veneration of the saints, such as reproductions of icons and small containers with consecrated oil or *hanut*[16], are relatively easy to obtain. Children can be very active in making use of these objects. They can give them as presents, exchange them with one another or they can decorate books or the walls of their homes with pictures of their favorite saints. These inexpensive objects and the numerous stories about miracles performed by the saints make the cult of the saints readily available to children. Children can be active participants in the rituals, thereby entering fully into the popular traditions of the Coptic Church.

Children are given rights and duties as members of the Coptic Church which they are gradually expected to perform. These right and duties, however, may vary from those of adults. One of the privileges given to children is free movement inside church during the liturgy; adults must respect the boundaries of the male-female partitioning of the church. In some ways, children's sexual status is ambiguous, and the rules concerning where women and men should stand do not fully apply to them. This also means that a child, male or female, may enter the *haikal* or sanctuary of the church. This room is usually reserved for priests and deacons, and entrance is strictly forbidden to women before menopause.[17] Children are considered to be in a state of innocence and, therefore, cannot be barred from the holiest part of the church.[18]

Attending the liturgy is often a family affair, and children are usually brought along with other family members. The liturgy itself is usually not less than two and a half hours long. The children spend part of the time socializing with each other, sometimes playing in the courtyard of the church, sometimes moving around among the adults. Parents and priests try to be lenient, but there is also an expectation that children should participate in the prayers and thereby develop their own inner, spiritual life. Indeed, the liturgy, with its set prayers, reciting of the Creed, signing oneself with the cross and veneration of the saints, is seen as a way of educating the children into becoming Copts.

Coptic children may describe their participation in the liturgy in a variety of ways:

Sherin, age 5: "In church, we pray and play."
Sherif, age 6: "I am waiting for the communion and, when the priest throws water up in the air, I know the liturgy is over. The water tells the angels to fly to God with our prayers."
Rami, age 8: "We pray, sing and take communion."
George, age 9: "I stay with my brother and pray with my hands lifted. Sometimes we find a prayer-book and look at it together."
Ghada, age 11: "I watch the priest and deacons when they prepare the communion. I like the incense best. It makes me happy."

The most important part of the liturgy is the communion. Children playing outside will be brought back in for the sharing out of bread and wine. Receiving the Eucharist is believed to be a moment of communion with the sacred, giving strength and protection against disease and misfortune. Many believe it also strengthens children to live as Christians in a Muslim society. Sunday school teachers often stress that receiving communion is important, and that one of the aims of their teaching is to make the children receive communion regularly.

One important exception to the general pattern of children participating with adults is the recent development of separate children's liturgies.[19] These liturgies are usually celebrated for children in Sunday schools or kindergartens. Caretakers or Sunday school teachers are present to ensure that everything runs smoothly. The liturgy itself is exactly the same as for adults, running for two to three hours. Only the sermon is adapted for a young audience. Some churches have consecrated an extra room especially for this purpose, and run a weekly children's service parallel to the liturgy in the main church.

An important preparation for communion is fasting, i.e., not allowing any food or liquid to pass the lips during a set period of time. Adults fast for at least nine hours before receiving the Eucharist. Children may fast for less, depending on their own wishes and their parents' attitudes. All children, including infants, usually fast for at least one hour before the moment of communion. In addition to this, there are long periods of fasting throughout the year when practicing Copts are expected to renounce all animal products. Children may take part in these fasting periods, at times even outdoing their parents in eagerness.

For children, fasting can be a way of practicing their Coptic Christian "skills." They show that they know what foods to avoid and fasting days to observe, and they are usually encouraged and praised for their efforts. Fasting may also socialize children to become aware of their Coptic identity. It can be their first encounter with the asceticism that forms an important part of the Coptic way of life. Children are taught that pleasing God requires great efforts, sometimes also privation. As Christians, they learn that they need to fight against temptation and overcome desire, and that one way of doing this is by observing the fasts of the church.

The Orthodox principle of access to the sacraments for all the baptized in the church is extended further than merely allowing children to receive the Eucharist. Children also participate in the communal anointment of the sick and needy (Sacrament of the Anointment of the Sick),[20] and may start using the Sacrament of Confession as early as the age of four or five.

There is no set age at which regular auricular confession becomes a duty, but there seems to be a general consensus that young children have a right to confess and a duty to do so from early puberty onwards. Sunday schools may arrange confessions for all children from the age of about nine. A confession usually takes the form of a conversation with a priest who offers advice and prays with the confessor. Many priests want community members to be linked to the church through personal bonds with their confessional father; today this general principle seems to be extended to children.

In addition to the five sacraments already mentioned (baptism, confirmation, communion, anointment of the sick and confession), the Coptic Church also celebrates matrimony and ordination to the hierarchy of the priesthood as sacraments. The Sacrament of Ordination includes the ordination of deacons. The Coptic Church has a long tradition of ordaining young boys, from the age of four or five, as child deacons (*shammas*). Today, this is not considered a sacramental ordination, but an initiation into the preliminary ranks of the ecclesiastical hierarchy. There are five degrees of the deaconate. Boys may successively become "singers" and "readers." Females can not be considered for any level of the hierarchy. In becoming a child deacon, the boy alters his status within the church and is no longer considered a layperson. Wearing the ritual white tunic and colored stole of the *shammas*, he will assist in serving at the altar. If he dies, the funeral prayers of the deacon will be read over him. In his spare time, he will often attend special classes to learn by heart the liturgy and special prayers. The young deacons are potential recruits to the priesthood. Their position is therefore seen as prestigious and they are generally believed to be both receivers and transmitters of *baraka* or divine blessing. Not all boys become deacons; it is a role reserved for the few, usually from well-respected families that are active in the church. For those boys that do become deacons, integration into the church through ritual activity is, to some extent, intensified.

The Coptic rituals that have been presented here can be seen as part of the process by which children are integrated into the church community. On the one hand, there are rituals of acceptance and welcome for the newborn by the family and the church. These rituals offer an opportunity for families to affirm their Coptic identity. The early childhood rituals emphasize that children are seen as valuable family and community members, who are yet vulnerable and in need of protection. Physical signs are used to mark the children's identity as Christian Egyptians. By the initiation of baptism, the child is received into the church, gaining all the rights of full church membership.

On the other hand, there are ritual activities in which older children can be active participants. Boys and girls take part in the same activities and are equally welcome to do so. As only boys are eligible for priesthood, however, this gives them certain privileges, such as serving at the altar as child deacons. The rights children were given at baptism are now supplemented by duties, for example, participating in communal worship and keeping the domestic dietary rules. By actively participating in these rituals, children can gain not only acceptance, but also admiration from their fellow Copts. In this way the rituals may work to reinforce attachment to their religious group.

## Integration through religious education

Teaching the faith has always been part of the activities of the Coptic Church. Before the growth of the modern school system, Coptic children were formally taught about Christianity in the *kuttab* or village school connected to local churches. From the middle of the 19th century, the Coptic

Church was active in establishing larger schools, usually open to Muslim and Christian pupils alike. Although the aim of these institutions was a secular education, religious lessons were also included in the curriculum. An ever growing number of Coptic children attended these school, as well as those run by benevolent societies, foreign missionaries and the Egyptian administration. Some schools offered Christian instruction to Christian pupils; others did not. A political debate about religious instruction in schools continued throughout the first half of this century. It was first settled under President Nasser, when Christianity become a compulsory subject for all Christian pupils.[21]

Parallel to the establishment of religious instruction in schools, another development was taking place. Since the late 1890s, informal gatherings of Coptic children for religious instruction had been organized by Habib Girgis, head of the Theological Seminary in Cairo. The group called itself "The Society of Love." Later, the name "Sunday schools" *(madaris al-ahad)* was adopted. In 1918, the group held its first general meeting: today, this is considered the birth of the Coptic Sunday School Movement.[22] In contrast to religious instruction in schools, over which the Coptic Church generally had very little control, the Sunday school could be used to teach the faith without undue restriction. Sunday schools have subsequently become the main arena for formal religious instruction of Coptic children.

In its early years, the Sunday School Movement was largely independent of the clergy. Its lay leaders belonged to the reform movement in the church, often standing in opposition to the conservative priests and bishops. Gradually, the movement left its anti-clerical stand. Several Sunday school teachers themselves joined monasteries or became priests. One of these ex-Sunday school teachers is the present Patriarch Shenouda III. Today, the movement has a central position in the Coptic Church and is given high priority and prestige. Priests and bishops have taken over responsibility for the work, with Patriarch Shenouda III the supreme head of the Sunday school or "School of Orthodox Church Education," as the movement is officially known. The organization of religious education has been highly successful. Today, all Coptic churches run Sunday schools (usually on Fridays, which is the official weekend in Egypt) that are attended by thousands of Coptic children, aged about four and upwards.

All children who are taken to church by their parents are expected to attend Sunday school. They become "Sunday school-children" *(atfal madaris al-ahad)*, supervised by their teachers who are responsible for a "class" of approximately 10 to 20 children. Being a Sunday school child carries a certain status. Facilities are made available to them in local churches, and great pride is expressed by priests and parents alike in the children's Sunday school activities. In this way, Sunday school can be described as having created a special "room" for children within the community, providing for their perceived needs.

One of the main aims of Sunday school activities is to transmit knowledge. The children might be baptized Christians, but living as a practicing Copt requires extensive knowledge about the faith and ritual praxis of the church. Sunday school instruction tries to ensure that children who are not taught enough at home get proper, Coptic Orthodox instruction in church. Children will learn Bible stories and their interpretation. They will also become familiar with the sacraments and the saints, and get introduced to the Orthodox praxis of prayer and fasting. The lessons are interwoven with instruction about moral behavior and ethical standards expected of "good Copts." This includes urging the children to be properly dressed, study hard at school and obey their parents. Children are told that good Christians are respectable and kind, and that they must strive to fulfil this ideal.

The Sunday school class may also make references to Islam. Teachers aim to make children aware that, since they are not Muslims, they should not identify too closely with all aspects of their surroundings. Certain aspects of the Christian faith can be taught with reference to Islamic beliefs. Most children know by heart passages from the Qur'an from their Arabic lessons. Teachers may juxtapose this with the Christian faith, for example, when teaching about the Christian dogma of Trinity or belief in the resurrection of Christ. Teachers may also discourage children from using Islamic terminology, and encourage them to use alternative Christian expressions.[23]

The Coptic Church strives to make Sunday schools attractive and available. Several church centers offer a service of collecting children from their homes for Sunday school. Where parents themselves fail to bring their children to church, individual teachers or a bus service fetch children in the morning and escort them home again, once the liturgy and the Sunday school classes are over. This is a new development in the outreach of the church, which reflects the importance given to early childhood religious education.

The organizers of Sunday schools try to make the classes attractive by combining religious instruction with games and outings. Songs, competitions with prizes and small parties are an integral part of most Sunday schools. For some children, especially those from poorer areas, Sunday school may represent the only extra-curricular activities they participate in. For many children, Sunday school has become a place to meet other children, socialize and explore their religious and secular environment. For example, a Sunday school may make a visit to a nearby monastery – an opportunity for strengthening and expressing Coptic identity, but it may also visit the local fairground and then help pay for the ticket.

In each Sunday school the children are divided into groups, usually segregated according to sex and age. Each group has one or several teachers, normally of the same sex as the children. This sex segregation is a general characteristic of both the Coptic Church and Egyptian society. It should be emphasized that although only the male sex is eligible for priesthood, religious education is deemed as important for girls as it is for boys.

The use of personal links to establish relationships has been pointed out as a trait of Egyptian culture.[24] The same can be said to characterize Coptic Sunday schools. Sunday school groups form small units within the church. Each unit is lead by a teacher who often strives to keep in close contact with the children, visiting them in their homes and getting to know their families. These units may become an important link between the child and the church – a link which is personified by the responsible adult. Ideally, each child should be linked to the church by way of personal contact with a priest (or confessional father). This may be difficult in large parishes. The priests, therefore, rely on Sunday school teachers to secure the attachment of children and their families, to the church.

Officially, all Coptic children should be given a chance to attend Sunday school, whatever their background. In reality, some parents may limit the extent to which their children can participate in activities outside the home, even if these are arranged by the church. Girls in particular may be subject to strict parental control. Furthermore, it seems that the type of activities offered in Sunday schools may exclude certain children. This seems especially to be the case for children from illiterate families. Fieldwork in Cairo has shown that some Sunday schools find it hard to integrate these children into their classes.[25] This may be because urban church centers focus attention on the importance of literacy and education, which may leave illiterate families on the periphery of church center activities. Some Sunday schools try to address the low attendance of children from deprived backgrounds by arranging special Sunday school classes for them, sometimes combined with a social program.

Children who attend Sunday school classes, year after year, often accumulate considerable knowledge about the teachings and praxis of the Coptic Church. In matters where parents may be more concerned with conventional ways of behavior, their children may have learned what the church considers to be correct praxis. Some children try to put pressure on their parents to conform with what they have been taught in Sunday school is right; some may outdo their parents in observance of prescribed fasting periods or daily prayers. While some parents express delight when their Sunday school children conform closely to Coptic ways of life, others may try to restrict their children from what they consider excessive religious exercises or even a challenge to their own parental authority.

Sunday schools convey to children that, as members of the Coptic community, they face demands both on a religious and social level. As baptized Orthodox Christians, they are meant to follow the ascetic and moral ideals of the church. From a young age, they are seen as responsible, moral beings. They are expected to conform to certain rules of behavior and to take part in the ritual life of the community by praying, fasting and participating in the liturgies. On the other hand, they are also reminded they should obey their parents and work hard at school. Their general behavior is thought to reflect both on their own families and the religious community to which they belong. Sunday school children are, therefore, faced with double expectations. They have to fulfil religious ideals that have value inside their community and to show the Muslim environment that Christians raise their children to become decent and successful citizens.

Seen as a whole, the activities of the Sunday School Movement aim to strengthen the children's Coptic identity. Through knowledge of their tradition, adults hope that the children will become attached to their church community. By allowing the children to spend time in church with other Coptic children, Sunday school leaders hope that each child will develop a sense of belonging to their religious group and that networks of friendship can be built between the children. The Sunday school teaches children that having a Coptic identity is valued within their church community. This can be especially important for children in Egyptian society, where being a Copt often means being the odd one out.

In the widest possible sense, the Sunday school transmits a world view and actively seeks to inculcate it in each child. This world view is a strong link to the church, as it can only fully be expressed through the community life and rituals of the Coptic Orthodox Church.

## Concepts of childhood

The integration of Coptic children into the church community builds upon commonly held ideas about what children are like and what features characterize childhood. Copts share some of these ideas with their Egyptian compatriots. Other sets of ideas are best understood in the light of the Orthodox Christian belief system.

The concepts in question do not make up a coherent system; they make up a mosaic of seemingly contradictory views about children. The theological teaching of the church stresses humankind's broken alliance with God and the need to restore and rebuild each person in the image of God. This view is complemented by more popular beliefs about children. These beliefs depict children as innocent and pure, often comparing them to angels. Though views of this kind are often expressed, they are seldom elaborated upon. Looking closely at the ritual life and activities of the church, it nevertheless becomes clear that both sets of beliefs influence the status children are ascribed, or can achieve.

The status most readily ascribed to a child is that of family member. A child is a daughter or son, and often a grandchild. It is as a family member that the child enters the church through baptism and confirmation. Most of the rituals of the church are celebrated as family occasions. Children are included as participants alongside other family members, often on the initiative of their parents. The family is seen as a cradle for the child and childhood is usually described with images of close-knit ties between family members.

The family is expected to cater to the child's spiritual needs. It is the parents' duty to make the sacramental rituals available to the child, as well as providing opportunities for religious education. On the other hand, it is the child's duty to obey her/his parents, and to fulfil the religious demands put to her/him. The parents can set the child on the right path; failing to do so is considered a danger not only to the salvation of the child, but also to that of the parents. An unbaptized and /or misbehaving child indicates that the parents have not fulfilled their religious obligations. A child participating in church activities, on the other hand, is considered to be on the right path, and this reflects positively on the parents. In this way, parents' and children's rights and duties are interwoven, reflecting a mutual dependency.

While the tendency to see individuals primarily as family members is shared by most Egyptians, the Copts emphasize the role of the family further by stressing that the family unit is, in principle, indivisible. The male/female couple are united by the Sacrament of Marriage, which sanctifies their union and the children born of it. As a model for the family unit, the image of the "holy family" of Nazareth is invoked. The Coptic Church upholds strict marriage laws and has put an absolute ban on divorce. Only if a spouse dies or renounces Christianity is the other partner allowed to remarry. These marriage laws are intended to secure a stable home environment for Coptic children.

Within the ideal of the family unit, a strong bond is assumed to exist between the mother and infant/toddler. The young child is believed to belong with the mother and the church celebrates their unity. This is especially evident in the baptismal ritual, as described above. The ideal of mother/child unity may also be a reason for the popularity of the "mother with children" saints.[26]

The sacramental practice of the Coptic Church to include all the baptized, whatever their age, in some respects puts children on an equal footing with other family members. So, too, does the theology of the church, which stresses the need for all human beings to seek purification and salvation. To reach the goal of sanctity, one needs to take part in the fellowship of the church, follow its teachings and participate in its rituals. With respect to this overriding priority, neither sex nor age is important.

In addition to the status of family member, with its set of duties and responsibilities, in popular Egyptian belief the child is also ascribed the status of being "of a purer kind". In comparison to adults, the child is seen as less sinful, less full of ungodly desires and less removed from the original ante-peccatum state of humankind. Put in positive terms, the child becomes a symbol of purity and virginity, likened to the saints and angels. "Children are like angels" (*Al-atfal zey al-malayka*) is an expression often used by Copts when they describe young children, especially with regard to their privileges in the church.

The idea of childhood as a reminiscence of a bygone state of perfection has ritual implications. Several of the rituals of the Coptic Church can best be interpreted in the light of the common belief that childhood is a state of proximity to God. One example is the Coptic funeral prayers. These prayers differ according to the deceased person's age, sex and, if applicable, monastic vocation or rank within the ecclesiastical hierarchy. For a departed child, the priest prays as follows:

> For a boy:"(...) Receive this sinless deposit of Thy child N., who hath [lived] in unfading beauty and untarnished virginity. (...) Have compassion on his childhood and count [him] among (...) those who are gathered in the places of rest in Thy Kingdom, who are 144.000 (....)"[27]

> For a girl:"(...) We beseech Thee (...) for this Thine handmaiden, the young virgin, the child of N. (....). May her entering in unto Thee be bright like an unquenchable lamp. Number her with her fellow virgins (...) in the unspeakable joy of those who have pleased Thee (...)"

The funeral prayers present the departed according to the category she or he belongs to (adult men, women, boys, girls, monks, nuns, and so on). For everyone, there is a recommendation to God that her/his soul be permitted to enter paradise, but it is a particular characteristic of the children's prayers that sinlessness and virginity is mentioned in their favor.[28]

The attitude that childhood is a state of innocence can also be seen mirrored in communion practices. Prior to the recent revival within the Coptic Church, it was common mainly to find children receiving the Sacrament.[29] Children were considered pure enough to receive the sanctified bread, while adult lay people were required to go through extensive preparations before taking communion. Today, the church has relaxed some of its demands concerning participation in the communion, and both adults and children receive the elements.

The freedom of children to move about inside church, crossing the boundaries of the male/female partition and even being allowed to enter the *haikal*, can be attributed to their status of purity. Being considered closer to God, children are given these extended rights that are not usually granted to laypeople.

Due to their affinity to the sacred, children are often referred to as *baraka* or divine blessing.[30] Capable of bringing blessings, they can, in certain circumstances, be used as mediators in rituals. The clearest example of this is the ritual performed in the last stage of the election of a new Coptic patriarch. In this ritual the names of three elected candidates are written on three slips of paper which are kept at the altar. After a liturgy the altar-lot is drawn by "a young child, ignorant of sin".[31] The name on the slip of paper he draws states who is to be the next head of the Coptic Orthodox Church.

In a ritual of a different kind, several children take part. The ritual is called *Salawat Abu Tarbu* or the Prayers of Abu Tarbu. It is a healing ritual for dog bites that has strong folk-religious aspects.[32] Seven boys, who have not yet reached the age of puberty, are called forward to participate. Following the instructions of the priest the boys imitate the movements of dogs; they bark and carry food in their mouths. The priest prays and reads the Abu Tarbu prayers. Without the miming children, this cannot be performed properly. Their purity, together with the prayers of the priest and the faith of the afflicted, are believed to help cure the diseases of dog bites.[33]

Although views of children's natural proximity to God are widespread, they are complemented by the fact that according to the theology of the Coptic Church, all children share in the fall from grace and are in need of the sacraments in order to be re-established as God's children. They also need to acquire knowledge about the faith which they are born into. Church membership from baptism onwards is not enough. Becoming an Orthodox Copt is not considered an automatic consequence of having Coptic parents. Organized religious education is therefore necessary. As shown earlier in this chapter, the church today makes a conscious effort to ensure that children born into Coptic families receive formal religious instruction. In other words, acculturation as a Copt is not considered automatic. Although children are believed to start their lives in a sphere of innocence, they are consciously socialized to ensure that they remain within the church community. Their status may be one of purity, but they are also seen as pupils or "trainees" in the world of Coptic Christianity.

As has been mentioned above, children are ascribed status as family members. They are in a state of innocence, but nevertheless need nurturing to grow up and become good Christians. In addition to this, some children may achieve a higher status. An example of this can be found in the stories told about child-saints. The child-saints are children who are considered saints because of their ascetic life-style and/or martyrdom. Well known child saints include the twelve year old Aba Nub, a martyr from the third century. Aba Nub is today one of the most popular Coptic saints. Reproductions of his icons are common, and a church built in his honor in the Delta region is a center of pilgrimage. Other child martyrs include the three year old Qiraqius, who encouraged his mother Yulita to die with him rather than worship the Roman gods, and the eight year old Dollasham, who was martyred with Bakhum, her older brother. Children are also known to have been martyred with their mothers. Of these, Umm Rifqa and her five children and Umm Dulagi and her four sons are the best known.

According to stories told about the saints, many of them began their careers in early life, practicing asceticism or joining monastic communities when they were still young. Apa Shenoute of Atripe is known to have fasted all day while still a boy herding his father's sheep, and Baraksiya is reported to have refused to leave the convent she visited at the age of nine. Modern saints also fit into this picture; former Patriarch Kyrillos VI (1902-1971) is said to have rejected luxuries as a child, while Umm Martha (1900-1988) entered a convent at the age of twelve.[34]

In the Coptic world view, the saints represent the highest degree of perfection possible to a human being. A saint has transcended sexual and material constraints, and is no longer marked by the sins and impurities of humanity. Purified by asceticism or martyrdom, the saints have already reached paradise. Children, in general, cannot be said to have conquered sin, nor are they believed to be continually striving to do so, as are monks and nuns in their monastic calling. But children are considered virgins without sexual desires, and they are not believed to lust after the things of this world in the same manner as adults. The ideal of human perfection, manifested in the person of a saint, is, to some degree, believed to be mirrored in every child. Therefore the child saint may be said to represent both man made holy and the child who naturally belongs with God.

Copts will often point out that "all kinds of people" – male, female, rich, poor, young and old – have sacrificed their lives to God. It is not age that matters, but willingness to put God first. Thus, a child can be an example to other believers, as maturity of age is not a prerequisite for saintliness. Dedication to God's will is more important and this is believed to be possible also for children. It is in the light of these beliefs about childhood that we must interpret both expressions such as "children are like angels" and the ritual activities of the Coptic Church that grant children rights and duties, as well as privileges.

## Revitalizing the community

Patriarch Shenouda III has publicly stressed the importance of including children within the church community, relating the integration of children to the success of the Coptic religious revival. As shown above, ritual activities and religious instruction both form a part of the integration process.

The amount of energy put into this endeavor may be interpreted partly as a reaction to what is considered to be a threatening Muslim society. Children are believed to be especially vulnerable to the influence of Islam. Therefore, parents and church leaders attempt to counteract this influence, using the means they believe to be most effective.

However, the Coptic Church is not only reacting to its environment, but is also acting in accordance with its own agenda. Actively including and teaching children has become a significant part of revitalizing the community at large. Children are consciously socialized as Copts in order that they may remain within the Coptic Church. Indirectly, the targeting of children is also a way for the church to reach and influence the parent generation. As has been shown, Sunday school children may communicate to their parents what they have been taught at Sunday school, and sometimes they may also be instrumental in tying their families closer to the church.

The family unit has always been important to the Coptic Church. Living in a hostile or indifferent society, the family remained a close knit unit which could keep the community alive. As family members, children have been cherished and included. In the present situation the church is no longer content to integrate children in an ad hoc manner. Rather, the children are focused upon as bearers of hope for the future of the Coptic Orthodox community in Egypt.

## Notes

1. Patriarch Shenouda III, cited by Barbara Watterson, *Coptic Egypt*, Edinburgh: Scottish Academic Press, 1988, 176.
2. See G. Coudougnan, *Nos Ancêtres les Pharaons...., L'Histoire Pharaonique et Copte dans les Manuels Scolaires Égyptiens* (Dossier du CEDEJ, Cairo: CEDEJ, 1988) on the presentation of Pharaonic, Coptic and Islamic history in Egyptian school books.
3. The interview was conducted during a nine month period of field work in Cairo in 1988/89. Information in this chapter is largely based upon this fieldwork which was carried out in a low-income neighborhood. Though residing in Cairo, several of the informants had strong links to rural Egypt. See: Nora Stene, "'Fordi Barn er som Engler...' En Religionshistorisk Studie av Barn i den Koptisk Ortodokse Kirke i Egypt. Ph.D; University of Oslo, 1991.
4. By "ritual," I understand any prescribed and formal behavior that has reference to the religious sphere. My definition is wide enough to cover the sacramental and liturgical rituals of the Coptic Church, as well as the rituals performed outside the church without the participation of priests.
5. The wash-basin prayers can be found in the liturgy book *Salawat al-Khidamat fi al-Kanisa al-Qibtiya al-Urthudhuksiya* (The prayers of the services of the Coptic Orthodox Church), Cairo: Maktabat al-Mahabba, undated.
6. It is conspicuous that several of the early writers that deal extensively with Christian seventh day rituals do not mention *salawat al-tisht*. This holds true for E.W. Lane, *The Manners and Customs of the Modern Egyptians*. (1836. Reprint. London: East-West Publications, 1981), E.L. Butcher, *The Story of the Church of Egypt*, (2 vols. London: Smith, Elder & Co., 1897), S.H. Leeder, *Modern Sons of the Pharaohs*. (1919. Reprint. New York: Arno Press, 1973), and W.S. Blackman, *The Fellahin of Upper Egypt. Their Religious, Social and Industrian Life today with Special References to Survivals from Ancient Times*. (London: George G. Harrap, 1927). It is possible that the ritual was seldom performed in their days. Interviewing Copts in villages in Upper Egypt, I was informed that the wash-basin prayers had recently been reintroduced to them by their relatives living in Cairo.
7. Boys are usually circumcized shortly after birth, girls at an older age, usually between 3 and 10,. On female circumcision in Egypt, see Andrea Rugh, *Family in Contemporary Egypt*, Cairo: A.U.C. Press, 1985, 160.
8. Coptic canon laws prohibits circumcision after baptism, though this is largely ignored today. On circumcision and the festival of saints, N. Biegman, *Egypt: Moulids Saints and Sufis*, London: Kegan Paul International, 1990, 23.
9. Bishop Ammonius was interviewed by the author on Febr. 13, 1989 in Luxor.
10. See G. Viaud, *Les Pèlerinages Coptes en Égypte*, (*D'après les Notes du Qommes Jacob Muyser*), Cairo: Bibliothèque d'Études Coptes, 1979, 76; on Coptic pilgrimages: "Des centaines d'enfants sont baptisés chaque jour du pèlerinage."

11. The birth of a boy gives 40 days of impurity, a girl 80 days, following Leviticus 12:1-5.
12. Today, the baptismal font is commonly found in the women's altar room, on the right-hand side of the church, to the east. Older churches have the font near the entrance, on the left-hand side, to the west. From the western side the heathen, unbaptized child should be brought into the church, which has its altar towards the east. Although this symbolism of the position of the font is well known to many Copts, it seems to have been discarded in favor of letting baptisms take place in the women's half of the church.
13. For further information on "children of promises," see N.H. Henein, *Mari Girgis: Village de Haute-Égypte*, Cairo: IFAO, 1988, 248.
14. See J. Muyser, "Surviviance de Tatouage Chrétien en Égypte," *Cahier Copte* 2 (1954) 11-23, and O. Meinardus, *Christian Egypt. Faith and Life*, Cairo: A.U.C. Press, 1970, 1-6
15. See Rugh, *Family*, and B. Thorbjørnsrud, "Messias Piker. En Analyse an Koptisk-Ortodoks Revitalisering i et Identitets Perspektiv." Ph.D. diss.: University of Oslo, 1989.
16. *Hanut* is a mixture of herbs, oil and spices used in yearly embalming ceremonies of the caskets where saints' relics are kept. The mixture is prayed over in church, and can usually be obtained in small quantities by laypeople at saints' festivals.
17. Girls are allowed into the *haikal* till the age of 12. This age limit is not usually explained by the onset of puberty, but by the venerated Orthodox tradition that the Virgin Mary lived in the Temple till she was 12 years old.
18. For earlier references to free movement of children in Coptic churches, see Leeder, *Modern Sons*, 171 and B. Watterson, *Coptic Egypt*, Edinburgh: Scottish Academic Press, 1988, 168.
19. I have observed children's liturgies in several parts of Cairo, as well as in Upper Egypt. The practice seems to have started in the latter half of the 1980s.
20. In the Coptic Church the Sacrament of the Anointment of the Sick can be administered to an individual, or it can be celebrated as a communal anointment of all the members of the congregation. This usually takes places in the fasting period leading up to Easter.
21. On this debate and the position of the Wafd-party, see B.L. Carter, *The Copts in Egyptian Politics, 1918-1952*, London: Croom Helm, 1986.
22. See Samir Murqus, "Tarikh Khidma Madaris al-Ahad wa atharuha al-Ta`limiya fi al-Fatra min 1900-1950," (The history of the Sunday schools and their educational basis from 1900-1950) *Majalla Madaris al-Ahad* 9 & 10, Cairo, 1984.
23. For example "firdaus" (the biblical word for Paradise) instead of "ganna" (the Qur'anic word for Paradise), and "salam lakum" instead of "salam `aleikum" (both phrases meaning "peace be with you").
24. See Rugh, *Family*.
25. Fieldwork of Thorbjørsrud (1989) and of Stene (1991).
26. The Coptic Synaxarion (Calendar of Saints) celebrates 15 different mother-martyrs, who died with their children.
27. The translation of the liturgies are taken from O.H.E. Burmester, *The Egyptian or Coptic Church, a Detailed Description of her Liturgical Services and the Rites and Ceremonies Observed in the Administration of her Sacraments*, Cairo: Société d'Archeologie Copte, 1967, 206-208. The number 144.000 refers to Revelation 14:1. According to Coptic tradition, the 144.000 are the children who were murdered by Herod in Bethlehem. They are considered martyrs by the church.
28. The marked difference between each category's funeral prayer becomes most apparent when directly compared to each other. Space does not allow this here,

but the reader is referred to the *"Salawat al-tajniz"* of the Coptic Church, English translation in Burmester, *The Egyptian or Coptic Church*.
29. See for example, A.U. Butler, *The Ancient Coptic Churches of Egypt*, 2 vol. Oxford, 1884, 291 :"Communicants are now very few, and for the most part children. Even little children receive (...). They walk round the altar, and continue receiving until all the wafer is consumed."
30. Children may be seen as *baraka* for a variety of reasons. They affirm their parents fertility, and give a much needed insurance for care in the future.
31. Quoted from "The History of the Patriarchs of the Coptic Church" in: Meinardus, *Christian Egypt*, 108 concerning the patriarchal elections in which an altar ballot was used, in the year 777.
32. "Folk-religious" refers to the fact that the ritual is marginal in relation to the doctrines and beliefs of the Coptic Church, and that it is believed mainly to be used by the lower social strata.
33. The liturgy of Abu Tarbu can be found in *Salawat al-Khadamat fi al-Kanisa Qibtiya al-Urthudhuksiya*, Cairo, undated. Although this ritual may not be common in Egypt today, it was observed in Cairo in 1988. The ministering priest also insisted that the afflicted was taken to a clinic for injections.
34. The information about the child saints is gathered from oral sources, as well as from the Coptic Synaxarion and smaller publications about the modern day saints. See M. and A. Bassilli, *The Life of the Great Saint Pope Kirellous VI*, London: St. Mark's Church, 1986, and *Dhikra al-Arba`in lil-Umm al-Qiddisa Martha*, Cairo, 1988. On the call to a monastic life during childhood, see P.A. van Doorn-Harder, *Contemporary Coptic Nuns*, Columbia, S.C.: University of South Carolina Press, 1995. It should be mentioned that Coptic monasteries no longer accept anyone under the age of 21.

Catherine Mayeur-Jaouen

# The Coptic Mouleds: Evolution of the Traditional Pilgrimages

## Description of a tradition

*Definition*
The precise meaning of the word *"mouled"* (from the Arabic *mawlid*, pronounced *muled* in Egyptian dialect) is "anniversary." It denotes the Egyptian form of pilgrimage to the tombs of the saints. Both the word and the tradition are common to Copts and Muslims.[1] Once a year, the mouled falls on the feast day of the saint, a day corresponding in principle to the date of his death or his martyrdom. This day is preceded by one or two weeks, sometimes a whole month, of diverse festivities which increase in number until they culminate in the last night, the famous "Great Night" *(al-layla al-kabira)*.

One must not confuse these mouleds with the pilgrimages of individuals or of parishes which are performed by the devout at any time in the course of the year. The Arabic language also distinguishes clearly between mouleds *(mawalid)* and visits to the tombs of the saints *(ziyarat)*. The Copts frequently use the word "excursion" *(rihla)* to designate parish pilgrimages.

The mouleds, unlike simple visits or pilgrimages, are characterized by a precise time and place, marked by a cyclic periodicity. In the exceptional cases of the Virgin Mary and St. George, several mouleds are celebrated in various places and at various dates, reflecting the importance and the popularity of these two patron saints of the Coptic Church. During the fast of the Virgin Mary (7-22 August), for example, the pilgrim can go to the different mouleds of Zeitun, Mostarod, Dronka, Bayad al-Nasara, and the like. The Virgin is also venerated by mouleds at other dates of the year, for example at Jabal al-Tayr before Ascension Day. Most of the other saints are venerated at only one place and one date.

All the Copts of Egypt are involved more or less closely in the mouleds, either by participating directly or because they have an indirect experience of the mouleds because they live near a pilgrimage site, or because of what others have told them. According to the place one lives and the family traditions of piety, one will tend to take part in one or other mouled.

The mouled is an integral part of the peasants' life, who celebrate several mouleds each year.[2] Often it represents the only genuine distraction possible to them. People from the towns often content themselves with a single annual pilgrimage, as close as possible to their town or neighborhood. But the parish excursions by bus allow the pious to become acquainted with a distant place of pilgrimage, too, so that the Copts possess a good knowledge of the religious geography of Christian Egypt, with its principal monasteries and its oldest churches, to say nothing of the supposed map of the Holy Family's journeyings when they were in exile in Egypt. Several places of pilgrimage, especially in Upper Egypt, are linked to the stay of the Holy Family in Egypt: at Jabal al-Tayr opposite Samalut, and at Deir al-Muharraq near Assiyut, two enormous mouleds commemorate the itinerary of the divine Child.[3]

The scale varies from a simple church surrounded by an enclosure to a gigantic monastery with fortified walls. Similarly, there are many different kinds of places: desert monasteries, countryside convents or urban parishes; finally, the sites often occupy two privileged positions, the banks of the Nile (as at Mit Damsis or Biba), and the sacred mountain (as at Dronka south of Assiyut, or at Manfalut).

There can be no doubt that the most important Coptic mouled today is that of St George at Riziqat near Luxor, from 10-16 November (1 to 7 Hâtur).[4] The Muslim tattooers who officiate there – well informed witnesses who surely cannot be suspected of partiality – readily assure us that not even the Muslim mouled of Tanta, where a million people come together, is as large as that of Riziqat. The other great mouleds are those which draw people from the whole country: that of the Virgin at Dronka near Assiyut (7-22 August), of St. George at Mit Damsis in the Delta (22-29 August), and finally St. Dimyanah near Bilqas in May. The other mouleds, sometimes of considerable dimensions, have only a regional reputation, such as the various mouleds of the Virgin or St. George, mouleds of Anba Shenouda and Anba Bishoy near Sohaj, and of Aba Nub at Samannud. There are also local mouleds which involve only one village or neighborhood.

The Nile Valley and the Delta are two distinct catchment areas that draw numerous pilgrims to the mouleds, but Cairo, where so many Copts live, is an important place of redistribution of piety. For example, Copts who come from Minya and live in the capital will certainly remain faithful to the mouleds of the region from which they come, but now they will also know the places of pilgrimage in Cairo and will perhaps have the opportunity to discover the great Coptic mouleds of the Delta, thanks to the activities of their parish or through relatives whom they meet in Cairo.

It is difficult to estimate the number of pilgrims; only those who remain in the same place for the whole duration of the mouled can be tallied with precision: but these are the minority, since most only make a passing visit, or content themselves with camping out during the last two days. At Bayad al-Nasara, a mouled of medium importance, ten thousand pilgrims have been counted. A rough estimate puts the number of persons gathered at one time at Dronka between 50 and 100,000 on the last day and the last night, but the comings and going of the pilgrims during the preceding fortnight may represent several hundreds of thousands of persons. It would be necessary to establish in detail what proportion of the visitors come several times or only once, how many spend a night, etc., but even the Coptic clergy itself can give only approximate estimates here.

## Characteristics of the Coptic mouleds

In some cases, the mouled is the feast of the patron saint of the village, when this is entirely or mostly Coptic, and then it is purely a feast for the local patron saint in which all the Coptic inhabitants participate; the rich often use the occasion of this feast to give alms and food to the poor. Following the Coptic calendar, the mouleds also fall on fixed dates, reflecting the rhythm of the seasons and the events of the agricultural process: in the village of Mari Jirjis, in Middle Egypt, the feast of the archangel Michael falls on 12 Ba`una and coincides with the beginning of the inundation, the feast of the harvest and the threshing of the barley.[5]

Most often, the followers of the saint do not live in the same place as the mouled, but must travel to get there. This journey, sometimes difficult and often expensive, is an important aspect of the mouleds. When the pilgrims come from the neighboring village on foot or on the back of a donkey, or come in a bus from a more distant town, they discover new paths and regions, sometimes renewing their ties to the countryside from which they originally come. Thus, the Copts perceive the Egyptian spatial dimension in their own way, finding the main Christian places there as havens of refuge and stopping places on their route.

It costs a great deal to rent a taxi or take a bus, and this is one of the highest expenses that the pilgrim must accept if he/she is to carry out a pilgrimage. In 1992, for example, it cost 140 pounds to rent a taxi for the return journey from Cairo and Mit Damsis. The expenses are reduced when the group shares the cost, but the pilgrims are not at the end of their troubles when they arrive at their goal. At Mit Damsis they must rent boats to cross the Nile, then take minibuses which lead to the twin pilgrimage sites of Sunbat: this all means several pounds more per person. Boatmen and taxi-drivers are almost always Muslims who have specialized in the Coptic mouleds. They wait for the cyclic return of the feasts and know their itineraries perfectly.

Sometimes, but rarely, the Coptic owner of a car or a lorry decides to take pilgrims to the mouled for free: this gesture is considered as an offering to the saint whose pilgrimage is being celebrated.[6]

When they have arrived, the pilgrims find a place to stay. Many Copts take part in the mouled as non-residents or merchants who run refreshment rooms, bookshops or stalls selling pious objects. In that case they pay taxes to the convent around which they are operating. Several kinds of lodging are envisaged for the crowd of pilgrims: they can rent houses or convent apartments reserved for them, or else, if they are poorer or more rural, they are content to set up their tents and spend the long nights of the mouled under the stars.

Other Coptic pilgrims – the majority – limit themselves to "visiting" the saint for an afternoon or a night in the period which is suited for doing what one has vowed (*nadhr*, plural *nudhur*) and giving ex-votos. The Coptic populace of the nearby town comes to seek recreation in an excursion which is both pious and entertaining. The family comes with children; engaged couples come; groups of friends and neighbors sometimes join in. In the course of the day, catechism classes may come to visit the church under the strict guidance of Coptic teachers. The evening and the night belong rather to young people, especially to the young men who are looking for a good time.

The Coptic mouled, like the Muslim mouled, is in fact the occasion for outdoor festivities which offer the pilgrims playgrounds, firing ranges, various games and stalls of every kind. The careless observer may think that many of these activities or even these rites are more profane than religious, but one must emphasize that this distinction does not exist in the pilgrim's spirit: for the followers of popular religion, buying a toy for a child at the mouled is just as much a *baraka* (something that brings a blessing) as the purchase of a rosary or a pious image. Although the fair is considered by today's clergy as something "profane," the pilgrims do not dissociate it from the rest of the activities they are offered.

The mouled is a totality where the soul and the body, the spirit and the senses must receive their due. As in the feasts for patron saints of medieval

Europe, devotion to the saint does not contradict the distractions of the world, and a successful mouled essentially involves having visited all the tricks on display, or having bought some sweets.

What does the pilgrim do at the mouled? He may be content with a short visit to the holy place, a prayer in the church, or buying a blessed loaf (*qurban*, which cost 15 piastres in 1991 and 25 in 1992). Where the possibility exists, he may buy holy water in a goblet, as at Mostarod, taking a good supply of this water in bottles brought specifically for this purpose. When the water from the miraculous spring is brought home, it is used as a source of healing.

In the church or the saint's tomb, the crowd visits all the icons, without forgetting any of them, and presses against the iron grille, which prevents access to a chapel, or against the iconostasis: touching it is an essential part of the pilgrim's visit, for the objects that can bring the *baraka* must be touched as long as possible. This is often accompanied by murmuring a prayer or a plea.

Candles play an important role, though diminished since electricity was introduced. It costs 10 piasters to buy a little candle. Despite repeated prohibitions, many pilgrims use the moist wax to write their names and their wishes, and often a date, on the glass walls that protect the holy icons. Others slip a note with their wish and their prayer into a chink in the frame of the icon. In the specific case of the mouled of Sunbat, a copper dome of about two meters encloses the relics of the saints who are venerated; at the top of the dome, at the average height of a man, there is a specially arranged slit to receive the little notes with ardent pleas which rain down on the relics.

The indirect relic is another pious souvenir of a successful mouled: traditionally, the pilgrims rub a scarf or veil against the tomb of the saint, and take this home in the hope of miracles. In some mouleds, the imagination and the organization of the clergy have taken over from these individual practices: at Samannud, for example, plastic sachets containing cotton are distributed to the pilgrims free of charge; this cotton is dipped in the oil which has come from the bones of the martyr Aba Nub, using a technique that was known in Europe during the Middle Ages. In Sunbat, scraps of the red shroud of St. Rifqa are distributed in similar little sachets. Since this shroud is changed each year, the number of the relics that are obtained is considerable.

After the visit, one goes round the fair and may make some purchases before going on to the important phase of the picnic for which the family has brought food and drink, unless it desires to buy food on the spot. Eating near a holy place, a tomb, or a church, is an essential rite in the Coptic mouled. No one takes part in a mouled without at least eating a piece of bread. One is enjoying the hospitality of the saint: partaking of food at the wayside or within the shade of the convent becomes a real rite of *baraka*. Many pilgrims buy the traditional chick-pea paste (*hommos*) or sweets (*halawa*) which are taken home from the mouleds as a souvenir full of blessing. The children who are newly baptized or circumcised during the mouleds have the right to receive toys.

People from the countryside make greater purchases at the big mouleds, which sometimes fulfill the functions of markets for them: earthenware for daily use, clothes, flutes, tambourines. Those who sleep there make use of the markets of fruit and vegetables which always are set up near the mouleds. Many people also go to mobile cafes, merchants of tea and water-bearers.

*Vows*
Vows play a considerable role in the mouled, since the time of the mouled is the most propitious for addressing a request to the saint and having recourse to his or her intercession. Most of the wishes expressed concern the birth of children and the healing of illnesses. Women who want children, single persons who want to get married, sick people looking for healing, students who want to pass their exams: all turn to the saints. Some saints and some mouleds have specialties, especially St. George at Mit Damsis, under whose auspices the priests healed possessed people in the course of impressive ceremonies of exorcism.[7] If the pilgrim favored by destiny has no particular vow to express (and this is very seldom the case), he will not disdain the blessed liquid, the *baraka*, which suffuses the mouled. No matter how high the spiritual elevation may be that is attained in the pilgrimage, culminating in enthusiastic masses and processions, the pilgrims are always interested: the relationship between the saint and the pilgrim constitutes an exchange of mutual giving.

If a vow has been made to the saint in the course of the year and one's prayer has been heard, one promises to repay the debt to him or her: literally, one says that one "owes" a vow to the saint (*lu nadhr `aleyya*). The poorest slip a little note of 25 piasters or a pound into the coffer which stands ready to receive this (*sanduq*). Others bring candles, and the richest or most devout bring a goat, a sheep, a cow or even a buffalo to be slaughtered at the mouled. These sacrificial vows (*nudhur*, pronounced *nudur* in dialect) are also called "victims" (*dhaba'ih*). If the meat of the slaughtered animals is sold, the price is given to the "Committee of the vows" or more simply to the priest who has the task of distributing alms; the meat is distributed free of charge or at a low price to the pilgrims. The mouleds are unique occasions for the poorest people to eat meat. At Dronka, the best organized of all the mouleds in Egypt, a special corner is reserved for the butcher's shop, which is a veritable slaughterhouse; elsewhere, "Committees of the vows" await the pilgrim who is willing to spend large sums or give other gifts in kind.

## Membership of a Christian community

The mouled is not only the occasion to express the fears and hopes of the individual; it is a collective experience and the occasion for renewing the signs of membership in the Christian community.

If a child has been born recently, its family takes the propitious occasion of the mouled to have it baptized. At Jabal al-Tayr, near Minya, the clergy estimate that about one thousand children are baptized each mouled, at the time of Ascension Day. The gigantic size of the new baptistery inaugurated in 1988 is sufficient proof that this affirmation is not excessive: six deep vats have been laid out there. The baptisms are carried out in relays, without any delays, by vigorous monks; each baptism lasts less than ten seconds. In the rural mouleds, one can note how old the children are at baptism – at least six months, and often from twelve to eighteen months – as well as the often puny condition of the children who are baptized.

One interesting detail is that one of the baptismal vats in Jabal al-Tayr is filled with unconsecrated water. It is for Muslims who come here to immerse their child when they are afraid of the child dying when it is young. This imitation of Christian baptism carried out by Muslims to obtain the *baraka* was already noted (and denounced) in the thirteenth century by the Hanbalite Ibn Taymiyya.[8] Traditionally, in the villages of Upper and Middle Egypt, the priest was regarded as a sorcerer and the Christian rites (especially those of Holy Week) as magic rites, so that the Coptic mouleds were the handy occasion for acquiring the *baraka*. Although the presence of Copts at the Muslim mouleds has always been rare or even non-existent, thanks to a minority reflex which is easy to understand, there is plenty of evidence that Muslims have regularly attended the Coptic mouleds.

Another *rite de passage*, circumcision for boys (*tahara*) and very often excision for girls (*khitan*), is carried out in the clinics or laboratories which are discreet but very active, and sometimes in private houses.

The Coptic mouleds, to a greater extent than the Muslim mouleds, constitute an important encounter among faithful. This, above all, is the place for meetings (even if only at a superficial level) between Copts of different regions, of different social classes and from different backgrounds: elegant ladies from the cities in printed gowns, peasant women badly dressed with silver rings squeezing their ankles and weighing them down, country people in the *jalabiyya*, civil servants in three-piece suits, young people in jeans and gaudy shirts, children at the breast. Mostly, these people only cross each other's paths, but they display their common membership in the same community.

The description which we have just given of the Coptic mouleds insists intentionally on the constitutive traits of the mouled, the things that seem least variable. The mouleds are the bearers of important traditions, some of which go back to the most distant past of Christian Egypt. Many observers, often including the Copts themselves, are convinced that nothing has changed or changes in the Coptic mouleds. The weight of the past seems to dominate popular religion. Nevertheless, the Coptic mouleds do change.

## Changes in the Coptic mouleds

Like the Muslim mouleds, and for reasons that are partly identical, the Coptic mouleds are experiencing a genuine reform. Many characteristics indicate a profound transformation, which began in the 1950s with the modernization of Egypt, that is far from completed today.[9]

*New developments and the restored equilibrium*
First of all, we find new cults which have come to rekindle the memory of older saints: the veneration of the crowds for the patriarch Kyrillos VI, who died in 1971, reawakens the veneration for the Roman soldier beside whom he was buried, Mari Mina, who once was the center of the most celebrated pilgrimage of antiquity.[10] The popularity of Abuna Fanous makes the crowds flock to the monastery of St. Paul, imitating the recent phenomenon at the rival convent of St. Anthony where the monk Abuna Yustus al-Antuni, who died in 1976, has become the object of a cult.[11]

But new mouleds have not been created in these last years, although many churches organize small local mouleds with a very restricted audience. On the other hand, the churches try to launch anew places of pilgrimage which have fallen into desuetude, such as that of Deir al-Janadla recently, where a little pilgrimage to the Virgin seeks to imitate that of Dronka.[12]

The only big mouled launched in the past twenty years is that of Our Lady of Zeitun, created on the site of the apparitions of the Virgin Mary in 1968 in this quarter to the north of Cairo.[13] The apparitions of the Virgin of Shobra at Cairo in 1986 have not awakened the same fervor, nor a pilgrimage.

Rather, one can see that an equilibrium is being restored: Jacob Muyser presented the pilgrimage of Anba Shenouda at Suhaj as the greatest in the Nile Valley in the first half of the twentieth century,[14] but this has been dethroned today by those of Dronka and Riziqat. Although the site of Dronka, a church in a grotto carved out in a quarry during Ptolemaic epoch, is very ancient and is held to be one of the stopping places of the Holy Family in Egypt, it has not always had the size it has today. It was re-initiated by the Catholic Copts and then by the Coptic Orthodox diocese, and Dronka has become a center among pilgrimages of the Nile Valley. From 1955 onwards, churches and convents and hospices for pilgrims have multiplied on the side of the cliff, disfiguring one of the most beautiful pilgrimage sites of Egypt with masses of cement. This extreme modernization of the mouled has nevertheless permitted a growth which the mouleds that are more deeply anchored in tradition find difficult to sustain.

*Modernization of life-style*

The modernization of life-style, which is an important factor in the changes that take place in the mouled, is not specific to the Copts alone; like their Muslim compatriots, they have seen in the course of a few years an uncontrolled demographic expansion, a tremendous urbanization, the development of villages into market towns or cities, and greatly increased access to commerce. Roads have improved. Traditional crafts gradually yield to manufactured products. The money sent by those who have left for Europe or North America to try their luck revolutionizes the way of life of those who stay behind. There is no longer any Coptic village, no matter how isolated, that has escaped these transformations.

The increasing proportion of city dwellers in the Egyptian population has its effect on those who take part in the mouled. Many visitors no longer accept the somewhat rudimentary conditions of the village pilgrims who come and pitch their tents in the shadow of the saint; they demand a certain comfort, and want to avoid mixing with the common people. Pilgrimage houses in durable materials have been built more or less everywhere to provide places for them to stay during the mouled. At the mouled of

Barsoum al-`Aryan, once located in a village and today drowned in an industrial suburb of Cairo at Ma`sara, the pilgrims take up residence for one or two months in perfectly ordered apartments where they bring a gas cooker and a refrigerator. Nor is it rare to see televisions under the tents of the pilgrims at Mit Damsis or St. Dimyanah.

Greater demands are made in the area of hygiene, concerning toilets and the slaughter of the sacrificed animals. In the past thirty years, the great centers of mouleds everywhere have had to install clinics where the pilgrims can be taken care of, and to provide ambulances.

It is indeed true that the great fields of tents at St. Dimyanah, Riziqat or Mit Damsis remain the preserve of the rural populations, who continue to flock in enormous numbers to the mouleds. But at last there is a movement which gradually separates peasants from city dwellers. We see a real spatial demarcation among the pilgrims at one and the same mouled. This is especially the case at Dronka where the village itself, on the outskirts of cultivated land, gives shelter to the fair and the tents, while the churches and convents protected by their walls on the sacred heights give shelter only to spiritual activities and guest-houses built of durable materials. Thus, within the same mouled two different spatial dimensions are marked out, rejecting the peasants in the mouled below in order to arrange the mouled above for the city dwellers. Not all communication is cut off, of course, and the peasants go to the masses in the grotto, just as the city dwellers do not disdain to walk down to the feast; but even an observer who knows little of the background will notice at once the different public in the two spaces.

Sometimes, the social differentiation of the mouleds is not something operating within one mouled, but between different mouleds, depending on whether they take place in the town or the countryside, or within one and the same town, in one neighborhood or another. Thus, the Virgin has two mouleds in Cairo on the same date: that of Mostarod concerns mostly recent emigrants from the countryside to the city, and the path to it is dusty and scarcely paved, along a stinking canal in a no-man's-land between the suburb and the countryside. At Zeitun, on the other hand, the completely new church is next door to the subway station in a more urban and more modern quarter which is less frequented by the common people.

## Clerical culture versus popular culture

The present evolution of the Coptic mouleds is not due only to the inevitable social differentiation imposed by the socio-economic transformations of Egypt today; it is equally due to a genuine explosion of popular Egyptian culture. A thousand traits of popular life, in the country and also in the towns, have been breached by modernization today, and even more by the contempt in which the popular culture is now held. On the part of some pilgrims, but especially of the clergy, a puritanism hardly known before is in place, and a growing censorship tries to check all the specifically popular manifestations of the mouleds.

It must be insisted that these changes are not peculiar to the Copts; the Muslim mouleds are prey to the same suspicions. Frequent articles in the semi-official Islamic press demand their suppression, denounce hypothetical abuses (usually of a sexual nature) and go so far as to accuse the mouleds of being anti-Islamic and of reflecting the crudest kind of paganism. This is the effect of Muslim reformism and Islamism which affects the entire educated and urbanized population to a greater or lesser extent. The effect of this propaganda has been to restrict the Muslim mouleds to the poor, the country dwellers and the illiterate.

The Coptic clergy cannot allow itself to make this kind of exclusion; the minority's need of unity is too great to permit dissensions that would result from anathematizing a praxis which is so useful in vivifying the faith of the pilgrims, molding together the ranks of the community, and filling the coffers of the dioceses. A major difference from reformist Islam is that the Coptic Church today does not make use of any religious argument which would make pilgrimages to the tombs of the saints illicit: the Christian tradition has no difficulty in admitting the cult of the saints, and in fact encourages it. On every other point, however, the clergy follows the attitude of the moderate Muslim intelligentsia: the mouleds can be kept, but they must be reformed by extirpating those aspects now considered blameful and by imposing the most rigorous control possible, insisting on the specifically religious part of the mouled and excluding as far as feasible all the "profane" aspects.

The evolution of the external feasts permits us to make these observations still more precise. The external feasts certainly remain an integral part of the mouled. Children and adults appreciate the feats of horsemanship or of balancing, the shooting galleries or the exercises where one must display one's skill. But these innocent activities are all being transformed. This is assuredly the aspect of the mouleds which has changed most in the course of the twentieth century, especially in the last thirty years.

One must not stop short at the superficial novelties – one notes, for example, that the children's toys sold in the mouleds are mostly now made of plastic, balloons or horses on wheels, miniature revolvers and Ninja turtles imported from the Far East, T-shirts with a logo in English. The sellers of drinks tend to offer video games as an attraction, costing ten piasters for the amusement.

But other changes go much further and prove that the popular tradition, once breached, is the victim of a genuine censorship. The belly dancers who made the evenings of the mouleds at Mit Damsis and Sunbat thirty years ago have disappeared; and the boats where parties were held during the night on the Nile at Mit Damsis as recently as 1950 are now inspected as soon as night falls. The shadow theater of the nineteenth century and the puppet shows have finished – foreign observers have always pointed out their crude and often obscene character – and the dancing horses have become ever rarer. The same kinds of change would be seen in the Muslim mouleds, due to the same concern for order and decency.

Were there ever itinerant Christian singers such as one still finds in the Muslim mouleds?[15] It is probable that they did once exist, and have disappeared; for who else would have composed and transmitted the numerous traditional ballads that relate the legends of the saints? The cassettes broadcast by microphone in the mouleds take their place today, but the change of content is very great! The sermons of the patriarch and the psalms of the parish have taken the place of the legends of the saints, which captivated their audience with their miraculous contents. They were very popular, especially in their musical expression and their use of the dialect. The pilgrims no doubt continue to sing hymns in honor of St. George, but the practice is decreasing. Other traditional amusements have disappeared, such as the eggs painted in yellow or cherry red, with which people played during the mouleds.[16]

The Coptic clergy is particularly careful to avoid all misunderstanding and to make no compromises with a tradition which is too popular and not approved of by the official church. The Coptic Church does need mass assemblies to assert its presence and its power and to sew together the bonds of the community, but it wants to control the way these take place. In the last ten years, the fields of tents and the external feasts have been strictly dissociated from enclosures of the convents.

At Ma'sara, the hawkers have even been pushed outside the enclosure of the convent of Barsoum al-'Aryan to the banks of a stinking canal. However, the organizers of the mouleds – essentially, the dioceses – receive considerable sums from their taxation of tents and barracks, hawkers and peddlers. But the general tone in Egypt is that of a growing puritanism, and the Coptic clergy does not want to be left behind by the Muslim intelligentsia which for its part denounces the Muslim mouleds under pressure from pervasive islamism.

The tattooers are one of the last corporations linked to the mouled which have survived this wave of censorship and modernization. The observation of their activities allows us some useful reflections on this popular culture which is in the process of disappearing.

It is well know that the Copts choose the privileged time of the mouled to have a little cross tattooed on the inside of the right wrist. The Christian stigmata, tattooed in thirty seconds with the help of an electric needle, does not cost more than fifty piasters. One hears from a distance the crackling of the apparatus and the crying of children: this is the corner of the tattooers, mostly Muslims, who await their clients by the dozen, showing small oil-paintings on glass which serve as models. We find popular motifs (the lion brandishing a sword, the serpent, the dancing woman, the bird) that are found equally in the Muslim mouleds, but we also find specifically Christian representations, crosses in various sizes, Christ on the cross, and the chief saints, especially St. George crushing the dragon.

In today's Egypt, where the gulf between the religions is continually growing, it is surprising to see Muslims tattooing small crosses on the little wrists of so many children. In the same way, the mixture of Christian and Muslim themes, religious and profane themes, disconcerts the external observer. But the mass of pilgrims finds the mixture of images perfectly normal. The tattooers, like the belly dancers or the comic actors of all kinds, know no confessional frontiers. The popular culture in Egypt has mixed Copts and Muslims together for a long time within the framework of the same references. The universe of the village was doubtless not idyllic, but the relations between the two communities were ritualized.

All this has not completely disappeared, as we see from the baptism of Muslim children in the Coptic baptisteries and the little crosses tattooed by the Muslims at the fair. It is still possible to write an ethnographic study of Coptic children which would be directly relevant to the whole of Egypt's peasantry. But this popular culture, which united Copts and Muslims within common references, is fragmenting more and more, so that the dissensions between the two communities become greater. The elites of both communities, Muslim thinkers or Coptic clerics, reject the forms of this culture and its disturbing spontaneity.

In the past, this cultural community which found expression above all in the mouleds was something felt by everyone, and the anthropologist Winifred Blackman could note in 1948 that the Muslims came to the mouled of St. George in Middle Egypt in numbers equal to the Copts.[17] This is no longer the case, and even if some Muslim women, in general mothers who are anxious before giving birth to their first child, go so far as to have recourse to the *baraka* of the Coptic saints, they represent an infinitesimal minority among the flood of the Christian pilgrims.

## The mouleds under increasing control

The Coptic mouleds, as a factor of potential social tensions, are the object of an increasing surveillance by the police or even by the army. Police busses are stationed at the entrance to the field where the mouled is held, while informers in civil clothes or mounted policemen comb the mouled to make sure that no disturbance and nothing suspicious disturbs the peace of the pilgrims. This police control, which exists equally in the Muslim mouleds, has a double object: it aims first to avoid the excesses inherent to the movements of the crowd, and which are reputed to be an inherent part of the mouleds (thefts, drunkenness, quarrels, prostitution, and sexual license). Likewise, the police presence claims to be defending the Copts against potential Islamist aggression, especially in Middle Egypt where interreligious clashes have increased in number after the events Minya in 1990 and then at Sanabo near Dayrut in 1992.

## Clericalization of the activities

The Coptic clergy plays a major role in the reform that has been undertaken. It tries to take hold of the phenomenon of the mouled and deprive it of some of its constitutive traits. Thus, the very term *mouled* is rejected by the priests, who wage a campaign on behalf of the less popular and more suitable terms *ihtifal* (official feast) or *tidhkar* (ceremony in memory of a saint). But the faithful continue to use the word mouled, a tangible sign of the limits of the reform.

The clerics attempt systematically to give a religious and moralizing turn to the amusements offered: for a modest sum one can enter tea-rooms where television screens continuously project edifying films about the lives of the saints and the patriarchs, as well as an American film about the life of Jesus, dubbed in literary Arabic. Although these contractions have not been a great success, they have in fact replaced others.

The entrance to the sanctuaries, previously practiced pell-mell, is more and more subject to regulations. The convents and the churches are closed for a part of the night, although they were open all the time in the past. Men and women are separated into organized lines to descend to the spring of Mostarod: the aim is to avoid all disturbing mingling of people, all dubious thronging together in the places of worship. Young men and young women equipped with armlets and scarves volunteer to help organize. At Dronka, special badges identify these volunteers who have the task of maintaining order, taking charge of the parking of cars and of the sale of food. Immense armies of scouts work under the aegis of the clergy to regulate the flow of the crowds and to direct the energies (supposed to be disordered) of the pilgrim mass.

The clergy also make use of the mouled to impose its own version of history, distributing gratis brief brochures which tell about the life of the saint venerated at the mouled and his or her miracles, or else the history of the sacred place. The city dwellers and those who are "educated," those who know how to read, get a supply of pious biographies, of cassette recordings of masses and psalms. All, whether illiterate or university educated, acquire pious objects – the inflation of religious trumpery (what would be called *bondieuseries* at Lourdes) is a striking sign of the contemporary changes. Various pictures of a Christ in the style of St. Sulpice, generally suffering, are offered in the form of icons or calendars. The Virgin and Child adorn handkerchiefs and scarves with the name of the monastery or the church visited. The Virgin with Child, St. George and his dragon, Mari Mina and his two camels, are the saints most frequently portrayed. The picture of Aba Nub, the child martyr of Samannud, has grown in popularity in the past few years. The veneration of the holy patriarch Kyrillos VI, who died in 1971, has an even more spectacular success.[18]

## The precarious unanimity of a Coptic world

Despite the growing dissensions, the mouled has become the time when the presence of a Christian world is manifested with fervent unanimity. The Muslims, once so numerous at the Coptic mouleds, are becoming rare. The clericalization of the rites leaves no place for them, but points, on the contrary, to the aim of reconstituting a Coptic Egypt, mythically smooth and intact. Within the courtyard of the church, within the enclosure of the convent, the faithful can still sing the psalms at the top of their voice, the microphones amplify prayers and litanies, the processions with icons are demonstrative. For once, the Coptic Church manifests its fervor and its religiosity publicly and ostentatiously.

The concerns of the present day are discussed aloud, the pilgrims enjoying the respite – so rare for the community – of finding themselves in the midst of thousands, tens of thousands, of fellow believers. The great Coptic mouleds are a manifestation of power and of unity which reflects the dream of a Coptic world that would be strewn with churches and crosses in neon light, administered by holy bishops, holy priests and holy monks. Even the smallest Coptic mouleds reproduce in miniature the atmosphere of the autonomous monastic cell.

The Coptic mouleds, like the Muslim mouleds, were once occasions for amusements and the expression of popular religiosity for peasants who often lived in isolated villages. Today, the horizons have been changed by the urbanization of life-styles, the improvement of transport by road, at a time when the interreligious tensions are increasing and the clergy has undertaken a systematic enrollment of young people in the last twenty years, making enormous efforts to train them.

It is certainly difficult to know what echo these different changes find in the pilgrims. The educated city dwellers are assuredly sensitive to these efforts and encourage them, but the country dwellers are not equally touched by the way the clergy has taken charge: they are frequently illiterate and cannot read the saints' lives which are distributed nor understand the commentary on a religious film in literary Arabic. They come in great faith and continue to practice ancient rites, living in tents and sacrificing animals. It is they who give the mouled its most remarkable vitality and its particular flavor. The Christian peasants continue to form the great battalions of the Coptic mouleds, but now an important part of the feast escapes them; the traditional mouleds are being profoundly reformed, and if they are maintained and even encouraged by the clergy, then this is so they can serve as a resource for a community anxious about its future.

## Notes

1. The existing bibliography about the Coptic mouleds remains rather poor. The only general work is by Gérard Viaud, *Les Pèlerinages Coptes en Egypte*, Cairo: IFAO, 1979 (120 pp.), which refers to a brief earlier bibliography; drawn up according to notes by *qommos* Jacob Muyser who died in 1956, the work has gaps, and in particular, it is beginning to be remarkably dated. It is nevertheless the only existing catalogue of the Coptic mouleds of Egypt, with maps and a calendar. The work is unfinished, lacking the synthesis which Muyser no doubt intended to write. Very fine photographs of the mouleds of Barsoum al-`Aryan,

Jabal al-Tayr and St. Damyanah can be found in Nicolaas H. Biegman, *Egypt: Moulids, Saints, Sufis.* London: Kegan Paul International, 1990 (175 pp.) (Dutch ed.: SDU, The Hague, 1990). But as its title indicates, this book refers primarily to the Muslim mouleds. As for J.W. McPherson, *The Moulids of Egypt, Egyptian Saints' Days* (1941, 351 pp.), obviously now a very old work, it is essentially devoted to the Muslim mouleds and mentions only the mouled of Mostarod.
2. Nessim Henry Henein, *Mari Girgis, Village de Haute-Egypte,* Cairo: IFAO, 1988, 251-252. This monograph about an entirely Coptic Egyptian village which has grown up under the shade of a convent gives a rapid but precise description of the mouleds attended by the peasants of the entirely Coptic village of Mari Girgis near Akhmim. The inhabitants celebrate three mouleds in the village itself, and go out to two others, including that of Anba Shenouda near Sohaj.
3. It is rather probable that the very ancient churches which occupied these sites were dedicated in primitive times to less prestigious Coptic saints whom the Virgin Mary has replaced, in order to affirm vis-à-vis the conquering Islam how ancient this chosen land was. The thesis which Ramez Boutros is currently writing will no doubt allow a better knowledge of the site of Jabal al-Tayr.
4. G. Viaud, *Les Pèlerinages,* 62. only devotes three lines to it, and calls the village Damaqrat.
5. Nessim Henry Henein, *Mari Girgis,* 252.
6. A recent incident near Damanhour has shown the risks which the pilgrims run at present. A small lorry from Damanhour in the Delta was getting ready to leave for the pilgrimage of Dronka in summer 1992, when the driver and his passengers were violently seized by Muslim extremists who were resolved to prevent the pilgrims from leaving. The police had to intervene and make the lorry take a roundabout route.
7. These ceremonies have been described and even photographed by G. Viaud, *Magie et Coutumes Populaires chez les Coptes d'Egypte,* Sisteron: Editions Présence, 1978. One may also consult the old but still useful articles by Elie Sidawi, "Le Mouled d'Abou Guerg," *Revue du Monde égytien,* I (1921), 146-152 and 225-234.
8. Muhammad Ummar Memon, *Ibn Taimiya's Struggle against Popular Religion,* The Hague and Paris: Mouton, 1976, 3.
9. Sidawi, "Les manifestations religieuses de l'Egypte moderne," *Anthropos XVIII – XIV,* (1923 – 1924) 283. Sidawi already observed that the mouleds at his time featured less shocking types of entertainment than the mouleds of the nineteenth century.
10. C. Pierre Maraval, *Lieux saints et Pelerinages d'Orient,* Paris: Le Cerf, 1985, 83.
11. Born in 1935, Abuna Fanous, a holy monk and wonder-worker, has enjoyed an exceptional reputation for several years now, despite the reluctance of the diocese, which exiled him for a time to Bush, near Beni Suef. There already exists an abundant bibliography about Yustus, including articles in European languages, which are usually plagiarized from the Arabic biography, *Al-Qiddis Yustus al-Antuni*: Abna' al-Baba Kirillus al-Sadis (ed.), Cairo, 1988.
12. G. Viaud, *Les Pèlerinages,* 55, already noted this earlier on. But it is only about ten years since the restoration of the convent, and the propaganda effort on behalf of the pilgrimage proves that attendance there is still very modest.
13. Cf. *Le Monde Copte 1,* 28-32, and Michel Nil, *Les Apparitions de la Vierge en Egypte, 1968 – 1969,* Paris: Téqui, 1980.
14. G. Viaud, *Les Pèlerinages,* 56.
15. Pierre Cachia is astonished that he did not meet any in the course of his research into the popular ballads in Egypt, but he notes the very large number of biblical legends transmitted in the patrimony of the Muslim singers at the mouleds:

*Popular narrative Ballads of Modern Egypt*, Oxford: Clarendon Press, 1989, 17.
16. Mentioned by W. Blackman, *Les fellahs de la Haute-Egypte*, Paris: Payot, 220. These painted eggs still circulate at Easter, but outside the mouled. Some of them are even found in bakeries run by Muslims in Cairo. This confessional mixture is always evidence of a very ancient practice.
17. Ibid., 223. The visits to Upper Egypt which gave rise to this testimony were made in the 1920s. In the case of the mouled of St. George, Blackman notes the abundance of horse races and carrousels, which (as far as I know) have totally disappeared today from the Coptic mouleds. She also alludes to rather reprehensible spectacles; here too, one would look in vain for a shocking scene in the mouleds which are now controlled both by the police and by the clergy.
18. In both cases, it seems that we have a reaction to the rise of fundamentalist Islam and to the pressures which the Copts feel more and more strongly. Aba Nub is the incarnation of the innocent martyr, and one hears of numerous tales of miracles which show that the Roman executioner is easily seen in the guise of a Muslim persecutor. As for Kyrillos, he is the incarnation of strong Coptic power which knew how to stand up against political power – in this case, to Nasser – and defend the interests of his community.

Nelly van Doorn-Harder

# Kyrillos VI (1902-1971): Planner, Patriarch and Saint

## Introduction: Coptic memories

"They [the Copts] felt like sons when they were in his presence."[1] These were some of the many lofty words that were spoken during the commemoration ceremony that is customarily held forty days after a person passes away. Many Copts felt orphaned because, for them, Patriarch Kyrillos had fulfilled the role of a father. Members of his flock daily thronged into his residence in order to seek his advice, blessing or consolation. According to the Copts, there was nothing he deemed insignificant. Copts like the story of the simple farming woman who once gave Kyrillos three eggs while he was celebrating a service. She said "Take these oh sayyidna and bless me." Kyrillos asked her "Are they well cooked? So that they won't soak my pocket?" Hereupon he put the eggs in his pocket and gave the woman his blessing.[2]

In his book about the Copts (1963) Edward Wakin comments on Kyrillos' asceticism and deep spirituality that: "From this spiritual height, he has surprised, stunned and chagrined the lackadaisical, the indifferent and the militant."[3] While still alive, Kyrillos' life-style made him an enigma for many. In the midst of church upheaval, political pressures and a grumbling Coptic community, Kyrillos VI managed to stay aloof from the intricacies of his high position and continued to pursue the life of a simple contemplative monk. This attitude and life-style gained him the respect of Egypt's president, Gamal `Abd al-Nasir (Nasser) with whose reign Kyrillos' period as patriarch coincided.

Kyrillos did not churn out a profuse body of writings, but taught through example and maxims. This method goes back to the desert fathers of the fourth century. Instead of addressing a general audience or situations in general, the fathers would answer a question with a specific spiritual advice or comment. Kyrillos' foremost example was the Syrian ascetic Isaac of Nineveh (died at the end of the seventh century). Isaac's work "goes back to primitive spirituality with no loss of originality."[4]

Throughout his life Kyrillos maintained a simple life-style of prayer, seclusion and sober meals. According to the Copts, he lived on one piece of bread with cumin a day during the fasting periods. They say that if a hungry person came by, he gave away the bread and only ate the cumin. His biographers mention that the bulk of his diet consisted of dry bread and spices, complemented with some vegetables and fruit.[5]

Today, Patriarch Kyrillos VI still keeps the Coptic hearts and minds spellbound. A flood of hagiographic literature about his life and miracles testifies to his immense popularity. A series of books enumerating miracles that are attributed to his intercession, both during his life and after his passing away, has already seen its thirteenth volume.[6]

Nevertheless, a proper biography of Kyrillos VI is still lacking. Most of the pictures that are transmitted about him only show his saintly dimension without addressing his qualities as an administrator or ruler, or mentioning the way in which he obviously planned his career. In spite of this narrow representation, it is widely agreed that Kyrillos VI played an immensely important role in the general revival of the Coptic Church. In fact, Kyrillos can not but have been a brilliant, astute ruler. He laid the foundation for the revival that we are currently witnessing, he groomed its current leaders, navigated the Coptic Church into a new era and gave Copts a general awareness of their Coptic identity.

This essay tries to provide a picture of Kyrillos' role in the current revival of the Coptic Church. The basis for the article mainly consists of written sources that are supplemented with stories from the vivid oral tradition that is still building up around him.[7] It hardly needs mentioning that this essay can only serve as an introduction to this fascinating pope.

## The period before becoming a patriarch

### Kyrillos' childhood

Kyrillos was born in 1902 and given the name of `Azir Yusuf `Ata. His family was wealthy and lived in the Delta. According to the Coptic stories, already at a young age signs of his future holiness and ascetic nature could be witnessed. During his childhood the Virgin Mary seems to have appeared to him regularly. The young Kyrillos liked to remind his family of the fact that their neighbors were poor people who were entitled to be given part of the family's food.

Upon graduation from high school, Kyrillos started his secular career in Alexandria as a clerk at the office of the Thomas Cook travel agency. During his short career at this firm, Kyrillos stood out as a devoted and reliable worker who, at the age of 25, shocked both family and colleagues with his decision to become a monk.[8] The patriarch at that time, Anba Yu'annis XIX (1928-1942), gave him permission to enter the monastery of Baramous that was renowned because of its spiritual leader, Father `Abd al-Masih al-Baramusi.

*Kyrillos the planner: his monastic career.*
In the monastery Kyrillos stood out as a diligent monk who, besides performing his prayers assiduously, liked to perform heavy chores, such as serving the older and disabled monks and providing them with their daily rations of water. When ordained a priest and monk in 1931, Kyrillos received the name of the fourth century martyr saint Menas (Mina). Until the tenth century, the tomb of St. Menas in Mareotis was a popular center of pilgrimage where people came to seek healing. Before he became a pope, Kyrillos was known as Abuna Mina al-Mutawahhid al-Baramusi, Father Mina the solitary from the Baramous monastery.

Immediately after his ordination, Kyrillos went to the prestigeous school for monastic studies in Helwan. This school had just been opened to raise the educational level of (potential) future episcopal candidates. Two year later Kyrillos returned to his monastery and stunned the monastic community with his wish to become a hermit. After moving into the desert, Kyrillos fell under the influence of Abuna `Abd al-Masih al-Habashi (the Ethiopian), a rugged hermit who excelled in ascetic and spiritual pursuits. This spiritual relationship turned out to be so fruitful that, according to Otto Meinardus, "the desert saint met the desert prophet."[9]

In 1936, Kyrillos sought to implement his own ideas of monasticism by heading his own monastery. He asked Patriarch Yu'annis XIX for permission to rebuild the ancient monastery of St. Menas at Mareotis. After the request was refused, Kyrillos retreated to a deserted windmill in Old Cairo that was built during the reign of Muhammad `Ali. He inhabited the windmill until 1942 when he was forced out because the British forces believed him to be a spy.[10] These six years of solitary life are considered the most formative in Kyrillos' career. During the long years of prayer, fasting and contemplation he developed his extraordinary spiritual gifts that already during his time in the windmill had started to attract great crowds who sought his blessing and miraculous powers. Innumerable miracles are believed to have happened during this period.

After his eviction from the windmill, Kyrillos raised money to build the present Church of St. Menas in Old Cairo with an adjoining student hostel.

With this project he started the implementation of his plans towards the revival of the Coptic Church. It was an attempt to give students spiritual guidance and educate them in the monastic life. This project continued when in 1944 Kyrillos became the abbot on the Monastery of Anba Samuel, a remote and primitive monastery, because the position of abbot allowed him to travel to and fro.

By the end of the World War II Kyrillos' career contained several components that were indicators of a future holy person or innovative church leader. His monastic career had been mostly spent outside his monastery of origin. In fact, apart from his wish to be a solitary, he had also been living outside his monastery due to conflicts of opinion between him and his superiors.[11] Kyrillos had a mind of his own and pursued his goals concerning monastic renewal with firm determination. Apart from following his conviction, Kyrillos grasped and manipulated the Coptic respect for the many holy men and women its tradition has produced. As Mark Gruber remarked about Kyrillos' stay in the windmill: "he was a master of the monastic symbol by convincingly exhibiting it under public scrutiny for years on end."[12] Without doubt, Kyrillos' solitary life was inspired by a sincere wish to pursue his higher spiritual goals. He understood, however, that an obscure hermit in the desert would not manage to advance church reforms. "Sainthood is a joint effort, not a one-man act."[13] By the time Kyrillos built the Church of St. Menas, Copts were sufficiently convinced of his holiness and hence sought his guidance and advice.

Through his student hostel Kyrillos started to advance new talents for the Coptic Church. He furthered the clerical ambitions of enthusiastic graduate students for whom there was no place yet in the existing monasteries. Whenever they expressed the wish to become monks, he sent them to the Monastery of the Syrians in Wadi al-Natroun. At that time this was the only monastery where graduate students could be placed, as its abbot, Anba Ta`ufilus, was the only abbot who appreciated higher education. Students that came under his influence during that period were Father Matta al-Miskin, the late Anba Samuel (who was the first bishop for social and ecumenical affairs) and the present Patriarch Shenouda III.

In fact, Kyrillos was undertaking tasks that the church hierarchy should have undertaken, hence his actions provoked irritation from the side of church officials. The church authorities perhaps thought to remove the charismatic monk from the public by making him the head of the remote Monastery of St. Samuel. But even in the remotest of all the Egyptian monasteries, throngs of Copts were quick to visit him. Moreover, nothing could prevent Kyrillos from passing the monastery's daily affairs into the hands of a prior while he himself pursued his projects in Old Cairo.

## The road to the patriarchate

During the period Kyrillos became known and popular among the Coptic population, the Coptic Church was led by a patriarch who became increasingly unpopular. Patriarch Yusab II (1946-1956) had worked his way up in the hierarchy. He had been the archbishop of Girga in Upper Egypt. Before he was elected patriarch, he twice served as the patriarchal deputy. Although only a monk is eligible for the office of patriarch, Anba Yusab managed to work his way onto the ballots. During his reign, the Coptic Church was teeming with stories about simony, scandals and corruption. In 1954, a group of young Copts kidnapped Yusab II and forced him to sign a document of abdication. On September 21, 1955, President Nasser agreed to relieve Anba Yusab of his patriarchal powers.[14] Yusab retired to a monastery where he died in 1956.

While a triumvirate of bishops continued to rule the Coptic Church, the monasteries and the Coptic population took time to reflect on the drawbacks of choosing a patriarch from among the bishops. Apart from the fact that Coptic Canon Law forbids the incumbent patriarch to hold a territorial bishopric, the Copts realized that a simple monk might be less prone to corruption. These events paved the way for Kyrillos to be hailed as the one whom Copts considered to be a sign of God.

The events around Yusab's dethronement took place at a time marked by profound instability, not only within the Coptic community, but in the whole of Egypt. After the 1952 revolution, Egypt entered a new era. There was hope that the inter-religious strife of the 1940s would end now that a regime with a more secular ideology had come to power. At the same time, especially the Copts experienced the detrimental consequences of the new government's policies of land reform and nationalization of businesses. Many prominent Coptic families lost their property and thus their socioeconomic influence.

*Kyrillos VI, the Patriarch:*

"This is a new test, a new task that God has given me."[15]

On April 19, 1959, a five year-old deacon, Rafik Bassili, took a slip of paper from a container that held three slips of paper with the names of the patriarchal candidates.[16] The boy had selected the paper with the name of Abuna Mina the Solitary. After a period without a leader and of confusion and discontent, the Coptic Church looked forward to a leader who would prompt respect and loyalty. The new patriarch was not going to disappoint them. Single-mindedly, without forgetting the religious and monastic dramatics, Kyrillos would pursue the realization of his ambitions for the Coptic Church. As he had stated at the beginning of his reign, this ambition was nothing less than "... to see the church in a spiritual revival that resembles the early days of the Apostolic Fathers."[17]

Coptic sources that want to give a concise description of Kyrillos' achievements, tend to focus on three issues: 1. the consecration of new *mairun*, (the holy chrism; a mixture of oil and balsam that is used for anointing in various church sacraments, such as baptism), 2. the settlement of problem of the *waqfs* (religious endowments) and 3. the improvement of ecumenical relations.

Each of these issues implies a field of activities: The matter of the *mairun* reveals Kyrillos' clerical and pastoral program. It is connected with the growth and revival of the Coptic Church itself. When more Copts are baptized, more priests and churches are consecrated, the supply of *mairun* is depleted within a few years. The need for new *mairun* testifies to the church's vitality.

The problem of the *waqfs* shows Kyrillos' way of negotiating church politics and problems within the Coptic community. Due to the expropriation of private lands after the revolution, many monasteries had lost their property. They were left with only the charitable endowments. The administration of these *waqfs* had long been the subject of dispute between the Coptic Community Council (*al-Majlis al-Milli*), which considered the monasteries as greedy, and the abbots of monasteries, who acted as trustees of these lands. Kyrillos solved this problem in 1960 by establishing a board consisting of monastic and lay members, that would administer these *waqfs*.

Barely three weeks after his enthronement Kyrillos also addressed the problem of the relations between the Coptic Church and other churches. His first move was to straighten out the strained relations with the Ethiopian Orthodox Church that had been under Coptic rule since its inception. In 1959 it became independent and Kyrillos consecrated the first Ethiopian patriarch. During his reign, Kyrillos also took steps to take the Coptic Church out of its isolation and become an active participant in international conferences. The Coptic Church already had become a member of the World Council of Churches and ecumenical discussions with leaders of Orthodox, Catholic, Anglican and Protestant churches were started.

*The monastic and church reform*

One of Kyrillos first actions as a patriarch was to lay the foundation stone for the re-building of the Monastery of St. Menas. Several Coptic and Western observers were dismayed by what they considered to be the political or social ineffectiveness of this gesture. According to Edward Wakin's interpretation, the Coptic community "was besieged, the minority anxious, the hierarchy, clergy and monks in disarray, the church wounded by turmoil, and the Patriarch lays a foundation stone in a deserted place for another monastery."[18]

What many observers in those days overlooked was that Kyrillos was not merely fulfilling his old dreams, but that he started the restoration of the Coptic Church by restoring its most central institution: its monasteries. To the Coptic community, the monasteries had always been the custodians of Coptic faith and tradition. Its leaders, the bishops and patriarchs, were chosen from among the monks. Married clergy regularly withdrew to the monasteries in order to renew their spiritual resources. For Kyrillos it was only natural to start restoring the church by improving the moral and educational level of its leaders.

One of the steps that led to the restoration of the monasteries was Kyrillos' decree that all monks who were residing outside their monastery of origin should return there. These included monks who lived as independent solitaries. Matta al-Miskin was leading such a group and refused to return to his monastery of origin. When, in 1969, Kyrillos made him the prior of the Monastery of St. Macarius and gave him a free hand in reorganizing the place, Matta al-Miskin gave in and moved to the monastery.

In 1960 he put an end to educational deficiencies among the married clergy by his decree that all priests must be graduates of the Coptic Clerical College. He stressed the rehabilitation of the religious life and observances. This also included early morning surprise visits to churches in order to impress upon parish priests the importance of observing the early morning liturgy on Wednesdays and Sundays.[19]

One of Kyrillos' goals was to draw the lax part of the community and the people in remote areas back into the sphere of the Coptic Church. He pursued this objective by intensifying the sacramental life of the church and by launching social-religious programs for the Copts in remote villages.

Already during his time in the Church of St. Menas, Kyrillos had stressed the importance of daily celebration of the Liturgy, as it cemented the bond between the Coptic community and its church. Only baptized Copts could partake in the Sacrament of Communion. Since baptism, confirmation and confession are interconnected in the Coptic Church, people were encouraged to have their children baptized, and take frequent communion so that they could become full members of the Coptic Church.

In 1959 the so-called "rural diaconal project" was launched. Trainees from the Clerical College were sent to villages that did not have their own church. They taught the villagers the basics of Coptic faith and provided social services. In their wake priests followed with a portable altar in order to celebrate the Mass and baptize children. Later on, Coptic training centers were set up where villagers could learn skills or crafts.[20]

All these clerical and social activities proved to have repercussions for the position of Coptic women. Until then, the only option for women who wanted to pursue a religious career had been to become a contemplative nun. With the increase of social and pastoral projects, women were needed to serve Coptic women and children. Female volunteers were recruited through the Sunday schools, Coptic charitable organizations, and local priests. As a result of these activities the community of the Daughters of St. Mary in Beni Suef was started in 1965, followed later by the movement for deaconesses (*mukarrasat*).

Furthermore, Kyrillos encouraged the contemplative nuns. His relationship with Mother Irini, the mother superior of the convent of Abu Saifein, who initiated the reform of the convents, is famous in Coptic circles. He encouraged her and other superiors to pursue their plans and allowed them considerable freedom with regard to the design and implementation of new ideas.[21]

In order to direct these new activities, for the first time in Coptic history, three extra-diocesan bishops were ordained. These were Anba Samuel for social and ecumenical affairs, Anba Gregorius for higher education and, the present patriarch, Anba Shenouda for religious education.

Not only had Copts started to frequent their church again, the community was also growing and it became apparent that more church buildings were needed. Obtaining permits to build them is a long and complicated bureaucratic process. In order to circumvent the usual red tape, Kyrillos directly addressed President Nasser and was given permission to build 25 churches a year.[22]

Kyrillos also obtained permission to build a new cathedral with an adjoining patriarchal residence. In 1968 the Cathedral of St. Mark was inaugurated in the presence of Egyptian and foreign dignitaries, including President Nasser and the Ethiopian emperor Haile Selassie. As a result of improved relations with the Catholic Church, Kyrillos was able to use the occasion to petition for the return of the relics of St. Mark. These had been kept in Venice since the ninth century. The return of these relics signified the ultimate recognition of the Coptic Church as the indigenous, historic church of Egypt.

In a few years, Kyrillos had managed to revitalize of the centers of Coptic life. The premises of the new cathedral accommodate several centers of Coptic Studies, such as institutes for graduate studies, Coptic language, art, music, liturgy, and archeology. Thus, the cathedral had become the urban, spiritual, and cultural nucleus of Coptic life.

In the desert, the buildings of monasteries were being restored and filled with enthusiastic monks who provided the Copts with spiritual guidance and vigor. The Coptic people were finding their way back into the churches where educated priests provided them with guidance and advice in several areas of their lives. They all felt secure because of their strong and dedicated patriarch who managed his flock like a father.

## Kyrillos the saint

"Baba Kyrillos looked right through you, nothing remained hidden from him." For the Copts this gift of clairvoyance was one of the affirmations of Kyrillos' holiness. These gifts pointed to his close contact with God and the favors he enjoyed from the saints. Especially his relationship with St. Mary and St. Menas are well-known in Coptic circles. He "talked" with the saints and sometimes appeared to believers accompanied by one of them.

Kyrillos used his unusual spiritual gifts to build and defend his church. According to one of the stories, a Muslim woman once tried to obtain his blessing by joining the Copts for communion. When she came to Kyrillos he refused to give her the Sacrament. People wondered how he had known that she was not a Copt. He said that when he wanted to give her the Sacrament, he suddenly realized that she lacked the signs of the *mairun* with which a Copt is anointed after baptism. The story also relates that Kyrillos was quite distressed after this incident. To him it was an abomination that the most sacred Sacrament, Christ's holy body and blood, might have entered an unclean person who was not purified by the proper Coptic rites.

Kyrillos carried his holy persona wherever he went. When he was asked to address an ecumenical meeting in Ethiopia, he delivered his speech in the form of an apophthegm: a word from a desert father. When addressing the audience about the working of the Holy Spirit, he conveyed his message through the following 'word:' "I feel that as the rains fall on the hills of Ethiopia and stream from there into the Nile so that the water reaches different countries and different nations, in a similar way the Holy Spirit is poured out over us who are present at this meeting and it streams to the [different] churches so that the water can reach our people..."[23]

Kyrillos was ever aware of the interaction between the holy man and his audience. He maintained a regular affirmation of his spiritual gifts. When, for example, in 1969 his body produced three kidney stones, he had them sent to a Coptic surgeon. The surgeon was appalled by the size of the stones and urged Kyrillos to break his fast in order to drink as much as possible. Kyrillos ignored this advice because, as he said: "How can I leave God?" "How can I leave Saint Menas?"[24]

The ultimate recognition of Kyrillos' capacity as a holy man came on April 2, 1968, when St. Mary, the Mother of Christ, started a series of public apparitions on the dome of a church in Zeitoun. Both the Egyptian Muslims and Christians were quick to interpret these apparitions as a special blessing and encouragement from St. Mary. After all, as the story goes, the first to see her were two Muslim mechanics working in a garage opposite the church. In that year Egypt was experiencing a national feeling of despair after the cataclysmic defeat during the Six-Day War with Israel in 1967. Now that Israel had occupied Jerusalem, Copts were barred from visiting this city. Kyrillos had a committee investigate the phenomenon and concluded that St. Mary had come "to spread blessing on this country" and that she had come to Zeitoun because now Egyptian Christians could not visit the Holy Land.[25]

In retrospect, the Copts believe that St. Mary came to honor their pope. For a period of more than two years, numerous miracles of healing and consolation took place among Muslims and Christians. A general revival of faith took place and the Copts were confirmed in their belief that Egypt is a special place for St. Mary because of her flight there after Jesus was born. Kyrillos himself merely sent a committee to check out the phenomenon. Obviously, his contact with St. Mary was close enough to know what she was up to.

## Conclusion

Patriarch Kyrillos' method of managing the Coptic Church was, even in the Coptic framework, unusual. During his reign hardly any inter-religious incidents can be mentioned. The main crisis that the Copts faced had been in 1955, before Kyrillos' enthronement, when President Nasser abolished the Muslim and Christian religious courts and changed the personal status law.[26]

Kyrillos' method of ruling, though beyond reproach, was single-handed. Although Kyrillos valued the talents and gifts people had, contradiction was impossible when his mind was made up. Had he not kept up his role as holy man all the way through, he might have experienced considerable opposition. Instead, he brilliantly manipulated his adversaries into cooperation and found creative ways to solve conflicts. Of course, Kyrillos could always count on the support of the Coptic community who never doubted for a moment that he was sent to rescue their church. Moreover, the consequences for people who tried to plot against the holy man could be disastrous. One of Kyrillos' biographers mentions the story of a bishop who tried to stir up trouble among the bishoprics. He mistook poison for medicine and consequently died.

On March 9, 1971, Kyrillos passed away after saying "May God take care of you" to everyone around him.[27] His body was laid to rest in the cathedral at the Monastery of St. Menas. In spite of the fact that Coptic Canon Law only allows the canonization of a saint fifty years after his or her passing away, Kyrillos already is considered among one of the foremost Coptic saints. Daily, crowds throng into the sanctuary and ask his intercession. This reality required a successor with a totally different style of ruling. Kyrillos' scepter was passed on to one of the people that he himself had groomed into leadership of the Coptic Church. Thus far, Shenouda III has followed a line of ruling and action mainly avoided by Kyrillos; he is a scholar, a teacher and takes on a high political profile.

## Notes

1. Hanna Yusuf `Ata, Rafa'il Ava Mina & Rufa`il Subhi, *Mudhakkirat `an Hayah Al-Baba Kirillus al-Sadis*, Cairo: publ. Abna' Al-Baba Kirillus Al-Sadis, 1985, 155.
2. Ibid., 64.
3. Edward Wakin, *A Lonely Minority. The Modern Story of Egypt's Copts*, New York: William Morrow & Co., 1963, 113.
4. Tomas Spidlik, *The Spirituality of the Christian East*, translated by Anthony P.

Gythiel, Kalamazoo, MI: Cistercian Publications, 1986, 15.
5. Hanna Yusuf `Ata, *Mudhakkirat*, 48.
6. Abna' Al-Baba Kirillas al-Sadis, (ed. & publ.) *Mu`jizat al-Baba Kirillus al-Sadis* (The Miracles of Pope Kyrillos VI), Cairo Vol 1-13 (undated, from around 1973 onward).
7. Most of the stories about Kyrillos VI were gathered during my stay in Egypt from 1987 until Jan. 1991. Two trips made in January 1992 and May 1993 provided further insights into the myths around Kyrillos VI that are still burgeoning. This article is based on written and oral sources. When the information provided forms part of the common Coptic stories about Kyrillos, I will not quote specific sources.
8. According to some sources Kyrillos joined the monastery already during childhood: Abbas Chalaby, *Les Coptes D'Egypte*, private publication, 1973, 124.
9. Otto Meinardus, *Monks and Monasteries of the Egyptian Deserts*, Cairo: A.U.C. Press, 1961, 157.
10. Ibid., 158.
11. The main cause for the conflict between Kyrillos and the abbot of the Baramous monastery was the abbot's decision to evict seven monks. According to Kyrillos, the abbot had not involved the patriarch in the dismissal and thus was acting against the Coptic Canon Law. Hanna Yusuf `Ata, *Mudhakkirat*, 27ff.
12. Mark F.X. Gruber, "Sacrifice in the Desert: An Ethnography of the Coptic Monastery." Ph.D. diss., State University of New York, 1990, 116. I owe several observations in this article to Gruber's analysis about the way Kyrillos made use of monastic symbols in order to find acceptance from the Coptic community and from several monasteries in the Wadi al-Natroun (who later backed him as a patriarchal candidate), see Gruber, 115-121.
13. Aviad M. Kleinberg, *Prophets in their own Country. Living Saints and the Making of Sainthood in the Later Middle Ages*, Chicago & London: The University of Chicago Press, 1992, 133.
14. The enthronement and the dethronement (which rarely happens, since a patriarch is installed for life) of the Coptic patriarch has to be ratified by presidential decree. For an example of such a decree see: Otto Meinardus, *Christian Egypt Faith and Life*, Cairo: A.U.C. Press, 1970, 140 ff.
15. Wakin, *Minority*, 104.
16. This tradition is based on the Acts of the Apostles 1:21-26, see: John Watson, "Signposts to Biography," and Nora Stene, "Becoming a Copt.", in this volume.
17. Wakin, *Minority*, 116.
18. Ibid., 112.
19. Ibid., 114.
20. Maurice Assad, "Prägung der koptischen Identität," in: Paul Verghese, *Koptisches Christentum*, Stuttgart: Evangelisches Verlagswerk, 1973, 114ff.
21. For an example of his communications with the mothers superior, see the letter Kyrillos sent to Mother Martha in: Rahibat Dair al-Amir Tadrus bi Harat al-Rum, *Al-Umm Martha*, Cairo: Viktur Kirillus, 1989, 23,24.
22. Mohamed Heikal, *Autumn of Fury*, London: Andre Deutsch Ltd., 4th ed., 1983, 158.
23. *Jami`a al-Ruh al-Muqaddas*, Cairo: Abna' al-Baba Kirillus al-Sadis (publ.), 1991, 26.
24. Hanna Yusuf `Ata, *Mudhakkirat*, 51.
25. Cynthia Nelson, "Stress, Religious Experience and Mental Health," *Catalyst* 6 (1972), 51.
26. The abolishment of the Christian religious courts was felt as a disadvantage for the Egyptian Christians, as Islamic law was already incorporated into the new

civil courts. This meant that Christians lost their equality and independence as far as their civil laws were concerned.
27. Father Raphael Ava Mina, *Pope Kyrillos VI and the Spiritual Leadership*, Cairo: Sons of Pope Kyrillos VI, 28.

John Watson
# Signposts to Biography – Pope Shenouda III

There can be no doubt of Pope Shenouda's influence on the recent life of the Coptic Orthodox Church. It is, perhaps, second only to that of his predecessor, Pope Kyrillos VI (1902-1971). The student lacks a critical biography of either man. Kyrillos was the 116th successor of Saint Mark as patriarch of the See of Alexandria and reigned from May 10, 1959 until his death on March 9, 1971. Shenouda was consecrated as the 117th Coptic Pope and Patriarch on November 14, 1971. The last four decades mark the height of the great Coptic renaissance. This essay will locate signposts to direct the reader towards the essential features of the life of Anba Shenouda.

Nazir Gayed, the future patriarch, was born on the August 3, 1923 in the important Coptic center of Assiyut in Upper Egypt. The family were devout Copts. Early pictures indicate a comfortable, middle-class background with Nazir wearing the tarboush, or fez, that badge of Ottoman conformity and respectability. His mother died soon after his birth, leaving a family of three boys and five girls. His father, Gayed Roufail, died a few years later when Nazir was still young. The child was raised by an older brother, Raphael, and his wife. Because of Raphael's work the family was required to move around Egypt. Nazir received a sound primary and secondary education in the Coptic School at Damanhur, the American School in Banha and Iman Secondary School in Shobra, Cairo.

In his twenties Nazir graduated from the Faculty of History of Cairo University. During this period he also completed his National Service as an officer in the Egyptian Army. He became a teacher in a high school and devoted his evenings to study at the Coptic Orthodox Theological Seminary. Some modest financial support came from journalism: for his entire adult life he was to be a wordsmith, producing an uneven output of many millions of words.[1] He was also recognized as a poet of quality. His academic achievement as a seminarian resulted in a rapid promotion from student to teacher at the Seminary in 1949. Nazir Gayed was twenty-six years of age. He carried a substantial teaching load but made time for postgraduate studies in Archeology and Classical Arabic at Cairo University.

Shenouda has retained his scholarly interests throughout his life and, in spite of the enormous demands of high office, he can be counted amongst the elite quartet of prominent living Coptic Orthodox theologians.[2] He is a natural teacher with a great gift for adaptation to the right level without patronizing his listeners. His many books are teaching books, often pedestrian and didactic in the extreme. His theology is essentially apologetic and dogmatic. Whole volumes are devoted to discussions of the poverty of Christology in the teaching of Jehovah's Witnesses: this is a recurrent theme and suggests that the sect is making inroads within the Christian churches of the Middle East, though not in Islam. Comparative theologies are directed against the inadequacies of Protestantism and Catholicism.

Reading through these many tomes, which are entirely predictable, it is necessary to note that there is no knowledge of historical criticism as a way of approaching the Scriptures, nor of the nature of historical theology. The world of Pope Shenouda the theologian is one of black and white: no grey exists. This must be accounted for, at least in part, by the context of Coptic Orthodox Theology. There is a marked tendency to "qur'anize" the Bible. If the Muslims have the infallible, unchangeable *Umm al-Kitab*, the Mother of the Book, as their source in Heaven, then the Bible must be equally without error. Islam, unmentioned, is the context of Coptic theology. The most influential Bible commentary in Egypt, translated in its many volumes into Arabic, is that of Matthew Henry (1662-1714). That work is profoundly Protestant.

It is a cause for concern, amongst theologically educated Orthodox of the Byzantine or Chalcedonian tradition at St. Vladimir's, New York and St. Sergius', Paris, that Coptic theology is so influenced by Protestantism. The major reforming pope of the 19th century in Egypt was Pope Kyrillos IV. He was enthroned as 10th Patriarch in 1854 after his education, secular and theological, by CMS missionaries from England. The CMS was the most conservative and evangelical of the English missionary societies of the nineteenth century. Kyrillos assumed the patriarchal office with a definite program to raise the educational standards of the Copts, especially the clergy. This was admirable, but there was a dark side to his rule. He was an iconoclast. He rebuilt the cathedral in Ezbekiah but prohibited the exposition of icons there. At the command of Pope Kyrillos IV, icons were publicly burned in the streets before the bemused Muslim population. Theology also developed a Puritan flavor. This tradition has affected the Coptic Orthodox Church. In the new climate of the late twentieth century, where the other

Orthodox churches are coming closer to the Oriental Orthodox, the element of Protestantism in Coptic Orthodoxy has become a ground for anxiety. A problem often referred to by Greek and Russian theologians is that the teaching of "Penal Substitution" is unknown to Orthodox doctrines of the Atonement outside Egypt.[3]

Shenouda's greatest book remains his first, "Release of the Spirit", a work of ascetic theology and the fruit of his eremitic life.[4] It is not available in an adequate English language version. The Copts persist in refusing the elementary principle of translation in which the translator works the text into his own first language. Translators whose language is Arabic usually translate Shenouda's works with disastrous results.

The Coptic Orthodox Church is a conservative body. It is unable to address, and is generally unaware of, the questions which are the primary premises of theological discourse and investigation in Western Churches. Orthodoxy, as seen by Pope Shenouda, is the bearer of the authentic apostolic tradition. He seeks to make a permanent distinction between the fundamental and the secondary: to know the difference between "how I feel" and "what the church has always taught." Orthodoxy is the carrier of a Patristic Theology where the contrast between prayer and thought does not exist. Coptic theology endorses the saying of the Egyptian Desert Father in the "Philokalia": "If you are a theologian, you will pray truly. And if you pray truly, you are a theologian."[5]

Whilst teaching in the theological schools of Cairo in the late 1940s and early 1950s, Nazir Gayed experienced a penetrating summons to the monastic life. At that time, the monastic life was no longer considered to be an appropriate path for educated Copts, but in one monastery Anba Theophilus Al-Suryani had other ideas and his enlightened approach was appealing to university graduates in medicine, engineering, agriculture, dentistry and the humanities. Nazir entered the Monastery of the Syrians in the Western Desert in July 1954. The monastery was to prove a model for the other monasteries which are now filled with university graduates. The monastic experience was central for Nazir. To an amazing extent, he continues to live a monastic life despite the restraints of the patriarchate. As Father Antonius Al-Suryani he received a further vocation to the life of a hermit and between 1954 and 1962 lived alone in a desert cave for extended periods. The deserts of Egypt have been a blessing upon Christianity. The power of the Coptic Orthodox revival derives from the desert monasteries. When the monasteries are strong in Egypt then Christianity is strong.

The infiltration of educated young men into the monasteries and subsequently into the hierarchy was crucial for the impending reforms in the

Egyptian Church. The weakness of this development is that too many young men have become bishops too quickly. A dramatic rise in the number of dioceses means that many young men have been consecrated bishops after a very short time as monks. Some must now join monasteries with the expectation of becoming bishops. Such men must regard the life of a monk as a means rather than an end. The presence of ambitious monks is always denied, but the desire for advancement, preferment and power is so universal that it is impossible to believe that these are absent from Coptic Orthodoxy. A handful of Coptic bishops behave with haughty and arrogant disdain, especially towards foreigners. They are wise enough to avoid this behavior in the sight of the present patriarch. He is a true monk, a man of poverty, purity and obedience, apparently by nature.

It is striking that the recent Coptic renaissance was largely initiated by two monks with a preference for the eremitic life: Pope Kyrillos VI and Pope Shenouda III. In the future study of the long history of Coptic monasticism it is likely to emerge that one of the most influential figures did not live in the patristic period but in the deeply troubled and materialistic twentieth century. For thirty-five years (1935-1970) the Ethiopian Abuna `Abd al-Masih al-Habashi lived a life of extreme asceticism in a cave about five kilometers from the Monastery of the Romans in the Western Desert. He was the inspiration for Anba Kyrillos, Abuna Matta al-Miskin, Anba Shenouda and numerous other monks. The need to be alone is a primary instinct in mysticism. The solitary's only need is to be known by God. It is the more remarkable that Kyrillos and Shenouda were called from the fearful void of the desert to the treadmill of ecclesiastical administration. Since 1985, His Holiness has occasionally referred back to the eremitic experience as the most important in his personal life. He has even looked, wistfully and nostalgically, across the desert to the place of his cave which is now, symbolically, in the middle of an armed forces battle training site.

It was Anba Kyrillos who called Abuna Antonius from the desert in September 1962 and ordained him as bishop for Christian Education. The new Bishop Shenouda was also to hold the post of Dean of the Theological College. His responsibilities included the oversight of the Sunday schools which are the centers for lay education in the Coptic Orthodox Church. He had been actively involved in the Sunday School Movement in Shobra since his late teens. The combined effect of the revived theological schools and Sunday schools had been to create what amounts virtually to a cultural and intellectual renaissance among the Copts. It has had political overtones. Power in the church resides in the monastic community but this family of monks was fed by the stream of educated candidates who were themselves products of the Sunday School Movement. Anba Kyrillos had an eye for potential leaders of quality and made a number of appointments which were to have great significance for the Copts. Much of the present strength and spiritual authority of the Coptic Orthodox Church derives from the insight of Pope Kyrillos. "A monk is one who regards himself as linked with every man, through always seeing himself in each", wrote Evagrius, the desert monk and spiritual writer of the fourth century.[6] This is especially true of these two popes whose combined influence reaches out from the desert into every area of church life.

When Pope Kyrillos died in March 1971, the long process of nomination, selection and election began in the Coptic Church. The nomination involves the entire church. The selection is undertaken by the Holy Synod after initial voting throughout the church. The election is liturgical. This electoral process has been the subject of some study and much speculation.

Muhammad Haykal, an important and influential commentator in the Arab world, has said that President Sadat regarded Bishop Shenouda as his nominee for the post and implies that the election was rigged. The election was to receive the presidential seal of approval though Sadat did not know Shenouda. The Minister of the Interior, Mamdouh Salem, had told the president that he could "guarantee" Shenouda. Robert Brenton Betts, the American authority on Christianity in the Arab East, believed that Shenouda was by no means a popular choice. According to Betts the favorite of most Copts was the monk Matta al-Miskin who, though popular with the Coptic masses, was viewed with suspicion by the church authorities and the state. Many regarded his political philosophy as Marxist and criticized him as a self-seeking demagogue. The candidate who received most votes, before the Holy Synod presented its short list of three, was Bishop Samuel, another monk of the Syrian monastery and an Episcopal appointee of Anba Kyrillos. He was responsible for Social and Ecumenical Affairs and functioned as the Foreign Secretary of the Copts. At the World Council of Churches Bishop Samuel was already regarded as Coptic Pope.

In the Acts of the Apostles (1:21-26) we read of the election of Matthias to the apostolic band by the casting of lots. The Coptic Orthodox Church is probably alone amongst the churches of the twentieth century in maintaining this tradition. On Sunday, October 31, 1971 an altar ballot took place in Cairo and a small boy, Emen Mounir Kamil, selected one of three pieces of paper. His choice bore the name of Bishop Shenouda, the bishop responsible for Education. The electoral process was complete. The bishop became His Holiness Pope Shenouda III.

The Coptic Pope occupies a unique place in Egyptian public life. He is the spokesman for an entire community. Pope Shenouda has always had his critics. He is, inevitably, attacked for being too soft as the mediator between the Copts and the government. For others, he is far too bellicose as the advocate who refuses to accept an inferior status for the Copts. The eminent academic P.J. Vatikiotis says that Shenouda was already known, at the time of his election, for his "rather aggressive activist views regarding the promotion and defence of the right of the Coptic community."[7] Vatikiotis points out that militant Coptic youth organizations proliferated under Shenouda and became increasingly vociferous in their demands for greater rights in the Egyptian body politic. Critics within the Coptic Church, like the distinguished academic theologian Dr. George Habib Bibawi, complained that Egyptian society was being given the impression of an awakening giant, threatening society at large and destroying the "classical friendship" in Egypt between Islam and the Coptic Orthodox Church.

Shenouda is an effective spokesman and representative for the millions of poor, inarticulate Copts who regard him as a folk hero. Apologists for the Pope will say that he only speaks out when others are silenced. Like his predecessors he has continually to be aware of the potentiality which exists, especially in the House of Islam, for the annihilation of Christianity. He has chosen the path of conciliation and works with many moderate Muslims who are his friends and allies. This does not prevent him from being a realist. He was deeply affected by the murder of Farag Foda, the prominent liberal Muslim writer, who was shot dead by Muslim extremists on June 8, 1992. Shenouda emphasizes the need to seek out "moderate Muslims," as he likes to call them. Foda had a personal logo on his note paper incorporating a cross and a crescent as a public testimony to his belief in the equality of Christians and Muslims. It was a statement not lost on Shenouda. One of the patriarch's central themes is that of patriotism. Again and again, he will refer to "Egypt our Mother." He has rejected the support of international groups supporting minority rights and is resentful of the suggestion that the Copts are like the Kurds in Iraq. He says that minorities are not numerical: the Copts are Egyptian through and through. The Copts are woven into the woof and warp of Egyptian history. In the reception room of the patriarchal residence in Abassiya, Cairo the same cross and crescent logo is fixed permanently to the wall.

Shenouda revolutionized the Coptic Orthodox Church. In the early years of his patriarchal ministry the church adopted a forward-looking policy. Major issues were directly confronted. The first of these concerned the basic human right of freedom of belief. In Egypt this meant the right to move freely between Islam and Christianity, rather than in the opposite direction only. Another sensitive issue was that of the alleged discrimination against Copts seeking posts in government and administration. A recurring problem was the use of the *Shari`a*, Islamic religious law, as a source of Constitutional Law. The Copts remained disturbed by the unreliability of any government census and the vexed question of assessment, which relates dangerously to all other issues.[8]

The issue which brought Shenouda into confrontation with Sadat was church building and repair. The legal foundation for the Egyptian state's control of church property is the Ottoman Hamayouni Decree of 1856, amplified in 1934 and a valid part of civil law. The law requires a presidential decree to build or repair a church. This had been settled privately by Pope Kyrillos with President Nasser. With Shenouda as pope, building was increasing. It was inevitable that some Coptic churches were built without presidential permission. It was, perhaps, equally inevitable that these churches should be subject to arson attacks by Muslim extremist.

As communal tensions increased, there were major Muslim offensives against the Copts in Khanqa, Cairo, Alexandria and Upper Egypt. At the same time, Islamic groups attacked government institutions. Some serious food riots, occasioned by governement withdrawal of subsidies on basic foods, and Sadat's peace mission to Jerusalem, further disturbed the atmosphere of a fragile communal climate. The crisis between Muslims and Copts came to a head in March 1980 when churches were attacked all over the country. Shenouda canceled all Easter celebrations in protest against the government's inability or unwillingness to protect his people. During Sadat's visit to America, two months later, immigrant Copts demonstrated openly against the visit of a "persecutor of Christians." The demonstrations received support in Congress. Sadat returned home accusing Shenouda publicly of conspiring to erect a separate Christian state in Upper Egypt. On June 6, 1981 a Coptic priest was murdered in broad daylight in Cairo. A few days later twenty Copts were killed and one hundred injured in the Zawiya al-Hamra district of the city. In August 1981 a bomb exploded in Shobra killing over a dozen Copts and injuring fifty more.

Faced with economic chaos, communal violence and a disastrous foreign policy, Sadat finally accepted sectarian strife as the principal concern of government policy. To some observers it seemed that he had merely found a distraction to divert the Egyptian people from the awful realities facing them. By Presidential decree No.493 of 1981, Sadat arrested and detained 1536 named people in one week, without charges or trials. Shenouda was arrested on September 5, 1981. President Anwar al-Sadat, a relatively young ruler of 62, was assassinated on October 6, 1981 in an attack mounted during a military parade in Cairo. The assassins were later found to be members of an Islamic movement.

Pope Shenouda was detained under house arrest in the Western Desert until January 5, 1985. Sadat appointed a committee of bishops to perform the pope's functions during his exile. President Mubarak retained the committee when he took over after Sadat's death.

The willingness of five senior bishops to serve the Egyptian government is revealing. The Coptic Orthodox Church is a divided church. Shenouda has made some efforts to be reconciled with those who supported his detention. He has not been entirely successful. Some of the antagonists have died, some are finding reconciliation very difficult and some are determined to oppose the pope.

In September 1981 the international, ecumenical contacts of the church were in the hands of Bishop Samuel, who joined Sadat's committee. The bishop was killed with the president. Other opponents, like Metropolitan Athanasius of Beni Suef, have made outward gestures of reconciliation. Metropolitan Mikhail of Assiyut regrets his criticisms of Shenouda. Bishop Yohannes, the Secretary of the Holy Synod in 1981, and Bishop Maximous are both dead. Bishop Gregorios, the principal academic theologian in Egypt, was alienated from the pope for many years. The man who may justly be regarded as the most famous Copt in the world, with the possible exception of UN Secretary General Boutros Ghali, is Father Matta Al-Miskin. He is the spiritual father of the Monastery of Saint Macarius, generally regarded by Western Christians as one of the dozen finest religious houses in the Christian world, but he has not met the pope for over a decade. Haykal portrays Father Matta as the principal religious adviser to Sadat. The disaffection of Matta and the inability of Shenouda to bring the two together are profoundly disturbing and augur ill for the future of the church. It is possible to hear Matta's supporters in the country referring to "Shenouda's churches."

The most common complaint against His Holiness is that he has departed from the "traditional" role of patriarch as a spiritual director, that he preaches everywhere and as much as possible and that he generally talks too much. It is certainly true that he can often be heard. Amongst Arab speakers, the pope is known for his captivating use of language, but it is not necessary to speak much Arabic to be aware of the exciting atmosphere created by this remarkable communicator. Shenouda is not Kyrillos and, no doubt, the next patriarch will be wise to abandon the Wednesday lectures in

Cairo and the Sunday evening sessions in Alexandria. Shenouda has his particular gifts and he employs them in the service of the Coptic Church.

Since his release, the patriarch has become much more involved in the life of the Coptic Diaspora and the World Council of Churches, of which he is currently one of the presidents. He is aware that only two or three priests in the Diaspora supported him in 1981. The majority, many still in place, opposed him and supported the committee. He received little support from the WCC; indeed, the leading Methodist ecumenist, Dr.Pauline Webb, was anxious, in 1981, to support Bishop Samuel against the pope. Shenouda will not allow such a situation to develop again, though he has proved unable to remove the many priests in the Diaspora who supported his detention. His Holiness has been engaged in some form of ecumenical theological dialogue for thirty years and describes it as "building bridges of love", but this work has intensified since 1985.

The Coptic Diaspora extends across Europe, Africa, the Americas and Australia. The pope has travelled extensively for ecumenical and pastoral engagements. A catalogue of this pilgrimages would fill a book. It includes: Kenya, Zaire and the Congo (1979), Russia (1972, 1988), Syria, Armenia and Lebanon (1972), the Vatican (1973), Ethiopia (1973) the USA (1977, 1989, 1991), Sudan (1977), England (1979, 1989, 1990, 1992), Germany (1990), Australia (1989, 1991), Scotland and Sweden (1992), and South Africa, Zimbabwe and Kenya (1994). If a similar scenario to that of 1981 should be seen again in Egypt, Pope Shenouda will know that his "friends" will be a much larger group than the tiny circle of Copts and Anglicans who supported him during his four years of exile.

Anba Shenouda has increased the college of bishops in Egypt. He has appointed many gifted young graduates as "general" bishops. These bishops have no geographical diocese, but are appointed to specialist ministries in education, social work, ecumenism and youth services. Some general bishops engage in pastoral work at home or abroad, acting for the patriarch in "locum tenens." All general bishops are nominated and consecrated by the pope. Patriarchal elections earlier in the twentieth century have shown that it is disastrous and canonically dubious to consecrate a diocesan bishop to be patriarch. At the same time, some Episcopal experience is desirable in a patriarch. Shenouda, like Kyrillos before him, seems to have secured the future by the appointment of general bishops. It is probably possible to guess who the next pope will be, and with a degree of accuracy.

Anyone familiar with the paintings of the orientalist artist John Frederick Lewis (1805-1875) will know his "Courtyard of the House of the Coptic Patriarch" (1864) which is full of activity: the dictating of letters, the groups of suppliants and the bustle of visitors. The juxtaposition of one race or creed with another is a recurring theme in paintings by Lewis. The suggestion is that the issues dealt with are not only spiritual or theological. They are also economic, social, ethnic. Pope Shenouda's residence is as hectic today. He tries to be accessible. On any one morning there may be foreign visitors, immigrant Copts, monks, nuns, priests, politicians, diplomats and bishops, and, at times, the sick seeking a blessing. Anba Shenouda's involvement with them all is very clearly that of a spiritual father and not of a hierarch. Others may try to protect him, but he is open to as many people as possible. It is an oriental court, but it is a friendly and open one. The pope can be watched as he seeks to find solutions to problems which are far from conventionally ecclesiastical. It is an environment which is far from the scholar's study or the hermit's cave. Vocation rules out personal preference.

As we have looked at the signposts of biography which bear the title 'Teacher,' 'Writer,' 'Solitary,' 'Politician' or 'Bishop,' we become aware of the integrity which characterizes this one life. Pope Shenouda's life is of one piece, of wholeness. His sternly moralistic and harshly dogmatic Orthodoxy is a seamless garment. This stubborn but impressive integrity lifts the purely Egyptian to the universal and Christian.

## Notes

1. At present, I know of forty-eight books in translation (English, German and French) and over fifty in Arabic. There is no published bibliography for Shenouda III.
2. According to me, this 'quartet of theologians' consists of Anba Gregorios (bishop for higher education; the professional, academic theologian), Abuna Matta al-Miskin (the ascetic, or spiritual theologian), Professor Isaac Fanous Youssef (the iconographic or visual theologian) and Pope Shenouda (the didactic or teaching theologian).
3. Penal Substitution alludes to the notion that Christ became our substitute, bearing the judgement we deserve in the light of our sinfulness and God's personal wrath. A key passage is Romans 3:23-26.
   Recent Coptic Orthodox exegesis has tended to be Protestant because it derives from Matthew Henry. There has been an internal Coptic controversy relating to the Doctrine of Atonement. A complete analysis on modern Coptic theology is still required.
   The traditional Orthodox position, according to Kallistos Ware is: "Where Orthodoxy sees chiefly Christ the Victor, the late medieval and post-medieval west sees chiefly Christ the Victim. While Orthodoxy interprets the Crucifixion

primarily as an act of the triumphant victory over the powers of evil, the west... has tended rather to think of the Cross in penal and juridical terms, as an act of satisfaction or substitution."

It seems to some commentators that the Coptic position at the moment is closer to Matthew Henry than to Kallistos Ware.

4. In Arabic: *Intilaq al-Ruh*.
5. The saying is from Evagrios the Solitary: G.E.H. Palmer, Philip Sherrard, Kallistos Ware (transl. and ed.), *The Philokalia*, vol. I, London-Boston: Faber and Faber, 1988, 62.
6. Ibid., 69.
7. P.J. Vatikiotis, *The History of Modern Egypt from Muhammad Ali to Mubarak*, Baltimore: The Johns Hopkins Univerity Press (4th ed.), 1991, 421.
8. See the article "The Renewal in Context," by Maurice Martin, S.J. for numbers about the Coptic population.

Nora Stene

# Into the Lands of Immigration

A recent phenomenon in the Coptic Orthodox Church is the establishment of new Coptic Church communities outside Egypt. This development has occurred with the increase in emigration from Egypt during the last three decades. The present situation poses a new challenge to the church and it raises several issues important to the study of contemporary Coptic Orthodox Christianity.

In the first centuries A.D. the church in Egypt extended its activities both north and south into Europe and Africa, but this was followed by centuries of isolation from the rest of Christendom. The Church Council at Chalcedon in 451, the Arab conquest of Egypt by 642 and possibly the sedentary nature of the population may all have contributed to this isolation. Coptic Christians, like their Muslim compatriots, tended to remain in their country of birth. In his classic study of Egyptian population dynamics, Cleland (1936) states: "Egyptians have the reputation of preferring their own soil. Few ever leave, except to study or travel, and they always return."[1]

During the last three decades this situation has altered, for Egypt today has large numbers of its nationals abroad. This article looks at the Coptic diaspora in the West.[2] After a brief overview of emigration patterns and profile of the diaspora church community, three issues are addressed: the self-image of the church abroad, the community's relationship to Egypt and, finally, some of its cultural expressions. In each case, discussion will be preliminary, indicating possible areas for further research.[3]

## Profile of the Diaspora

Emigration from Egypt by Coptic Christians needs to be seen in the context of general Egyptian emigration patterns. Broadly speaking, two periods of emigration can be detected. The first belongs to the era of President Nasser (1952-1970), during which a limited number of young Egyptians were encouraged to study abroad and school teachers were sent out to work in neighboring Arab states. Migration was politically controlled, mainly through exit visa requirements.[4] Nasser's nationalization policies also led to a number of well-to-do families leaving Egypt to settle in the West. Amongst these were Coptic families. The presence abroad of economically resourceful individuals from this early phase of emigration has been important in the establishment of Coptic churches in the West, that followed at a later stage.

The second period of emigration began in the early 1970s. Along with President Sadat's "open door" policies came an easing of emigration restrictions. One result of this was a growth in the number of Coptic communities worldwide. This fact was reflected in a rapid increase in the construction or acquisition of new Coptic churches in various parts of the world.

Overall Egyptian emigration has since continued, but numbers are generally believed to have fallen in recent years.[5] Although statistics on the migration of Coptic Christians are unavailable, however, the community is generally seen to be "expanding outside Egyptian borders."[6]

The size of the Egyptian Coptic population outside Egypt is difficult to determine due to a lack of reliable sources. Local priests often count their congregation in "families" and decline to give exact number of individuals. Father Mina of the Coptic St. George Church in Brooklyn estimates that one million Copts live outside Egypt.[7] The Coptic Encyclopedia does not give exact figures, but a compilation of figures given in the Coptic Encyclopedia for North America, Europe and Australia amounts to approximately 200.000-300.000.[8] Historian A. O'Mahony gives a number of approximately 300.000, though he does not specify if this number is for the West only.[9]

Copts of all social classes have emigrated, but it is still possible to suggest a social profile for the Coptic diaspora in the West. The requirements for obtaining a visa for Western countries have favored the resourceful and educated, those with proficiency in a foreign language and those who already have relatives abroad. A large number of Copts have gone abroad for higher education and have ended up staying in their host countries. The result has been the establishment of communities whose members are engaged in professional jobs, including medicine, trade and commerce. As mentioned earlier, wealthy families that may be the patrons of new church buildings also form part of the communities, as well as a number of working class families and individuals.

Emigration of Copts has come about for a number of reasons, most of which apply to Egyptian emigration in general. Ralph R. Sell lists the following: demographic transition with rapid population growth; the legitimation of inter-Arab movement during the Nasser period; and individualism and removal of state restraints during the *infitah* years of Sadat.[10] The "open door" policy of Sadat allowed individuals to seek to satisfy their financial and professional goals outside Egypt. For the Coptic community the additional factor of being non-Muslim in a predominately Muslim society has played a role. Many have felt their own and their children's future to be uncertain. With the Egyptian population identifying more strongly with Islam, many Copts have felt marginalized. Seeing their future prospects threatened, some have taken the option to emigrate.[11]

Although this article focuses on emigration to the West, it should be mentioned that the West has not been the exclusive destination of emigrant Copts. There are Coptic communities in most of the countries of the Middle East, from Iraq to Libya. There are also Coptic churches in both Brazil and the Caribbean. Africa presents a special case, as it is considered a "mission field" for the Coptic Church; communities of local converts have been established in several African countries. However, the largest Coptic communities are probably to be found in North America and Australia. While most Western European countries have Coptic communities, possibly the largest is the London congregation that numbers 5.000-7.000 individuals, according to the local priests.

In sum, Copts abroad form a relatively young diaspora community, numbering several hundred thousand people. The early emigrants of the 1950s and 1960s have been followed by large numbers since the 1970s, and the last decades have seen the establishment and expansion of Coptic communities, particularly in the West.

## "From one end of the universe to the other"

The line above is the title of the news page in the Coptic Patriarchate's monthly magazine in English, *Keraza*, which is distributed to the diaspora communities. These words may reflect a new self-image presented by the church. Having broken away from its traditional confinement in Egypt, the church appears to be looking for new roles to play and ways of portraying its image in the West. This section outlines some of the elements that may be playing a part in this re-structuring of the Coptic Church's self-perception. The self-image discourse is reflected in the literature produced by church centers, both in the diaspora and in Egypt. It can also be heard in the formal and informal talks and discussions taking place amongst Copts.

A striking feature in the presentation of the Egyptian Coptic Church outside Egypt is the positive valuation given to the present situation.

Emigration from Egypt is usually presented as an opportunity, not an outcome of difficult or pressing circumstances. The relationship of the diaspora communities to Egypt will be discussed below, but here it is sufficient to stress how joyously the establishment of new churches in far off corners of the world is recounted.[12]

The Coptic Church's past days of glory are often remembered in the context of the international role then played by the church. Special emphasis is put on the contribution to Christianity in the field of theology made at the early church councils.[13] Similar treatment is given to the influence of early Egyptian monasticism on Europe and to the fact that itinerant Egyptian monks reached as far north as Ireland.[14] This role is seen to be continuing today, with the Coptic Church again making international contacts.

One example of the importance given to the early "European connection" is the recent popularity of the Theban martyr saints of Upper Egypt, particularly St. Mauritz (Muris) and St. Verena. The Theban saints are said to have arrived in Switzerland in the company of a Roman legion in the year 285 A.D. Mauritz was a soldier and Verena is said to have been a nurse. According to the legend, they were both beheaded when they refused to sacrifice to heathen gods.[15] Their story is often retold by expatriate Copts and they have become a motif of recent icon paintings.[16] An altar to St. Mauritz and St. Verena has recently been consecrated (1994) in the church of the Bishopric of Ecumenical and Social Services in Cairo. This bishopric has extensive links to the international network of the Coptic Church. For many Copts, the Theban saints may represent a link between their Egyptian roots and their new domiciles in Europe.[17]

Travelling saints or monks of the first centuries A.D. are said to have "spread the gospel" and to have been "pioneers of the faith."[18] Present day emigration from Egypt fits this image of a church reaching out. As part of this image, great emphasis is placed upon the Coptic Church sharing in ecumenical dialogue, both with other Orthodox churches and with the Catholic and Protestant churches. The Coptic Church is often portrayed as a leading figure in these debates.[19]

A consequence of the expansion of the Coptic Church has been the admission of converts into the diaspora communities. Most often these are spouses of Copts that have joined the Coptic Orthodox Church at marriage or at the baptism of their children.[20] Some individuals or families have joined the Coptic Church after becoming acquainted with it in its Western context. Though converts are relatively few in number, some take a very active part in the life of the church. Some hold important positions as ordained deacons or Sunday school teachers. It is too early to say what effect converts may have on the Coptic Church, but their inclusion may be a sign of the new international profile of the church. By dispelling the image of a national church exclusively for expatriates, converts may become one of the elements that confirm the role of the diaspora as an "international body" with a new and positive role to play in the West.[21]

## Back home – relationships to Egypt

In spite of a new self-image as an international community, in the official discourse of the church Egypt is usually referred to as the true homeland of the Copts. The community in the West is called "the church in the lands of emigration." Terms such as "in exile" or "diaspora" are avoided. This may be interpreted in the light of Patriarch Shenouda's wariness of anything that might imply criticism of the state of affairs in Egypt. The church prefers to stress the continuous loyalty of Copts to Egypt and the voluntary nature of present day emigration patterns.

Opinions vary as to whether the emigration of Copts is a permanent feature or not. Some writers, such as Bishop Gregorius, expect emigrants to plan to return to Egypt: "To my understanding the Copts love their country, Egypt, and do not like to leave it (...) whenever they found it more convenient for them to go back to their beloved country they did not hesitate to return.[22] Others, like Abuna Tadros Malaty clearly envisage, the establishment of Coptic communities worldwide as a permanent feature. Malaty advocates studying the needs of the church abroad with a "futuristic view."[23]

In writings of a theological or spiritual nature, Egypt is often portrayed as a place of particular blessings. Quotations from the prophets of the Old Testament are popular, such as Isaiah chapter 19: "On that day shall there be an altar to the Lord in the midst of the land of Egypt" (verse 21), and "Blessed be Egypt, my people" (verse 25). Bishop Mousa writes in *Keraza* on the same subject: "However far Egyptians emigrate, neither they nor their descendants would ever forget their Egyptian origin, for how could they forget their being Egyptian with all the spiritual, Biblical and native blessings which this carries?"[24]

On a more personal level, the relationship of expatriate Copts to Egypt may sometimes be marked by a certain ambiguity. Although generally retaining strong ties with Egypt, the increasingly Islamic character of present day Egypt can nevertheless be problematic for Copts. Patriotic feelings may be mixed with disillusionment and a sense of alienation. The migration experience itself, in which sustained effort is put into adapting to a new environment, may also affect attitudes towards the home country.

One issue which brings into focus the relationship to Egypt is that of language. Arabic is the mother tongue of the first generation of expatriates, but different European languages are increasingly in use, while promotion of the liturgical language Coptic is also discussed. This issue is of concern both because of the possible bilingualism of the second generation (or lack of it) and the on-going debate about which language(s) to use in church services.

If likened to other immigrant minorities in the West, one might expect the Coptic community to give high priority to keeping Arabic alive as its language of communication.[25] But the use of Arabic is complicated by several factors. On the one hand, Arabic serves as a vehicle of identity, a link to the past, Egypt, the Middle East and the Arabic-speaking church leadership. For many, the beauty of the church liturgy is linked to the use of Arabic hymns and prayers. On the other hand, Arabic is perceived as tied to Islam and Muslim culture and to the demise of the earlier Egyptian language, Coptic. Younger generations may be unwilling to put effort into learning Arabic, with the result that English or another European language is increasingly used. In the Coptic community in London, it has been observed that, while some families promote bilingualism in their children, the majority seem to be of the opinion that the second generation will not be Arabic-speaking. This is sometimes viewed with sadness or resignation, but it has not led to a communal effort to teach Arabic.

The question of which language(s) to use in the Coptic Liturgy is widely discussed. Several translations of the Liturgy into European languages are available, as well as transliterations of Arabic and Coptic. A liturgy with a combination of Arabic, Coptic and European languages is not uncommon. In some cases comprehension by a monolingual younger generation is given priority; non-European languages then take second place to prayers and worship in the new mother tongues. Current discussions are reflected in the writings of Abuna Tadros Malaty, who believes that the use of Arabic in the Liturgy should be restricted: "I do not think that one (the older generation) should insist on enjoying worship practices in a language known to him at the expense of his children's salvation."[26]

The attitudes of emigrant Copts to the Coptic language differ from those regarding Arabic. Coptic is sometimes referred to as the real language of the Copts and its extinction as a spoken language is lamented. As a liturgical language it is kept alive mainly by memorization. The Coptic Liturgy is taught to deacons and sometimes to Sunday school classes or the whole congregation. Specially interested individuals, families or groups may arrange to study Coptic, learn to read it and use simple phrases in conversation. Such endeavors are admired, as Coptic has an enhanced status not granted to Arabic.

The discussions and choices that are made concerning language will continue to form part of the negotiation of Coptic identity in the diaspora communities. The position of Coptic may strengthen in the diaspora, possibly at the expense of Arabic. Both are Egyptian, non-European languages that can serve as identity markers. Another possible development is the consolidation of European languages, not only as mother tongues, but also increasingly as vehicles for Coptic Orthodox worship.

The nature of the diaspora communities is not that of isolated entities developing on their own in new surroundings. In addition to a continuous influx of new migrants from Egypt, the (Egyptian) clergy also play an important part in development within the diaspora. Resident priests are often sent from Egypt where they have had their training. Only a small number of priests are from diaspora communities themselves. Most regions do not have a local bishop, but fall administratively directly under the patriarch. Bishops that reside in the West belong to monasteries (like Anba Karas, Abbot of St. Anthony monastery in California) or are "general bishops" (like Anba Youssef, responsible for the southern region of the U.S.A.). A "general bishop" may be relocated to other areas if the need arises. In this way the reins of control are kept firmly in the hands of the Egyptian hierarchy. A steady stream of visiting priests and bishops maintains close connections between the church at home and abroad. The pastoral visits of Patriarch Shenouda himself reinforce this central control.

## Cultural production

The term "cultural production" refers here to the combined efforts of community members to create signs of their common culture. In the case of the Coptic community, the first act of communal activity is commonly the securing of church buildings where the Coptic Liturgy can be read. Sometimes churches are borrowed or rented, but the aim is often to buy and transform church rooms into distinct Coptic places of worship. The priests take a central role in this endeavor, although the financial means usually come from the lay members of the community. This striving to find a suitable place for church worship reflects the importance of the clergy and the church rituals. Without a priest, children cannot be baptized, confessions cannot be heard and Holy Communion cannot be received. These ritual activities continue to form the center of Coptic religious life outside Egypt as well as within its borders.

Coptic churches outside Egypt are intended to cater to a range of activities. Rooms are needed where bread can be made for the Liturgy, for communal eating after service, Sunday school activities and meetings of different kinds. Feast days bring together large numbers of people, adults and children, who have to be accommodated. The need for a meeting place as well as a church may spur the community on to acquire large properties with overnight facilities. In the United Kingdom two such centers exist. Such places have clear potential for contributing to "community building," though the financial and practical difficulties of running the properties may cause initial difficulties.

The establishment of monasteries and seminaries outside Egypt may be seen as an extension of the activity of acquiring churches.[27] Little has been published on the nature of these institutions, for example the number of monks permanently inhabiting the monasteries, or the way the monks are recruited. Nevertheless, such enterprises carry symbolic significance for the Coptic community, as monasteries are seen as the spiritual centers of the church.

Whenever a Coptic church is established, whether as a purpose-built church or a converted room, it is decorated with icons. Icons are often painted specially for the church in question. They may be imported from Egypt or painted on location. These icons can be said to transform the church rooms into genuine Coptic places of prayer. With their symbolism they express the orthodox teaching of the church. Consecrated for use in church buildings, they are also an integral part of worship as practiced by Coptic Orthodox Christians. As visual images, they are specially Egyptian Coptic, but they also appear to cross cultural barriers, appealing to individuals from different backgrounds. The activity of icon painting has become established in the "lands of emigration", though still on a small scale. With an increasing number of churches being constructed or bought, there might be room for extensive activity in this field in the future.

A third sphere of activity that deserves attention is the printing and production of books, leaflets and magazines. Great effort is put into translating religious texts, including the liturgies, prayer-books and devotional readings of different kinds. Some books are translations of church publications in Arabic, others are original works in Western languages. Written by members of the community for other members of the community, these publications give important information about the concerns and interests of the diaspora community, and point to several areas for further study.

Community action undertaken by Copts may also be an area for further research. The English language church magazine, *Keraza*, has included several articles on community services provided by the church to the Coptic community in Australia. These include the opening of a primary school for approximately 140 Coptic children in Melbourne and a hostel for the elderly in Victoria.[28] Although this type of activity may still be sporadic, it may be one of the ways in which Coptic communities express their cultural concerns in the future.

## Conclusion

Some areas for further research have been mentioned above. There are more, not least of which might be questions concerning the re-creation of Coptic life and ritual by the second and third generation of Copts. Taking into consideration the strong central control noted earlier, study of the Coptic diaspora will need to be seen in relationship to developments within Egypt. The opposite case may also hold true. Studies centering on the Coptic church in Egypt may need to consider the diaspora communities and the impulses, resources and developments that may be filtering back to Egypt. Notably, this may concern the position of women, the relationship to non-orthodox Christians and attitudes to secular society. New priests who are themselves second generation diaspora Copts may be instrumental in new developments. Whether these will influence the Coptic Church at large or whether the main initiatives will still come from Egypt remains to be seen.

The profile of Coptic activists in the U.S.A. during the Sadat years shows the potential for diverging developments in the diaspora. While the church in Egypt carefully sought to balance its relationship with the authorities, American Copts wanted a more confrontational line. The political situation both within and outside Egypt may, in the future, cause communities established on different continents to develop characteristics of their own.

As yet, the diaspora communities are still in the making, adapting their Coptic heritage abroad and working out what roles to play in the "lands of emigration".

## Notes

1. W. Cleland: *The Population Problem in Egypt*, 1936, 36. Quoted in R.R. Sell, *Gone for Good?*, Cairo: 1987, 27.
2. The question of emigrants from the Coptic communities in Ethiopia, Eritrea and the Sudan falls outside the scope of this article. Due to the political circumstances in each of these countries their situation differs from that of the Egyptians. References to the "Coptic Church" are therefore to the Egyptian Coptic Church.
3. This article is largely based upon fieldwork carried out in London's Coptic community during 1993/94. The findings from this fieldwork form the basis of a PhD in progress on the issue of the religious socialization of Coptic children in diaspora.
4. Sell, *Gone*.
5. Saad Eddin Ibrahim, in: A. Stephens, "Brain Drain," *Cairo Today*, June 1992.
6. Patriarch Shenouda III, "migration," in *The Coptic Encyclopedia*, 1620-1624, Aziz S. Atiya, (ed.), New York: Macmillan, 1991.
7. E. Norden, "America's Oldest (and Newest) Christians, *The American Spectator* (June 1993) 24-28.
8. Article "Migration."
9. A. O'Mahony, "From Survival to Revival: the Copts of Egypt, *Living Stones* 9 (1993) 16.
10. Sell, *Gone*, 46-49.
11. See: M. Zaki, "The Denial of a Coptic Minority," *Civil Society*, vol. 3, (May 1994) 26-29.
12. This situation contrasts with the self-presentation of other Oriental Orthodox Churches, such as the Armenian and the Syrian Orthodox Churches, which both stress their involuntary exile from countries of origin. Also see, for example, T. Malaty, *Introduction to the Coptic Orthodox Church*, Alexandria, 1993.
13. See: Shenouda, Patriarch, "Glories of the Coptic Church," lecture given at the University of Michigan, May 2, 1977, printed in *The Coptic Orthodox Church*, pamphlet from St. Mark's Church, London, undated. Also see: A.S. Atiya, *The Copts and Christian Civilisation*, printed at St. Mary and St. Anthony Church, Solihull, U.K., 1985.
14. Athanasius, Bishop, *The Copts through the Ages*, Cairo, undated.
15. See: O. Meinardus, "An Examination of the Traditions of the Theban Legion," *Bulletin de Societé d'Archeologie Copte 23*, (1981) 5-32.
16. For example, their icons can be found in the small Coptic church of Coulsdon, south of London, in the United Kingdom.
17. Whether the Theban saints have reached the same degree of popularity in Australia or the United State needs to be explored further.
18. Athanasius, Bishop, *The Copts*, no page ref.
19. From *Keraza*'s editor, 1994 no.1, p.5: "The Church is once returning to its place as an or perhaps the, ecumenical leader, as it was in the early centuries of Christianity."
20. The Coptic Church practices (infant) baptism by full immersion. It does not recognize the baptism of non-orthodox Churches, and priests will usually insist that converts are (re) baptized according to the Coptic ritual.
21. J. Watson reflects this view when he writes: "The Coptic Orthodox Church is an international body transcending all barriers which are social, political or racial," (*Prisoner of Conscience: Christian Patriarch*, Kent, 11). An interesting comparison

might be made between the Coptic Church in diaspora and other emigrant church communities from the Middle East. Points of comparison might be reinterpretation of past history, particular types of saints that increase in popularity, and the perceived role of the community in the West.
22. Quote from Bishop Gregorius' article "The Copts in Cyprus" (undated manuscript). This article is about Copts in Cyprus in the 12th to 17th centuries A.D. In an interview with the author on June 14, 1994 Bishop Gregorius expressed the same sentiments about present day emigrants.
23. T. Malaty, *Introduction*, 294.
24. *Keraza* 5 (1993) 4.
25. The Armenian Orthodox community in London puts effort into teaching Armenian, sometimes at the expense of religious teaching (see S. Pattie, "Faith in History, Armenians rebuilding Community in Cyprus and London, PhD thesis, University of Michigan, U.S.A., 1990). Language learning is also given high priority by the Greek Orthodox community (K. Kotsoni, *The Greek Orthodox Community in Leeds*, Leeds, 1990). Similar patterns are also found with different groups from the Indian subcontinent (see: Jackson and Nesbitt, *Hindu Children in Britain*, London, 1993).
26. Tadros Malaty, 1992, 296.
27. In 1994, there are reported to be monasteries in the U.S.A., Australia, Germany and Italy, and seminaries in the U.S.A. and Australia. There are no reports of convents for nuns.
28. *Keraza*, 2 & 4, 1993.

Anitra Bingham-Kolenkow

# The Copts in the United States of America

Patriarch Shenouda III introduced the article on "Migration" in the *Coptic Encyclopedia*[1] by talking about people "seeking better opportunities" and under "economic and social influences" when leaving Egypt. Priests and monks were sent from Egypt and the Coptic communities grew.[2] Patriarch Shenouda also tells how they sought places of worship (often given by or bought from other Christian denominations and later building their own churches). Father Gabriel Abdel Sayed tells of the thousands who came (160-180,000 total by 1989[3]) with many churches, especially in the New York-New Jersey area and around Los Angeles. This is still a time of growth (with new churches being formed in the most populous areas), but more a time of consolidation since some communities have been in existence for twenty-five years or more. Two divinity schools (Los Angeles and New Jersey) and a California desert monastery have been established.

## Background: the Copts in Egypt

Egypt is a largely Muslim country. Copts are a little over six percent of the population. Some are rich; you see visitors' Mercedes cars if you visit a Coptic monastery. Some are poor; Cairo garbage collectors and low-paid professionals have an average salary of maybe twenty to one hundred dollars a month.

The Copts in America talk about persecution in Egypt. They do not mean persecution like that of the millions of Christians killed in Russia under Stalin. Nevertheless, they suffer occasional discrimination, harassment and sometimes acts of violence, from which they feel the government does not sufficiently protect them.

Major immigration to America began in the late 1960s. Previously there had been greater restriction on emigration from Egypt with a select few allowed to go abroad for study. This changed in the 1960s; the Nasser government allowed large numbers of professionals (doctors, pharmacists, chemists, engineers) to emigrate because of lack of jobs in Egypt. The "Six-Day" War with Israel slowed emigration, but in 1968 and after many came to Canada and then New Jersey and Los Angeles. The Coptic Church could not supply enough priests for these burgeoning new communities; the late Father Raphael Nakhla travelled from Canada to New Jersey for liturgies.

Immigration to the United States has been more common for the affluent and educated.[4] The official requirement is to have family members who will support you or a job waiting in the United States which cannot be filled by a United States resident. Those who had been rich by Egyptian standards may take entry level American jobs (grocery clerk, dry cleaning and gas station jobs), often recommended by the priest. However, most see America as a place where they will be able to make good money eventually – and where their children will have good jobs: "There is no future for us in Egypt now."[5] Copts sometimes contrast the religious who enter monasteries with the materialistic who go to America, but the reality is that most Eygptians now ask how they can get to America.

## Copts in America

The stories of the life Australia's immigrants found in P. Anderson, et al. *Eastern Orthodoxy in Australia*[6] tell of transition situations similar to those found by Copts coming to America. This is true, although many Copts were trained as doctors or engineers, knew English (doctors and engineers are taught in English in Egyptian universities) and eventually found high paying jobs. They often found help and hope in the church where Arabic was spoken and where people talked of God as well as problems – and helped them to find jobs.

As in the Greek Orthodox community in Australia described by Anderson, Coptic wives in America often were lonely at home and isolated because they did not speak English. Their husbands were busy and had people who translated for them on the job. Some went to local colleges or high schools to learn English. Many worked. Coptic churches organized English classes (and Arabic classes for their English speaking children). In America the Coptic Church serves as an Arabic speaking resource even for Egyptian Catholics and Protestants.

The church also served as a meeting ground between generations. The youth felt their parents did not understand what it meant to be part of school and American society. The parents felt the children were breaking away from their families in an uncontrolled way, wanting freedom; sex and drugs were feared). A good priest was a mediator, getting to know the youth and having them feel he wanted to hear their opinions. Where monasteries in Egypt have been resources for youth there, Coptic summer camps and retreats become important in the United States (although large groups of youth also visit the California monastery). The camps provide relaxed community experience; they enable Coptic youth to think about ideals and become acquainted with other young people, priests and bishops. Said a priest, "they can talk about what embarrasses them to the friendly ear of a priest from another area" – or see that other young people have the same problems. As in Egypt, this is a time for the youth to meet their peers from other churches in situations of "idealism." (Such gathering places are common for ethnic religious groups, as, for example, the Jews in New York). Children may resist being a part of the church or (in contrast) go into religion even more than their parents (and become monks).

People found their mates through the churches; churches become a way of perpetuating national communities. At the same time, the church felt threatened when people met and married outside the church (the church felt as though it had lost the people). On the other hand, a number of Egyptians came to the United States because they were able to find an American wife and thereby get the proper visa or a green card. And some of these wives and husbands have proved great helpers to the priest in getting to know the outside community and in translating the Coptic Liturgy into English. One priest had a group for "American" wives and found them enthusiastic and helpful with libraries and polishing sermons.

A priest said the Coptic family was the biggest resource for the church and for America. "The Egyptian family is stable. The language keeps the first generation together in the church. They have no permission to remarry."[7] The priest told a story of a researcher who interviewed school girls about sexual experience before marriage. A Coptic girl said that her church taught her to keep the body clean before marriage. The researcher congratulated the parents. Indeed, the Coptic Church works hard to keep families together. It has meals after mass every Sunday and family retreats as well as the camps. Church festivals are also a time for families to work together on church projects.

## Priests and helpers

The church sent over its best priests and most learned scholars. The late Father Gabriel Abdel Sayed (New Jersey) had been a professor, Father Antonios Ragheb (New Jersey) had been famous for his spirituality and work with young people in Egypt. The pope sent his deacon, Father Shenouda Anba Bishoi (who had taught at the Cairo Divinity School), to Chicago. The late Father Bishoi Kamel (one of the most charismatic of Coptic priests, famous in Egypt for his sermons) came to Los Angeles in October 1969 and the following feast of St. Mark consecrated St. Mark's Church there. (Monks and priests in Egypt told me of the Egyptian fame of all these priests). Father Ishaiah Mikhail Bibawy, the translator into Arabic of many books about the desert fathers, came to San Francisco, as did Father Mattias Wahba who was writing a Ph.D thesis on St. Athanasius. Father Tadros Malaty (a writer on church history and the Bible) was active on both coasts as well as in Australia. Bishop Tadros (who came as an engineering student) tells of being cared for by the now Bishop Dioscoros (both bishops were engineers in Los Angeles). Father Bishoi Gobreial of St. Mark's Los Angeles (then lay) tells how he worked with them. A number of monks came as priests.[8] Some immigrants returned individually to Egypt, became monks and are now serving in Australia and Brazil.

In the years before 1993, Bishops Bishoi, Hedra, Tadros and Ruweis came from Egypt to work on administrative problems. In 1993, Bishop Youssef (formerly a priest in the States) was appointed to the Southern states. Bishop Karas had already been appointed as bishop of the monastery of St. Anthony. There is still a need for bishops in the metropolitan areas of the East and West coasts. Patriarch Shenouda himself has come regularly in recent years to visit the churches.

One particular resource for spiritual direction have been bishops and spiritual leaders who came to the United States for medical treatment or education. Chicago and Cleveland (where bishops have been for medical treatment) have become places for Copts to visit them.

Mother Irini, mother superior of the convent of Abu Saifein in Cairo, received medical treatment in the United States over a number of years; she gave spiritual direction, especially because there are no women's monasteries in the United States.

There were a few deaconesses, like Sister Nadia Amin, who served in Chicago. She clearly was a great help in listening to the women of her congregation. Sister Ruth of the Daughters of Mary in Beni Suef came to Chicago to study social services and care for the aged. Sarah and Ayed

Henry (who had been active in social and ecumenical services in Egypt) also came to study in the United States. Wives of priests served as helpers and listeners.[9] It is indeed helpful to have an older (and consecrated) woman to listen to women.

Immigrating religious should be well prepared. The church has not always been careful (either in Egypt or America) about preparation of priests for their particular area of service. It was easy for priests to get a visa but often there was very little church support, monetarily or personally. Priests often felt isolated. There also needs to be preparation not only in language but in what Robert Bellah the American sociologist, calls "cultural literacy" and business administration.

Many priests got along very well. They built churches and encouraged their congregations. General advice given by priests to new priests showed the adjustments they needed to make. The situation was quite unlike Egypt where the black dressed priests were the vulnerable representatives of a minority church – but very well taken care of and admired by parishioners. In America, the priests were in no danger and needed to adjust to the lack of respect as well as help from parishioners who were adjusting themselves. In America the church was a "weekend" church, with less activity during the week. Recommendations were to get out on one's own, find American friends.

A major feeling was that America in general and his congregation in particular were materialistic. On the question of materialism and America: Yes, there is materialism and members of your congregation have to struggle particularly as they are from a foreign country. Give religious meaning to their struggles. Teach them about American asceticism. (Indeed, America has a tradition not only of Catholic but of Protestant ascetic communities – Shakers, Amish, Hutterites, etc. – which has interested some Copts, as a contrast to the prevailing materialism). Ask them where they find beans and lentils for fasting; do they know the nutritive value of beans with rice? A temptation is wealth – especially to eat or relax with people who are rich, with lobster for fasting food; of course your people want to give you the best, but ...! Do not ignore the rich; they also are members of your congregation, but pair them with the poor and eat as a trinity (poor, rich and yourself).

## Equipping the church for a new land

One major need was translation and publication of writings from the Coptic tradition. Several translations of the St. Basil Liturgy were printed (including the 1992 Papal edition). The Agbeya (book of hours) was published in New Jersey, Los Angeles and San Francisco. The Psalmodia translations edited in Australia and Canada were used also in the United States. The large green book used in the Passion Week was translated in Chicago and Los Angeles.

There has been increasing focus on translation of church writers into English. Many books of Pope Shenouda are translated into English (the Pope himself speaks excellent English). Father Matta al-Miskin's writings likewise have been translated – not only small pamphlets, but also *The Life of Prayer* (largely translated in *St. Mark Monthly*). Father Tadros Malaty's writings have been published in English and Arabic, back to back. All these and others are remarkably prolific authors; I have watched Father Tadros going over page proofs while listening to a speech. Pope Shenouda not only writes Tuesday and Wednesday lectures, but actively supervises the English *Keraza* magazine at a desk in the print shop. (This has a different format than its Arabic counterpart and has color pictures).

The Patriarchal Print Shop sends shipments of magazines and books it prints. Independent printing is also done in the United States. Many churches produce not only liturgies but stories and writings of famous leaders, such as Pope Kyrillos VI, Bishop Johannes and Father Bishoi Kamel. Father Mattias Farid Wahba printed writings of Athanasius, Cyril Alexandria and Ephrem Syrus.

Hany Takla and others organized the St. Shenouda Society in Los Angeles, a group that not only translates and publishes but also has a microfiche library of all the Coptic manuscripts available in the libraries of the Western world. Several magazines are published by American Copts: *The Copts* (New Jersey; political, reprinting of news articles), *Coptic Church Review* (New Jersey; with contributions on church history also from Canada and Egypt) and *Coptologia* (Pennsylvania). Aziz Atiya gathered Coptic and non-Coptic scholars to produce *The Coptic Encyclopedia* (8 vol., 1991). The fifth International Congress of Coptic Studies (Washington, D.C.,1992) attracted American Copts as well as scholars from around the world.

The churches not only have libraries but their stores are crammed with both Arabic and English material for grownups and children (including Bishop Demetrious' lessons in Coptic), many small (and large) sacred pictures, ancient and modern (like those of Isaac Fanous and his students which adorn the churches), prayer beads and other religious articles (often made in Egypt), books, religious movies, and catalogues of Arabic speaking businesses. Audio tapes are sold. Copts love to listen to liturgies (by the Pope or their favorite priests) and songs for children on long journeys. In Egyptian monasteries, monks spend the whole night singing Advent songs to Mary – with small groups asked to sing the more complex parts. American tapes of the hymns have printed on their covers, "Form your own group." Both in America and Egypt students also play rock versions of hymns and "praises" with their cymbals and triangles.

The Orthodox churches have taken a conservative yet mediating way concerning certain social issues, saying "no" to abortion, "yes" to birth control; having both married and unmarried priests; working with the World Council of Churches and sharing biblical fundamentalism with the evangelicals, yet with spiritual or scholarly interpretation (and often some worry that those evangelicals may convert their flocks). Bishop Antonios Markus went to Fuller Theological Seminary to study missions. On the East coast, students have gone to the Orthodox St. Vladimir's (which should serve as a resource center for their own central city divinity school) and other seminaries.

The Copts in America are a church with much potential energy. There is the immigrant energy plus ancient tradition – to focus on the needs of society. In addition to the general Orthodox spirituality (of church fathers, liturgy and divinization of the human), Coptic martyrdom and minority situation joined with charismatic leadership have provided a special edge. There is much that needs to be done in the United States, especially in those areas which have been the centers of Coptic growth (Los Angeles, New York-New Jersey). An Egyptian monk once said to me, "But Americans might be prejudiced against me because I am dark." In Afro and Puerto Rican areas, dark active people in monks' clothes might be particularly appreciated. Perhaps among such people this African-born church may find a special role.

## Notes

1. New York: Macmillan, 1991; 5:1620-21.
2. Coptic means Egyptian Christian. Copts are largely Orthodox Christians, with relatively few Catholics and Protestants. (In the United States, these latter often join with the Arabic speaking Orthodox for fellowship.) When Copts speak of America, they mean the United States in contrast to Canada, as will this paper.
3. Ibid. 5:1621-2. There are nearly sixty churches in the United States (11-12 each in

New York-New Jersey and California, and the number continues to grow). Some are churches with two priests, some with a visiting priest; some small in (e.g.) an ex-Methodist church (renovated according to the Coptic rite, with icons and often chandeliers); elsewhere many thousands crowd into large new churches (esp. New York-New Jersey and Los Angeles, with Florida and Texas growing fast).

This paper will not be as much about figures (often unreliable; also United States government figures are for both Muslim and Coptic immigrants; further there are illegal immigrants) as a paper trying to listen to the accounts of priests and people coming to the United States. I thank all the people who have talked to me, especially Father Mattias Wabba and Father Bishoi Gabreial on the West coast and the late Father Gabriel Abdel Sayed, Father Markus Girgis and others on the East coast. Pope Shenouda now has asked each church to write its history, to be gathered into a book under his editorship.

4. A priest quoted the *Wall Street Journal* that Egyptians were the best educated of immigrant groups (25% higher degrees). Dr. Emil Tanago (a urologist) was honored by the Egyptian and other governments; Laila Kamel (M.A. Berkeley) was one of six recipients of the Goldman award (for her work with Cairo garbage collectors' recycling). A recent article in *American Spectator* (June 1993) 24-29, gave a picture of large families, pride in traditions, strong educational background and good priests. For at least a generation, the immigrant family tends to keep its strength.

5. Recently it is more difficult to come. Even through the 1970s it was easy for professionals to immigrate to the U.S.A., only having to wait for a visa up to four months. In Egypt people used to wait one year for jobs; now they may wait five.

6. Sydney: Australian Council of Churches, 1966. Cf. Oscar Handlin's *The Uprooted* (Boston: Little, Brown, 1952); L.G. Brown *Immigration: Cultural Conflicts and Social Adjustments* (New York: Longmans, Green, 1933), reprinted in *The American Immigration Collection* (New York: Arno, 1969). Brown emphasizes the transplantation of social centers (churches, etc.) as easing transitions (11). Cf. *Coptic Encyclopedia* 5:1622-23 on Australia.

7. Although an upper class Egyptian Copt said that there was much divorce among her friends, there is also pressure for "good behavior" in a minority community; Copts want to distinguish themselves from the Muslim ease of divorce.

8. They were less expensive and considered more easily moved. Life was very different from the monastery. Some felt lonely (they should have been sent two by two or attached to a monastery, as in Germany). There is a great need for priests partly because some, who might have become priests in the past, became monks in the regrowth of enthusiasm for the monastic life. There are relatively few priests or monks and nuns in Egypt in comparison to the population (less than 5,000 in five million), even if placed side by side with the decreasing number of Catholic religious in relation to the Catholic population in the United States.

9. In the Coptic Church, as in all Orthodox churches, there are married as well as monastic priests. Wives of priests also need training.

Mat Immerzeel

# Coptic Art

A remarkable feature of the interior of Coptic churches and monasteries is the overwhelming presence of art. The eyes of the visitors are struck by an astonishing mixture from the past and present: icons, wall paintings, carved wood and stuccoes, but also printed reproductions and fabrics. One is tempted to walk around in churches as if they were museums, but such an attitude neglects the existence of a deeper dimension: these images had and still have an important function within the church building and the liturgy. Art is an integrated part of the religious life of the Copts, as in that of other Christians in the East.

## About the Objects

In discussions between Westerners and Oriental Christians some confusion might arise about the use of the word "icon." What Westerners have in mind is the more reduced meaning of the icon as an object: a wooden panel on which a holy representation is painted. Meanwhile, Copts and other Christians from the East consider all holy images as icons, such as wall paintings, mosaics, fabrics, and even photos and reproductions. To avoid any mix up, "icon" here will only be used for a painted wooden panel.

The expression has a Greek origin: it means "image" or "representation." In contrast with the situation in the Roman Catholic Church, where representations are objects of devotion, the image has the same status as the word and the sacraments in the Oriental churches. In the Coptic Orthodox Church, however, the official use is more limited and the icon itself is never venerated. Icons of saints are carried around in churches on the day of their feast, or in the most important periods, like Advent, Easter and the forty days after.[1] Through its consecration a holy image becomes more or less the gateway to a higher world, because the depicted person – Christ, the Virgin Mary, saints or archangels – is supposed to be present in reality. One can pray in front of it, or leave a written message to the saint on or next to his or her image. Important are the virtues of the saints, as they are a source of inspiration to the Copts to follow their example.[2] Although it is not officially encouraged, touching an image – the most direct contact with a saint apart from touching a relic – is widespread.

The communication is two-sided; through their image the saints might manifest themselves to the people, e.g. by a miracle.[3] Holy portraits establish the contact between the believers and the saints, and for this reason the presence of icons in private environs is as important as in churches.[4]

A unique object that always can be found on the altar in Coptic churches is the so-called *Kursi* (pl.: *karasi*), the "Throne of the Chalice."[5] A *kursi* is a small altar-casket with a hole at the top, which contains the chalice during the liturgy. Such boxes are made of metal, stone or wood. Wooden *karasi* are often provided with representations at the four sides, made by icon painters. The themes depicted differ from case to case, though the Last Supper is always present. Its eucharistic symbolism relates this theme to the liturgical purpose of the object and the chalice.

Several Coptic churches, in cities as well as in monasteries, are decorated with centuries-old or modern wall paintings. In the case of a wall painting, the paint is directly applied to a layer of plaster that covers the wall. A common expression is *fresco*. This word, meaning "fresh" in Italian, refers to a particular painting technique that was developed in Italy: the paint is applied when the plaster is still wet, which results in a stronger fixation of the pigments. In Egypt, however, this method was unknown; consequently, the expression should be avoided in the case of Coptic wall paintings.

The visitor to the workshop of an icon painter will be astonished by the enormous quantities of eggs in his/her atelier. The eggs are not destined for human consumption; they are the stock of the painter for the preparation of the paint. This paint, called *tempera*, consists of a mixture of egg yolk and different pigments. *Tempera* was generally used in the East and the West before the invention of oil paint, but in the East it never disappeared.

Some of the oldest icons are painted with so-called encaustic paint, a mixture of melted wax and pigments, which had to be applied very rapidly before the wax stiffened. One is surprised to see the still vivid colors of encaustic paintings, such as in several of the oldest icons and a wall painting in the Syrian Monastery. Like *tempera*, the wax method was not specific to Egypt; some icons in the Greek-Orthodox Monastery of St. Catherine in the Sinai were very likely imported from Constantinople. The encaustic technique died out many centuries ago. It will take years of study to master this extremely difficult method again. Modern icon painters prefer *tempera*, although some are experimenting with oil paint, gouache or pastels.

The decoration of public buildings and private houses with mosaics was widespread in Antiquity. In the early Christian period and the later Byzantine Empire mosaics were applied to the walls and to the apses of churches. This old tradition was brought to life again in recent times. In the past, mosaics were composed of large quantities of colored stones, pieces of glass and fragments of pottery. Nowadays, such materials are difficult to find, or too expensive to produce. Coptic mosaic makers content themselves with prefabricated pieces of colored plastic that are imported from abroad. Others prefer natural materials from the desert, e.g. shells or sand with different colors.[6]

Modern Coptic art is characterized by the continuation and re-introduction of old techniques, although the use of modern materials is not completely avoided. The results of the efforts of icon painters and mosaic makers have remained unchanged: the iconography, i.e. the nature of representations, and the religious purposes of the objects have their roots in the past. A past, however, that is still far from being fully understood and explained.

## The history of Christian art in Egypt

### Early Coptic art (5th-7/8th century)

It has been suggested that already in the first centuries A.D. Christian art existed in Egypt, but archaeological evidence for this supposition is lacking. Its origin must not be sought in Egypt, but mainly in Rome. The early Christian art of the Eternal City, with its countless Christian sarcophagi and wall paintings in the catacombs from the 3rd and 4th centuries, was an important source of inspiration to later generations. Rome was the traditional capital of the Roman Empire, but after 395 A.D., when the empire was split between a Western and an Eastern part (the Byzantine Empire), the role as forerunners in the creation of new items of Christian art was partly taken over by the new capitals: Ravenna for the West and Constantinople for the East.

Christian art very likely did not appear in Egypt on a large scale before the period of early Coptic art that started in the fifth century and flourished until the 8th. From this era remains a wealth of wall paintings, stone sculpture, fabrics and woodwork. Monasteries, such as the Monastery of Saint Apollo in Bawit (near Assiyut) were richly decorated with limestone reliefs and wall paintings that belong to the most important monuments of early

Christian art.[7] Although early Coptic art evidently shows its own characteristics, it has strong roots in the art of late Antiquity. A remarkable feature is the emphatic presence of mythological themes, often with an erotic content (e.g. Leda and the Swan) or Dionysian scenes. Decorative elements, such as vine-scrolls and interlaced patterns, were also copied from traditional motives.

Some of the oldest icons (6th-8th century) were found in Egypt. Although it has often been argued that icons were an Egyptian invention, this is hardly probable. As stated before, several icons in the Greek Orthodox Monastery of St. Catherine in the Sinai were most likely painted in Constantinople. In Rome, too, several icons are conserved, of which the oldest is dated in the beginning of the 7th century.[8]

An argument in favor of an Egyptian origin was the discovery of pagan "forerunners:" the famous Fayoum portraits, painted panels and even a triptych with the images of deities, dated between the 1st and the 4th century A.D.[9] The almost total absence of such discoveries outside Egypt can, however, not serve as a proof of this hypothesis. The dry Egyptian climate is very favorable to the conservation of organic materials. In other regions, with different climatological conditions, wooden panels and fabrics would simply have vanished in the course of time.

This is certainly not the only reason why some of the earliest icons were found in Egypt. The Christian world was rent by a theological struggle concerning the propriety of the use of representations of saints. In the Byzantine Empire this led to a crisis called Iconoclasm that started in 726 and lasted until 843 A.D. During this period, all religious art was banned; existing objects with the images of Christ and saints were destroyed, whilst the supporters of the cult of icons were subjected to persecution.[10]

Until 642 A.D., when Egypt came under domination of Muslim rulers, it was a part of the Byzantine Empire. Thus, during the Iconoclasm, the country was out of the reach of the Byzantine emperors. It seems that Coptic art, and also some icons in the Monastery of St. Catherine, fortunately escaped intentional destruction.

The rejection of representations of human beings by the iconoclastic movement was shared by the Muslims, which explains the entirely ornamental character of Islamic art. This attitude certainly had consequences for Coptic art as well. However, it seems difficult to blame the new rulers for the general lack of Coptic art after the 7th century. Periods of tolerance and interdiction alternated, but generally speaking, from time to time the Copts had limited possibilities to decorate their churches and monasteries.

*Coptic art between the 8/9-18th century*
From the period between the 8th and the 12th/13th centuries traces of Christian art in Egypt are scarce. Recently, in 1991, a splendid wall painting was discovered in the Western apse of the Church of the Holy Virgin in the Syrian Monastery (Wadi al-Natroun). Represented is the Annunciation – the Virgin Mary and the Archangel Gabriel – accompanied by four prophets. Its late Antique style and painting-technique – for the main theme the encaustic technique was used – allow us to suppose that this wall painting was created in the 8th century.[11]

The Church of the Holy Virgin is endowed with yet other precious treasures from the Coptic past. Other wallpaintings of uncertain date are hidden from the eye by a layer of plaster or by a second layer of wall paintings. The Syriac inscriptions on the upper layer of representations indicate that they were painted when the monastery was occupied by Syrian monks, probably in the 13th century or perhaps earlier. The Annunciation was covered with a representation of the Ascension. When this upper layer was damaged by a fire in 1988, the separation of both wall paintings became urgent. This difficult job was accomplished by a French-Dutch team of restorers and archaeologists. At present, the Annunciation is restored in full glory, whilst the Ascension is on show in a corner of the church.

An example of a positive effect of the presence of Muslims is the impressive decoration in stucco in the sanctuary and a side chapel of this church.[12] It must be somewhat younger than the Annunciation, but it is entirely comparable to similar works of Islamic art in Cairo and other locations in the Muslim world. In spite of the fact that the chronology of the wallpaintings and the stuccoes is still subject to discussion, it is evident that the art of the Syrian Monastery represents an intriguing meeting point of several periods and cultural influences.

The present knowledge about Coptic wall paintings still shows many blank spots. Historical and archeological evidence seems to indicate that many wall paintings were created in the period between the 12th and the 14th centuries. Examples are those in the monasteries of Saint Anthony and Saint Paul near the Red Sea, and in the four monasteries in the Wadi al-Natroun.

It is remarkable that, at first sight, icons on wood seem to be excluded from the artistic activities in the mentioned period. We are confronted with an enormous gap in time between the earliest icons (6th-8th century) and those from the 18th century, when icon painting started to flourish again in Egypt. Apart from sporadic icons imported from Greece, Crete or other Mediterranean regions, no genuine Coptic examples are conserved that can be dated with certainty in these "Dark Ages of Coptic icon painting." Nevertheless, their existence is confirmed by written sources. Icons were seen by contemporary writers, and they were admired by visiting pilgrims from Europe.[13]

In the course of time the destruction of objects and the buildings in which they are kept is inevitable, but this does not explain the systematic absence of icons for more than ten centuries. A logical explanation is that they were intentionally destroyed, though not necessarily always on order of intolerant Muslim rulers. According to some reports, old icons that were no longer in use served to feed the fire on which the holy *Mairun* (the holy oil used in the sacraments) was prepared.[14] If this really was a common act, it can be understood as the transmission of the holiness of superfluous icons to the holy *Mairun*.

Furthermore, we cannot exclude the possibility that the Coptic Orthodox Church has known its own sporadic periods of iconoclasm. For example, in the 19th century the destruction of icons was ordered by Pope Kyrillos IV, because in his opinion they received too much veneration.[15]

It is not very likely that in the future old icons will be rediscovered in the storerooms of churches and monasteries, but in the case of wall paintings the situation is more hopeful. Whilst many of them have certainly been lost in the past, others remained visible for centuries.

In several churches wall paintings were hidden from the eye by a layer of plaster or paint. A reason for this "mild" kind of iconoclasm was perhaps that the destruction of wall paintings was not without danger for the architectonic structure of the walls and apses underneath. The cutting away of the supporting layer of plaster would have been a rather radical, messy solution that required additional restoration work.

In the long run, the covering with plaster or paint was the best method to preserve wall paintings for future generations. Protected from the touch of pious visitors, dust and smoke, they are patiently awaiting the arrival of skilled restorers. Recently, wall paintings came to light in the monasteries of St. Bishoy and Baramous; as mentioned before, the Syrian Monastery still conceals a part of its treasures.

*Icons from the 18th and 19th centuries*
Shortly after 1740 A.D., a fertile period of icon painting started. The most famous icon painters from the 18th century are Abraham or Ibrahim al-Nasikh ("the writer") and Yuhanna Armani al-Qudsi ("the Armenian from Jerusalem"). Both artists and their assistants painted hundreds of icons, triptychs and *karasi*. Ibrahim also illustrated and copied manuscripts. They were

the real masters of Coptic icon painting until about 1780 A.D.[16] Another icon painter from the same period was Mattari, whose work is present all over Egypt. There is some evidence that he was working in an Armenian tradition.[17]

This brings us to a remarkable point: both Yuhanna and Mattari came from Armenian circles, and they were certainly not the only icon painters working in Egypt that had a non-Coptic background. The dominant 19th-century artist was Anastasi al-Rumi ("the Greek"). Like Yuhanna one century before, Anastasi had moved from Jerusalem to Cairo.[18] So our main question is: how Coptic was Coptic icon painting? Can we really speak of a "Coptic style" if a considerable number of the icons made on behalf of Coptic customers were painted by "foreign" masters? It is not clear what the relationship between the workshops of Jerusalem and Egypt was in the 18th and 19th centuries, nor for what reasons painters moved from Palestine to Egypt. Were they invited by the Copts, or were there economic reasons for their migration? It will probably need years of research to answer these questions, but one thing is clear: as is the case with early Coptic art and certainly also with the medieval wall paintings, the production of more recent Coptic icons has to be studied in a wider geographic and cultural context.

It seems that the production of icons lasted until the 1870s. By that time the art of icon painting in Egypt was declining. A revival was seen only about 90 years later.

## Modern Coptic art

*The Neo-Coptic School*
Until the sixth decade of the 20th century Coptic art was hibernating. It was awakened by Isaak Fanous, who was appointed director of the Art and Archaeology section of the Patriarchate's Institute of Coptic Studies in 1956.[19] Fanous started his career with an intensive study of Christian iconography in Paris, as well as of the cultural heritage of Egypt. He created a flourishing school of Neo-Coptic art that was more or less officially declared to be the one and only tradition. Most of the modern icon painters – monks, laypeople and even foreigners who felt attracted to the Coptic Orthodox Church – received their education from Fanous at the Institute of Coptic Studies.

Within Egypt, Fanous and his pupils are certainly supplying a need. The construction of new churches and the renovation of older buildings demands a considerable quantity of representations. The same goes for the newly founded churches and monasteries abroad. The emigration of Copts to North America, Western Europe and Australia pressed the Coptic Orthodox Church to found churches, chapels or monasteries in or near foreign cities with a large concentration of Copts. Those new buildings, or older churches bought from other Christian communities, are in need of icons, wall paintings, mosaics and stained glass windows. So, Coptic painters are not only working inside Egypt; they also travel from one country to another, where they are warmly welcomed by the local Coptic communities. Fanous and his pupils have left their artistic traces all over the world.

The style of the Neo-Coptic School is characterized by a certain simplicity and severity, elements that are derived from older paintings. The use of colors depends on the artist. The work of Fanous himself shows a delicate balance, whilst other artists prefer a vivid mixture of red, blue, green and brown, set against a golden background and emphasized by dark outlines. To reinforce the direct contact between believer and saint, the holy figures are always looking straight at the beholder, with wide-open, oval-shaped eyes. Another particular aspect is that they seem to radiate a mysterious light. This intended effect expresses spirituality, not only of the represented saint or the artist, but also of the Coptic faith and its theology.

In the past, the Coptic Orthodox Church never had written instructions about the correct ways of representing the saints. Consequently, the rules are actually fixed by Fanous and the Coptic Church. The iconography is based on traditional items, known from older icons and wall paintings: the Virgin Mary holding the Child, other themes concerning the Virgin, the Enthroned Christ, the Last Supper, Coptic saints and the archangels. The golden background is filled with symbolic representations that are related to the saint's life or martyrdom.

An important theme is the Flight to Egypt, mentioned in Matthew 2:13-15. The tradition of the Holy Family's stay in Egypt is very strong, because it relates the country to the earliest days of Christianity. The local element is emphasized by adding pyramids and palm trees to the background.

Many icon painters, in particular the nuns and monks, consider artistic work as a part of their religious life.[20] Some are gifted artists, whilst others have more problems in gaining the desired results, but all believe the painting process, which entails continuous prayer and fasting, to be as important as the result. Painting is nothing less than a prayer! The instructions given by Fanous in his lectures and icons are a resource to his followers; each of them has developed his own style and spiritual expression within the borders fixed by the Neo-Coptic School.

*The importance of tradition in Neo-Coptic art*
The Copts consider themselves as the heirs of the ancient Egyptians, as unique as those from an Islamic, Greek, Armenian or Jewish background. This "back-to-the-roots" movement is rather recent. Otto Meinardus remarked that the notion of the Copts being "the sons of the Pharaohs" was absent in ancient writings.[21] An explanation of the present attitude can be found in a combination of a political tendency towards nationalism and the scientific study of the past. From the 19th century onward, archaeological discoveries considerably enlarged the knowledge on Egypt's Pharaonic history. This influx of new historical information had important consequences for the self-confidence of the Copts. It strengthened them in their opinion that the Coptic Orthodox Church was above all a national church.[22]

According to Fanous, Coptic art had strong roots in the art of the Pharaonic period. His aim is to return to these roots, and to purify the iconographic heritage from all non-Egyptian influences, such as the traces of the Byzantine and Western cultural heritage.[23] It seems, however, that the task of creating a purely Egyptian art with which the Coptic icon painters charged themselves is somewhat too heavy: a complete purification is impossible.

The present borders of Egypt are very recent. After the Pharaonic period, the Valley of the Nile and its surrounding deserts saw the coming of the Hellenistic culture, the Roman empire, the Byzantine Empire, the Islamic rulers, the crusaders, the army of Napoleon and finally the Western colonialists. As in many other countries, Egypt's culture is composed of a variety of introduced elements. To separate the different aspects, scientific research depends on the possibility of dating objects correctly, or of confirming or rejecting their local origin. As was stated before, however, for the study of Christian art in Egypt there are many lacunae. It might be understood better if developments in neighboring regions (e.g. Syria, Palestine, Nubia and Ethiopia) are related to those in Egypt. It seems to be impossible to trace any direct relationship between Pharaonic and Coptic art without the danger of simplification.

What are the alleged Pharaonic elements in Coptic art? They must certainly be something more profound than the presence of pyramids on the background of icons of the Holy Family in Egypt, because the introduction of this scenery is very recent.

It has been postulated that the religious character of Pharaonic art relates it to Coptic art[24], but this is not true. Religious aspects, including mythology, have always been a dominating factor in the artistic expressions of all cultures. In this matter the situation in Egypt is far from unique.

Another statement concerns the influence of Pharaonic iconography on Christian themes. Evidently, many early Christian representations had a "pagan" origin. They were based on mythological scenes, derived from the iconography of other late Antique religions, or from imperial iconography (see below). One should realize that during and even long after Antiquity, repetition was more appreciated than originality. In modern Coptic art this is still so, because religious art must express something higher than the creativity of an artist alone.

The symbolic meaning of representations should be understandable to anyone, so for the development of early Christian art the best possibilities to develop new iconographic themes were offered by the absorbing of the traditional symbolic language. The main problem in the Egyptian context is the question whether Pharaonic motives were still known and "readable" in the period of early Coptic art.

A supposed example of a Christianized Pharaonic theme is that of the goddess Isis nursing her son Horus. We know from many discoveries that this motif was still very popular in the Roman period, even outside Egypt. Its symbolic meaning was without doubt generally understood, the more so because in the European part of the Roman Empire local goddesses were represented in the same situation, with one or even more children.

The oldest known representations of *Maria Lactans*, the Virgin Mary nursing the Child Jesus, appeared in early Coptic art in the 5th or 6th century. The temptation to search for an Egyptian connection is very strong[25], though a direct influence of the Pharaonic representation has not been demonstrated. It must also not be forgotten that a mother feeding her child was a part of daily life. The motif could have been re-invented at any time, without the intervention of "pagan" examples.

A second theme with a supposed Pharaonic origin is the representation of the so-called holy horseman: a soldier-saint riding a horse and often killing a dragon, a snake, a devil or another symbolic representation of Evil. Such saints have always been very popular in the Middle East. The most famous soldier-saint is St. George, whose image is spread all over the world.

The symbolism of Good gaining victory over Evil was common before the coming of Christianity. Of course, the good person was always placed at a higher level than the bad one. In Pharaonic art Horus was depicted riding his horse and killing his adversary Seth, personified as a crocodile. It is supposed that this Pharaonic scene was Christianized.[26] However, in and after late Antiquity comparable representations were used as political propaganda. Roman emperors and Sassanid kings were represented sitting on their horses, with their defeated adversaries at their feet. It makes more sense to suppose that Christians used this political iconography for their own purposes. Christ was considered as the new, Celestial Emperor, and as a result of this doctrine many early Christian iconographic elements were derived from imperial art.[27] The theme of the holy horseman fits fully within this tradition; the possibility of any Pharaonic influence can almost certainly be excluded.

The above-mentioned examples reveal a discrepancy between modern scientific research and what can be considered as an "Egyptocentric" view. This controversy should not, however, be seen as a difference between the East and the West. The supposed relationship between Pharaonic and Coptic art was not a Coptic invention. It already appeared in scientific studies on the subject in the 19th century, and is closely related to the search for the Germanic and Celtic roots of antique and Christian art. It cannot be denied that such influences existed, e.g. the use of certain decoration patterns, but in modern research their importance is not relevant any more. However, a (modest) revival of the search for "national" influences can be noticed in ultranationalist movements. The arbitrary use of scientific data to support a nationalistic or religious ideological point of view, however, only leads to short-term victories. It will not convince those who think otherwise. In Egypt, it might even disturb the delicate relations between Christians and Muslims.

Nevertheless, the "Egyptocentric" view also has positive effects. Several Egyptian scientists and students, Copts as well as Muslims, are open to the cultural heritage of both religions. For example, I recently noticed a group of Muslim schoolchildren in the Coptic Museum. They were patiently sitting on the ground, making drawings of the monuments on display. Obviously, students are stimulated to dicover their country's diversified past.

*Posters, puzzles and earrings*
A visit to a Coptic monastery or church should always end in its small bookstore. Here, a remarkable mixture of objects is offered for sale: the Bible and other books, music-cassettes and video-tapes, but also posters, postcards, puzzles, ballpointpens in the shape of a cross, key hangers and earrings with the images of saints. The mass production of such objects hardly entitles them to be called "art," but a brief reference is justifiable in this article.

The merchandise is marked by a somewhat confusing combination of holiness and triviality. Amongst the reproductions we find old icons and wall paintings, more recent Neo-Coptic pictures and, above all, examples of what can be considered as popular taste. An important source of inspiration for the latter is the neoclassical art in Europe of the 19th century, well known from Roman Catholic *in memoriam* cards: the images are characterized by soft colors, as well as sweet, realistic faces and a preference for the dramatic.

The presence of posters and printed textiles in Coptic churches is often overwhelming. All kinds of reproductions can be found in Coptic community buildings, private homes and shops. Like painted icons, such images are an assurance of the presence of the saints in daily life. The image is more important than the artistic value; its blessing action is even heightened if a signature, greeting or dedication of a bishop is written on the reverse side. A Coptic taxi-driver is always recognizable by the postcards or stickers with the images of saints in his car. Thus, the saint's protection during the struggle with the neverending traffic jam in Cairo is guaranteed.[28]

Most Copts are not able to buy expensive handmade icons, but the industry of cheaper mass-fabricated objects offers enough possibilities to fulfil their needs. Tourists are pleased as well. A postcard with the image of a saint is much more original than one with the ever present pyramids, and what could be a better souvenir of Egypt than an image of the Virgin Mary printed on papyrus?

## Actual iconographic doctrines

The people, responsible for the countless popular images, are anonymous, with the exception of one: the Italian Renaissance master Leonardo da Vinci. One of the most popular themes in Egypt is the Last Supper, and it is remarkable how many reproductions of Leonardo's Last Supper, doubtless the most famous interpretation of this theme, are present in Coptic churches and private environments. The Copts share this preference with other Oriental Christians, e.g. in Syria. Reproductions are printed on paper or on linen, embroidered, cut in wood, molded in metalwork, or even copied by hand. If quantity were the standard, Leonardo would be the most popular Coptic painter in the world.

Leonardo's Last Supper has recently attracted the attention of the ecclesiastical authorities: Pope Shenouda III has expressed his desire to remove all copies from churches. His objections concern the well-filled table around which Christ and his apostles are sitting, whilst the present doctrine of the Coptic Church requires the presence of only one loaf of bread and one chalice filled with wine. A well-filled table, however, was also the tradition in Coptic icon painting in the 18th and 19th centuries. The consequence of the official point of view is that most of the older icons representing the Last Supper are not suitable any more for liturgical use.

It seems that the problem with Leonardo's Last Supper is more profound than is realized by the Copts. Although the theme is very important because of its eucharistic symbolism, Leonardo concentrated his painting on the moment at which Christ declared: "One of you shall betray me." One of the disciples is responding with "Lord, is it I?" (John 13:26).[29] This iconographic innovation is a demonstration of Leonardo's creativity, but it cannot be denied that it leads our attention away from the eucharistic meaning. For this reason only, and not because of the incorrect number of objects, this particular painting is not so suitable for use within Coptic churches.

This example of the official rejection of a particular iconographic element reveals another weak point in the tendency towards purism referred to by Fanous. It is certainly not the only one. In September 1994 Pope Shenouda III visited Leiden University, and at this occasion he gave a lecture about his vision of Christian iconography. He mentioned several examples that require some modifications, among them the Temptation of Adam and Eve. According to the Pope, it is correct that both are represented naked. It is, however, wrong to provide them with navels, for Adam and Eve were created by God and not born from a woman.

Another example mentioned by Pope Shenouda is the representation of John the Baptist as "The angel of the desert." The word "angel" means "messenger" in Greek, and indeed, both John and the angels are divine messengers. But John the Baptist was not a messenger from Heaven. Consequently, unlike "real" angels, he does not need wings. However, icon painters in the Middle East have interpreted the expression "angel of the desert" too literally: they depicted the saint with wings. Hence, Pope Shenouda concluded that a winged John the Baptist was incorrect.

Modern icon painters are following the instructions of the Coptic Church by painting purified representations, but the problem is what to do with the old, "wrong" ones. Since the earliest days of Christian art Adam and Eve had navels, whilst John the Baptist is depicted with wings up to now. Which is stronger, the tradition or the new doctrine?

I recently had a discussion with a monk about the publication of an 18th- century icon representing an "incorrect" Last Supper. His recommendation was not to publish it. Nevertheless, other fathers did not share his opinion. To them, there is a clear difference between modern opinions and the documentation of the past. The "incorrectness" of a representation can be a reason to remove it from a church, but it cannot be ignored as a fact. In the worst case, someone might take the decision to "correct" a wrong interpretation. We can only hope that others will prevent him from doing this.

The attitude of the Coptic Church about how to deal with its cultural heritage is ambiguous. The Copts are free to support any modern theological doctrine on iconography, but history, even their own, can never be rewritten. In order to restore the balance between the past and the present, the church is in need of an open discussion on this matter with specialists – archaeologists, art historians and theologians. In fact, this discussion exists already; it was opened by members of the Coptic community themselves.

## The ENCCAP project

A main problem for the Copts is that in Egypt the possibilities for a scientific study of the Coptic cultural history are limited. At the University of Cairo, Coptic art is a branch of Islamic art. Moreover, scientific publications on Coptic art are not easy accessible, as they are mostly written in German or French.

Although the Coptic Orthodox Patriarchate has tried to solve this problem by the creation of the Institute of Coptic Studies, the patriarch and many other Copts considered the situation unsatisfactory. To improve the knowledge of the Coptic cultural past within the Coptic community they sought the help of Western specialists.

Since the early 1980s, a relationship has developed between the Coptic Church and the early Christian art section at Leiden University (The Netherlands). In 1989, three Coptic monks were invited to study early Christian and Coptic art at Leiden University. To facilitate their stay far away from the desert, they were lodged in the Abbey of Saint Adelbert in Egmond-Binnen. For the occasion a Coptic chapel was constructed in the abbey.

The success of this modest project inspired the Patriarchate and Leiden University to a follow up with a project called the Egyptian-Netherlands Cooperation for Coptic Art Preservation (ENNCAP).[30] Its aim was to improve the knowledge on the history of Christian art in general and Coptic art in particular within the Coptic community, and to develop an adequate expertise in documentation and conservation skills within Egypt for Christian art.

Lectures on Christian art were given by scholars of Leiden University to monks from several monasteries, students of the Institute for Coptic Studies, and other motivated Egyptians. In addition, the students were taught how to document objects, and how to save icons, wall paintings, manuscripts and other historical documents from further deterioration.

When Pope Shenouda III was still a monk in the Syrian Monastery, he started to collect the old objects in the monastery. Under the leadership of

Father Martyros, the present curator of the collection, the monastery is now creating a modest, though attractive museum. Monks of other monasteries are likewise encouraged to create their own museums with the support of ENCCAP.

## Notes

1. N. van Doorn, "The Importance of Greeting the Saints. The Appreciation of the Coptic Art by Laymen and Clergy," in: H. Hondelink (ed.) *Coptic Art and Culture*, Cairo: Shouhdy Publishing House, 1990, 101-118, spec. 103.
2. Ibid., 103-104.
3. J. den Heijer, "Miraculous Icons and their Background," in: *Coptic Art and Culture*, 89-98, and: Van Doorn, "The Importance," 105-106.
4. Van Doorn, "The Importance," 109.
5. P. van Moorsel, "Ein Thron für ein Kelch," in: *Tesserae. Festschrift für Joseph Engemann*, Aschendorffsche Verlagsbuchhandlung, Münster, 1991, 299-303 (Jahrbuch für Antike und Christentum Ergänzungsband 18).
6. A. and B. Sadek, "Le Musée de la Poussière," *Le Monde Copte* 24 (1995), 91.
7. K. Wessel, *Koptische Kunst. Die Spätantike in Ägypten*, Verlag Aurel Bongers, Recklinghausen, 1963; P. du Bourguet, *L'Art copte*, Paris, 1964; A. Badawy, *Coptic Art and Archaeology. The Art of the Christian Egyptians from the Late Antique to the Middle Ages*, The MIT Press, Cambridge (Mass.)/London, 1978.
8. J. Beckwith, *Early Christian and Byzantine Art*, Harmondworth 1990, 88-91.
9. L. Langen, "Icon-painting in Egypt," in Hondelink, *Coptic Art and Culture*, 55-72, spec. 56-59.
10. Ibid., 63-64.
11. Several articles dedicated to the Annunciation are included in *Cahiers Archéologique* 45 (1995).
12. S. Fleury, "Die Gipsornamente des Dar es-Suriani," *Der Islam* 6 (1915), 71ff.
13. Langen, "Icon-painting," 64-65.
14. Ibid., 65.
15. Ibid.
16. P. van Moorsel – M. Immerzeel – L. Langen, *Catalogue général du Musée Copte. The Icons*, Supreme Council of Antiquities/Leiden University, Cairo, 1994, 16-18.
17. Van Moorsel-Immerzeel-Langen 1994, 47-48; P. van Moorsel – M. Immerzeel, A short Introduction into the Collection of Icons in the Coptic Museum in Old-Cairo, in: *Coptology: Past, Present and Future. Studies in Honour of Rodolphe Kasser* (ed. S. Giversen, M. Krause, P. Nagel), Leuven 1994, 35-44, spec. 39-40
18. O. Meinardus, The Iconography of Astasi ar-Rumi, *Studia Orientalia Christiana Collecteana* 14 (1970-71), 379-397; Van Moorsel-Immerzeel-Langen, *Introduction*, 52-53.
19. "Un copte d'aujourd'hui," *Le Monde Copte* 2 (1977), 12-15; S. René – C. Chaillot – M. René, "Isaac Fanous," *Le Monde Copte* 19 (1991), 5-13.
20. C. Chaillot, "Moines iconographes coptes contemporains," *Le Monde Copte* 18 (1990), 33-36.
21. O. Meinardus, "L'art copte au cours des trois derniers siècles," *Le Monde Copte* 18 (1990), 89-99, spec. 97-99.
22. Ibid.

23. René, Chaillot & René, *Un copte*, 8.
24. B. Sadek, "Vers un art copte contemporain. Compte rendu de la thèse de Mme J. Ascott," *Le Monde Copte* 19 (1991), 215-226.
25. Ibid., 17.
26. Ibid.
27. J. Engemann, "Die imperialen Grundlagen der frühchristlichen Kunst," in: *Spätantike und frühes Christentum*, Frankfurt am Main 1983, 260-266.
28. Van Doorn, *Importance*, 109.
29. H.W. Jansson, *A History of Art. A Survey of the Visual Arts from the Dawn of History to the Present Day*, Thames and Hudson, London 1981, 419-420.
30. The project is financially supported by the section Directorate General for International Cooperation of the Netherlands Ministry of Foreign Affairs (DGIS), as well as by private funding by the "Sonnewijck" Foundation through the Foundation Christelijke Kunst en Cultuur in het Nijldal (Christian Art and Culture in the Nile Valley; CKCN).

# List of Contributors

*Anitra Bingham-Kolenkow* (passed away September 1996), was a specialist on New Testament and Christian Origins. Since 1982 she spent up to six months a year in Egyptian Coptic monasteries. Dr. Bingham-Kolenkow was a visiting scholar at the Dominican School of Philosophy and Theology and the Graduate Theological Union at Berkeley, U.S.A.

*Nelly van Doorn-Harder*, teaches Islamic Studies at Duta Wacana University in Yogyakarta, Indonesia. Dr. van Doorn-Harder is the author of *Contemporary Coptic Nuns* (1995) and has written several papers on the contemporary Coptic Church.

*Mark Francis Gruber*, is Assistant Professor, Department of Sociology and Anthropology, Saint Vincent College, Latrobe, Pennsylvania, U.S.A. Professor Gruber has published several articles on Coptic social studies and is the author of *Sacrifice in the Desert: An Ethnography of the Coptic Monastery* (1990).

*Mat Immerzeel*, an Archaeologist and Art Historian, specializes in Coptic art. Professor Immerzeel currently teaches at Leiden University in the Netherlands where he is a staff member of the project for Coptic Art Preservation (ENCCAP).

*Dina el-Khawaga* is a political scientist from Institut d'Etudes Politiques de Paris. She is currently teaching at the University of Cairo, and is the author of *Le Renouveau Copte. La communauté comme acteur politique*, Paris 1993.

*Maurice Martin* is a specialist on Coptic Christianity and has written widely on contemporary and classical Coptic topics. He is currently heads the research library at the College of the Holy Family in Cairo, Egypt.

*Catherine Mayeur-Jaouen* is Professor at the Sorbonne University in Paris, France. Professor Mayeur-Jaouen is the author of *Al-Sayyid al-Badawi, un grand saint de l'islam égyptien* (Institut français d'archéologie orientale, Lé

Caire (1994)), and has written widely about Coptic and Islamic topics.

*Saphinaz-Amal Naguib* is Professor at the Faculty of Arts, Oslo University, Norway. Her main research interests are Egyptology, Coptic and Copto-Arabic hagiographies. Professor Naguib is the author of *Le clergé féminin d'amon thébain a la 21e dynastie* (1990) and *Mirroirs du Passé* (1993).

*Christiaan van Nispen tot Sevenaer* is Professor of Philosophy at the Coptic Catholic Seminary in Cairo, Egypt. Professor van Nispen tot Sevenaer has written extensively on Muslim and Christian Middle Eastern issues.

*Samuel Rubenson* is a Research Fellow at the Theological faculty of Lund University in Sweden. Dr. Rubenson has published several articles on Coptic studies and is the author of *The Letters of St. Antony. Origenist Theology, Monastic Tradition and the Making of a Saint* (1990 and 1995).

*Nora Stene* is a Research Fellow at the Department for Cultural Studies of Oslo University, Norway. She is currently working on a research project on Copts in diaspora in Western Europe.

*Berit Thorbjørnsrud* is a Research Fellow at the Department of East European and Oriental Studies, University of Oslo in Norway. She is currently working on modern Coptic Orthodox perceptions of the person and the body.

*Kari Vogt* is Associate Professor at the Department of Cultural Studies, University of Oslo in Norway. She has written widely on Chistian and Islamic issues, and is one of the two authors of *Women's Studies of the Christian and Islamic Traditions* (1993).

*John Watson* is an Anglican theologian with a specialist knowledge of the Coptic Orthodox church. Dr. Watson has written several biographies of contemporary Coptic saints and leaders.